PLEDGING
ALLEGIANCE

Books by Sidney Blumenthal

OUR LONG NATIONAL DAYDREAM
THE RISE OF THE COUNTER-ESTABLISHMENT
THE PERMANENT CAMPAIGN

PLEDGING ALLEGIANCE

The Last Campaign of the Cold War

SIDNEY BLUMENTHAL

HarperCollins*Publishers*

PLEDGING ALLEGIANCE: THE LAST CAMPAIGN OF THE COLD WAR. Copyright © 1990 by Sidney Blumenthal. All rights reserved. Printed in the United States of America. No part of this book may be used or reproduced in any manner whatsoever without written permission except in the case of brief quotations embodied in critical articles and reviews. For information address HarperCollins Publishers, 10 East 53rd Street, New York, N.Y. 10022.

FIRST EDITION

Designed by Ruth Kolbert

Library of Congress Cataloging-in-Publication Data

Blumenthal, Sidney, 1948–
    Pledging allegiance / Sidney Blumenthal.
        p.   cm.
    Includes bibliographical references and index.
    ISBN 0-06-016189-2
    1. Presidents—United States—Election—1988.   2. United States—Politics and government—1981–1989.   3. United States—Foreign relations—1981–1989.   I. Title.
E880.B57   1990
324.973'0927—dc20   89-45025

90 91 92 93 94 CC/HC 10 9 8 7 6 5 4 3 2 1

For My Sons
Max and Paul

Contents

ACKNOWLEDGMENTS   *ix*

1 A LONG TWILIGHT STRUGGLE   *1*

2 WAITING FOR GORBACHEV   *18*

3 THE VISION THING, OR
   WHATEVER   *49*

4 THE NIXON SUCCESSION   *77*

5 THE PRETENDERS   *92*

6 THE STRATEGIES OF ZEUS   *108*

7 THE VACUUM   *133*

8 BORN IN THE U.S.A.   *163*

9 THE CAT IN THE HAT   *175*

10 GOTHAM   207

11 THE END OF IDEOLOGY   227

12 THE BIRTH OF A KINDER,
    GENTLER NATION   248

13 THE DEAD DEMOCRATS   284

14 ABSENT AT THE CREATION   320

    NOTES   355

    BIBLIOGRAPHY   367

    INDEX   375

Acknowledgments

I encountered civility and frankness among political practitioners in my work on this book. Almost without exception, they went out of their way to share their knowledge and insights. Regardless of partisanship, self-interest or ideology, they displayed a democratic camaraderie, a feeling of participating in a great common enterprise. I am grateful to all who were willing to help me understand the events in which they were involved.

Many of the ideas in *Pledging Allegiance* were thrashed out in long discussions with my friends, especially Lee Auspitz, Thomas Edsall, Hendrik Hertzberg, John Judis, Robert Kuttner, Dan Morgan, John Ritch, James Rubin, William Schneider, Hillel Schwartz, Derek Shearer, Larry Smith, Ralph Whitehead, Leon Wieseltier and Juan Williams. They devoted many hours of their time to hearing me out, filling in the gaps of my knowledge and challenging my misconceptions. I am particularly indebted to James Chace, whose encouragement and observations were indispensable to me.

Without the generosity and public-spiritedness of Richard Dennis and the friendship of Charles Wolff, the obstacles facing me in the writing of this work might very well have been insurmountable.

During the 1988 campaign, I was fortunate to have worked at *The Washington Post* with Jeffrey Frank, an editor of uncommon intelligence and sympathy. I am also appreciative of the assistance of the professional librarians of *The Washington Post*.

I am grateful for the hospitality and openness of the Institute of the U.S.A. and Canada studies whose resources were put at my disposal while I was in Moscow. I am particularly grateful for stimulating conversations with Sergey Plekhanov, the institute's deputy director, and Vladimir Pechatnov, an analyst on American politics and a scholar on the thought of Walter Lippmann.

Ted Solotaroff, my editor at HarperCollins, helped me shape the vision of the book into one about American politics at the greatest turning point in forty years. His criticisms and suggestions have been unfailingly astute; his commitment never flagged. Janet Byrne, the copyeditor, has done a superb job in saving me from errors, both egregious and small.

Kathy Robbins, my literary agent, has been a valuable counselor, not only about manuscripts but about people.

Above all, I am indebted to my wife, Jackie, who is my wisest adviser. Our entire lives have been lived in the shadows of the Cold War. This book is dedicated to our sons, Max, born in 1977, and Paul, born in 1981, who will live most of their lives in the twenty-first century.

I see what you are not making,
oh, what you are so vividly not.

HENRY JAMES
The American Scene

1

A Long Twilight Struggle

I

It was a cold day in an uncomfortably overheated room. The 1988 presidential campaign had ended three weeks earlier. For those who must provide a professional analysis, enough time had elapsed for the election to be viewed in the long perspective of history. This group of about a dozen experts often did not sound all that different from the many other such groups from Cambridge, Massachusetts, to Austin, Texas. Their offices were cluttered with well-thumbed copies of *The Almanac of American Politics*, stacks of *Time* and *Newsweek*, the *Congressional Quarterly* and the *New Republic*, and clippings from the *New York Times* and *The Washington Post*. These political junkies had inside sources in Washington; they spoke knowingly, with a grasp of the fine shadings separating various positions and postures, and of the whole parade of personalities that had marched through the campaign. They chuckled over the foibles of Gary Hart and Dan Quayle, shook their heads over Michael Dukakis's haplessness, expressed a cynical appreciation for George Bush's cynicism, worried that press coverage was being reduced to sound bites, wondered why liberalism seemed to have such reluctant defenders, and debated whether it was the Republican Party "lock" on the Electoral College, the unanswered negative campaign, or peace-and-prosperity that won Bush the White House. All of the important questions raised by the campaign appeared to have been raised and cogent judgments rendered. In short, these experts knew their business. They sounded almost like "Washington Week in Review" or an extended segment of the "MacNeil/Lehrer Newshour."

Almost. The English of these experts was fluent, even colloquial, but it was clearly not native. Nor, once they had covered the usual campaign topics, was their ultimate concern that of American specialists. These were the leading Soviet experts on their country's principal foreign policy interest. They worked at the Institute of the U.S.A. and Canada Studies, an official institute located in the former Moscow mansion of the Tsarist aristocratic Volkonsky family, fictionalized in Leo Tolstoy's *War and Peace.* The large seminar room was as nondescript as a typical one in any American university or think tank, but the weight of Russian history in the atmosphere was undeniable, even overwhelming.

The task of the institute's experts was to comprehend America and to communicate their views to the Central Committee and the Soviet president. Long before the advent of Mikhail Gorbachev and glasnost, they had been granted a remarkable freedom. They were allowed to peruse American publications at will and to travel extensively within the United States. The Politburo, after all, could not afford to mislead its advisers or shield them from the American rival. But in *zastoi,* or "the time of stagnation"—the Brezhnev era—some of them were lying, perhaps even without knowing they were doing so. It was a form of justification and self-protection, but presented as irrefutable, the higher truth, adduced from the science of Marxism-Leninism. In applying a vulgar Marxism to American politics, they saw events as mere manipulations of ruling class circles at the commanding heights of the economy: the big bankers, industrialists, the military, and so forth. The inevitable conclusion was that democracy was little more than a shadow play.

This debased method was part of the reason the Soviets generally preferred that a Republican be elected president. The Republicans were far less confusing to understand and handle than the Democrats. They were obviously the party of the ruling class; the connection between the economic base and the political superstructure seemed direct. A Republican in the White House confirmed the dogma: A Republican was president because in a capitalist country a Republican should naturally be president. Stability in the U.S.–Soviet relationship, according to this line, followed. The administrations of Richard Nixon and Gerald Ford—and Jimmy Carter—seemed to prove the rule; that of Ronald Reagan was the exception, until his last-minute change of mind.

The reductive approach to American politics, however, was now out of fashion with most of the experts, not only because it was misleading about American realities but because it was a remnant from the recent, discredited Soviet past. The experts had abandoned vulgar Marxism like a dead skin. Their view of events abroad was still shaped by events at home, but they were no longer lying about others because they had stopped lying about themselves.

The experts at the U.S.A. Institute are members of the Moscow intelligentsia, the community that is a main support for perestroika and glasnost, which are more than specific policies; they are also the latest manifestation of the Westernizing impulse of the Russian intellectuals. The specialists on America are wholly immersed in the current ferment of Soviet politics. One scholar of U.S. constitutional law has emerged as a leading advocate of, as he puts it, "the rule-of-law state, rather than the rule-of-state law." Another regularly writes scathing articles assailing the right-wing Russian nationalists. Yet another, an analyst of the U.S. electoral system, tirelessly argues with conservatives in favor of the virtues of democracy, which they insist is little more than disorder, and has managed a successful campaign for a candidate for the new Congress of People's Deputies. These Soviets, who formerly thought of themselves only as experts or Communists, have taken on the mentality of citizens.

What they noticed most about the 1988 presidential campaign was neither the personalities of the candidates nor their tactics, but what had been ignored or evaded. This was the issue the Soviet policymakers believed was central, and it consumed them night and day. The issue was the ending of the Cold War.

They had trouble understanding why American politics didn't register this epochal transformation, why the largest event in the world, as far as they were concerned, was absent from a campaign in which "national security" was an obsession. Why, they asked, was American politics content to be trapped in the past, when the Russians were desperately attempting to escape? Why wasn't Gorbachev's effort to withdraw from the Cold War as rapidly as possible acknowledged in the American political dialogue? The stonewall stance perplexed and worried them.

"Has America lost direction?" asked a Soviet expert. "Why did foreign policy issues play such an insignificant role in the campaign? Can America confront its problems?"

This statement was not made in the mocking tone often prevalent in the past. An America that could not confront its problems used to be offered as proof of the Soviet position. What else could be expected? Such were the contradictions of capitalism. But the current plaintiveness of the Soviet expert seemed to be sincere. An America that was blind might pose a greater threat to the Russians than an America with accurate vision. An America trapped in political anachronisms would likely thrash around, making it more difficult for the Soviets to withdraw from the conditions of the Cold War. Such an America might endanger the precarious effort to reform Soviet society, and pull the world backwards. Or, its great evasion might make America irrelevant. One of the experts confessed that some of his colleagues used to wonder if the Soviet Union would, as they put it, "ever get its Kennedy." Now, he said, they speculated whether America would "ever get its Gorbachev." "To have your own Gorbachev," he said, "you must live through the period when an alternative is being formed. You must address issues." The experts' view of America was now being shaped by the transformations of their own country.

"What kind of Soviet Union would the West like to see develop from perestroika?" asked an expert. The question disclosed the age-old Russian sensitivity to Western opinion, a desire for both acceptance and security. What kind of Soviet Union? The predicament facing it has seemed to be that described by Yale University historian Paul Kennedy in his book *The Rise and Fall of the Great Powers.* In it, he uncovered a pattern, from the 1500s to the present, in the behavior of powers whose preeminent status in the concert of nations could not be sustained. Their obligations and interests exceeded their technological and economic strength. They were especially sapped by an excessive military claim on resources. The imbalance between means and ends is due to what Kennedy called "imperial overstretch." The Soviet Union, he observed, was suffering acutely from this syndrome. If it continued on its course, its slippage would be drastic. It must either cut its military as a condition of economic reform or face "imperial decline."

"The essence of it is very correct. I like it," said Georgi Arbatov, the director of the U.S.A. Institute and an adviser to Gorbachev, endorsing the Kennedy thesis. It was May 1988, and Arbatov was in Washington, reflecting on what he said was "the end of the Cold War."

"Internal and economic problems have become the number one priority practically for all countries," he said. "A lot of things regarded as normal have become a luxury—the use of military force, any adventure abroad." After the Soviets' ill-fated and financially draining misadventures in the Third World, the lesson was painfully clear.

The Cold War, according to Arbatov, had taken on an air of unreality. "The Soviet Union may be a developing country," he said. He added slyly: "And the United States may be becoming a colony of business interests from Japan, West Germany and maybe South Korea." The Cold War "just prevents us from dealing with it. It's becoming clear that there are real sources of trouble. The source of the nations' problems is not just their enemy. Psychologically, it's easier if you have an enemy. Both sides did."

Then, he repeated a clever "threat" he had made that had achieved some notoriety: "We are going to do something terrible to you. We are going to take away your enemy." This last phrase resonates through forty years of American history.

II

What do the gropings of a people of a half-developed country, halfway around the globe, rummaging in the darkness of their hidden past, and dreaming all the while of VCRs and fresh oranges, have to do with the Iowa caucuses?

The period from 1985 to 1990—from Gorbachev's assumption of power through Bush's—marked the Cold War's waning. The 1988 presidential campaign, the political centerpiece of this anxious, confused time, was a stunning exercise in the absence of leadership—a failure to come to terms with the new realities of the world as it was and as it was becoming. Pledging allegiance to the shibboleths of the past became the measure of patriotism and prudence. The campaign itself was lived in the last age, as if the Cold War were raging and Stalin alive.

Though the campaign seemed to be insignificant because of its evasiveness, its very emptiness suggested its importance. The candidates' attempts to escape the demands of history by clinging to irrelevant issues were desperate; a crisis of national purpose was postponed, but hardly averted. History is nowhere suspended or ended, not least in America. But to admit the Cold War is over is to be forced to envision American politics in a radically different way.

Since the end of World War II, American politics has been framed by the Cold War, and every presidential campaign has been waged in its terms. The Cold War was about more than the balance of power. It was a metaphysical system in which the world was perceived as a frozen tableau of enemies. The Cold War defined a moral cause, which all other policies must in some way serve. National security became a claim above all others—a means perceived as the ultimate end. But there were different visions of the Cold War, and they served as the foundation of postwar domestic politics. Though their meaning has faded, their hold has only just begun to loosen, as the 1988 campaign and the early Bush presidency demonstrated. The political consequences of the peace have barely begun to be felt. America is as much the prisoner of its past as Russia.

The architects of the American Century were the heirs of Franklin D. Roosevelt. They understood, before Germany and Japan surrendered, that America was going to be the most powerful nation in the world, that an American Century was about to dawn. The archetypal figure of this era was Dean Acheson, FDR's assistant secretary of state and Truman's secretary of state. Acheson was not initially hostile to the Soviets, but Stalin's aggressiveness provoked an American response. "Only slowly," wrote Acheson in his aptly titled memoir, *Present at the Creation,* "did it dawn upon us that the whole world structure and order that we had inherited from the nineteenth century was gone and that the struggle to replace it would be directed from two bitterly opposed and ideologically irreconcilable power centers."

The basic U.S. policy in the Cold War was defined in 1947 by George Kennan, the State Department planner, writing under the pseudonym "X" in a piece published in *Foreign Affairs*—perhaps the most influential magazine article in recent American history. Kennan depicted the Soviet Union as paranoid, messianic and expansionist, driven above all by the imperatives of Marxist ideology. The appropriate U.S. response to this "implacable challenge," he wrote, was "containment." Foreign policy was to be devoted to manning the watchtowers along a perimeter guarding the West from encroachments from the East. It was a holding operation, calculated to prevent the enemy from infiltrating and advancing.

The label "the Cold War" was first applied to the conflict that same year by the influential columnist Walter Lippmann. In a series of articles on Kennan's piece, soon published as a book simply enti- tled *The Cold War*, Lippmann criticized the ideas that were rapidly settling into conventional wisdom. The Red Army was occupying Central Europe, he wrote, not because of the strictures of Marxist ideology but because this had been the route to Hitler's bunker in Berlin. Lippmann foresaw the containment doctrine turning into a global anti-communist crusade—a "strategic monstrosity," he called it—that would lead to "recruiting, subsidizing and supporting a het- erogeneous array of satellites, clients, dependents and puppets." When the dictators who were backed in the cause of anti-commu- nism faced internal revolt, the U.S. would be forced to choose be- tween "defeat" or support "at an incalculable cost on an unintended, unforeseen and perhaps undesirable issue." (Kennan, in time, came to share Lippmann's critique.) Prophetically, Lippmann, who had been a member of Woodrow Wilson's team at the Paris Peace Conference that ended World War I, suggested the outlines of a solution to the Cold War: a settlement of Europe, with the withdrawal of the Sovi- ets from Central Europe, and the reunification of a demilitarized Germany. For the Cold War to end, the U.S. and the USSR did not have to resolve all their tensions. "For a diplomat to think that rival and unfriendly powers cannot be brought to a settlement," wrote Lippmann, "is to forget what diplomacy is all about." His cool analy- sis, however, was almost immediately submerged at the time by the rush of events. And every one of his fears about the conflict he named was eventually realized.

The political mood of early Cold War liberals was perhaps best captured by the young historian Arthur M. Schlesinger, Jr., in his book *The Vital Center*. He attempted to chart a strategy for the "democratic left" that would maintain the momentum for reform while fending off the "challenge of totalitarianism." The task of liberalism after Roose- velt, he emphasized, was radically different because of the Cold War. "How to produce a vigilance that never falters?" he asked.

By the time the containment policy was in place, liberals were already under siege from conservatives, who found a galvanizing cause in the Cold War. The leader of the Republican Old Guard was Senator Robert Taft, who had called the New Deal a "philosophy of totalitarian government." Now he charged President Truman with following a "pro-Russian" line and accused Secretary of State George C. Marshall of holding a "pro-Communist position." But Taft's answer to contain- ment was the isolationism he had advocated before the war, and he opposed the Marshall Plan and NATO. Taft viewed the growth of the national security apparatus as a logical continuation of the liberals' program of big government.

Former Communists soon imported into the already conspiracy-minded right wing the most paranoid attitudes of communism itself. The leading theoretician of their position was James Burnham, a former Trotskyite and OSS agent; according to him, the makers of the American Century had forged a policy of surrender. In 1947, just as the Truman administration was formulating its Cold War policies of containment, Burnham published *The Struggle for the World*, in which he referred to the conflict between East and West not as the Cold War but as World War III. The choice, as he posed it in the title of a subsequent book, was *Containment or Liberation?* He urged rolling back communism—neither isolationism nor containment. "Who," asked Burnham, "will willingly suffer, sacrifice, and die for containment?"[1]

The principal theme of the new Cold War conservatism was the betrayal of the West by the liberals, who were identified with the communists. Without ever producing a shred of evidence, conservatives claimed that Roosevelt had signed secret accords at the Yalta Conference in 1945 that delivered Central Europe to the Soviets. In this political myth, Yalta became the equivalent of Munich—the sellout of the democracies that only encouraged totalitarian aggression. The actual Cold War architects were now charged with harboring the enemy within, especially in the State Department, which was claimed to be running a policy of appeasement and retreat. Acheson called this "the attack of the primitives." Out of power for a generation and despairing of ever overcoming the New Deal, the Republicans believed they had finally found a way to roll back the Democrats. Thus the early Cold War provided the source material for the modern negative campaign.

Such an approach had been tried before the war, but with little success. In the 1936 campaign against Roosevelt, for example, the right wing rehearsed charges that still loudly echoed in 1988. "Many good Democrats do not see the 'Roosevelt Revolution,' because they are so blinded by faith in the Party label he wears," wrote Elizabeth Dilling, a prominent conservative, the Phyllis Schlafly of the day, in *The Roose-*

---

1. In 1983, President Reagan awarded Burnham the Medal of Freedom, citing him for having "profoundly affected the way America views itself and the world." At the ceremony, Reagan added, "And I owe him a personal debt, because throughout the years traveling the mash-potato circuit I have quoted you widely."

velt Red Record and Its Background. She devoted an entire section of her tract to proving "Roosevelt [Is] Not a Democrat." She pasted on him the S-word ("Roosevelt's Tactics Resemble Socialists' ") and the C-word ("Communist Party Backs His Program"). Even more insidious, she claimed, was the influence of the American Civil Liberties Union. "ACLU—'Pulse' of the Roosevelt Regime" read another whole section. Roosevelt's softness on communism was related to his softness on crime. Dilling cited a case in which, as governor of New York, he refused to extradite a Communist labor agitator to a state where he had been indicted on criminal charges—an early "furlough" incident. Roosevelt, moreover, had associated with "radical" black leaders, "Red Negroes," as Dilling called them. "The studied, insincere and obsequious flattery by the Roosevelts and their radical supporters of the Negro people is without precedent in any American political party," she wrote. The 1936 campaign, however, did not revolve around the issues of the S-word, the ACLU, softness on communism and crime or closeness to black leaders but around Roosevelt's agenda for reform.

Now the Cold War and the atomic bomb gave drama, urgency and seeming credibility to the right-wing approach. Negative campaigning itself, of course, was nothing new; it was as old as the Republic. There had been personal slander against Washington, Grant and Cleveland; accusations of corruption were made against Van Buren and Hayes. Racial smears had been made against Lincoln and Harding. Foreign radicals were said to be conspiring with Jefferson toward revolutionary ends. Nativist fears had been whipped up against Al Smith. Negative campaigning even extended beyond the candidates to their parties. Before the Civil War, the Democrats called their opponents the Black Republican Party; after the Civil War, the Republicans called the Democrats venomous Copperheads. But with the beginning of the Cold War in the late 1940s the historic tactics of negative campaigning were integrated into a far more coherent and overbearing strategy. Whereas previous negative campaigning had acknowledged the legitimacy of opposition, now opposition itself was cast as deceitful and unpatriotic.

The liberals never truly recovered from the early onslaught. They developed a defensive flinch, as if they had to prove their loyalty. Even before the entrance on the scene of Joseph McCarthy, the Democrats presented the Cold War as an ideological crusade. In selling the initial Cold War policies in 1947 to a reluctant Congress, dominated by Republicans still attached to their prewar isolationism, Truman resorted to Manichean rhetoric. "At the present moment in world history," he said in his speech announcing the Truman Doctrine, "nearly every nation must choose between alternative ways of life." Then, his Justice Department created a Loyalty Review Board to judge the patriotism of federal employees and an Attorney General's list of subversive organizations. The U.S. Commissioner of Education also announced plans for a "Zeal for American Democracy" program to inculcate patriotic thoughts in the minds of high school and junior college students. The week before Thanksgiving, the administration staged rallies in Washington where thousands of government workers took "freedom pledges" and sang "God Bless America." These measures and spectacles were calculated, at the same time, to sell the Cold War program, stigmatize the misbegotten challenge from Truman's left by former vice president Henry Wallace and preempt the Republicans' use of the loyalty issue in the upcoming 1948 campaign and beyond.

But the overheated political atmosphere did not cool down. In 1950, when North Korea invaded South Korea, the Cold War finally assumed global dimensions, no longer confined to Europe. American boys were fighting Communists in Asia. It seemed to validate the drastic view that the Soviet Union sought to dominate the entire world. After that, the Cold War liberals' zealous rhetoric often obscured their inherent realism even from themselves.

It was in this atmosphere of suspect loyalty that Richard Nixon's career flourished as a crusader against Communist subversion. His national reputation was secured by investigating Alger Hiss, a former New Dealer and State Department official who had been present at Yalta as a member of the U.S. delegation. His conviction for perjury before the House Un-American Activities Committee seemed to many to prove the entire case made against the Democrats by the Republican right.

At the 1952 GOP convention, the conservative standard-bearer Taft was defeated for the presidential nomination by Dwight Eisenhower, who, writes his biographer Stephen Ambrose, had been "one of FDR's principal agents in carrying out his foreign policy in Europe during the war [including Yalta], and Truman's Chairman of the JCS [Joint Chiefs of Staff] when China was 'lost'." In his efforts to accommodate and appease the right, Eisenhower slated Nixon as his running mate and allowed the conservatives to write the Republican Party platform. That document accused the Democrats of having "shielded traitors to the Nation in high places" and declared, "There are no Communists in the Republican Party." It also promised that a Republican administration would "repudiate all commitments contained in secret understandings such as those of Yalta which aid Communist enslavement" and cursed the policy of containment as "negative, futile and immoral." In the campaign, Nixon continued to play his role as inquisitor, accusing the Democratic presidential candidate Adlai Stevenson of holding "a Ph.D. degree from Acheson's College of Cowardly Communist Containment." He blamed the Democrats generally for "the unimpeded growth of the Communist conspiracy against the U.S."

Cold War anxieties of the late 1950s established the momentum that culminated in the 1960 campaign. In 1957, the Soviets launched the first satellite into space, *Sputnik*, a sphere about the size of a beachball. The country had an anxiety attack. Two months later, a top-secret report to President Eisenhower on national security was leaked to the press. The Gaither Report (after its chairman, H. Rowan Gaither, Jr., the chairman of the Ford Foundation) claimed that the Soviet economy was more dynamic than the American and that the Soviets had a dangerously big lead in missiles and warheads. Panic now set in. "It was like looking into the abyss and seeing Hell at the bottom," said Robert Lovett, who had been Truman's secretary of defense. In fact, there was no missile gap; there were only projections, based on faulty numbers, of what the authors of the report assumed about Soviet behavior, which was itself unfounded. Nonetheless, Eisenhower appointed a Commission on National Goals, which was told to locate them. But this quest was misplaced. The Cold War, after all, defined the national purpose.

At issue in the Eisenhower succession was which junior officer of World War II would revise the American Century. John F. Kennedy's theme was to get the country moving again; his national security policy was to close the missile gap. Richard Nixon's countertheme was "Peace without Surrender." In his inaugural address, Kennedy described the Cold War as a period that was indefinite, "a long twilight struggle." He was all trumpets, calling for a willingness to "pay any price, bear any burden." His election marked the zenith of the American Century.

In 1963, after the Soviets provoked voyages to the brink over Berlin and Cuba, Kennedy signed a nuclear test ban treaty with Khrushchev and was speaking about "a strategy for peace" and making the world "safe for diversity." It was clear that he was seeking a new direction.

The Kennedy legacy that Lyndon Johnson made the most of was U.S. involvement in Vietnam, which he dramatically escalated. He conceived of the Vietnam War not as a distraction from his main work but as the culmination of the Great Society—its extension to the Mekong Delta. Over the years, the Cold War had become more than a policy; it was a way of knowing, an epistemological system. Every stirring, in every corner, was seen as an aspect of the all-enveloping struggle. Vietnam could only be perceived on an East–West axis, an outpost of Chinese Communist or Soviet imperialism, one or the other, or both, depending upon the year one heard the official briefing. Vietnam could not be seen on its own terms, and the tragic experience of French colonialism could not be admitted as relevant. To do so would have required the overthrow of an entire system of thought, leaving American national security managers without a formula for understanding the world. The Vietnam War was ultimately fought for an idea, a corollary of the Cold War.

American politics were now a storm of moralistic charges and countercharges. The Vietnam War split the Democrats into hawks and doves—a split far deeper than any division within the Republican ranks. For a generation after the Democrats' loss of the White House, the party remained riven. The winner of 1968 was the loser of 1960. This Richard Nixon claimed to be a "new Nixon." But he remained a one-man collective memory of the Cold War in American politics.

The unraveling of his presidency was the unraveling of its history up to that point. What was called "Watergate" was only incidentally about a break-in by Nixon's paramilitary operatives—the Plumbers—at the offices of the Democratic National Committee. The underlying issue was the Vietnam War, which Nixon rightly understood as an episode in the Cold War and which he also understood as the essence of domestic politics. The first break-in of Nixon's Plumbers was not at the Watergate but at Daniel Ellsberg's psychiatrist's office. On the White House tapes, Nixon obsessively referred to the Hiss case. Just as Hiss had conveniently served in the effort to discredit the New Deal, raising Congressman Nixon to national prominence, Ellsberg, the leaker of the Pentagon's secret history of the Vietnam War to the newspapers, could be used to depict the entire opposition to President Nixon as unpatriotic.

Jimmy Carter gained the White House by promising purity of heart. But the divisions within the Democratic Party left over from the Vietnam War had not been resolved. Carter attempted to achieve unity by pasting the antagonist views together in his speeches. His moralism, however, was inadequate in controlling the growing international chaos that had been wrought by Nixon's realism. Carter's approach was contradictory, incoherent and unsettling, and by 1979, he was already politically overwhelmed.

In early November, Senator Edward Kennedy—prodded by the

congressional Democratic leadership, the party's activists and the major constituency groups—announced his candidacy for the presidential nomination. The same week Ayatollah Khomeini's Revolutionary Guards seized American diplomats as hostages at the U.S. embassy in Teheran. A month later the Soviets invaded Afghanistan. A month after that Carter withdrew the arms control treaty he had negotiated with the Soviets—SALT II—from consideration by the Senate. These blows inflicted more severe damage on Carter's presidency than *Sputnik* and the Gaither Report did on Eisenhower's. Within hours of the Afghan invasion, Carter told a reporter: "This action of the Soviets has made a more dramatic change in my own opinion of what the Soviets' ultimate goals are than anything they've done in the previous time I've been in office." Carter's sincerity, the core of his political appeal, now seemed a form of naïveté. Though he fended off Kennedy in the primaries by brandishing the symbols of national security, these very symbols were turned against him in the general election.

Ronald Reagan pledged to restore the metaphysical simplicity of the Cold War. His politics involved a massive misapplication of memory and a reiteration of the right-wing charges leveled against the Democrats since the inception of the Cold War. In the 1980 campaign he compared Carter to Neville Chamberlain, the British prime minister whose policy of appeasement failed to satisfy Hitler's appetite. This logically made Reagan Churchill and the Soviets Nazis. "We're seeing the same kind of atmosphere we saw when Mr. Chamberlain was tapping his cane on the cobblestones of Munich," he said.

According to President Reagan, the Soviet Union was "the evil empire . . . the focus of evil in the modern world." America, he said, misappropriating a phrase of Lincoln's, was the "last best hope of man on earth"—the redeemer nation, embarked on a holy crusade. Reagan promised to restore the American Century, the supreme American position after World War II, when Europe and Japan were in ruins, by returning to earlier Cold War policies as he understood them. For the first time during the Cold War the extreme right was in power.

III

The politics of the 1980s were dominated by opposite visions of the Soviet Union. To neoconservatives it appeared as a vigorous, waxing superpower—monolithic, unchangeable and unyielding. The nightmare of life in the East bloc was most vividly painted by Jean-François

Revel in his book *The Totalitarian Temptation*, which became an essential text in the neoconservative canon:

> The transition to totalitarian rule is by definition irrevocable except in the case of some cataclysm like a world war. . . . it becomes impossible for residents of a totalitarian state to conceive of, or to remember, a society different from their own. Their capacity to dream as well as to think begins to fail. Their spirit is battered by propaganda and enfeebled by cultural isolation; nostalgia for the past and the utopian dream of the future are both beyond their reach. Such people can no longer imagine either past or future.

This idea of totalitarianism was also the basis of Jeane Kirkpatrick's sweeping condemnation of Carter's foreign policy, which became an ideological factor in the 1980 campaign. In an article in *Commentary*, she charged that the president's policies had undermined the authoritarian allies of the U.S. in Iran and Nicaragua, and that Carter had in general presided over "a declining American position" in the face of "a dramatic extension of Soviet influence." She explained: "The foreign policy of the Carter administration failed not for lack of good intentions, but for lack of realism about the nature of traditional versus revolutionary autocracies and the relation of each to the American national interest." In a tone of complete assurance, she wrote that "the history of this century provides no grounds for expecting that radical totalitarian regimes will transform themselves." Kirkpatrick's article was commended to Reagan to study by his advisers, and upon his election he appointed her ambassador to the U.N.

Reagan also ringingly endorsed a "critically important" campaign polemic by the neoconservative editor of *Commentary*, Norman Podhoretz. His tract, *The Present Danger*, warned that the balance of power had ominously tilted in favor of the Soviet Union and that should the "fierce effort" to reverse it fail "we would know by what name to call the new era into which we have entered . . . the Finlandization of America, the political and economic subordination of the United States to superior Soviet power."

That the Soviet Union was more powerful than the U.S. was demonstrated with statistics by a group called the Committee on the Present Danger, whose distinguished members included many neoconservatives as well as William Casey, who was appointed CIA director, and Paul Nitze, who had helped formulate the original Cold War policy, wrote the Gaither Report, and was named the administration's chief nuclear arms negotiator. The Committee's calculation of Soviet superiority was ultimately based on the claim that there was a direct correlation between the numbers and throw-weights of missiles and strategic geopolitical power. This precept of nuclear theology could never be empirically proved but only affirmed, as if it were an irrefutable truth. It was expressed in a metaphor—the window of vulnerability. Though there was a Soviet buildup in the 1970s, the window of vulnerability was as mythical as the missile gap of the late 1950s. The U.S. capacity for launching a second strike in a nuclear exchange, in fact, was never in doubt. Reagan, however, attempted to close the window of vulnerability with the biggest military buildup of the postwar era.

Hardly anybody in Reagan's Washington suspected that the Soviets might not escape the dialetics of history. When Mikhail Gorbachev assumed power, the idea that he might be anything but a worthy successor to Stalin was widely ridiculed. George Will, the leading conservative columnist, who had coached Reagan in his presidential debate with Carter, promoted Revel and Kirkpatrick, and called Leonid Brezhnev "the most effective politician of the last two decades," contemptuously dismissed all hope for Gorbachev:

> After Stalin, the last Bolshevik, came Khrushchev. . . . Then came Brezhnev and Andropov and Chernenko, the last leaders who were—what?—brutalized or sensitized or something by the war. Now comes Gorbachev, and from Western leaders comes the "new generation" theory: Be of good cheer, because the new generation is, well, younger. . . . Besides, his wife has a well-turned ankle—a matched set in fact. I am not being sexist. I respect her for her mind, but ankles are geopolitical facts.

There were other facts, such as Gorbachev's vision of the Soviet Union, which was diametrically opposite the neoconservatives'. While they stood in awe of Soviet power, he saw a stagnating, weakening country headed toward catastrophe. His vision mirrored Marx's of the revolutionary crisis in the penultimate chapter of *Capital*:

> . . . new forces and new passions spring up in the bosom of society; but the old social organization fetters them and keeps them down. It must be annihilated; it is annihilated. Its annihilation, the transformation of the individualized and scattered means of production into socially concentrated ones, of the pigmy property of the many into the huge property of the few, the expropriation of the great mass of the people from the soil, from the means of subsistence, and from the means of labor,

this fearful and painful expropriation of the mass of the people forms
the prelude to the history of . . .

The word Marx uses to conclude is, of course, "capital." But if the
words "Soviet communism" were inserted instead, the passage would
read as a telescoped description of Soviet history, from the overthrow
of the old order to the construction of Stalinism—"the prelude" to the
current crisis.

Gorbachev had a view not only of the past, which he considered
marked by Stalinist criminality ("enormous and unforgivable"), but of
the future. The USSR, having suffered through the failed industrial
revolution of Stalinism, now faced the postindustrial age. Gorbachev
knew he must push Russia to the West and into the twenty-first
century. Time and again, he raised the specter of the new century to
justify change. In 1984, the year George Orwell feared totalitarianism
would completely harden its power and a year before Gorbachev became the Soviet leader, he was already speaking about the need to
prepare for the next century. "What is at stake today," he said, "is the
ability of the Soviet Union to enter the new millennium in a manner
worthy of a great and prosperous power."

Though Gorbachev did not immediately bring dishwashers into the
average Russian's kitchen, his policies did something more important.
The heart of totalitarianism was now stone dead. At the core of the
Cold War was an almost mystical ideological polarization. But all
around Moscow the huge lettered propaganda slogans adorning the
public buildings came down shortly after Gorbachev came to power.
Atop the five towers of the Kremlin the five red stars still blazed all
night. Children were once told that the red stars represented the five
continents, which would one day form a single global Soviet republic.
No more. The belief in the inevitability of history through prescribed
stages toward communism had been relinquished by the Soviet leadership. The "Grand March," as the Czech writer Milan Kundera sardonically called it, was forsaken. With that, totalitarianism lost its spiritual
cause and was truly finished. Even if a reaction inside Russia were
successful, what would be restored would not be Stalinism; it would be
a kind of tsarism with a hollow crown.

Once Gorbachev insisted on fundamental changes and public debate, the Cold War lost its mooring to any monolithic structure. Not
only had Gorbachev managed to emerge from its center, but an entire
cohort stepped forward to support him.

"My fellow Americans," said Ronald Reagan, giving a voice level for a radio broadcast on August 11, 1984, a few months before his reelection by landslide, "I am pleased to tell you that I've signed legislation that will outlaw Russia forever. We begin bombing in five minutes." Fortunately for himself and the rest of us, he was being facetious. What happened to Ronald Reagan and the Cold War in his second term was far from what he or anyone else could have predicted, jokingly or otherwise: the disgrace of the Iran-contra scandal, from which he, though not the Cold War, would be rescued by Mikhail Gorbachev.

2

Waiting for Gorbachev

VLADIMIR:	Let's wait and see what he says.
ESTRAGON:	Who?
VLADIMIR:	Godot.
ESTRAGON:	Good idea.
VLADIMIR:	Let's wait till we know exactly how we stand.
ESTRAGON:	On the other hand it might be better to strike the iron before it freezes.
VLADIMIR:	I'm curious to hear what he has to offer. Then we'll take it or leave it.
ESTRAGON:	What exactly did we ask him for?

Waiting for Godot, SAMUEL BECKETT

I
_____

With Ronald Reagan's landslide election in 1984 all things seemed possible for the Republicans. Many Democrats, having suffered two shocks in a row, were doubly intimidated. In possession of only the House of Representatives, they had been worn down by the Sisyphean task of resisting Reagan's popularity. They could stop this or that policy, but they could not stop Reagan. Sensing an opportunity, some Democrats began to cozy up to the Sun King. Their efforts to create grand compromises, with themselves as the grand compromisers, made it difficult for their party to sustain a position on a whole range of issues, from the MX missile to contra aid. The president seemed to be in complete control. *Fortune* magazine even hailed him in a cover story for his "management style." It was hard to argue with success. The picture of the jaunty president was especially highlighted by the contrast with the grim Soviet leader, Konstantin Chernenko, who could barely speak or walk. What was approaching, said Reagan in his second inaugural, were "golden years."

Two years later, Reagan's presidency seemed reduced to rubble. The monarchical president, who had been impervious to slings and arrows, wandered about in a daze. Eventually, he managed to restore his presidency and his poll ratings in time for the last reel but only by undergoing a major transformation. His fall came through the attempt by his trusted CIA director, William Casey, to wage the Cold War by any means necessary. His deliverance came through a *deus ex machina*, Mikhail Sergeyevich Gorbachev, who was determined to end the Cold War. Reagan was Reagan again, but only after he repudiated the master concept of his ideology: the belief that the Soviet Union was an "evil empire."

The period between Reagan's fall and rise was the seedtime of themes for the 1988 campaign. It was an unsteady, equivocal period. The themes that had their beginnings here—competence, patriotism and suspicion—were not the basis of a new era but the anxious signs of the one that was passing. George Bush, who was flustered by the circumstances that gave rise to these themes, wound up as their ultimate beneficiary. His inheritance would have been ashes, however, if Reagan had not been saved from scandal by Gorbachev.

Reagan's fall, of course, had its origin in the Iran-contra scandal. To the general public, the scandal was about Iran. All the polls showed that it was mainly Reagan's transfer of weapons to the Ayatollah that led to the public's revulsion. Reagan had come to power partly on his promise to erase the humiliation of the Teheran hostage crisis. By arming the Ayatollah he betrayed his promise and his image. To the press and the Congress, the scandal was mainly about illegally aiding the contras and was perceived through the prism of the Watergate conspiracy. The presumption in the Watergate investigations, however, was that Nixon was responsible; the charge against Reagan was that he was irresponsible, which became his ironclad defense. His problem was his innocence, which made his acquittal easy but led to the question of whether the president could govern. Reagan's leadership did not engage the citizenry but was an attempt to disengage and soothe them. Now he roiled them. Substance overwhelmed style, the scandal overwhelmed the scenario. Yet, unlike Nixon, Reagan divulged what seemed to be the worst news first: that the money from the sales of arms to Iran had been used to help fund the contras. The search for the smoking gun was made to seem redundant, the investigations anticlimactic. Reagan was as confounding in his failures as he was in his successes.

William Casey, the director of the CIA, died before he finished the most grandiose project of his career or could testify about it. Nobody has fully explained it since: not the Senate Intelligence Committee; not the President's Special Review Board; not the congressional committees investigating the Iran-contra affair; and not the special prosecutor. What the mumbling, shuffling spymaster had done may never be revealed. He is beyond the call of any interrogator; documents were shredded, key witnesses lied, and the congressional investigation was botched. Though it is generally considered to be a settled affair, the Iran-contra scandal is filled with black holes. Every part of it eventually leads into utter darkness.

Casey believed that the Cold War was a hot war. "This is not an undeclared war," he told a group at New York's Metropolitan Club in the spring of 1985. "In 1961, Khrushchev, then leader of the Soviet Union, told us that communism would win—not through nuclear war, which could destroy the world, or conventional war, which could quickly lead to nuclear war, but by wars of national liberation in Africa, Asia and Latin America. We were reluctant to believe him then—just as in the 1930s, we were reluctant to take Hitler seriously."

The future was the continuation of the past: the battle of good and evil. Within Fortress America, the forces of good were on the right. Casey, an OSS agent during World War II, a time when an emergent superpower did not restrict its spies, was one of the earliest Cold War conservatives. In 1955, he was the lawyer who filed the incorporating papers for William F. Buckley, Jr.'s *National Review,* the first journal of the conservative movement. Casey wanted to do more than contain communism. He wanted rollback. He could feel the enemy closing in. He ended his personal letters with the flourish: "God Save America!"

The enemies outside were reinforced by battalions within—the liberals, the press, the Congress—or, as Casey grumbled upon leaving a congressional hearing, "the assholes." He lied to the Senate Intelligence Committee about the CIA's mining of the Nicaraguan harbors, and he deeply resented being chastised when he was found out. The latest Boland Amendment, which prohibited agencies of the government from militarily aiding the contras, only deepened his contempt and wrath. Seemingly disparate incidents—the blasting of a marine barracks in Beirut by a truck bomber, the hijackings of a TWA airplane and the *Achille Lauro* cruise ship—reinforced his view that the conspiracy was widening. And yet Congress, after Watergate, had passed laws forbidding all manner of what are known in the intelligence trade as "black" operations, including assassinations. Casey's sense of the spy game, going back to his OSS days fighting Hitler, demanded a way around the restrictions set up by the enemies within. As Lieutenant Colonel Oliver North, Casey's action officer on the National Security Council, was to testify:

> Director Casey had in mind, as I understood it, an overseas entity that was capable of conducting operations or activities of assistance to U.S. foreign policy goals that was a stand-alone. . . . That was self-financing, independent of appropriated monies and capable of conducting activities similar to the ones that we had conducted here.

This full-service covert action agency was known to those who ran it as the Enterprise. It was independent of Congress and the president, with Swiss bank accounts, munitions, airplanes, a landing strip, a ship, and secret agents around the globe. It raised, according to the select congressional committee investigating the scandal, about $48 million in two years through the sale of arms to Iran, the CIA and the contras, through contributions from foreign governments, and by bilking gullible conservative donors. Strategically placed members of the administration driven and blinded by ideological zeal, such as Assistant Secretary of State Elliott Abrams, fell into the gears of the scandal. Others participating in aspects of the scandal, who began to have doubts, were self-censoring. "Where I went wrong," testified former national security adviser Robert McFarlane, about his conviction that the contras were a hopeless cause, "was not having the guts to stand up and tell the president that. To tell the truth, probably the reason I didn't is because if I'd done that, Bill Casey, Jeanne Kirkpatrick, and Cap [Caspar] Weinberger would have said I was some kind of commie."

Selling arms to Iran to finance the contra operation fostered the creation of the Enterprise. Once the group was established, the men behind it envisioned a whole array of secret projects. The Enterprise was something like SPECTRE, the worldwide covert action organization depicted in Ian Fleming's James Bond novels, pledging allegiance to no government.

Some money from the Enterprise's accounts apparently paid for the contras' resupply, an effort on the part of the Enterprise to gain further control over them. Yet it does not appear that any Enterprise money went directly to the contras. Rather, it went to cloak-and-dagger operatives and secret companies. When the Iran-contra scandal was uncovered, there was at least $8 million still in its accounts. What that might have financed can only be speculated upon. Certainly, Casey and North were desperate to find new ways to counter terrorism and communism in the Third World that were not subject to the supervision of the U.S. government.

On December 17, 1986, Casey was scheduled to testify before the Senate Intelligence Committee, which was conducting the first inquiry into the scandal. That morning, he collapsed, was rushed to the hospital and never recovered. He died six months later of brain cancer. Though the mystery of Casey's conspiracy may never be fully deciphered, its political effects are evident. The ultimate expression of Cold War conservatism led to its ultimate rejection.

The scandal's aftermath was to impact on the campaign. It set the stage by moving all the scenery, altering the lighting and rehearsing the actors with miscues. When the curtain finally went up, the campaign participants stumbled over the furniture, wandered out of spotlights and mouthed lines that kept audiences sitting on their hands. The political press corps were like critics who did not know if they were reviewing Samuel Beckett, David Mamet or Neil Simon. The campaigners' confusion was partly due to an inability to comprehend that the era of the Cold War was drawing to a close.

For Republicans, modern times began in 1980 with Ronald Reagan's election. Reagan's rise had seemingly obliterated the legacy of Richard Nixon; as Republicans marched into partisan battle, they held aloft Reagan's image as both a banner and a shield. With Reagan, everything seemed possible; without him, nothing. The Republican domain was unthinkable without a radiant Reagan at its center.

On November 25, 1986, Ronald Reagan held an unscheduled press conference at which he relinquished the stage and the microphone to Attorney General Edwin Meese, who announced that the money raised by selling arms to Iran had been diverted to aid the Nicaraguan contras. Reagan was not available for questioning by reporters; he had fled. He no longer knew the script or even who was producing this play; he could not speak his lines or act his role. The Republicans could not believe their eyes and ears. It seemed to be a waking nightmare. On December 1, Reagan's approval rating, as measured by the *New York Times*–CBS News poll, collapsed from 67 to 46 percent—the greatest and swiftest decline ever recorded for any president.

Every election is a referendum on the administration that has just held office, for the victorious opposition always seizes upon the failures of the incumbent regime. In 1968, as war and riots raged, Richard Nixon promised to "bring us together." In 1976, in the wake of Watergate, Jimmy Carter promised "a government as good as its people." In 1980, as almost everything seemed to be slipping out of control— "America Held Hostage," as a nightly ABC News program was called—Ronald Reagan urged: "Vote Republican, for a change." And in 1988?

The first theme of the campaign was established by the President's Special Review Board to investigate the Iran-contra affair. Also known as the Tower Commission, after its chairman, John Tower, the diminutive former senator from Texas who was still a giant of the Washington establishment, the board's other eminences included Edmund Muskie, former senator and secretary of state under Carter, and Brent Scowcroft, national security adviser under Gerald Ford. In the section titled "A Flawed Process," the commission used words such as "contradictory," "inadequate," "too informal," "chaos," and "unprofessional" to point up a "failure of responsibility," which was ultimately charged to the president's "management style," a euphemism well understood in Washington to refer to his passivity, ignorance and inattention. This was not simply a report on the scandal by a group of disinterested observers. It was the judgment on Reagan by the Washington establishment—the powers that were, are and will be. They had a different understanding of power than Reagan and the Reaganites. Power, as they understood it, neither began with his election to the presidency nor would end with it. So the standards applied to Reagan were not his standards. By criticizing Reagan for his "management style" the

Tower Commission was doing more than faulting him for his style. Reagan's image was as a man of strength and power, which lent him an air of natural self-confidence. The commission was saying that, in the terms of Washington, Reagan exercised little power. He was absent from the office he held. In effect, he was his own pretender. This revelation crumbled his image.

Reagan's handling of the commission's report lent credence to its accusation about his "management style." When presented in a closed session with the commission's findings, he denied to its members that he had traded arms for hostages. But the assembled board told him that indeed he had. Was he unaware of his own actions? Reagan sat back, subdued and befuddled. An hour later, at the press conference at which the report was presented, Tower said that Reagan "clearly didn't understand the nature of this operation, who was involved, and what was happening." Reagan was humbled, and he pledged to study the report. His homework was to learn what went on in his own administration. Almost overnight, he lost his vigor, becoming an old man, out of touch, unsure of himself.

The Democrats were jubilant. In public, they wore long faces; in private, they danced on the tables. Nothing they had ever said about Reagan had stuck; he was "the Teflon president." The Democratic pollsters had advised the Democratic politicians that Reagan's policies might be unpopular, but he was not. Still, attacking only Reagan's policies was unsatisfactory because they could not be met head on if he himself had to be avoided. No Democrat felt safe. Now Reagan had been brought down. The blow that had felled him had not been delivered by the opposition but by Reagan's own men. The Washington verdict that Reagan's "management style" was at fault made a Democratic succession to Reagan seem likelier. It might be 1976 all over again—the Watergate disaster, the Democratic triumph. Not only could the prostrate Reagan be sidestepped, so could his discredited conservatism. The Democrats could campaign against misgovernment and offer themselves as professionals. This campaign was not to be about ideology, but competence. It was a theme awaiting a candidate. In the meantime, the spillage from the scandal seemed endless. "Just sit back and don't spoil the view," said one influential Democratic strategist.

II

"COUP D'ÉTAT" screamed the headline of the newsletter published by Howard Phillips, the chairman of the new right Conservative Caucus. It was the first publication truly to voice the fears of many activists. "The real significance of the 'Contragate' crisis now confronting the Reagan administration," wrote Phillips, "is the decision of the president to seek surcease from his liberal critics by surrendering virtually total control over U.S. foreign policy to George Shultz and the Wall Street establishment which Shultz represents." The scandal was a repetition of Watergate, another liberal coup, toppling another antiliberal president. Though the liberals had been defeated at the ballot box by Reagan, they had not stopped their efforts to thwart the popular mandate for an unthrottled conservatism. They succeeded in Watergate and they were succeeding again. "In both cases," wrote Phillips, "power passed from the elected leader of Main Street America to the media-confirmed surrogate of an unelected establishment elite." Reagan's smiles and salutes and catches in the throat were now meaningless. "Conservatives find it increasingly difficult to stand by a man who has deserted them," wrote Phillips. "Eventually, the conservative regime falls, while the liberal policy and personnel which it has installed continue."

Phillips came from a faction of the conservative movement—the new right grouping of organizations fueled by the money raised by computerized direct mail. But his opinion was not unrepresentative of the more dedicated conservative cadres. The momentum of the movement that seemed centripetal in the period leading up to Reagan's election had reversed and was now centrifugal.

For decades, the conservatives had struggled to reach national power. They began as a scorned minority of a minority, inhabiting the frozen wasteland on the edge of Republican territory, a few scattered individuals who, as they huddled together for warmth, could agree about little more than the satanic nature of communism. They argued about labels, whether to call themselves liberal or conservative, about the proper place of the market and tradition, about loyalty to the Republican Party, and whether Abraham Lincoln was a saint or a devil. Slowly and with great effort, their movement overcame its isolation and its natural tendency to divide over doctrinal differences. They founded magazines, journals and think tanks. They established political action committees and cultivated religious sects. They raised tens of millions of dollars and achieved control over a host of foundations. They stroked and promoted candidates, framed their issue positions and wrote their speeches, while seeking to discredit and defeat others. In 1964, with Richard Nixon temporarily in oblivion and the moderate Republicans divided, the conservatives gained dominance over the Republican Party convention and nominated their champion, Senator Barry Goldwater, who was far more interested in making his points than in winning power. His defeat did not disappoint them; they felt this was nothing but a milestone.

In 1968, Nixon returned from the dead to arouse and perplex them. They loved him for his enemies, and he loved to throw them against his enemies. He constantly plotted how to use the right as a weapon. The problem for the conservatives was that Nixon lacked the principles for which they supported him. Their instinct was to exonerate him of accusations because of their hatred of his accusers, despite their familiarity with his frequent political betrayals. After Watergate, during which virtually all conservative publicists engaged in convoluted apologetics, they wanted to forget him, but never to forgive his enemies. Through their desire to settle scores Nixon's resentment lived on—another of his political afterlives. Reagan's election in 1980 was greeted by conservatives as their vindication. As they had always believed, the majority was conservative, after all; it had simply been manipulated, misled and silenced by the liberal establishment.

This belief was the sine qua non of conservative politics. One of Goldwater's books was entitled *The Conscience of the Majority,* and his campaign slogan—"In your heart you know he's right"—expressed the wish-fulfillment of conservatives. But it was only when the Democratic coalition was shattered by racial discord, the Vietnam War and the emergence of the counterculture that conservatives were able to take political advantage. The potential of social polarization as an electoral strategy was first detailed by a young Nixon campaign aide, Kevin Phillips, in his influential 1969 book, *The Emerging Republican Majority.* In it, he argued that the GOP could become the majority party by forging an alliance of resentment between those who voted in 1968 for Nixon or George Wallace. The Dixiecrats and the plutocrats, the urban ethnics and the Sunbelt evangelicals could be combined in a common reaction.

But Nixon's two triumphs had not brought the conservatives what they wanted. He was especially disdainful of them when he was popular. Their rewards were largely symbolic and rhetorical. His administration was mostly staffed by the usual Republican types, drawn from the large law firms and corporations. These partisans of the status quo were not movement conservatives; they were, in fact, their natural adversaries within the GOP. By 1980, however, the conservative infrastructure built up over the years—a counterestablishment against the presumed liberal establishment—yielded a harvest. For the first time, a corps of right-wing cadres was prepared to enter the government. These conservatives were not devoted to an abstract sense of public service, or to making the government run more like a business. To them, the movement that had taken over the party was the true "conscience of the majority." The government had assumed a zombie-like life of its own and was taking its marching orders from the liberal establishment. The conservative mission was to make the government act as the instrument of their ideology, which they presented as the only true patriotism. Thus they sought to create a Movement State.

There were problems from the beginning. Reagan was distant and passive even in the staffing of many of the most important posts within his administration. Of those aides closest to him in his first term, only the bumbling presidential counselor Edwin Meese was devoted to conservative patronage. A number of those appointed were eccentrics; a few were corrupt; many more were politically inept and quickly turned into burn-out cases. Still, thousands of conservative political appointees honeycombed the administration, turning departments into bureaucratic war zones. Tooth and nail they fought the civil service and the traditional Republicans. In the Department of Education, for example, the movement conservatives met weekly to plot how to undermine its moderate Republican Secretary, Terrell Bell, former commissioner of Utah's System of Higher Education. Bell, in his memoir, described how he infiltrated an informer into their midst and found that their network extended throughout the executive branch, "in influential positions in OMB [Office of Management and Budget], the Justice Department and the West Wing [of the White House]." Their special targets were appointees who did not share their ideology. When events did not cooperate with one of their policies they blamed those who did not agree with it. If the construction of the Movement State met obstacles, Americanism as they understood it was being betrayed. Their agenda was advanced behind the figure of Reagan. Their battle cry, raised at a rally of political appointees by the militant Secretary of the Interior James Watt, was "Let Reagan Be Reagan." An entire worldview was encapsulated in that slogan: the Reagan iconography, the struggle for the Movement State and the belief that a far-flung conspiracy was plotting against it.

By Reagan's second term, the Movement State was stalled. The supply of potential conservative appointees was running dry. Not even the Heritage Foundation, continually shoveling résumés into the White House, could provide the troops. The problem was not just a shortage of personnel. By late 1986, the conservative movement was spinning apart. Faction was set against faction, sect against sect. The old right, which had run the movement when it was tiny, felt dispossessed by the more cosmopolitan neoconservatives. The old rightists despised the newcomers, seeing these former leftists as usurpers, using their control over foundations to freeze the old right out of the money. For their part, the neoconservatives, many of whom were Jewish, viewed elements of the old right as anti-Semitic. As the old rightists cast the neoconservatives as aliens, the neoconservatives cast the old rightists as nativists. The factions fought publicly over key positions, such as the chairmanship of the National Endowment for the Humanities, which the neoconservative William Bennett won. And they went at each other ideologically in their respective leading journals, *National Review* and *Commentary*.

As they squabbled, the American Enterprise Institute, once the leading conservative think tank, suffered a financial crisis and the resignation of its president. This crisis was precipitated by the withdrawal of funds from major donors who believed that AEI was drifting away from Reaganism in a quest for respectability. Money and moral woes strained other conservative groups as well. The National Conservative Political Action Committee (NCPAC), which had produced slashing negative television commercials against Democratic senators in 1980 and 1984, was deeply in debt. Its founder, Terry Dolan, died of AIDS, and his slow, semipublic death provided the occasion for antigay right wingers to attack NCPAC libertarians within the movement.

In the meantime, the direct mail operation of Richard Viguerie, upon which most of the new right was dependent, went bankrupt. Hundreds were laid off and Viguerie was sued by a conservative group for creating "bogus entities" to raise money. Also, as during their rise in the late 1970s conservatives could not turn to their main source of cash: the Southwestern independent oil operators. That industry was in recession. The religious right, which had been created by the new right, had assumed its own dynamic, tapping great sums of money from true believers. One of its leading figures, Pat Robertson, was preparing to run for president. The approaching campaign was not unifying the movement but accelerating its centrifugal force.

The schisms within the movement created a huge opening for an outside power: the Unification Church of the Reverend Sun Myung Moon, the self-proclaimed South Korean messiah, whose ultimate goal is a global theocratic dictatorship. Untold millions were channeled through Moon to the conservatives. Viguerie, for one, restored his solvency through payments from the Moonies. (Before he died, Terry Dolan took more than $700,000 from the Moonies.) Many other right-wing groups became Moonie dependencies, taking money outright or staffing their organizations with Moonie volunteers. The Moonies also published the *Washington Times,* the conservative voice in town, and two magazines, *Insight* and *The World and I.* Moon became the greatest source of money and the biggest private employer of conservatives in the capital. The largesse was spread so widely, extending to salaries, donations, free travel expenses, and exorbitant payment for certain articles, that hardly any conservative publicly criticized the operation. At the same time, political operatives associated with the Moonies became key organizers within the religious right. Andrew Ferguson, a rare conservative who was unwilling to bite his tongue, wrote in the *American Spectator* that "Moon gave conservatives many reasons to ignore the unpleasantness and refrain from questioning his growing involvement—millions and millions of reasons, all (as the old joke has it) with little pictures of George Washington on them." Thus the movement that had crusaded against un-Americanism became, in part, a financial dependency of a foreign power with a hidden agenda.

In the deep background, meanwhile, the Enterprise was being assembled. It contained spores that had drifted over from the movement, but it was in its own orbit. It used the conservative movement primarily as a cash cow and a laundromat. The Enterprise's agent was Carl "Spitz" Channell, a former NCPAC operative, who set up a number of political action committees and raised $10 million, mostly from right-wing blue-haired widows, on the promise that they would be buying weapons for the contras. Most of the money was lavished by Channell on himself and his lovers; some money made its way to the contra leaders; and some was "washed" through a Cayman Island bank account to the Enterprise.

The Heritage Foundation, at the instigation of Robert MacFarlane and Oliver North, transferred $100,000 to a front group controlled by Channell's partner, Richard Miller, who, after pocketing $20,000, deposited the rest in a secret bank account, congressional investigators reported. Sending along the check, Heritage's President, Edwin Feulner, wrote, "My colleagues and I have discussed your proposal in some detail and we are pleased to respond in a positive way."

When this was disclosed in depositions taken by the investigators, Representative Richard Cheney, the ranking House Republican on the committee, rushed to the defense of the preeminent conservative think tank. If its records were requested, he threatened, he would retaliate by calling up the records of the Brookings Institution and every nonconservative think tank in Washington. His gambit worked. The Heritage Foundation's role in the scandal, in which the demands of the Movement State took precedence over any claim of scholarship, was never further probed.

But with the disclosure of the Enterprise, the effort to build the Movement State was in a shambles. Decades of labor seemed to have come to naught. The making of a conservative governing class in the executive branch, especially in the realm of foreign policy, ground to a standstill. Retreads from the Nixon and Ford years began to reappear in familiar roles: Howard Baker as chief of staff, Frank Carlucci as national security adviser, Richard Thornburgh as attorney general.

Members of the Enterprise, a collection of arms dealers and rogue intelligence agents passing themselves off as idealists, claimed that their actions, however unlawful, were undertaken for a higher patriotic cause. Conservatives did not feel outraged at the Enterprise but at Congress, which was investigating, and at the State Department, which the Enterprise had tried to circumvent. The world according to the conservatives appeared more starkly divided between good and evil than ever before. The battle against communism was again being lost at home; sniveling legislators had stabbed the country in the back. It was in the disintegration of conservatism that the issue of loyalty, which reached a crescendo in the presidential campaign, came to the fore. A new, strong leader, conservatives demanded, was needed to stand for the flag against the subversive elites. From where would the leader spring? The march of the pretenders began. The first was heralded by Howard Phillips: "Into this vacuum has stepped one Patrick J. Buchanan, now the White House director of communications . . . the logical successor to Ronald Reagan in the hearts and minds of the Republican rank and file."

As the ranks of sunshine patriots dwindled, the moment of the foul-weather friend arrived. "The greatest vacuum in American politics is to the right of Ronald Reagan," said Buchanan, as he plotted his future in his windowless office in the West Wing of the White House. His career strangely reflected the oscillations of conservatism. Whenever conservatism soured, he inevitably rose to the surface.

The Reagan aide who had been the Nixon aide provided the continuity between Watergate and the Iran-contra scandals. For Buchanan, Watergate was "the lost opportunity to move against the political forces frustrating the expressed national will." The lesson Buchanan drew from the Nixon disappointment was that to "effect a political counterrevolution in the capital . . . there is no substitute for a principled and dedicated man of the right in the Oval Office."

In early January 1987, Buchanan left his office in the West Wing, wandering across the street to Lafayette Park, to lead a fevered conservative rally in support of Reagan. "You will not bring this president down!" he shouted. "What liberalism and the left have in mind," he wrote in an op-ed piece in *The Washington Post*, "is the second ruination of a Republican presidency within a generation."

Buchanan, however, was thinking beyond Reagan. The man of the right was not George Bush, who was lying underneath the fallen presidency. It was not Representative Jack Kemp, whose arcane talk of supply-side economics was not galvanizing the activists. And it was not Pat Robertson, whose faith might be powerful enough to rebuke a hurricane, but not the Internal Revenue Service, which was auditing his Freedom Council for improper political activities. The Republican primary voters, Buchanan was convinced, were being "radicalized" by Reagan's ordeal; "an explosion" was about to occur. None of the GOP presidential hopefuls expressed this primal rage.

Buchanan was raised on curdled conservatism. In his family the household gods were Douglas MacArthur, Joseph McCarthy and Francisco Franco. After attending the Columbia School of Journalism, Buchanan became an editorial writer for the St. Louis *Globe-Democrat*, occasionally writing vicious little pieces about the Rev. Martin Luther King, Jr.

In 1966, when Nixon was at the beginning of his miraculous resurrection, Buchanan became the first full-time member of his fledgling campaign staff. He was known as "Mr. Inside" because he specialized in writing speeches that brought right-wing crowds to their feet. During the 1972 race against George McGovern, Buchanan was an endless source of ideas for negative campaigning. His participation in what was called the "Attack Group" prompted his summons before the Watergate investigating committee. He was defiant. As far as he was concerned, it was the committee that was on trial. "The mandate that the American people gave to this president and his administration cannot and will not be frustrated or repealed or overthrown," he said. He urged Nixon to burn the White House tapes. In the confusion immediately following Nixon's fall, before Gerald Ford had taken complete hold of the presidency, Buchanan attempted to be appointed ambassador to a country whose policies he defended: South Africa. Members of Ford's incoming staff, however, caught on to the paperwork by holdover Chief of Staff Alexander Haig that had already approved the nomination, and the new president rejected it.

Under Jimmy Carter, a host of conservative columnists were elevated to prominence, including Buchanan, who was unrestrained in his invective. Upon Reagan's election, these conservative publicists became peers of the realm. The president drove up Connecticut Avenue in his limousine to dine at George Will's house. He appeared at the anniversary dinner of William F. Buckley, Jr.'s *National Review*, of which he was a charter subscriber. The television appearances and lecture fees of the right-wing columnists rose astronomically. Buchanan's annual income was an estimated $400,000. His fame was won as a regular member of "The McLaughlin Group," a weekly television show influential in setting the tone of Reagan's Washington. It was hosted by John McLaughlin, a former Jesuit priest whose parish had been Nixon's White House in its final days. Buchanan was his bunkermate. "The McLaughlin Group" featured conservative animadversions in the form of parodies of liberalism. Buchanan was a star.

In 1985, at the beginning of Reagan's second term, Buchanan was appointed his communications director. He prepared for the job by rereading James Burnham's *Suicide of the West,* an apocalyptic tract in which Burnham elaborated his notion of the Cold War as the Third World War. Inside the White House, Buchanan urged Reagan to stand tall at the Bitburg cemetery when he laid a wreath on the graves of Nazi SS soldiers. He urged the president to stand tall against economic sanctions against South Africa. And he cast contra aid as a Manichean issue, which "will reveal whether [the Democratic Party] stands with Ronald Reagan and the resistance—or Daniel Ortega and the communists."

With the scandal's revelation, Buchanan appeared as the man on horseback—the "man of the right." For a time, his outbursts were unavoidable on television: all the network news programs, the talk shows and even the half-time show of ABC's "Monday Night Football." In Orange County, California, his sister, Angela Jackson, the former treasurer of the United States, began organizing prominent conservative activists. Howard Phillips of the Conservative Caucus was excitedly on the telephone. The Manchester, New Hampshire, *Union Leader* was encouraging. And the political operatives around Senator Jesse Helms offered their services. On January 14, a meeting on the potential candidacy took place at Buchanan's McLean, Virginia, home. A Republican defeat was in the air; the moment was ripe. The model for a Buchanan run was not the triumphant Reagan of 1984 or 1980 but the radical Reagan of 1964. In the closing hours of Goldwater's campaign, as defeat seemed certain, Reagan had made his national political debut in a televised speech—"The Speech"—in which he laid down the tenets of conservative fundamentalism for the next generation. "Some of our own have said 'Better Red than dead.' . . . Should Christ have refused the Cross?" he demanded. The Republicans in 1988, it was generally agreed at the meeting, would lose the presidency. But Buchanan could rise, like Reagan, as the conservative standard-bearer. A few present argued that Jack Kemp should be given his chance, that Buchanan's candidacy would unleash a conservative civil war. At that, John Lofton, a columnist for the *Washington Times*, declared, "Let the bloodbath begin!" For a few days more, Buchanan stood on the verge. The entire Republican Party quivered. Then, suddenly, the man on horseback abruptly dismounted. He had apparently suffered a failure of nerve; yet the theme of resentment lived on.

There was soon another pretender. Ronald Reagan called him "a national hero." But Oliver North averred that he was acting out the scenario that William Casey had suggested in case the activities of the Enterprise were exposed: "the fall guy scenario." On the first day of the Iran-contra committee hearings, Representative James Courter, a movement conservative, expressed his disillusionment with Reagan. "Ronald Reagan," he lamented, "lacks the courage of Reagan's convictions." Who had Reagan's convictions, if not Reagan? The conservatives felt that they had tumbled through a time warp. It was the McCarthy era, the time of show trials. But they were sitting where the accused Communists and fellow travelers had sat. And their enemies were sitting where Joe McCarthy and Dick Nixon had presided.

The new man on horseback literally wore his patriotism on his sleeve. The conservatives ransacked their minds for images. They idolized him as a Reagan, a Rambo, a Charles Lindbergh. North claimed that he would obey any order from the commander-in-chief, including one to stand on his head in a corner.[1] He challenged the terrorist Abu Nidal to hand-to-hand combat. He wondered aloud if he had put all the incriminating evidence through the shredder.

North beguiled the conservatives from the moment they laid eyes

---

1. Later, during his trial, in the effort to save himself, North charged his commander-in-chief with covering up and lying, and he subpoenaed Reagan's testimony.

on him. The White House Office of Public Liaison, dominated by movement conservatives, discovered him in the early 1980s and frequently used his services as a speaker on behalf of contra aid. Soon he was delivering his patented briefing, complete with slide show, before large conservative groups. The tremulous catch in the voice and the pictures of Soviet guns never failed to move these audiences. The contra war, he explained, was the hot war, was the Cold War, was the war on terrorism. "The Cubans have decided, the Soviets have decided, the Bulgarians, the East Germans, the Libyans, the PLO. It is now up to the Congress to decide whether or not we are able to do something about what is going on in Nicaragua."

North had a sense of drama, especially of self-dramatization, but not of politics. He never understood that checks and balances were the essence, not the antithesis, of the American system. He had the Praetorian guard's contempt for politicians and their half-measures. The lieutenant colonel came to stand for Reagan's foreign policy, which was presented as a grand strategy culminating in the Reagan Doctrine, the rollback of communism in the Third World. But it was not really a foreign policy at all. It was, instead, the substitution of the military for diplomacy, from the Middle East to Central America. U.S.–Soviet relations were reduced to an arms race. When military means failed, as in Lebanon, or seemed inadequate, as in Nicaragua, the administration was at a loss for a policy. In the latter case, the Congress stepped in, with legislators holding forth and passing bills. Rather than resort to diplomacy, both in the region and with the Congress, the administration engaged in charades while its policy went underground. The Praetorian guard assumed more and more influence.

For decades, the conservative rhetoric about betrayal, appeasement and stabs in the back referred to events surrounding World War II, conflating Munich and Yalta. North updated the analogies. His motivation, as he told the Iran-contra committee, had its source in the Vietnam War:

> We didn't lose the war in Vietnam. We lost the war right in this city. . . . I came back from a war that we fought in Vietnam to a public that did not understand, in my humble opinion, they had been lied to. The American public did not know what we suffered, what we endured, or what we tried to achieve. And I think the same thing prevails for the Nicaraguan resistance today.

Nicaragua was Vietnam revisited; in the life-and-death struggle with the Sandinistas, the contras were being betrayed in Washington. "The

Congress of the United States," he said, "left soldiers in the field unsupported and vulnerable to their communist enemies. . . . You then held this investigation to blame the problem on the executive branch."

Since the end of the war, conservatives had argued that U.S. power was being weakened by a hesitance to use force, a condition they termed the Vietnam Syndrome. Oliver North, however, suffered from a different Vietnam Syndrome. In 1974, after tours of duty in Vietnam and Okinawa, he entered the Bethesda Naval Hospital for more than three weeks, officially diagnosed as suffering "emotional distress." The proximate cause was apparently his wife's determination to leave him. North's biographer, Ben Bradlee, Jr., cited several sources on his break-down. According to one, North was incoherently ranting, dashing about naked, and waving a pistol, threatening suicide, before being hospitalized. Another source was quoted as observing North in the hospital recreation room, where he often pulled up a chair next to himself, upon which he draped his uniform, bedecked with medals. North's résumés failed to note his hospitalization, and Bradlee quoted sources who said that North managed to have it erased.

In 1978, North became a born-again Christian. He joined a charis-matic church that practiced speaking in tongues and faith healing by the laying on of hands. He was certain that his version of patriotism was divinely inspired and that his mission was predestined. Bradlee quoted a Reagan administration official in whom North confided: "I heard him say that he had been wounded in battle and he felt that he had been spared by God in order to do something important, and this was it."

North, it was often said, was the son Reagan wished he had. The "national hero" was Reagan's illusion, a fantasy of derring-do unreeling in his private screening room. But the notion of North as Reagan's son was also an illusion promoted by North himself. He told many conservative leaders that he had watched the televised landing of stu-dents rescued from Grenada alone with the president in the White House. When one student kissed the ground, Reagan said: "You see, Ollie, I told you not to worry. You can trust Americans." North also told a group of born-again Christians that he and Reagan had fervently prayed together, just the two of them. North, in fact, had never met with Reagan alone on any occasion, according to the White House log.

North's lies and exaggerations about matters large and small were endless. He even recounted a tale about his dog, dead by poisoning from terrorists. But the mutt, according to neighbors, had, alas, died of old age. Having been personally deceived by North, however, did not disillusion the conservatives, who demanded that the principal action officer of the Enterprise, now the self-described "fall guy," be treated as a hero.

He appeared before the Iran-contra committee on July 7, 1987. It was the first confrontation between the themes of competence and ideology, and it ended in a triumph of the latter—of image over reality, audacity over law.

The dimensions of North's victory were framed before the opening gavel fell. To placate the White House, the committee agreed to limit its existence to ten months, which rushed its inquiry. It allowed the White House to vet all documents before it saw them, and permitted North's attorney to edit his client's notebooks. Then it struck a disadvantageous deal with North. He was granted immunity; he would not be questioned prior to his appearance by the committee staff; and the questioning would be limited to a period of thirty hours. They had no idea what to expect. Inside the committee, the debate was fierce. Its position of self-inflicted weakness was strenuously opposed by most of the House Democrats on the panel. Most of the Senate Democrats, led by Daniel Inouye, were intent on demonstrating their "fairness," that is, nonpartisanship. Their House colleagues were not so intent on posturing as statesmen. But they deferred to the judgment of the House committee chairman, Representative Lee Hamilton, lionized for his crewcut rectitude. On issue after issue, Hamilton caved in. According to sources who participated in the committee's inner deliberations, Hamilton's fear of confrontation and of somehow upsetting the arms control negotiations with the Soviets that were quietly underway had disastrous consequences. For members to have publicly challenged the conditions of North's appearance would have meant challenging Hamilton. Out of protocol and respect, they kept silent. Years of retreating before Reagan prepared the Democrats on the committee to retreat before North.

For five years, North had worn a business suit to his job on the National Security Council. In combat with the committee, he donned his uniform again. The lawyers who questioned him were concerned with the facts and the law. He responded with long perorations about patriotism, the danger of communism and terrorism, his love of God and family. His attorney, Brendan Sullivan, snarled at committee members who tried to move the inquiry back on track. He was not put in his place by the chairman, Senator Inouye; Sullivan's intimidations, therefore, never failed. North sat alone, but he filled the television screen. Here was a religious charismatic with glistening eyes, an unswerving patriot with medals to prove it. The committee appeared faceless and heartless, a kangaroo court. It seemed like a Kafkaesque bureaucratic nightmare, with North the brave individual against the system. The issue of what Senator Sam Nunn called the "junta"—the shadowy underworld of the Enterprise—was lost. Instead, the patriotism of the investigators was called into question.

This issue was directly addressed only by Senator George Mitchell, who chided North: "Although He's regularly asked to do so, God does not take sides in American politics. And in America, disagreement with the policies of the government is not evidence of lack of patriotism." But this was too little and too late.

North's appearance, which shattered the committee, was a peculiar foreshadowing of the 1988 campaign. The theme of "management style," or competence, did not withstand the blast of patriotism, no matter how distorted or spurious. The committee made this possible by its political incompetence, which was ultimately traceable to its preemptive fear. Even though the Movement State was a shipwreck, the menacing cultural symbols of Cold War conservatism could still be floated.

III

The Republican charges of softness and betrayal, which dominated the general election campaign, were first rehearsed by the right wing in the wake of the Iran-contra scandal against Ronald Reagan. To be sure, the usual suspects were rounded up. "It's getting harder and harder for all sides to tell the Democratic line from the Soviet one," read an article in the *National Review*. Congress was regularly excoriated as the Imperial Congress, usurper of the functions of the executive. And press-bashing was unrelieved. But Reagan was blamed more than any individual as the source of disillusionment. "If Reagan is the Reagan of mythology, it's time to strap on the gun and reenact 'Death Valley Days,' " said Representative Newt Gingrich, the leader of the movement conservatives in the House. Reagan's inability to act out conservatives' dreams perplexed and then angered them. The coolest analysis was offered by neoconservative "godfather" Irving Kristol, who attributed "the basic flaw of the Reagan presidency" to his failure to achieve the Movement State. " . . . his major appointments in the foreign policy area—in the Pentagon and the State Department—have been from the traditional-conservative wing of the Republican Party. The result is that Mr. Reagan has not only found his hands tied by Congress—he has managed to tie his own hands as well."

North's forceful appearance before the committee investigating the

Iran-contra scandal increased conservative disillusionment with the dimming Reagan. The lieutenant colonel had done everything that the president had not. In August, one month after "Olliemania" swept across the television screen, Reagan implicitly acknowledged that his Central American policy was in tatters by agreeing to the peace plan engineered by Costa Rican president Oscar Arias. The right was in a fury.

"Support the contras—IMPEACH REAGAN!" read a button proudly worn by movement conservatives. "Reagan's Bay of Pigs," read the headline on an editorial in the *Wall Street Journal.* "Fiasco," it began. "There is no other word for it." The editorial continued: "This is appeasement. . . . The Brezhnev Doctrine wins." That week fifteen conservative leaders were invited to the White House to be reassured of Reagan's steadfastness. He read a prepared statement pledging support for the contras, took no questions and departed. For an hour afterward, the conservatives sat in the room with Chief of Staff Howard Baker, heaping bitter accusations on him and the president. Full-page advertisements filled the *Washington Times.* "Munich in Managua," read the headline on one taken out by the right-wing Accuracy in Media. The "lesson of Munich," it said, "was forgotten by our president." R. Emmett Tyrrell, Jr., the editor of the *American Spectator,* in a piece entitled "The Coming Conservative Crack-Up," traced the problem to the shortcomings in constructing the Movement State. "They have not even thought of maintaining enduring institutions comparable to those of the Liberals," he wrote about his fellow conservatives. "There is something decidedly shaky and ephemeral about all their think tanks, their magazines, their activist groups." The Reagan presidency, wrote Joseph Sobran, a senior editor of the *National Review,* in his syndicated column, "shows every sign of ending sadly, in frustration, if not worse. . . . There was no Reagan revolution, only a Reagan rest stop."

Reagan now presided over a posthumous presidency. Instead of shrugging off criticism with quips and jokes, as he used to do, he began talking about his death. As he left Washington for a vacation at his ranch, following the North hearings, he announced that he would not be covered, like a corpse in a coffin, with "dust and cobwebs." Upon his return, hearings commenced on the nomination of Robert Bork to the Supreme Court. The conservative Bork would be defeated, Reagan declared, only "over my dead body." But Bork was defeated, and many conservatives blamed Reagan for insufficient support. Bork lashed out at the "ultra liberals" and the White House, claiming that his pleadings that it "become more active" had been in vain. Then, for one last time, Reagan pressed the issue of contra aid, declaring that he had taken a "solemn vow" to advance it "as long as there is breath in this body." But it was defeated.

North and Bork were both acclaimed as conservative martyrs, but they had very different understandings of their roles. North made himself out to be the "fall guy," that is, the stunt man, who stepped in to protect the leading man from injury (until the trial). Bork made himself out to be his own man, then changed his views on civil rights and privacy before the Senate Judiciary Committee and, after his rejection, demanded to know why Reagan had not stepped in to protect him.

But Reagan was waiting for a director, a script, a role to be played. The supporting actress, Nancy Reagan, desperately wanted him back in his familiar role, and she began the hunt for someone to recast his presidency.

The chief of staff when the Iran-contra scandal broke, Donald Regan, former chief executive officer of Merrill Lynch, had been Secretary of the Treasury in Reagan's first term. When he and James Baker decided to switch positions for the second term they presented the matter to Reagan as a fait accompli. The president acquiesced without questions. Regan had a Boston Irish background and was as ashamed of his humble origins, though he had gone to Harvard, as he was proud of his "fuck-you money," as he liked to put it. He was a martinet with little experience in the political arts, and he treated the scandal as an unfriendly takeover. His main interest appeared to be protecting his own reputation. He regarded the First Lady's influence as an intrusion on his turf, thereby precipitating a fight he could not win. Regan learned of his defenestration from a television news report. A year later, he attempted to even the score by publishing a book in which he revealed Nancy Reagan's reliance on an astrologer.

Regan's replacement was Howard Baker, the former Republican majority leader, a man of the party. He came from eastern Tennessee, a bastion of unbroken GOP strength since 1860, and was the son-in-law of the late Senator Everett Dirksen, the Republican minority leader. He had also been the ranking Republican on the Watergate committee, where his job was to protect the party from the scandal. In the Iran-contra affair, his job was the same. In the former, the president had to leave; in the latter, the president had to stay. Baker's appointment vastly relieved establishment Washington and, by the same token, sent the right wing into a rage. As majority leader, he had systematically administered euthanasia to the conservatives' social issues agenda. As chief of staff, he was deft at listening to their complaints while quietly putting the knife to them within the executive branch. To the right wing, Baker was worse than a Democrat, worse than a liberal; he was a Republican for whom time did not begin in 1980. But Baker had no program of his own beyond damage control.

The First Lady, in the meantime, discreetly sought advice from the wily Robert Strauss, former Democratic National Committee chairman, who is a friend of all presidents who wish to be his friend. She also called on the longtime Reagan scenarist, Michael Deaver, whose use, however, rapidly diminished as he sank into his own scandal over influence peddling. Regan and Baker, Strauss and Deaver—these were all character actors. None of them had the power to create a new production in which Reagan might star.

It took the president some time to grasp that even as the scandal was center stage, another script for him was being written.

Though he was confused, hurt and talking about death, Reagan was not defeated. He was more than an inveterate optimist; he was at heart a utopian. He had a dream. It was not the old one of rolling back communism; this was another vision entirely, one that his aides always considered ridiculously, even dangerously naïve. Gorbachev, however, came to understand this vision. Through his growing comprehension of what the president believed, Gorbachev emerged as Reagan's ultimate handler.

During his first two years in the White House Reagan twice asked the national security apparat to give him a plan to eliminate nuclear weapons. But this presidential request twice disappeared down the memory hole. Reagan was thinking the unthinkable. But he was hardly a committed arms controller. In fact, he campaigned against that intricate, incremental and arcane diplomacy as a form of appeasement. His mind contained absolutes. If he could not be superior in nuclear weapons he wanted to abolish them.

His strategic policy was driven by the notion advanced by cold warrior Paul Nitze since 1950 that the U.S. was vulnerable to Soviet nuclear strength. In the mid-1970s, Nitze argued that the Soviets possessed more nuclear warheads than the U.S., a superiority that could enable them to launch a devastating first strike—a scenario captured in the metaphor of the "window of vulnerability." Only when the "window" was closed would the U.S. be strong enough to halt the geopolitical extension of Soviet influence. Nitze's notion was more a theory about American psychology than a calculation of Soviet nuclear capability. The precise index of weakness measuring the opening in the "window" involves comparisons in the number of land-based missiles and warheads. Virtually all of the Soviet arsenal can be counted in this way. But the U.S. arsenal is based on what is called the "triad"—land, sea and air. The "window," therefore, measures only one part of the "triad." Nitze's position envisioned a craven America, refusing to respond to a nuclear attack with its remaining forces. Moreover, the theory's principal axiom—that the Russians can launch an incapacitating first strike—was unsupported by any technical evidence. In order to test the notion, they would have to fire one thousand missiles in a precision attack across the North Pole. The Soviets, however, have never fired a single missile across the pole, and they have never launched more than ten at a time. The "window" was a thoroughly hypothetical idea that explained little about U.S. strength. But it became the Reagan administration's strategic premise.

It was principally carried out by Richard Perle, the clever assistant secretary of defense, a neoconservative who had spent many years in Washington as an aide to Senator Henry Jackson while constructing a network of his own in Congress, the bureaucracy and the press. Perle was adept at stopping all initiatives toward arms control, which was much easier work than pushing them forward. When he failed to halt the gears of the arms control bureaucracy, he advanced proposals that the Soviets were almost certain to reject. One of these, dubbed "double zero," proposed that the U.S. and the Soviets both eliminate their intermediate range missiles from Europe—an idea that trumped Perle's interagency rivals, was put on ice by the Soviets and justified U.S. deployment. The arms race went on.

With the "window of vulnerability" reigning as nuclear strategy and the ingenious Perle dominant within the bureaucracy, a conservative version of deterrence prevailed. It was to be confounded by none other than Reagan. In 1983, inspired by the theoretical nuclear physicist Edward Teller and a small group of right-wing enthusiasts, Reagan announced the U.S.'s intention to build a seamless shield in outer space that would deflect all incoming missiles. He proposed the Strategic Defense Initiative, or Star Wars, without calling on any of his national security experts or giving his secretaries of state and defense more than twenty-four hours' advance notice. Only the fantasist president believed in the perfect astrodome, where life would go on as usual even if the nuclear missiles were flying. The others rationalized Star Wars as yet another element in deterrence. But Reagan meant to replace deterrence with defense—the most radical change in nuclear strategy since the Soviets exploded their first bomb. Reagan called Star Wars "my dream," but he mistook the means for the dream itself. A world without nuclear weapons was his true dream, as Gorbachev discovered.

The Soviets reacted with shock and horror to Star Wars. They did not believe that the U.S. meant to erect an impermeable curtain in space. They understood this as an effort to make a first strike even more devastating, a drastic escalation of the arms race.

The first summit between Reagan and Gorbachev took place in Geneva in November 1985. Reagan's aides were obsessed with photo opportunities. Standing in the cold, Reagan did not wear an overcoat while the younger Soviet leader did. This signified American vigor. Then, at the suggestion of the president's staff, Reagan and Gorbachev sat before a roaring fireplace. This signified warmth. Reagan made no proposals and, from his staff's point of view, no mistakes. Gorbachev, for his part, explained the Soviet trepidations about Star Wars. It appeared to be a successful encounter because nothing changed. But the surface was deceptive. A chemistry developed between the two leaders. "There was," said a Soviet embassy source, "a psychological interdependence." For Reagan, the meeting was crucial. Personal experience often defined his views, overriding even ideological imperatives. After sitting and talking and shaking hands with Gorbachev, the Soviet leader was no longer an abstraction, a symbol. He was a real person. "I think I'm some judge of acting," Reagan said afterward, "so I don't think he was acting. He, I believe, is just as sincere as we are." And Reagan told Gorbachev many tales about the old Hollywood, the likes of which he had never heard before. Reagan hardly appeared monstrous. On the contrary, he was a pleasant surprise.

In their fifty-four-minute private conversation Reagan revealed his utopian side. He had seen even farther than the end of the Cold War. He explained that he had glimpsed a new age in which nuclear weapons were banished and the two superpowers truly cooperated. He had seen, perhaps, the 1951 movie *The Day the Earth Stood Still,* in which an alien threatens destruction of the planet if all nuclear weapons are not done away with. Perhaps Reagan did not have the movie in mind—who knows?—but he did suggest the bare bones of its plot or, in the language of Hollywood, the treatment.[2]

2. Garry Wills suggests that Star Wars had an earlier reflection in a movie in which Reagan starred as a fearless government agent. "In his 1940 Brass Bancroft movie, *Murder in the Air,* Reagan protected the secret of a wonder weapon against those who would steal it from America—an 'inertia projector' that would bring down enemy airplanes by knocking out their electrical systems. . . . What is Star Wars but another,

A month after the summit, he told high school students in Fallston, Maryland, what he had proposed to Gorbachev. "Just think," said the president, "how easy his task and mine might be in these meetings that we held, if suddenly there was a threat to this world from some other species from another planet outside in the universe. We'd forget all the little local differences that we have between our countries and we would find out once and for all that we really are all human beings here on earth together. Well, I don't suppose we can wait for some alien race to come down and threaten us. But I think between us we can bring about this realization."

In the meantime, in Moscow, the coil around Gorbachev tightened. Within the Politburo, Reagan's military buildup was viewed as a "disincentive" to negotiate, especially by the conservatives. The arms race bolstered their position by increasing the military share of the economy and the political influence they derived from that. To reduce their stockpiles might mean a reduction in their influence over the course of the Soviet state. For years, before the U.S. buildup, the Soviets had made agreements with the U.S. Now they argued that the U.S. "could not be trusted with arms control," according to a Soviet source. On the other hand, Gorbachev inherited from Brezhnev a foreign policy that had isolated the Soviet Union. The war in Afghanistan seemed an unending nightmare. "We created a united front of nations against us," a Soviet diplomatic source said, on the day the Red Army left. Most important, the summit altered Gorbachev's perception of Reagan. The president's wholly unexpected talk about invaders from space contributed to Gorbachev's belief that Reagan could be convinced to make a daring deal. The Soviets recognized that if Reagan left the stage without having signed an arms reduction agreement, his successor would have enormous difficulty doing so; Reagan would have legitimated breaking with the line of presidents since Nixon who had done so. "It was important that with this man," said a Soviet diplomat, "we should achieve something."

On July 25, 1986, Reagan wrote Gorbachev suggesting that all ballistic missiles could be eventually abolished. This gesture was encouraged within the bureaucracy by the cynical Perle, who saw it as another notion the Soviets would reject. From Reagan's treatment, Gorbachev wrote a script. The first draft was submitted to Reagan at Reykjavik in October 1986. Everything, both sides agreed before hand,

---

more complex projector meant to trace, in lasers and benign nuclear 'searchlights,' the image of America itself across the widest screen of all."

was subject to negotiation. Amazingly enough, it was. In the first act, Gorbachev proposed a fifty percent cut in strategic arms and the elimination of intermediate range missiles in Europe. In the second act, Reagan, riffing on the concept, proposed eliminating all ballistic missiles in ten years. In the third act, Gorbachev proposed eliminating all nuclear weapons in ten years. "All nuclear weapons?" replied Reagan. "Well, Mikhail, that's exactly what I've been talking about all along . . . get rid of all nuclear weapons. That's always been my goal." But in the final act, Gorbachev insisted that this vision of the future was contingent on Reagan's agreement to ban research and testing of Star Wars components outside of the laboratory for ten years. Reagan drew back. He refused to give up the space defense. One dream collapsed upon the other. The summit, in a flash, was over. The projector broke, the screen went white. In the car to the airport, Reagan muttered, "Laboratory, laboratory, laboratory."

At first, the American delegation appeared stunned and defeated. Something more dire than a failed summit loomed: a public relations disaster. Then, what Donald Regan called "the shovel brigade" began its work. This was not a setback, but a tremendous victory. It was a Cold War *High Noon* in which the president did not back down. For a few more weeks, Reagan's image held steady. Less than a month later, the Iran-contra scandal was exposed.

Gorbachev was on the spot. His summitry with Reagan was his first major foreign policy initiative. He stood before the Supreme Soviet offering excuses for why it had fallen apart. Gorbachev had followed Reagan's treatment, but his script was filled with too many surprises. In order to make himself look good, he had to make Reagan look good. Of all the handlers, Gorbachev had the greatest motive. He needed the president, and he needed to provide a script the president could follow.

Now more than ever, the president needed direction. He was bewildered as the scandal dragged him through scene changes he didn't understand. "They still like me, but they don't believe me," he reflected sadly. When Reagan sank to his lowest point, Gorbachev, with an eye cocked at the ticking clock, began furiously rewriting. He dropped his objection to Star Wars, convinced by Andrei Sakharov that it was more a fantasy than a threat. And he narrowed his focus to the Intermediate Nuclear Force (INF) treaty, accepting the "double zero" proposal that Perle had dropped as a monkey wrench in the works. In practical terms, it made a small difference in the size of the nuclear arsenals, less than a four percent reduction. But it did eliminate an entire class of weapons. And the treaty would make all the difference politically.

Reagan was back in a starring role. He remembered that he was the leader of the Free World; the audience was believing again; and he was realizing his vision. "I occasionally think," he told the United Nations General Assembly in September 1987, "how our differences worldwide would vanish if we were facing an alien threat from outside this world."

Two months later, the curtain went up on the Washington summit. The man on horseback in July was replaced by the man in the black Zil limousine in December. The conservatives acted as a naysaying chorus. Howard Phillips and Richard Viguerie, new right stalwarts, berated Reagan as "nothing more than a useful idiot for Soviet propaganda." The phrasing was a perversely brilliant stroke. "Useful idiot" was one of Lenin's signature phrases, referring to capitalist dupes. Disillusioned right wingers contemptuously called Reagan "Reagachev." "Appeasement is as unwise in 1988 as in 1938" read a full-page ad in the *Washington Times* taken out by the Conservative Caucus a month after the summit. Under a black umbrella, British prime minister Neville Chamberlain's accoutrement, which became the symbol of the Munich betrayal, stood portraits of Chamberlain and Hitler. Under Chamberlain was Reagan; under Hitler, Gorbachev. The right wingers were throwing Reagan's own rhetoric back at him. In 1964 Reagan had said: "The specter our well-meaning liberal friends refuse to face is that their policy of accommodation is appeasement, and appeasement does not give you a choice between peace and war, only between fight and surrender." For decades Reagan employed these terms for political advantage, not hesitating to compare Jimmy Carter to Chamberlain in 1980. Now, over and over, Reagan spoke about how he was making "history."

To the delight of the audience, he was laughing and telling jokes again. On December 7, 1987, in the East Room of the White House, Reagan played Gracie Allen, Gorbachev played George Burns. "Doveryai no proveryai," said the president, a Russian phrase he learned that meant trust but verify. "You repeat that at every meeting," said Gorbachev. (Laughter) "I like it," said Reagan. (Loud laughter and applause) Scratch, scratch. The treaty was signed.

"I've often wondered," said Reagan five months later, "what if all of us in the world discovered that we were threatened by a power from outer space, from another planet. Wouldn't we all of a sudden find that we didn't have any differences between us at all?"

A month later, in June, Reagan went on location to Moscow. It was there he told the press that "of course" the Cold War was over and that the "evil empire" was a phrase from "another time." He also displayed an unusually acute self-consciousness about the transformation of his own role. "In the movie business," he observed, "actors often get what we call typecast. The studios come to think of you as playing certain kinds of roles, and no matter how hard you try, you just can't get them to think of you in any other way. Well, politics is a little like that too. So I've had a lot of time and reason to think about my role." The "studio" that "typecast" Reagan was American political society, especially the conservative movement. The producer who saw his potential as a leading man in a different feature was Gorbachev.

From the moment of the signing of the INF Treaty, Reagan's popularity began to rise. It continued to do so from summit meeting to summit meeting with Gorbachev. The Iran-contra scandal receded into the past. The indirect effect of Reagan's revival on the coming campaign was momentous. Bush was always Reagan's dependency. The vice president was powerless to change the relationship. He had little capacity to generate energy of his own. He secured it from whatever sources were available. When Reagan was restored, his light once again fell on his number two. The period of Reagan's remaking was the making of much of the Bush candidacy. Without the conservative crackup, accelerated by the Iran-contra scandal, the right wing might have been able to build up another candidate. Without the treaty, Bush might have had to carry the heavy burden of a tainted presidency. Without the Gorbachev presence, Bush might not have been lifted by Reagan's renewed popularity or found a means to dramatize his foreign policy credentials, which were the basis of his presidential image.

Seeking the mantle of the Reagan succession was mostly an illusory quest. The problem rested in the idea that becoming president meant becoming like Reagan. Unfortunately, Reagan was never what he appeared to most of the people most of the time. How could anyone be Reagan, when Reagan was not Reagan? His image was strong, but he was among the weakest chief executives. By all accounts of those who worked closely with him, he was passive, lazy and stage-directed. His aides cleverly played with the forms, but squandered the institutional power of the presidency, in particular the executive's control of the departments and agencies, which became a battleground of budget negotiations with the Congress, of patronage grabs and corruption. The true state of affairs was illustrated by the savings and loan and Department of Housing and Urban Development scandals a year after Reagan left office. In fact, the Reagan White House never had an important legislative success except those brokered by the Republican-controlled Senate. When the GOP lost the Senate, Reagan's record of getting his programs through Congress sank to the lowest recorded for any president in the postwar era. His popularity masked his institutional weakness. When his poll numbers fell in the Iran-contra scandal, he had little recourse but to turn to former Senate majority leader Howard Baker. The appointment of Baker was an admission of what had been the underlying reality all along.

Gorbachev's diplomacy, then, provided Reagan with a bravura last act. His revived popularity proved that it was not linked to his rigid embrace of Cold War conservatism. But if this were so, what remained of Reagan's coattails to grasp? He had fostered a crisis of solvency, a wild imbalance between means and commitments, accelerating America's relative decline in the world. Yet insolvency became the core of the Republican political advantage, blocking social reform and entrapping Congress in an endless, dreary budget impasse. In foreign policy, however, Reagan's presidency might be carried on in the ending of the Cold War, a process he had helped begin. Reagan himself spoke of the Cold War's waning, but he left no larger framework of public understanding. The candidates were left hanging on the edge of a new world.

During the Washington summit, Gorbachev worked out of the Soviet Embassy on 16th Street, several blocks from the White House. On the third day, he conferred on the telephone for almost two hours with members of the Politburo back in Moscow. George Bush waited for Gorbachev in an anteroom. It was the only occasion for the vice president to meet with him privately. Georgi Arbatov, the U.S.A. Institute director, a traveling member of the Gorbachev entourage, spotted the lonely Bush. They launched into a conversation about U.S.–Soviet relations.

"We shouldn't have illusions about the future," Bush said, according to a Soviet source who was present. "We should lower expectations."

"I think it's quite different," replied Arbatov. "The danger is cynicism. We don't have time to lower expectations. It's a luxury we can't afford."

They shook hands and Bush continued waiting. The Soviets considered Bush's comments "conventional wisdom." He seemed to them not to have the vision to sense the world that was coming into being.

Soon, Bush was greeted by Gorbachev. So were his five guests, three of whom were from the early primary states of Iowa and New Hampshire. They ate caviar and blinis. Then Bush sat with Gorbachev in his black Zil as he rode back to the White House. The crowds on the sidewalks waved. "It's too bad," said Bush, "you can't stop and go into some of these stores because I think you'd find warm greetings from the American people."

Gorbachev thought for a moment and shouted at his driver, "Stop the car!" He bounded out of the car and strode into a startled crowd on the corner of Connecticut and L streets. As Gorbachev shook hands like a wardheeler, Bush belatedly got out and looked around, seeming slightly dazed at the strange sight of Americans thronging the Soviet leader. The crowd did not notice Bush. He started to shake hands, too. He drew close to Gorbachev. Duke Zeibert, the owner of a power-lunch restaurant, appeared on the balcony above the scene. "Come on up and have lunch!" he yelled. "We have borscht!"

Gorbachev and Bush, standing side by side, like running mates, waved. Then they retreated into the limo. "Do you do this a lot?" wondered Bush.

"Oh," said Gorbachev. "I do it a lot. I do it in Moscow and I do it every time I go to the provinces. So I believe in it. I believe that's the way you ought to do it. Leaders should be equal."

3

The Vision Thing,
or Whatever

Senator Paul Laxalt was Ronald Reagan's "First Friend." They had both risen from humble backgrounds to become governors of neighboring states, California and Nevada. They shared the same politics, the same outlook. They were home on the range, tall in the saddle, their talk a banter of jokes and asides. Reagan liked being at ease, and he was at perfect ease with Laxalt.

It was July 1980. The two men were literally on top of their world, in a tower suite in the Renaissance Center Hotel in Detroit, a short limousine drive from the Joe Louis Arena, where the Republican Party was preparing to nominate Reagan. As they savored the moment, Laxalt asked his friend for a favor. The nominee had only one real decision to make in Detroit, the selection of his running mate, and, according to a member of Reagan's inner circle, Laxalt could stand almost any choice except one: George Bush.

The pals in the hotel suite were said to have derided Bush's reedy voice, his boyish enthusiasm, his colored cloth watchbands. To them, Bush appeared to be a hopelessly effete product of his class.

After Bush had beaten Reagan in the Iowa caucuses, he had yammered on about how he now had the momentum—the "Big Mo'." He was running on his past appointments and his slogan: "A President We Won't Have to Train." This proved to be ideal for Reagan: a contest of privilege versus opportunity, the establishment tool versus the self-made man. During the next primary, at a debate in Nashua, New Hampshire, Bush walked right into Reagan's Sunday punch. "I paid for this microphone," he angrily told the moderator who tried to cut him off. It was a direct quote from the movie *State of the Union*—and enabled Reagan to do what he did best, in this case play Spencer Tracy playing a presidential candidate who was running against the vested interests. Reagan had immediately seized the moment and the nomination from Bush, who suddenly became a diminished figure, incapable of sustaining a competitive mythology. Thus the first person to cast Bush in the role of wimp was Reagan.

Reagan had two preferences for vice president. The first was Laxalt. But this selection would have made no political sense, Laxalt being a virtual carbon copy of himself. Reagan's second choice was Jack Kemp. The popular representative from upstate New York, a former professional quarterback, had worked for him as an aide when he was governor of California, and had withdrawn from the Republican race in deference to Reagan. He also had much to give the ticket. Kemp stood for the doctrine of supply-side economics, which provided a world-historical justification for the regressive tax cuts Reagan wanted. Moreover, the new economic elixir was drawn from the Fountain of Youth; once imbibed, it lent the aging trouper the gloss of innovation. Unfortunately, there were rumors about Kemp. When Reagan was governor his political staff was revealed to contain a number of homosexuals who were driven from office. The rumors about Kemp's involvement in the "homosexual ring," though completely unfounded, still persisted. According to a member of his entourage, Reagan did not want these charges flying around. Kemp's family would be hurt by the accusations, even if they were disproved. He was young; he was attractive; he would have other chances. So Reagan passed over Kemp.

In the meantime, some of the bored television correspondents covering the packaged event began promoting the rumor that Reagan would pick former president Gerald Ford as his running mate. The former rivals would campaign and govern as "co-presidents." (The reporting of this story was encouraged by Ford and Henry Kissinger, who visualized himself as a prime minister in a co-presidency.) Reagan, however, was thinking of no such option. Enter Richard Wirthlin, his pollster. He had tested only three names: Gerald Ford, Howard Baker and George Bush. Reagan didn't like any of these choices. But he also didn't think much of the office of the vice presidency, regarding it as something like that of lieutenant governor. Reagan's lieutenant governor had been a cipher named Houston Flournoy. The vice presidency mattered only as a political question. In Wirthlin's poll, Bush showed best. The political motive won out over the personal objection. Reagan picked up the telephone and dialed Bush. After hanging up, Bush leaped in the air. One of Reagan's aides was dispatched with the unpleasant task of informing the volcanic Laxalt that the pledge had been broken.

Bush was appointed Reagan's heir by virtue of arithmetic. His poll numbers were superior because he had lost without giving offense. His name recognition was high, and so was his recognition as a member of the Republican establishment. He was placed in the line of succession to the presidency partly for the same reason that Reagan and Laxalt had spurned him. This was to lead Bush into a political quandary. He was uncomfortable in the patrician role he had been assigned by fate. He walked like a patrician; he looked like a patrician; he had the accents of a patrician; yet he did not really talk like one. He tried to sound like one of the boys, the good ol' Texas boys, which he decidedly was not. After his 1984 vice presidential debate with Geraldine Ferraro, he announced, "We kicked a little ass." Bush's expression was one no good ol' boy would likely make about a woman. Instead he came across as a gentleman for whom chivalry was dead. He seemed to be attempting to shed his skin, to become new again. And nothing made him seem more uncomfortable.

"I'm following Mr. Reagan—blindly," the vice president said. Serving under Reagan was both a reward and a punishment. The contrast with Reagan was among Bush's principal political problems as he set out on his 1988 campaign. Reagan, the son of an alcoholic small-town salesman, was hardly born to rule, but he was comfortable playing the role of the strong leader who was all of a piece because he was comfortable playing roles. Reagan's model was the archetypal patrician in politics, Franklin D. Roosevelt, who was also all of a piece. But George Bush seemed to be a man in pieces. FDR was never more patrician than when he exercised his democratic touch. Bush inspired skepticism whether he was showing his blue blood or his red.

The most consistent image he projected was that of an amiable wimp. Once he announced his candidacy, it was generally agreed by the press, his opponents and his own managers that this image was his greatest obstacle. According to most serious people who had observed him up close over a period of years, Bush was a weightless trimmer. A high-level Reagan administration official who became a key adviser to Bush's campaign said in late 1987: "Bush is an intellectual wimp. When faced with a conflict among ideas his tendency is not to try to get analytical leverage or to formulate the nature of the problem and the choices. His tendency is a political tendency. He tries to have it both ways. He doesn't know his own mind." A member of the cabinet in the Ford administration who campaigned for Bush said: "If leadership consists of having views and a desire to impose those views on society because they're right, that's not George Bush. He has no natural aversion to drift." A senior strategist of the Bush campaign privately described the candidate as a "transitional" political figure whom he expected would make a "transitional president." There were very few people at this level who did not like Bush; there were also very few who felt he had the gravity of the event-making leader.

Bush compounded his troubles by his unfortunate flair for the ridiculous statement. "If I have a tendency, and I confess to it, to avoid going on and on with great eloquent statements of belief," he explained. Bush did have that tendency. He had others as well. He could be crudely inappropriate: "Boy, they were big on crematoriums, weren't they?" he said after a tour of Auschwitz. He could be silly: "The caribou love it," he said in defense of the Alaska pipeline. "They rub up against it and they have babies." He could be almost inarticulate: "Yeah, I think there's some social change going on . . . AIDS, for example, uh, is a, is a, uh disease for, disease of poverty in a sense. It's where the hopelessness is. It's bigger than that of course." He was given to malapropisms: "America's freedom is the example to which the world expires." He read his stage directions aloud: "I just have to be vague about the answer, but I certainly empathize with the problem." When faced with what he wished to avoid or could not explain, Bush fell back on the word "thing." At a drug rehabilitation clinic he was introduced to an addict and started talking about "that withdrawal thing." In attacking liberals on foreign policy, he mentioned "the post-Vietnam thing." And when a friend suggested that he take some time to think about what he would do as president, Bush blurted, "Oh, the vision thing."

His spontaneous responses were occasionally absurd. *"Finis!"* he shouted at a rally, as he ripped in half a leaflet he had grabbed from the hands of a fifteen-year-old Iowa girl who identified herself as a supporter of Jack Kemp. "Comme ci, comme ça," he told a third grader in a Harlem elementary school, when she hesitated to answer a question he had posed about spelling. He frequently conveyed a barely repressed panic in his nervous giggling, giddy smiling and windmill arm-flapping. His media advisers labored to tranquilize him. The metaphors and similes used in his set speeches to make him seem more coherent were obviously crafted by others. It took him many rehearsals before he could recite them without stumbling. When he left his text he was often at sea. His priorities, he said, campaigning in South Carolina, were "education, or whatever, and jobs, whatever." "Whatever" was his fill-in-the-blank answer to "the vision thing."

The use of the vernacular by the genteel is always an effort to cover vast social distance. Bush's imprecise language revealed his uncertainty about the journey. So did his well-publicized love of pork rinds, horseshoes and country music. His yawp was not a sign of primitivism but of a fear of being perceived as overcultivated. His social imagination, however, was so flat as to appear stunted. He had little intellectual curiosity and rarely read a book. His thinking was diffuse and did not naturally attach itself to ideas. The lesions in his language reflected lesions in his thinking.

No criticism over the years rankled Bush more than Garry Trudeau's "Doonesbury," which depicted him as invisible. Trudeau came from a similar background, being a graduate of St. Paul's and Yale. The worst vice at Phillips Andover Academy when Bush prepped there was a "bad attitude," a combination of class disloyalty and nonconformity bred by free-thinking. (Bush's attack during the campaign on "Harvard boutique liberalism," seemingly antiestablishment in intent, was really an assault on "bad attitude." It was not antiestablishment at all, but an oblique assertion of caste superiority. For many who attended Yale when Bush did, Harvard seemed to be a repository of "bad attitude.") To Bush, Trudeau was a traitor to his class. (George Bush, Jr., another Yalie, rising to the defense of his father, made a private threat to beat up Trudeau.) As the campaign got under way, Bush said of "Doonesbury":

> I used to get very tense about that. My mother still does. She's 87. She doesn't like it when people say untrue and ugly things about her little boy. Having said that, it doesn't bother me any more. You know why, because we took a tremendous pounding, not just from elitists like "Doonesbury," coming out of the elite of the elite, but untrue allegations, and you know why I don't worry about it anymore? Because the

American people don't believe all this stuff. They don't believe it. So I'm saying, why should I be all uptight, when people don't need a filter, you know?

Trudeau of Yale was thereby turned into a treacherous elitist; Bush of Yale into a wholesome man of the people. Very little was more revealing of Bush's insecurities than his loathing of the cartoonist.

George Bush was the first member of his class to become president since John F. Kennedy, the first Republican since William Howard Taft (also a Skull and Bones man). He was the presumptive heir of the wise men of the eastern establishment who had created the postwar order. His lineage as the son of Senator Prescott Bush of Connecticut was impeccable, his three foreign policy credentials as ambassador to China and the United Nations and director of the CIA were ideal. He seemed poised to step in as a maker of a second "Creation," now made possible by the ending of the Cold War. But the unifying theme in Bush's political career was not policymaking but loyalty. The period in which he had risen highest as a functionary was marked by the steep decline in influence of the wise men and those who thought as they did. The Reagan era was ruled by a different vision, a right-wing ideology that had been partly constructed in reaction to them. Bush's fealty to Reagan v.as so total that he seemed to fit effortlessly his role as diplomat. His subservience throughout his career to others' policies and views had been his main qualification. Now it had put him in line for the presidency. He did not have the vision for a new "Creation," just "the vision thing."

It is significant that the issue precipitating Bush's break with the wise men was his ambition. In the mid-1970s, at a small meeting of members of the Council on Foreign Relations, the heart of the eastern establishment, Bush had a sharp altercation with William Bundy. The Council had been the bastion of the postwar consensus. But it had been split by the Vietnam War, and the pieces weren't being put back together again. The rule of the establishment was shattered. And it had apparently lost the confidence of George Bush, according to a member who recounted his outburst. William Bundy was by then the editor of the Council's prestigious quarterly, *Foreign Affairs*. During the Vietnam War, he had been the assistant secretary of state for East Asian affairs. His brother, McGeorge Bundy, had been the national security adviser in the Kennedy and Johnson administrations. The Bundys were Lowells, Boston Brahmins, and members of Skull and Bones. And William Bundy was married to Dean Acheson's daughter. Bush, of course, was a member of the Council. But he was angry, and he lashed out: "You Bundys had your chance," he said. The source of the story does not recall that any particular issue of substance prompted Bush's remark. His motive appears, as the remark suggests, to have been political opportunism.

Throughout his career, as we shall see, Bush himself had tended to drift to the right to defend against attacks that he was an establishment figure. In the 1980 GOP primaries, Ronald Reagan and his entourage directly assailed Bush for his membership in the Council and the Trilateral Commission, another bogeyman. Bush succumbed to the smears, before Reagan had selected him as his running mate, by quitting both organizations. Henceforth, for the duration of the Reagan administration, he would be his own ghost.

In 1986, on the 75th anniversary of the founding of the Carnegie Endowment for International Peace, an important institution in the foreign policy establishment, its president, Thomas L. Hughes, wrote an elegiac essay, "The Twilight of Internationalism," which perhaps best summarized the vision that Bush had abandoned:

> . . . what has declined is American internationalism—the disposition, mindset, or world view that for decades regarded as self-evident, and that almost automatically supported, the following verities: international cooperation, consultation, and conciliation; international law, institutions, and treaties; international negotiation, norms, and dispute settlement; economic interdependence, growth, and freer trade; international development, aid, and technical assistance; diligence in seeking arms control; and restraint in the use of force, except when responding to clear provocation and then, if possible, employed under multilateral auspices.
>
> By midcentury, this internationalist ethos embraced American mainstream conservatives and liberals alike. Most Republicans and most Democrats likely to lead the country were part of this idiom and outlook. . . . Today these internationalist impulses have pretty well exhausted themselves in mainstream American political life. . . . Instead, they are the objects of derision and contempt.

In the 1988 campaign, Bush hailed the wise men but did not draw upon their legacy in approaching the end of the Cold War, the conclusion of the struggle they had helped to frame and control. His personal and political evolution had led him far away from their views. His predicament with "the vision thing" was more than an immediate and ephemeral campaign problem. It was a matter of misalignment with his background.

II

The decline in the political energy of the bipartisan consensus of the postwar era can be measured in the distance between Prescott Bush and George Bush. At six foot, four inches in height, the father loomed over his son. "Big guy, tough," the vice president told interviewer David Frost. "One time when I was less than truthful he picked up a, I don't know whether it was a squash racket or a, looked like a big stick." Another reminiscence, recalled to Garry Wills: "It never occurred to me to differ. I mean, he was up here and I was this little guy down here."

But more than Prescott Bush's physical presence and sternness were felt by George Bush. His career was a terrifying challenge. The elder Bush had vaulted himself into the establishment; his heir awoke there. It was always difficult for George to transcend his imperious father. His departure from the world of his father, particularly his removal to Texas to prove himself as a businessman, was both a tribute and a rebellion. Over time, George strayed from his father's legacy, even while seeming to fulfill it.

Prescott Bush was a representative Republican figure of the postwar consensus at its zenith. He was the son of a Columbus, Ohio, steel manufacturer; attended Yale, where he was tapped for Skull and Bones; and in World War I, served as a captain. Afterward, he set out to make his fortune. He began with a St. Louis hardware firm, and by 1925 he had become a Wall Street banker, vice president of W. A. Harriman Company, run by a Yale friend, Roland Harriman. Five years later, when the bank merged with Brown Brothers to become Brown Brothers, Harriman, he became a partner. (Roland's brother, W. Averell Harriman, became a Democratic governor of New York and was one of the wise men instrumental in the making of the postwar order.)

In exclusive Greenwich, Connecticut, where Prescott had settled, he served as the moderator of the town meeting for seventeen years. He came to the attention of the Republican Party because of his prowess at fundraising. In 1950, he won the GOP senatorial primary by beating Clare Booth Luce, the wife of *Time* magazine publisher Henry Luce and one of the most outspoken conservatives of the time.

Prescott Bush's political career had two particularly dramatic moments. The first occurred during his first campaign for the Senate. It is recounted by George Bush: "Drew Pearson [the syndicated columnist] on the Sunday before Election Day, 'revealed' that my father was involved with Planned Parenthood. My father lost that election by a few hundred out of close to a million votes. Many political observers felt a sufficient number of voters were swayed by his alleged contacts with the birth controllers to cost him the election."[1]

The second dramatic moment in Prescott Bush's career involved his stand on McCarthyism. In his successful campaign for the Senate in 1952, he made a point of separating himself from Joseph McCarthy, then at the height of his powers. McCarthy's subsequent witch-hunt for Communists in the State Department and the army deeply offended the newly elected Senator Bush. He made efforts to prevent McCarthy's abuses. Finally, in December 1954, the bipartisan consensus drew together against the point man of the Republican right. On the floor of the Senate, Senator Bush spoke in favor of the censure of McCarthy: "Either you must follow Senator McCarthy blindly, not daring to express any doubts or disagreement about any of his actions, or in his eyes you must be a Communist, a Communist sympathizer, or a fool." The line was drawn; the consensus held. Prescott Bush's sense of public service, early apparent in the Greenwich town meeting, was not some vague sense of duty. Ultimately, for him, it came down to certain irreducible principles, especially civility.

George Herbert Walker Bush, according to his father's wishes, followed in his footsteps. He was trained in the complete curriculum of the patrician: the right schools, the right sports, the right war. During the Depression, he was chauffeured to private school. (Bush once recounted to Reagan how his chauffeur raced him through snowstorms to get him to school before the other children in their limousines—a story that convulsed Reagan with laughter.) At Andover, Bush was imbued with standards of right conduct and noblesse oblige. In World War II, he served in the navy as its youngest pilot. His plane was shot down during a bombing run. His two crew members died; he was rescued by a passing submarine. Unlike Reagan, who spent the war making motivational movies for the army at the Hal Roach Studio in Culver City, Bush was a war hero. Perhaps more than any other experi-

1. Though George Bush initially followed Prescott's example in supporting "the birth controllers," becoming actively involved with Planned Parenthood in Houston, according to members there, his position "evolved," as he put it. After being chosen as Reagan's running mate, Bush adjusted his view to fit that of the antiabortion movement.

ence in his life, this ought to have put to rest the accusations of his being a wimp. But in his telling of the story during the campaign, Bush made himself seem silly instead of heroic. "I was shot down, and I was floating around in a little yellow raft setting a record for paddling," he explained, two months before the Iowa caucuses. "I thought of my family, my mom and dad, and the strength I got from them. I thought of my faith, the separation of church and state."

After the war, he went on to Yale, where he was elected the captain of the baseball team. He was extremely popular among his social peers. But having proved himself at Yale to be his father's son, he now tried to carve out his own identity.

In 1948, Bush set out for Texas with his wife Barbara in their Studebaker. He did not want to be thought of as "Pres Bush's boy," he said. The journey from east to west conveys the classic American myth of escaping the confines of class and making oneself over; even a patrician can be transformed. Later, Bush boasted that it was here that he was able to "make it on [his] own." But he did not completely cut off his links to the past; on the contrary, his family connections and old school ties were the basis of his adventure.

His first job was with an oil business owned by one of his father's Yale classmates and fellow member of Skull and Bones. Bush did not like the gladhanding and salesmanship required of him. He formed a partnership for his own oil company, raising the initial capital from his investment banker uncle, G. Herbert Walker, Jr., and from family friends associated with the Brown Brothers, Harriman bank such as Eugene Meyer, the publisher of *The Washington Post.* Bush lived among other easterners who had come west to make a quick killing, in a section of Midland, Texas, with streets named for Ivy League schools. When Bush sold his interest in his firm twelve years later, before the oil boom, he realized a profit of $1 million—a modest amount by the Texas standards of the day. Still, he had succeeded on his own and was independently wealthy.

The Republican Party in the early 1960s was like a small oil company about to go big-time. Within it, the old and the new forces were at odds. Wealthy moderates in the party feared being inundated by right wingers from the new suburbs. In Harris County (Houston), a delegation of moderates asked Bush if he would take on the task of taming the influx of rabid John Birch Society members by running as the GOP county chairman. Some of those who coaxed Bush into politics later felt he had given in to the Birchers because he gave some of them committee posts. It was the first instance of his yielding to the right wing.

Bush discovered that almost everything about the eastern establishment manner was politically unacceptable in Texas. He had made the transition from the Yale Club to the Bayou Club of the Houston elite without much difficulty. But he could not similarly convert family credentials into political currency. He betrayed himself every time he opened his mouth and rolled his New England vowels. As a politician, he was driven by a sense of inadequacy born of privilege. In the effort to win, he was constantly striving to be someone he wasn't, conforming to something he half-understood. Bush the politician was strangely other-directed, the opposite of the Yankee inner-directed type. His behavior depended upon picking up cues and signals from others, whom he frequently read in a confused way because of the distorted lens of his background.

In his entire career, Bush never ran as a moderate Republican or won a statewide race, as had his father. Bush emerged as a politician in the same year as Ronald Reagan. In 1964, he endorsed Barry Goldwater for the GOP presidential nomination over Nelson Rockefeller, the New York governor who was leading what had been until that moment the dominant wing of the party, the wing to which his father always belonged. Under Thomas Dewey and Dwight Eisenhower, the moderates had beaten back the conservatives. But the center of power on the Republican right was shifting from the Middle West to the Southeast and across the Sunbelt. New money was challenging old money; a powerfully organized new conservative movement threatened the grip of the eastern establishment.

Civil rights had now become a cutting edge issue between the two factions. Bush's position was a break with more than the moderate wing of the party; it flouted his father's record. Only four years earlier, in 1960, Prescott Bush had joined with just seven other Republican senators and the northern Democrats in an attempt to block a southern filibuster on a civil rights bill. Now George won the GOP senatorial primary against his conservative rivals by assailing the proposed Civil Rights Act of 1964 as "politically inspired and destined to failure." He said, "I believe the government is trying to usurp the rights of the people." (At the time, Bush held memberships in three segregated private clubs.) But he was easily defeated in that year of the Democratic landslide by the liberal Senator Ralph Yarborough.

Two years later, Bush won a congressional seat in a conservative, safely Republican Houston district. He was distinguished by his zero rating with the liberal Americans for Democratic Action except for one errant vote: for open housing. For this act, Bush was harshly attacked by the right. As it happened, Bush had flip-flopped, initially opposing the bill and then supporting it when he saw that it was going to pass.

His rightward drift continued. In 1968, when he was endorsed for reelection by the Ripon Society, the vanguard of Rockefeller Republicanism, he wrote the group a letter demanding that the endorsement be rescinded, apparently fearing guilt by association.

Bush's career entered a new phase with the election of Richard Nixon. In the midterm election of 1970, the Nixon White House ran the pioneering negative campaign against the Democrats on the basis of what was called the "social issue." According to a memo from presidential assistant Charles Colson to the president, the phrase "law-and-order" was to be reiterated to make "the public believe that Democrat, Liberal permissiveness was the cause of violence and crime." Underlying this theme was the issue of race. The president himself took to the hustings to heighten the atmosphere of divisiveness. But it was crucial to the success of this polarizing strategy that the candidates themselves broadcast the theme.

Nixon had personally encouraged Bush to make the race for the Senate, not particularly because he saw him as an effective spokesman for law-and-order but because he regarded him as a generally attractive candidate. Asked later his motive for running, Bush joked: "Upward mobility."

He positioned himself on the right, anticipating a rematch with the liberal Yarborough. But Yarborough was toppled in the Democratic primary by the more conservative Lloyd Bentsen. "If Bentsen is going to try to go to my right, he's going to step off the edge of the earth," Bush said. But Bentsen cast him as Nixon's handpicked candidate, lacking independence. Bush seemed vaguer rather than clearer about what he stood for as election day approached. The judgment back at the White House was that Bush had not gotten nasty enough. "He refused to allow us to use some very derogatory information about Bentsen," wrote Colson in a memo to the president. " . . . We probably should have forced him to do more." Bush had acted more like Prescott Bush's son than Nixon's.

After his defeat, according to Nixon's senior aide John Ehrlichman, "Nixon delivered a soliloquy that Bush had talent, money, the background and inclination to do well in public life, and we ought to do what we could to help him along." The president despised and feared the eastern establishment in direct proportion to his desire for acceptance by it. The White House tapes were filled with ranting monologues about how the establishment was out to get him. Bush was part of the establishment, but Nixon saw him as someone who would be willing to do as he was told. His sense of loyalty, bred in him by his family, and at Phillips Andover Academy and Yale, could be used politically against the establishment. In his own small way, Bush was in rebellion against the establishment, too. In a 1971 memo to another presidential assistant, Colson wrote: "We should always consider using George Bush more often as a good speaker. . . . he takes our line beautifully."

A month after Bush's loss he sought to trade on his background for a cabinet post: U.S. ambassador to the United Nations. In an audience with the president, according to a memo written by Chief of Staff H. R. Haldeman, Bush "pointed out that there was a dearth of Nixon advocacy in New York City and the general New York area—that he could fill that need in the New York social circles he would be moving in as ambassador." Nixon and Haldeman responded by staging the equivalent of a mock execution. The U.N. job was withdrawn from Bush. Instead, he was offered a job as a presidential assistant of "unspecified general responsibilities," that is, a glorified gofer. Bush was willing to accept the lower post. Three hours later he was called back and given the U.N. job. Bush had to pass this test of humiliation before being sent to the oak-paneled private clubs of Manhattan where Nixon was regarded as a gate-crasher.

Bush did not assume his post as someone dedicated to the mission of the United Nations, which was among the great legacies of American internationalism. He was not carrying on the Rooseveltian tradition that lay at the heart of the bipartisan postwar consensus but was acting as Nixon's agent.

At the U.N. Bush's most notable accomplishment was completely unwitting. While the president and Secretary of State Henry Kissinger were secretly preparing to open relations with the People's Republic of China, Bush was sent out to defend Taiwan's effort to remain a member of the U.N. This was a cause dear to the right wing since the days of the China Lobby, of which Nixon had been a chief advocate. Bush was never informed of the impending shift in policy, which he served by misdirection. He deceived as he was deceived. It was another ritual humiliation, another test. He was angry at being used, but he admired Kissinger enormously and wished to emulate him as a statesman. "On to the next event!" Bush told his U.N. staff.

With his landslide victory in 1972, Nixon planned to consolidate his regime. He sought to reduce the power of the departments and agencies by centralizing it in his White House staff. He wanted to extend his recent triumph to the party as a whole by bringing it more under his control. And he wanted to inflict severe damage on the establishment, his nemesis. Nixon trusted few, even inside his own administration. The day after his election, he demanded the signed resignations of his entire government. "Eliminate the politicians," he told his assistant, John Ehrlichman, about reappointments. "Except George Bush. He'd do anything for the cause."

On November 20, 1972, Bush was flown by helicopter to meet with the president at Camp David. Nixon had another test for Bush. The U.N. staff, the president said, was infested with disloyalists. They had to be disposed of. The man who had first risen to national prominence hunting Communists wanted to know if Bush would engage in a ritual denunciation by naming names. "Give us the names of loyalists," Nixon demanded. Would Bush demonstrate his loyalty to the president by betraying the loyalty of those who had served under him at the U.N.? These American diplomats were hardly Communists, but in Nixon's world they were seen as "enemies." On the spot, Bush offered up a name. And he agreed to write the "tough political memo" Nixon requested.

Bush wanted a new position. His first choice was deputy secretary of state, Kissinger's number two; his second was deputy secretary of the treasury. Even though Bush had been humbled in the playing of the China card, he wished to position himself as Kissinger's understudy. "Will you let me decide?" asked Nixon, speaking like a father who knows best for a son. His choice for him was the chairmanship of the Republican National Committee. Bush would now act as Nixon's agent in the party, where he would try to organize a lasting political realignment in the country. If Bush took this job, Nixon tantalizingly suggested, he would receive a cabinet post after the 1974 midterm election. Bush conceded his destiny to Nixon. "I'll do what you tell me," he said. "Not all that enthralled with RNC but I'll do it."

The new RNC chairman advised the president in early 1973: "Watergate, Executive Privilege won't be an issue in '74. Never get questions on it." But virtually all of Bush's time was consumed by Watergate. As he served as the president's apologist, Nixon was engaged in the coverup. During Watergate, two patricians with New England roots took divergent paths. Attorney General Elliot Richardson, ordered by the president to fire Special Prosecutor Archibald Cox, resigned. Richardson put loyalty to principle and country above loyalty to person and party. Within the Republican Party, Richardson became a nobody, a man who could not be trusted. (Among Reagan's first acts as president was the junking of the Law of the Sea Treaty, painstakingly negotiated over years by Richardson.) George Bush, too, had to choose during Watergate. Time and again, he proved that he could be relied upon. The reward was appointment to higher and higher office.

With a new president, Bush sought a new job. He waited by his telephone at his family's summer home in Kennebunkport, Maine, hoping for a call from Gerald Ford asking him to serve as vice president. But the White House staff feared that if he were named, the illegal campaign contributions Bush received under Nixon's Operation Townhouse would pull Ford back into the Watergate controversy. So the call went instead to Nelson Rockefeller. As a consolation prize, Bush asked to be appointed U.S. ambassador to China. This enabled him to benefit from the change in China policy he had been sent to argue against at the U.N. It also removed him from the scene of Watergate. But within months he became restless in China and wanted a new job.

In the aftermath of Watergate, Congress investigated the CIA and uncovered numerous abuses. The agency needed a new director to soothe the legislators and to restore its public image. In its Cold War beginnings, the CIA had been a patrician stronghold, as much a part of the establishment's cosmos as the private clubs in midtown Manhattan, the investment banks on Wall Street and the estates in Connecticut. Serving in the CIA was the most discreet form of public service. It was not the low-status work of warfare but the highest; in a word, "intelligence." The CIA was a creature of the Cold War, a war seemingly made to order for its cerebral, clandestine techniques. But now the agency had run amok. To return to first principles, it needed the leadership of a patrician. Ford selected Bush.

The Democrats in the Senate put a condition on his confirmation, that he act the role of the establishment figure who was above politics. He could not, the Democrats stipulated, run as Ford's vice president in 1976. Bush had harbored hopes for just that possibility, and he resisted making this commitment. But Ford ultimately insisted.

At the CIA, Bush was a diplomatic success in calming the Congress. But, more important, he presided over an imbroglio that was his greatest substantive contribution to the rise of the right wing. During the period of détente, the conservatives denounced the CIA's assessment of Soviet military strength as a vast underestimate. The drumbeat on this issue was constant from the President's Foreign Intelligence Advisory Board, a group of private citizens dominated by right wingers who regularly met with the president. (PFIAB included Clare Booth Luce, whom Prescott Bush had defeated long ago within the Connecticut GOP.) In 1975, PFIAB had demanded that the CIA create a counter-commission to review Soviet military strength. William Colby, then director of the CIA, had rebuffed the suggestion as an assault on the agency's institutional integrity. The new director, George Bush, quickly caved in. The nine members of the "B-Team" he appointed were all cold warriors devoted to disproving the conclusions of the CIA's own experts, the "A-Team." Its report portrayed a Soviet Union of overpowering might that must be met with a huge U.S. military buildup. For the right, this was an enormous propaganda coup and helped foster an atmosphere for massive Pentagon spending.

"The B-Team never did what they were supposed to do," recalled former admiral Daniel Murphy, who was Bush's CIA deputy and vice presidential chief of staff. "They wrote in their pet projects. They never did their job. It was a lot of publicity. Bush probably thinks it was more worthwhile. . . . That's very typical of George Bush."

"I used to see Bush from time to time," said Richard Pipes, a Harvard historian, who was the National Security Council expert on the Soviet Union during Reagan's first term and the director of the "B-Team." "I just don't know what Bush's positions are. I'm not sure that anyone knows."

Two weeks after Jimmy Carter's election Bush made a pilgrimage to Plains, Georgia, where he implored the president-elect to keep him on as CIA director. "If I stay on," Bush promised, "I won't run [for president] in 1980." He pleaded with Carter to take control of his fate. But Carter turned him down. Thereupon the disappointed placeman began his quest for the presidency.

Bush's message in 1980 was his résumé. His media adviser, Robert Goodman, dubbed him the "American eagle." His television ads were filled with balloons and flags: "This time there will be no repeating past mistakes. This time there can be George Bush. A president we won't have to train." But running for the nomination against Ronald Reagan, Bush felt the need to deny his background. "They say I'm a patrician," he told a reporter. "I don't even know what the word means. I'll have to look it up." It was then, in order to counter the attacks on him as an establishment figure, that he dropped his memberships in the Council on Foreign Relations and the Trilateral Commission.

He won a startling victory in the Iowa caucuses, but it was mostly a function of scheduling. Reagan hardly visited Iowa at all; Bush practically moved in. After his Iowa win, however, he refused to spell out his program with specifics. "If they can show me how it will get me more voters someplace, I'll be glad to do it," he told an interviewer. But his expediency was too transparent for his own good. Bush's "Big Mo' " out of Iowa lasted exactly two weeks, until the next primary in New Hampshire.

Six months later, at the GOP convention, Bush, again the placeman, anxiously waited by the telephone for Reagan's call.

III

Vice President Bush served the president like a dutiful son. In December 1984, a month after Reagan's forty-nine-state landslide, Bush summoned Lee Atwater, who had been hired as his campaign manager. "I told him," recalled Atwater, "that one of the things he would be criticized for was not espousing his positions on the issues." According to Atwater, Bush replied: "My number one job for two years is to support President Reagan. I have to be the lead surrogate for the Republican Party in the 1986 election. Then, in the summer and fall of 1987, I'll outline my positions. By the fall, my positions will be very clear to the voters."

Following his plan, Bush prepared to unveil his views in a series of commencement addresses in May 1987. His senior advisers knew that Bush had no overarching vision. They did not believe he ought to make one up. Instead, they suggested that he speak to a variety of issues that would develop into a few basic political themes. What these themes were none of them really knew. In his first speech, Bush said, "We cannot deal with the future unless we let go of the past." Was he paraphrasing the philosopher George Santayana's epigram: "Those who forget the past are condemned to repeat it"? Was Bush groping for a way to say that he was not Reagan? Or was Bush saying that he had no future unless he buried his past? His staff was baffled. They didn't know what he meant; Bush himself could not explain to them what he had just said. He tried again in another speech: "When I talk about the future, I don't mean we should turn back on the past, or the present for that matter. Some things should remain as guideposts so that we know where we come from as a nation and who we are as a people." But Bush did not explain what "things" in the past or the present might serve as guideposts to the future.

Bush, however, had two enormously positive assets, both of which implicitly pointed to his patrician background. Within the GOP, his claim to the Reagan succession partly rested on royalist principle. As vice president, he was next in line to the monarchical president; it was Bush's turn; he had been loyal and honorable; he had earned the promotion by his "good" attitude. For many Republicans, giving the nomination to Bush was a matter of fair play. His second advantage was that many of the right wingers who supported Bush were, as a senior Bush strategist put it, "authoritarians and he's vice president."

There was the danger, his handlers worried, that he would be perceived as no more than the sum of his inheritance, his schooling and his appointments—a scion of the establishment who had not earned his way. But if this identity were placed against the backdrop of international affairs the perception radically changed. Bush's stature suddenly became immense, for he became the foreign policy wise man. "The larger the share of the voting decision is made up by foreign policy the better off we'll be," Robert Teeter, Bush's pollster, predicted. It was through this image, he said, that "we could control the agenda." Ultimately, foreign policy meant U.S.–Soviet relations. "The more important the question is, 'Who deals with Gorbachev?,' the better that would be." Bush's ability to negotiate with Gorbachev was his unique claim as to why he should be president. But Bush did not accept the implication that what he would be negotiating was the end of the Cold War.

Bush regarded the president with a mixture of disdain and awe. Reagan paid little attention to details and had a prejudice in favor of quirky ideas, like supply-side economics, or "voodoo economics," as Bush put it in the 1980 primary campaign. Reagan did not conduct himself as the inside political player that Bush believed himself to be. Yet Reagan had succeeded as a political personality where Bush was confounded. The president had a charisma that Bush marveled at and wished to possess. He faced the electorate as a man without a mystique. He wrapped himself in Reagan's mantle, but aspired to be like Reagan only in his popularity.

Bush had understood the center of American politics to be Washington's court society since he had been a young man. As well as being a Connecticut Yankee, he was a child of the capital, intimate with it as a result of his father's business and political success. Washington is a place of elaborate etiquette and ceremony, in which one's status is determined by institutional station. How people master their situations within this orbit is decisive in how they are judged, as Bush knew when he defended Nixon during Watergate. Bush's action was not governed by issues or ideology, but by his desire to sustain his standing in Washington as a player. Emotion, even belief, had to be curbed for the sake of status and power; the game must go on. Reagan was more than a Washington outsider. He constantly projected a stereotype of the

Washington insider as a foil which he campaigned against. Bush as vice president strictly followed Reagan's lead. But the central figure in his political education was not Reagan but Richard Nixon. It was during his presidency that Bush truly entered Washington's society as a player. Under Nixon, he was schooled in realpolitik in foreign policy and cynicism in domestic politics. What he had not learned was "the vision thing."

Bush's true identity as a member of the eastern establishment, Nixon acolyte and Washington player was unacceptable as a democratic persona. Like a political man of the Victorian age, he had separated his public mask from his private self. But the insider still remained uncertain how to conduct himself as a character on the stage facing an audience of strangers.

His career had thrived on the disintegration of forces greater than himself. He stood upon the debris of moderate Republicanism and liberal internationalism. From the beginning, when the moderate Republicans of Harris County enlisted him to contain the Birchers, he was elevated for his appearance as a figure of reassurance and stability. The more things fell apart the higher he rose. Bush was far more successful in taking advantage of the disarray than in clarifying himself or the larger world. Now, he had to maneuver through the rubble of the conservative movement.

Since his entrance into politics, he had never failed to capitulate to the right's major demands, but never won their trust. As his campaign prepared for the nominating race, the movement was already split by ideological squabbles; then, the Iran-contra affair and other scandals rained on the movement in a torrent. Bush's strategy, masterminded by Atwater, was to prevent the conservatives from mounting a united front against him. Bush sought to sow disunity by gathering conservatives into his camp.

Simply on the basis of being Reagan's shadow he could count on a sizeable following of conservatives, who naturally transferred their loyalty from number one to number two. But the others could be moved only by ideological solicitations. Bush's condescension toward the movement had occasionally seeped out. "I'm a conservative, but I'm not a nut about it," he had said. And he once classified the right wing as the "extra chromosome set." But throughout the Reagan years he had put his background at the service of the radical right. Bush was determined that no conservative could ever say that there was any space between himself and the president, which would provide the excuse to support another candidate.

He especially attracted those conservatives who felt their social status raised by proximity to the patrician. The case for a politics of status within the Republican Party was pithily put in January 1986 by Robert Bartley, the editor of the *Wall Street Journal:* "In background and demeanor . . . Mr. Bush certainly does not fit the mold of conservative activist. He lacks the streak of the rebel. . . . Yet to those of us who see nothing wrong with and even belong to the Trilateral Commission, this is not necessarily a disadvantage. Indeed it is entirely fitting that a successful rebellion start to don an establishment mantle." By appealing to the right's status anxieties, Bush hoped to accomplish his first strategic task. It was, a senior Bush manager confided, the campaign's intention "to discombobulate and destroy the conservative movement." The more the conservatives attached themselves to him, the more acceptable he seemed to them, the more they would be divided.

Bush's divide and conquer strategy extended politically from the capital to Fort Mill, South Carolina. On December 11, 1985, Bush appeared at the Washington Hilton to pay homage to someone who had loathed him in life, William Loeb, the deceased owner of the Manchester, New Hampshire, *Union Leader,* the bellwether of conservatism in the first primary state. The memorial prompted a huge turnout, more than one thousand minions of the right. For their benefit, Bush gave an unparalleled self-abasing performance. "Bill Loeb thought I was too preppy, too much of a cheerleader," he said. "Here's the quote: 'incompetent, liberal, masquerading as a conservative, a hypocrite . . . double-standard morality, involved up to his neck in Watergate, part of the self-appointed elite, the candidate of the Trilateralists and Rockefeller barons . . . a spoon-fed little rich kid who has been wet-nursed to success.' . . . I didn't mind it when he called me 'a ninny.' No, excuse me, that was Tony Lewis. . . . Or when he said, 'Bush has put his manhood in a blind trust.' Oops, wrong again. That was Doonesbury."

Some conservatives nodded their heads in silent agreement as Bush read each insult. Some thought that his imperturbability was cleverly calculated to discredit them. But most were delighted that he paid tribute to them through the ghost of Loeb. Bush's strategists believed that he had gone "a half-step too far," as one admitted, but argued that the ploy had worked.

Bush was also assiduously building his base in the religious right. The GOP party apparatus in the South was almost all on the vice president's side. By combining the politicians' support with the evangelicals' he would make himself impregnable on Super Tuesday, the southern primary. If he won either Iowa or New Hampshire, he could march into the South as the inevitable nominee.

For the television evangelists, "the vision thing" had a different meaning than it did for Bush. There was Oral Roberts' vision of an 800-foot-tall Jesus who appeared to him in a dream and commanded him to beg millions of dollars from viewers or else die. There was the vision that told Pat Robertson how to divert a hurricane. There was Jimmy Swaggart's vision of homosexuals roasting in Hellfire. There was Jerry Falwell's vision of Lynchburg as a holy city of Virginia, the model of America as a Christian academy. And there was the holy spirit that showed Jim and Tammy Faye Bakker the shimmering vista of a Christian theme park-cum-water slide. So far as it is known, George Bush's most intense religious training was compulsory chapel at Andover, where he was subjected to droning sermons on the undemanding strictures of upper-class faith. For these Episcopalians, God is like the founder whose portrait hangs in the board room; he's there, but he doesn't bother anybody. For someone of Bush's class and denomination, full immersion calls to mind Berlitz language training rather than hardshell Baptists. And yet the Bakkers' complacent vision had much in common with Bush's, even if their vulgarity would never be admitted at the Yale Club, or even the Bayou Club.

In November 1985, Bush held an hour-long private meeting with Jim Bakker. Afterwards, Bush described it as a "very enjoyable, very friendly, no-agenda kind of a meeting." He said he watched the Bakkers' PTL Club on TV "from time to time" and "certainly wouldn't be opposed" to the idea of sending them money. Two months later, Barbara Bush played hostess to Tammy Faye at the vice president's mansion at the Naval Observatory. At the same time, three of Bush's top advisers were put on the PTL payroll at an expense to the television ministry of more than $200,000.

Bakker was not the only evangelist Bush had cultivated. Jerry Falwell had been receiving the treatment for years. When Falwell's Moral Majority, which had fallen into disrepute, was recast as the Liberty Federation, Bush addressed its founding convention in January 1986. "America," proclaimed the vice president, "is in crying need of the moral vision" of Jerry Falwell. In March 1987, when Bakker resigned as the head of PTL because of his affair with the church secretary, Jessica Hahn, Falwell took over. The morning after, Falwell received Bush's call of support.

By then, Bush was well on his way to consolidating his conservative support throughout the South. "Going South," a senior Bush handler said, employing the Bush idiom, was a way to deal with "the class thing." But even as his allies on the religious right descended into temporal scandals of money and sex, the vice president was being pulled into the maelstrom of the Iran-contra affair.

Bush's principal credential was now cast into doubt. He was the foreign policy professional who denied knowledge of the Reagan administration's foreign policy. "Mistakes were made," he said passively, explaining nothing. He claimed to be "out of the loop." Loyalty was his shield.

Bush seemed to have been touched by pitch. With one hand, he appeared to have brushed away the Iran part of the scandal; with the other, the contra part. On July 29, 1986, Bush had traveled to Israel, where he met with Amiram Nir, the Israeli prime minister's deputy on counterterrorism. Nir was acting as a negotiator between the Americans and the Iranians in the arms for hostages deal. Before the Nir–Bush meeting, the U.S. position was that it would not release weapons to Iran unless all the hostages held in Lebanon were released. Nir explained to the vice president that if the Iranians received the shipment, they would arrange the freeing of two hostages. Soon afterward, the U.S. acceded to Nir. The weapons were transferred, the two hostages released. Bush, for his part, claimed he never understood that the deal was one of arms for hostages until the Senate Intelligence Committee began investigating in December 1986. And yet his deputy, Craig Fuller, who was present at the Nir meeting, wrote a memo that described in detail the character of the deal. If Fuller understood, why didn't Bush? Or was he dissembling?

At the same time, Bush's national security adviser, Donald Gregg, was revealed to have had extensive contacts with Felix Rodriguez, who had been a key agent in the contra resupply effort run by the National Security Council. What was the chain of command here? Was this a rogue operation, or did Gregg know what Rodriguez was doing and inform Bush? What did the vice president know and when did he know it?

Investigate! bellowed Senator Robert Dole, who suddenly emerged as Bush's chief rival. The camera turned to the Senate minority leader. Bush's men wondered how to retaliate. Their wheels whirred in vain as the clippings about Bush's role in the scandal accumulated.

The various conservative pretenders to Reagan's mantle scurried to and fro, unsure whether to attack Reagan, defend him, or simply mourn his passing. The conservative movement, already a cockpit of petty rivalries, began to break apart. Many conservatives removed Reagan's picture from their walls and replaced his smiling countenance with that of Oliver North. Reagan seemed increasingly out of touch and irrelevant. His "posthumous presidency" made the Iran-contra affair particularly acute for Bush. From the beginning of the administration until its end, Bush was perceived as Reagan's reflection. Just as popularity for one was transferred to the other, so was trouble.

"Whatever lingering illusions we may have had about the invincibility of the Reagan mantle or the permanence of a broad-based GOP realignment must be put on the shelf," read a strategy memo of February 20, 1987, written at the direction of Lee Atwater. But what did the shattering of these "illusions" mean? Could Bush now separate himself from Reagan, and if so how? Some within his entourage urged him to create a new identity by demanding new responsibilities from the president, but how this would give him a new image remained uncertain. Bush took none of this advice. Reagan, after all, remained enormously popular within the Republican Party. If the vice president separated himself he would lose the Reagan mantle and still be tarred with the scandal. He would have been, said pollster Robert Teeter, "a man without a country."

Bush went into "a tailspin on ice," in Atwater's words. Teeter termed it "a holding pattern, a freeze." Bush could not deal with "the vision thing" and at the same time deflect questions about the Iran-contra affair. Meanwhile, his battle intensified with the press, which raised his weakness as an issue. The week he announced for the presidency, in October 1987, *Newsweek* blared on its cover: "Fighting the Wimp Factor." Bush did not help himself. When asked by *Newsweek* correspondent Margaret Garrard Warner why he entered politics, he blathered: "It's hard to describe. . . . I got intrigued with it, I felt fascinated, believe in the country, in its strength, in helping people. You know, all the reasons people go into politics. Challenges and rewards."

Bush started contending with his wimp image. He warmed up by trying to shift the subject from his moral and intellectual courage to his physical courage—his heroism in the war—which had never been questioned. He also began to overcome his habit of self-effacement, drilled into him by his parents and school. In the past, upper-class figures in politics had sidestepped the image of the eastern gentleman by adopting other ones. Theodore Roosevelt had been a cowboy, Rough Rider and big-game hunter. John F. Kennedy had traded on his being a war hero and placed his upper-class background in the context of the immigrant saga. Bush's image-shifting, as we have seen, was to become a Texas good ol' boy, but mostly he created cognitive dissonance. Upon losing an Iowa straw poll, he said without a trace of irony: "A lot of people that support me—they were off at the air show, they were off at their daughter's coming-out party, or they were off teeing up on the golf course for that all-important last round."

On October 28, 1987, at the first debate of the Republican candidates, Bush struck a surprising blow against his wimp image. He did so by getting someone else to play his role while he played the bully. Pierre Samuel Du Pont IV was the heir to the chemical fortune, schooled at Exeter, Princeton and Harvard Law, and the former governor of Delaware. His staff called him "The Duper," after his prep school nickname. With his stiff bearing and slicked-back hair, he looked like the straight man in a Marx brothers' movie. As a governor of Delaware, Du Pont in fact had compiled a record of considerable achievement. Early on, Bush strategists feared that he might use his executive competence to position himself as a moderate. They estimated he might win at least fifteen percent of the Republican primary vote this way. If a moderate with this strength combined with a conservative who won a third of the vote, Bush might be stopped at the convention.

But Du Pont proved to be a curious parody of Bush. He tried to reinvent himself as a new man, a man of the right. "He got sucked into the right wing," a gleeful senior Bush strategist recounted. Not only did Du Pont thwart his own potential, but he contributed to the hoped-for conservative crackup by further fragmenting the movement. Du Pont introduced himself to the primary voters as a candidate of "new ideas" and "populism." His "new ideas" had been gleaned by his staffers, who raced through the conservative think tanks in Washington, picking up the most extreme economic proposals. He was in favor of making social security voluntary—among many other schemes of "privatization." Far from being the feared moderate, Du Pont's "new ideas" thrust him back into the class politics of the reactionary Du Pont family. Covering Du Pont's campaign was like watching an egg that would not hatch.

At the same time, Du Pont, like all politicians, wanted to be seen as a man of the people. He preferred to be called "Pete." But Bush called him "Pierre," making him the wimpy rich preppy. Then he dismissed Du Pont's social security idea as "nutty." Thus Bush was able to distance himself from his own negative images of the wimp in thrall to the right.

In the next debate, Bush did something more substantive. At the time, he was the only Republican candidate supporting the Intermediate Nuclear Force Treaty. He called upon the others to join him in his support; none of them would. Clinging to the orthodoxies of Cold War conservatism, Jack Kemp attacked the treaty as a potential "nuclear Munich." Dole equivocated. And Alexander Haig, with as many impressive jobs on his résumé—former NATO commander, White House chief of staff, secretary of state—as Bush, was dive-bombing. To Haig, Gorbachev was just "Stalin in Guccis." In New Hampshire, Haig circulated a leaflet: "Haig vs. Bush. The winner has to take on Gorbachev. . . . Who do you want on our side of the table when the chips are down? Someone who's made a difference, or someone who will just fill a chair?" In the first GOP debate, Haig described Bush's manner of expression as a "whimp." An unstable, trigger-happy figure—"I'm in control here," he had said in the White House shortly after the president had been wounded in 1981—Haig could not help himself by hurting Bush. But he could inflict damage.

Bush had not really dispelled this image of "just filling a chair," which had been his defense in the recent Iran-contra scandal. He was still "running against himself," said a senior Bush handler. And Bush remained suspended on a string tied to Reagan, for better or worse. During the Iran-contra affair, it was for the worse. When Gorbachev landed in Washington for the December summit, it was for the better. The Reagan factor had thrown the greatest doubt on Bush's candidacy throughout 1987. But in 1988 it suddenly turned into his greatest asset. Of the pretenders to Reagan, only Bush had not separated himself from the president at this crucial juncture. Now he was very much in the big picture, shaking hands with Mikhail Gorbachev.

In his first television commercials, Bush broadcast two images of himself: the self-made man and the wise man. "All I wanted was a chance to succeed. . . . I know that's what the people of South Dakota want," he said in one ad. There was no mention here or in any of his speeches of his father, of Andover, Yale, and Skull and Bones, of Brown Brothers, Harriman and Uncle Herbie Walker's venture capital, of the Council on Foreign Relations. In another spot, Bush appeared with a parade of world leaders, from Margaret Thatcher to Lech Walesa to Mikhail Gorbachev. Bush was doing what presidents do because he knew how to do it. "I am convinced," he said in the ad, as it flashed his handshake with Gorbachev, "the people of Iowa care as deeply about peace as I do." The people could prove their good intentions by voting for Bush. His slogan: "Ready on Day One to Be a Great President." This was a variation on his 1980 theme: A President We Won't

Have to Train. But, with Gorbachev present, the reference to Bush's background did not appear forced or empty. The Russian leader had given Bush an appropriate way to dramatize the image of the statesman. "Nothing could have helped us more," said a Bush handler. "Nothing was more important." But Bush wanted the benefit of association with Gorbachev without considering its meaning.

With the Washington summit, the Reagan presidency was restored without Reaganism. There had been summits in the past, but this one was truly a watershed. It was about far more than the INF Treaty; it was about the end of the Cold War.

For George Bush, however, these world-historical events seemed to be simply an element of his campaign strategy. Arms control, after all, was not an issue that he had identified; it identified him. He did not need to understand anything new, much less present a "vision." He was already prepared—"ready on day one." The search for "the vision thing" was a redundant exercise. He acted as if nothing fundamental was changing in the world, except perhaps his image.

A month after the summit, on January 5, 1988, Bush delivered a speech to the National Press Club in which he attributed Gorbachev's policies to "our strength . . . our steadiness . . . [our] resolve." Bush made no reference to Soviet history, society or politics. What Gorbachev was doing was simply a reflection of his respect for U.S. power and will. Then, he equated Gorbachev's Russia with Hitler's Germany: "It would be easier, safer, more diplomatic to remain silent about such matters—to negotiate our treaties with the Soviets and never raise the question of Nicaragua or Afghanistan or human rights. But that would be untrue to ourselves and to the lessons of history. In September I visited the death camp at Auschwitz." Bush proceeded to enumerate the horrors in detail—"mounds of human hair, the eyeglasses and the toothbrushes and the tiny children's shoes." Without a transition, he raised Gorbachev's name and his policy of glasnost. Gorbachev, said Bush, may have "an almost Western style that makes him different from his predecessors. But make no mistake about it, he is no freedom-loving friend of democracy. He is . . . an orthodox, committed Marxist. . . . We must never confuse style with substance. . . ." Almost as an afterthought, Bush added that in case Gorbachev "can transform Soviet society [a subject Bush did not discuss at all], we will be waiting for him . . . ready to move from an era of confrontation to one of cooperation. In the meantime, we must remain ever watchful." Thus, at the start of the campaign year, Bush's view of the end of the Cold War was a parsing of skepticism.

But Bush's fate was linked to the Cold War's fading more than he realized. In time, Reagan's popularity, renewed by the summit, would rub off on the vice president. The osmosis process, however, was not occurring swiftly enough. In a campaign, events do not arrive and depart in an orderly way, as though they were on a tight train schedule. The chronology is jumbled, the narrative line a scribble. What seems to have passed can suddenly return. The coming of Gorbachev did not lay a neat wall between the past and present. Almost as soon as the Soviet leader left Washington for Moscow, Bush was plunged into another round of Iran-contra scourging. New reports filled the press. "He should release all his notes, all his memoranda," demanded Dole.

Bush steeled himself for an interview with Dan Rather on the "CBS Evening News." "I don't think they'd do that," he said, when his handlers informed him that he was going to be attacked for his involvement in the Iran-contra scandal. Roger Ailes, his media adviser, who had scripted his evisceration of Du Pont, rehearsed him for the duel with Rather. As the Bush team expected, on January 25, CBS led into the interview with a six-minute report on Iran-contra. Rather then turned to Bush, who was ready. "It's not fair to judge my whole career by a rehash on Iran," he said. "How would you like it if I judged your career by those seven minutes when you walked off the set in New York?"

The anchorman was an ideal political foil for Bush—a hate object for the right wing, personifying the satanic media. By hitting back at Rather, Bush was also striking at his own wimp image. After the encounter, Bush privately called Rather "a pussy." "The bastard didn't lay a glove on me," he crowed to his aides. On the stump the next day he gloated, "I ought to get combat pay for last night." To Bush, the incident was another ordeal by fire by which the patrician is made strong, like being a fighter pilot or moving to Texas. In the meantime, the facts about the Iran-contra scandal were lost in the battle of personalities between the vice president and the anchorman.

Bush's thrusts and parries were all tactical. He was aiming to control the tenor of the headlines in the morning papers and the sound bites on the nightly news. At best, as in his "combat" with Dan Rather, he was able to dominate the cycle for more than a day, even winning the cover stories of the newsweeklies. But Bush's tactics did not amount to a new politics, much less a new vision.

The eastern establishment, the bipartisan consensus and the moderate wing of the Republican Party were no longer available to him. Long ago he had dissociated himself from them, and they no longer figured in politics. Bush had to sustain himself by other means. After the wise men came the political consultants, and their techniques for positioning him replaced the policies of statesmanship.

The world of his father was gone, but Bush still sought the support and advice of a political father-figure. Unfortunately, this father kept his distance, because he did not believe Bush was brutal enough to win.

4

The Nixon Succession

The 1988 Republican presidential campaign was the Reagan succession. That was partly why the candidates were searching high and low for a "vision." They wanted their own version of "morning in America" set against a background of blue sky and windswept beach. But that beach was haunted by a hunched, brooding figure, walking in the sand in his black wingtips. For the Republican legacy was not only Ronald Reagan's; it was also Richard Nixon's. It was morning in America all right—3:00 A.M.

The cycles of American history, according to historian Arthur Schlesinger, Jr., are formed by periods of progressive movements and reaction to them, of public action and private pursuit, of affirmative government and drift. Within the GOP, there is a political rhythm that fosters a different cycle—the Nixon cycle. For the entire period of the Cold War, from start to finish, Nixon was the essential Republican. Even as Reagan departed from the White House to sun himself in his Bel Air compound, Nixon was still asserting himself: his book *1999: Victory without War* was displayed on the racks at airports, his article on how to deal with Gorbachev was featured in *Foreign Affairs*. President Bush called him for advice, Reagan only out of courtesy. Nixon outlasted everybody.

The Nixon model, like clockwork, reappears in periods of retrenchment, when the Republican Party is seeking relief from its charismatic leadership. After Eisenhower, the party naturally turned to his charmless number two. After the Goldwater candidacy of 1964, the party sought relief from too much failed ideological rapture with the "new" Nixon. And after Reagan, the party, as if suffering charisma sunstroke, sought shade. They couldn't have Nixon, but perhaps they could cool off in his shadow. The return to Nixonism was the return to normalcy. Accordingly, Dole and Bush, each of whom were the reincarnation of parts of Nixon, fought for a place out of the sun.

Nixon was the master of the politics of resentment. In others' successes he saw only his own failure; in others' virtues he saw only his own flaws. His personality exercised a sway over the party that is hard to underestimate. The Republican activists may have basked in the warmth of Eisenhower and Reagan, but they identified with the insecurity of Nixon. They saw their own opportunity in the rise of the lower-middle-class man whose upper lip was drenched with sweat as he battled against the sophisticated, morally corrupt establishment: the Nixon story from the Alger Hiss case to Watergate.

Nixon was the founding father of the modern negative campaign, which is rooted in the Cold War. The impugning of an opponent's patriotism, the accusation of being soft on communism, the charges of appeasement and betrayal—all these were perfected by Nixon only a few years before Joseph McCarthy began his crusade and two decades before that transplanted Californian, Ronald Reagan, ran for public office. "REMEMBER," read an ad in Nixon's first race, in 1946 against Jerry Voorhis, " . . . his voting record in Congress is more Socialistic and Communistic than Democratic." Nixon was tutored in this method by the Socrates of slurs, Murray Chotiner, one of the original political consultants in California, the crucible of the trade. Chotiner was the original Lee Atwater. "There are many people," taught Chotiner, "who say we want to conduct a constructive campaign and point out the merits of our own candidate. I say to you in all sincerity that, if you do not deflate the opposition candidate before your own candidate gets started, the odds are that you are going to be doomed to defeat. . . . It is not a smear, if you please, if you point out the record of your opponent. . . . Of course it is always a smear, naturally, when it is directed to our own candidate." This brand of campaigning was not mere name-calling but the systematic denigration of an opponent using all the techniques of marketing. It is the politics of resentment for a media-driven age.

As president, Nixon shrewdly recognized that he needed something positive to offer. When it was suggested to him by Daniel Patrick Moynihan that he might become a conservative reformer like Benjamin Disraeli, Nixon tried on the role and admired the fit. His administration consolidated and expanded Lyndon Johnson's Great Society. And Nixon ended up proposing programs, such as the Family Assistance Plan, that are too radical for the Democratic Party of today. But he didn't really care that much about the poor. He saw the Disraeli-like reforms as a way to buy domestic peace. Then he could follow his Bismarckian longings in the great game of nations.

The Cold War was Nixon's reason for being. He needed the long twilight struggle, both to wage it and to continue it. He had to have the perpetual enemy, the deadly threat. Nixon could be trusted with the Soviets. Only he understood their cynicism; only he could negotiate; only he was tough enough. But the Cold War must be endless; for if it were ever over, then Nixon's function would cease. He would simply be history.

The Nixon succession was interrupted by Watergate. If the scandal had not intervened, the party was prepared for a contest between Nixon's secretary of the treasury, John Connally, one of Lyndon Johnson's understudies, whom the president admired for his toughness, and the vice president, Spiro Agnew, who held the historic Nixon post of hatchet man. But Agnew pleaded no contest to charges of larceny and resigned before Nixon did. Connally spent $12 million in the 1980 primaries and won one delegate's vote. He then went bankrupt in the oil bust. Only Watergate had made it possible for Reagan to gain eventual control of the national party. His apologists presented his politics as novel and innovative, but virtually every important aspect of them—from the obsession with media imagery to the attempt to foster a realignment on a Sunbelt base—had been established by Nixon. Now, with Reagan departing, the Nixon succession was resumed, with the disgraced president's two former party chairmen as the leading contenders.

II

"Dole—he must go," said Richard Nixon. It was late November, 1972. Nixon had just been reelected president, and he was purging his administration and party. Senator Robert Dole was the chairman of the Republican National Committee. But he had a problem, in Nixon's eyes. "Image," said the president.

The similarity may have been what was unnerving. Dole, like Nixon, was a child of the small-town Protestant ethic. Every step of his rise was marked by difficulty; in repose his face was a scowl. Nixon's overwhelming desire in his second term was to wrap a mystique around himself. He aspired to become an American de Gaulle, the only foreign leader who had paid him any attention during his purgatory in the 1960s. When the president gazed at Dole he saw the unvarnished Republican Party as well as the old Nixon. The plainness of Dole's anger and self-pity exposed much of what the president wanted to disguise in himself. Nixon's preferred mask was classiness; his choice for the RNC chairmanship was George Bush.

Before that moment, Dole had merely disliked Bush. Afterwards, he loathed him. Dole had run for the Senate three times and won; Bush twice and lost. In Dole's eyes, Bush had earned nothing. In a typical act of Nixonian sadism, Dole was told to go to New York to try to persuade Bush to leave his post at the U.N. for Dole's own RNC job. Dole followed orders. He did not learn until later that Bush had already accepted and that he had allowed Dole to go through the humiliating exercise without telling him. Insult was added to injury. The self-made man was wronged by the entitled man. "I didn't dream it up to go after Bush," Dole reflected. "But it's true: He started at the top and he stayed there. Why should he even be there?"

The battle between Dole and Bush for the presidential nomination was the Republican class struggle in its rawest form. Since Lincoln, with the accidental exception of Theodore Roosevelt, the Republican Party had always nominated a candidate who could claim a modest small-town origin, preferably in the Middle West. Even Thomas Dewey, who looked as though his birth had been announced with a bond offering in the back pages of the *Wall Street Journal*, hailed from a small village in Michigan. The class struggle between Dole and Bush was a cultural war fought over the issue of authenticity. Dole was the more authentic and, ultimately, it was because of that that he was undone.

This cultural conflict might have created the misimpression that the battle between Dole and Bush was a reengagement of the struggle between the historic wings of the GOP, once represented by Senator Robert Taft of Ohio, the midwestern conservative, and Governor Thomas Dewey of New York, the eastern moderate. But that schism, running back in the party to the post–Civil War period, had finally been dissolved by the Cold War. The divided factions of the GOP were hardened by the division of Europe into implacable blocs. Robert Taft, the lineal inheritor of the leadership of the Old Guard from his father, President William Howard Taft, upheld the old isolationism in an utterly changed world. He opposed the Marshall Plan and the formation of NATO as a dangerous European entanglement that was inflating big government at home. The rival wing of the party, in the meantime, supported the internationalist foreign policy of the postwar consensus. In the early presidential campaigns of the Cold War, in 1948 and 1952, Taft attempted to storm the convention and was repulsed. Dewey's final victory over Taft was at the 1952 convention with the nomination of Dwight Eisenhower, which also elevated onto the national stage as his running mate the enduring figure of the age. Nixon transcended and revised the old party split because of his complete identification with the new world order: the Cold War. But he did not later control the party through the force of his personality; nor did he dominate by the force of Cold War conservatism. He also manipulated the institutions and factions of the party so that he could bridge them all. He won the support of the right-wing without ever becoming its captive. And he constantly sought the approval of the establishment he held in contempt. He had the ability to rise above principle at any turn. By virtue of their backgrounds, Dole would appear to have been Taft's heir and Bush, Dewey's. But what had intervened was Nixon. The blood motive in the rivalry between the chief Republican candidates could be traced to their days as Nixon's protégés. Both Dole and Bush could make rightful claims to his legacy, at the center of which was a dark, empty space.

If Bush had a problem with "the vision thing," Dole had one with "the vision gap." This "gap" was discussed in the press and within his campaign. Nobody ever explained what the "gap" was between, or what the "vision" would fill when it was supplied. But it was something that Dole had to have.

Dole himself strained to produce what others would call a vision. In the magnificent office of the minority leader in the Capitol, he pointed to the doors leading to the terrace, overseeing Independence Mall. "I went out on the terrace," Dole said. "Nobody else around, looking at the Washington Monument, thinking of these lofty thoughts of why I was running for president." He pondered, he mused, he reflected. And only one idea came to mind. "How," he said, "do I beat George Bush?"

A "vision," everyone else in his campaign agreed, had to do with more than crushing Bush into fine dust. It had to do with the future, whatever that might be. Dole's media consultants, Mike Murphy and Alex Castellanos, labored for months to come up with the long view. Long before the events of the campaign began, they had, for all intents and purposes, given up. "Instead of inventing a grand 'vision,' keep it simple," they wrote in a private campaign memo dated June 3, 1987. "Let Senator Dole hold a little bit of the future up for people to see. Announce the Dole for President Committee's 'Commission on the Future,' or 'Commission on America in the Next Century,' composed of 20 leading experts in their fields." This idea, like most, came to naught.

Perhaps a long campaign video would fill the vision gap. "Generally, I think we're heading in the right direction," wrote William Lacy, a top Dole manager, in a private memo of July 30, 1987. "There's one major concern: The film must be very powerful (in the way the Reagan '84 film was) and have a Big Finish. I don't see—nor can I figure out—the Big Finish." In the video's final sequence, Dole appeared in a wheat field talking vaguely and repetitively about "the future." "We're on the threshold of many opportunities," he concluded. But everyone in the campaign agreed that this was not the longed-for vision.

On the stump, Dole turned the notion into a joke about his own cynicism. "We thought about having a vision-of-the-month club just for the media," he said. "They'd say: 'That's the wrong vision,' and I'd say: 'That's all right, I got another one.' " When he passed a Pearle Vision Center in a mall, he told the reporters he was going to go in and buy one.

Dole's actual vision was not one his handlers wanted to acknowledge. They showed pictures of his experiences growing up in the heartland and as a war hero, and accompanied these scenes with kitsch rhetoric about "values." But the campaign never presented the real education of Bob Dole; that was a story of bleakness and pain. He was raised in poverty during the Depression in Russell, Kansas, a small town origi- nally called Fossil Station but renamed after a Civil War veteran who never bothered to visit. Doran Dole operated a creamery for farmers, a business that depended upon barter. The children were awakened at five in the morning to complete their chores before school. Kenny Dole, Bob's brother, whose oil lease business, operated out of a store-front on Main Street, was barely eking by in late 1987, and who was selling limestone "Dole '88" paperweights for ten dollars, remembered: "All we know is work. Wish to hell we could have done something else. . . . If you went to a restaurant, your mother was lazy. 'Just put some water in the gravy,' my mother said. 'We'll get by.' " In 1937, the family moved into the basement of their own house in order to get the rent for the upstairs. Still, Bob was the star athlete of his school and had made it to the state university. Then came the war.

He was with the elite 10th Mountain Division in Italy when he was hit by a shell. Paralyzed from the neck down for a year, he lay on a hospital bed for another two years and was never again to have use of his right arm or be without pain. Unlike Bush, Dole never portrayed himself as a hero, or referred to his physical bravery. He simply said he "got shot." "Why me?" Dole wondered. "I don't really accept it yet."

Dole's defiant response to the world often took the form of sardonic jokes. His sensibility owed its power to its emotional minimalism, which assumed grotesquely convoluted proportions. He was Grant Wood out of Fritz Lang, *American Gothic* gone to *Metropolis.* The suspense of listening to Bob Dole was wondering when he would suddenly veer from pure emptiness into pure savagery. It could happen at any moment. His monologues, more often than not, were dark commentaries on political cant. "I have a record of leadership, but he doesn't," Dole said in one of his typical monologues about Bush. "I assume it's getting to him. It's going to be a big issue in this campaign. That's what it's all about: leadership. I can't help it if he hasn't pro-vided any."

The pattern of the attack was inimitable. Dole's self-deprecation in the form of one-liners was almost always wielded as a razorlike weapon. "I was almost ready to vote for you after I read that," Dole said to Bush in a debate, holding up one of Bush's campaign brochures. Dole spared no one, not even the supposedly untouchable president. When Bush crowed in an Iowa debate that Reagan had called upon Bush to act as his stand-in when he could not appear at an event himself, Dole quickly cut him down to size: "Did he call collect?" He shouted "Good news!" when a man in a New Hampshire crowd told him Edwin Meese had endorsed Bush. Beyond the one-liners, Dole frequently lapsed into diatribes on why unhappiness was the essence of existence and why only somebody who had suffered as he had was qualified to be president. If

Reagan campaigned on the pleasure principle, Dole campaigned on the pain one. "You've all made it the hard way," he told a Republican crowd. "And, if you haven't, you're still trying to make it the hard way. Or, maybe the hard things haven't happened to you yet. But they might." This was not a threat, but Dole's way of relating. "And I don't think it would be too bad to have someone in the Oval Office who sort of got there the way you did."

Dole's so-called meanness was really his way of being sincere. When he uttered his famous gaffe in his vice presidential debate with Walter Mondale in 1976, calling U.S. involvement in wars in this century "Democrat wars," he conveyed more than he could express. He associated his opponents with the most painful episode in his life, which turned his youthful athletic frame into a shell of itself. The cosmos was unfair and capricious, and Dole was unforgiving. There was something in his hatred of "Democrat wars" and his hatred of George Bush that was more profound than partisanship or political ambition. They were images of his torment. It might even be said that it was a vision, more fevered than anything a political consultant could conjure.

Dole's managers treated him delicately as they attempted to reform his image with the help of media advisers and speech coaches. They believed that if they could get him to subdue his "meanness" he might be able to take on a vision that they had crafted. But Dole's vengeful outbursts and biting comments were his irrevocable ways of coping with his own fearful vision.

III

In no way did Bob Dole see himself as a pretender to Ronald Reagan. He believed that Reagan's policies had been so harmful that only "bitter medicine," as he put it, could cure them. He did not share Reagan's abhorrence of big government. Nor did he believe that poverty was caused by the indolence of the impoverished. He had a genuine compassion for the poor and the disabled, traceable to his own crippling, a connection he often drew himself. In fact, Dole had been the co-sponsor with George McGovern (a loathsome figure to the Reaganites) of the bill establishing food stamps. Dole's leadership in the Senate was crucial in winning the extension of the Voting Rights Act against the opposition of the Reagan administration. On civil rights, Dole still thought of the GOP as the party of Lincoln, not of Meese. But nothing inspired his contempt for the Reagan presidency more than the deficits Reagan had produced. Dole called Reagan's way the "easy way." The skyrocketing national debt and its beneficiaries deeply offended his ethic of honest work and sober economics, learned at his father's knee in rural Kansas. Twice in the early 1980s, he forced Reagan to sign tax increases he had directed through the Senate, though the president pretended they weren't tax bills. After Walter Mondale called for raising taxes and went down to ignominious defeat, Dole publicly said Mondale had been right.

Vice President Bush occupied the job that Nixon had held in 1960, which gave his political predicament a certain Nixonian cast. Bush was a trapped politician who at the same time had to articulate the case for continuity and change. He also approached U.S.–Soviet relations as a realist Nixonian, not a utopian Reaganite—something Bush never made explicit for fear of separating himself from Reagan in the public mind. Early on, Kissinger's former deputies—Brent Scowcroft, William Hyland and others—had rallied to Bush's side. But it became evident that as Nixon followed the early skirmishing between his former underlings, he clearly preferred Dole. "Prescott Bush, the old man, was tough as nails," he told a friend, having worked closely with the senator in the 1950s, when he had presided over the Senate as vice president and occasionally gone golfing with him. "I just don't know what happened to George," Nixon then remarked. He was drawn to Dole for the same reason he had dumped him in favor of Bush for the RNC chairmanship. "Bob is tough," he said. "Nixon," said the friend, "liked Dole for his dark side."

Dole, in turn, was eager to consult with Nixon and made a visit to Saddle River, New Jersey. For hours the old campaigner, now in exile, held forth on politics and policy. The deficit, he advised, had never been an effective issue. Dole needed to talk about something that conveyed the sense that he had a larger purpose. But Nixon did not have this something at hand to give to Dole.

With neither a vision nor an effective organization, Dole still had himself. "You can't go home again?" Dole asked in a campaign commercial. Novelist Thomas Wolfe had first presented this proposition as a declarative statement. Dole turned Wolfe's phrase into its obverse to point up his new slogan: "He's one of us." Dole explained it to a crowd in New Hampshire by speaking about himself in the third person: "He's had some hard knocks in his lifetime. Nobody gave him anything." If Dole was one of *us*, who was Bush one of? And if Bush wanted to go home, where exactly would that be?

The Iran-contra affair had placed Dole before the public as he had not been since his ill-starred performance as Gerald Ford's running mate. For almost a year, there was rarely a week in which he was not featured as a guest on one of the Sunday morning interview programs or ABC's "Nightline." The scandal, as Dole saw it, was another aspect of the class issue, another instance of Bush unfairly coasting by, not being called to account, hiding behind his father, Reagan in this case. By the end of 1987, as Dole continued to pound away on the issue, he did not grasp that the political scene was fundamentally changing to Bush's advantage without his having to do anything but stand pat while Reagan abandoned his dogmas of a political lifetime for a place in history as a man of peace.

When Mikhail Gorbachev landed in Washington his itinerary included a visit to the Senate. He was keenly aware that the SALT II Treaty, an arms control deal negotiated by President Carter, had met with enormous conservative resistance there. (The Russians themselves had gone far to undermine the last Democratic presidency. As the SALT II debate was building, they invaded Afghanistan, which prompted Carter to withdraw the already embattled treaty. Brezhnev had skewed priorities so that U.S.–Soviet relations ranked lower than Afghanistan.) Gorbachev wanted no troubles for the INF Treaty. When, at his meeting with Senate leaders, Dole said he wanted more time to study the treaty, Gorbachev pulled him into a side room to lobby him alone for ten minutes. When they emerged, Gorbachev offered him his hand and wished him good luck. "Thank you," replied Dole. "I'm winning."

For Dole, foreign policy was mainly a matter of political expedience, of what policies would play to Republicans. His view lacked nuance and creative impulse. Mostly, he went down the line with the right wingers. "Where do I sign?" was his attitude, according to a conservative Senate source. Dole's reduction of foreign policy to political tactics was illustrated after his trip in 1987 to Nicaragua, when he called for "a little three-day invasion" and then dismissed his remark as "just giving an opinion."

His idea of the Soviets was in part a projection of his own notion of power. "What alarms me most about Mr. Gorbachev, for all that he brings that is new," said Dole in his major foreign policy address during the campaign, "is that he also brings something that is very, very old: the convictions of a committed, dedicated, tough as nails Communist." His description of the Russian leader as "tough as nails" happened to echo, word for word, Nixon's description of Prescott Bush.

Thus Dole treated the INF Treaty simply as an opportunity for tactical maneuver. He had seen arms control treaties in the past, and this one touched only a very small number of nuclear weapons. Politically, however, it signaled a sea change. Dole had no sense that something momentous was happening. The idea that the Cold War might be ending was alien to him. He was obsessed with the shortest of short-term angles. Of course, he would eventually have to support the treaty. He was, after all, the leader of the president's party in the Senate. In the meantime, he expressed nothing but skepticism. He postured as being the toughest on the Russians in the hope of reminding Republican primary voters of Bush's wimp problem and of playing to the right-wing grandstands. Meanwhile, Bush, merely by remaining in Reagan's shadow, managed to claim the president's success with the Soviets for himself.

Dole did not much understand the political uses of issues. He understood bills and amendments to the bills and continuing resolutions. When he addressed the issues one could often hear the creaking of the gears and pulleys of the purely legislative mind. He was the master of the Senate who never realized how far that position, however powerful, could be from center stage.

Dole's campaign had attempted to identify him as the small-town candidate—"He's one of us"—while the Bush campaign tried to get Dole to be his saturnine self. Dole, under stern instructions from his handlers, tried to smile more and not say what naturally came to his mind. The Bush campaign, at Atwater's instigation, devoted its energies to creating situations that might provoke Dole to fits of sarcasm or anger. On February 3, for example, Bush's Iowa state chairman, George Wittgraf, was trotted out to say that Dole in 1976 had "single-handedly brought the Republican ticket down to defeat." Wittgraf also tried to rile Dole by attacking his wife. Elizabeth Hanford Dole, Dole's second wife, a power in her own right, was an important part of his aura. She had quit her job as Secretary of Transportation to work on the campaign. Now Wittgraf issued a press release noting that "three federal agencies are examining aspects of Elizabeth Hanford Dole's now defunct blind trust" (no wrongdoing was ever found); that the Doles were wealthy; and that they lived in the Watergate complex. The next day, on the floor of the Senate, Dole angrily confronted Bush, presiding as the Senate president. He rose to say that Bush owed "my wife an apology"; that Bush was "mean"; Bush was "personal"; Bush was "groveling in the mud." But Bush replied: "I don't want to engage in negative campaigning."

In the days that followed, Dole's anger mounted. Bush had suffered little and done less. "I'm a little disadvantaged," Dole said, "because I have to work for a living." Even Bush's association with Reagan was unmerited. "When Ronald Reagan wants his program passed, he doesn't call George, he calls Bob." But Dole had waffled on the INF Treaty and Bush had been steadfast. It was impossible to drive a wedge between the president and the vice president.

It was precisely Bush's identification with Reagan that swept Dole to victory in the Iowa caucuses. The prosperity of the Reagan years had been unevenly spread across the country, and it had skipped Iowa. Bush was at the disadvantage of Reagan's unpopularity. The vice president finished a dismal third, behind Dole and television evangelist Pat Robertson. The day after the caucuses, on February 9, Bush landed in New Hampshire with a new message. "He's one of us!" he claimed about himself.

Dole arrived at the cavernous National Guard Armory in Manchester that night full of confidence. He was greeted by a buoyant, flag-waving crowd of about one thousand. In the front row sat some half-dozen graying veterans of the 10th Mountain Division. Perhaps their presence encouraged Dole to revert to being himself. In any case, he delivered a rambling, self-lacerating monologue. "Is it a fair system?" he began. "No, they should have started in Kansas. . . . They say Bob Dole won [in Iowa] because he was a neighbor. I was a neighbor in 1980 and I lost. . . . I'm not trying to spread doom and gloom. I'm an optimist." As though to contradict his point, he offered a metaphor for the federal deficit. Imagine, he said, a young man pounding on an iron door, looking through its bars, seeing nothing but bones, and screaming, "What have you done to my future?" Finally, Dole had managed to create a "vision" of the future—the future as boneyard.

"I want to close on an optimistic note," he went on in his incoherent way. "You see it can happen in America. . . . You don't have to be rich and powerful. . . . When I got out of the hospital I went home to hide. . . . All I wanted to do was go off somewhere. Russell, not too much action. You can hide there pretty well." Dole then digressed to describe his political origins, how a local Republican approached him. "He said I should be a Republican. I said, 'Why?' He said, 'There are twice as many Republicans as Democrats in Russell, Kansas.' I made a philosophical decision on the spot. I became a Republican." Dole droned on: "Why do I want to be president? I think we're on the threshold of greatness. . . . Oh, you've got problems, but we've got a lot of opportunities. I want to be part of it. I can get elected in 1988. . . . Electability is very important. . . ." His speech did not come to an ending so much as grind to a halt.

The next day, Richard Wirthlin, Dole's pollster, informed him that victory was his. Wirthlin was also Ronald Reagan's pollster. Throughout the 1980s, his numbers revolved around the implicit assumption of Reagan's presence. It was not that Wirthlin wanted to put the best face on the numbers, but that the best face could always be expected to turn them around. For Dole to win, he was now advised that he simply had to be affable and not allow the hatchet man inside to emerge. If he smiled, he could be Reagan. Thus the fatal mistake.

The Dole campaign had prepared a negative ad about Bush, showing a figure walking in the snow but leaving no footprints. "After a lifetime of walking in the shoes of giants, isn't it interesting that George Bush has never left a single footprint behind?" said the voiceover. But the spot aired only once. Dole did not want the aspersion of meanness cast on him. With Wirthlin's poll in hand, he anticipated only the happy ending. He was just months away from being elected president.

Bush's handlers now went on the offense, led by pollster Robert Teeter. Bush became tough again. He charged every failure of the Reagan administration to Dole's leadership in the Senate. Dole's strength thus was turned into weakness. Bush himself was cast as a blue-collar type, driving a tractor trailer around a parking lot, with Secret Service agents on the running boards. On February 13, a thirty-minute show was broadcast, featuring citizens posing prearranged questions to the candidate. "Ask George Bush" was directly modeled on the shows that Bush's media adviser, Roger Ailes, had contrived for Richard Nixon in his 1968 campaign. The final programmed questioner asked Bush if he was a member of the "old eastern establishment." "Some of them," he replied (without identifying the "them"), "are going after me because my mom and dad could look after me when we were born. I had nothing to do with that. When I ran for office in Texas they said this guy's from New England. I said, 'Wait a minute, I couldn't help that. I wanted to be near my mother at the time.' " He was one of them, but it was an accident of birth for which he was deeply sorry. To clarify the point, Barry Goldwater was flown in to endorse Bush for president, returning the favor that the young Bush had extended to him in 1964, when Bush first repudiated his father's wing of the party. "I believe in George Bush," said Goldwater. "He's the man to continue the conservative revolution we started twenty-four years ago." His statement was promptly transformed into a commercial and rushed on the air.

The "new Bush" proved his newness through self-deprecation. Teeter imported Peggy Noonan, a former Reagan speechwriter, to craft the words. In his closing statement in the debate of February 14, Bush delivered them. "I don't talk much, but I do believe," he said, without explaining what it was he believed. "I may not articulate much, but I feel." For good measure, he quoted Lincoln, "Here I stand, warts and all." But the true echo was not with Lincoln. It was with Nixon's Checkers speech, a self-justifying plea intended to turn the political tables. Bush's weakness was being made into strength.

Then came the coup de grace. Over and over again, on the weekend before the New Hampshire primary, snowbound voters were blitzed by a negative television ad produced by the Bush campaign about Dole. On the INF Treaty: "Bob Dole straddled. . . ." On taxes: "Bob Dole straddled. . . ." And on and on. Bush had initially hesitated to commission the negative spot, but his handlers insisted. The choice, as they posed it, was between winning and losing, and Bush's qualms were soon overcome.

On February 16, Bush won the primary by nine points. Late that night, on an NBC special, Tom Brokaw asked Dole if there was anything he would like to ask his rival. "Stop lying about my record," he snarled. Dole was back in character. Bush flew directly to Texas, where he unveiled his slogan again: "He's one of us."

Dole connected his losses with the sources of his bitterness. "I've felt better," he said. "Nothing's easy in life for me." In March, before the Illinois primary, he found himself standing outside the Wesley Pavilion in Chicago, where he had been treated for his war wounds, and began talking about "optimism."

By then Dole was forty points behind in Illinois. He insisted that his campaign stage a thirty-minute broadcast from Knox College in Galesburg, the site of one of the Lincoln–Douglas debates. Doing so, on one day's notice, would require the construction of a veritable television station. "The show is going to be tough," warned Michael Murphy, Dole's media adviser. "It's not like we're going to blow our lead," Dole replied.

"I didn't expect this job to be handed to me," the candidate began. "I expected to earn it." He mentioned Lincoln. "He worked hard . . . born in poverty." And then the screen flickered. Dole was trapped in a freeze frame, his mouth gaping half open, the top of his head cut off by a black strip, as his voice droned on. Then the original eighteen-minute Dole video started unreeling. Dole's campaign was in rerun. "You can't go home again?" asked Dole again. Then, just as suddenly, the picture was restored. Dole on tape was yanked in midsentence: "I happen to believe. . . ." Dole live was talking about the Wesley Pavilion. "I started right there . . . I went back." At last, this was the Big Finish his campaign handlers had had such trouble imagining.

It was more than losing that stoked the rage of Bob Dole. What had lain beyond the edge of his hospital bed was the void. And now it had assumed a human form. Yes, Dole explained, Bush had "his organization," "name recognition" and was "close to Ronald Reagan." But that was not his secret of success. Dole had once journeyed to the heart of darkness, and now he glimpsed the horror again. He saw this vision in the face of his foe. "There's nothing there," said Dole. And nothingness, as he understood it, was triumphant.

Having won the Nixon succession in his battle with Dole, Bush went on to a much easier task, eliminating the politicians who saw themselves as Reagan's most appropriate successor.

5

The Pretenders

I

Jack Kemp and Pat Robertson represented the cultural contradictions of conservatism. Kemp stood for the free market, which was relentlessly uprooting society. Robertson stood for a traditional, even biblical, authority. At the heart of these profoundly different conservative visions was a stark dualism, a division of the world into good and evil, lightness and darkness. What animated the dualism was the endless conflict between the Free World and communism. Without this enemy, the vision lost its compelling drama. Once there was no "evil empire," it would be hard to muster a political crusade.

Reagan had been the great dissolving agent of the differences among conservatives. He could represent at the same time the apocalyptics, who believed they would be beamed up to heaven before the battle of Armageddon, and the supply-siders, who believed in "voodoo economics," in George Bush's phrase, which purported to demonstrate that revenue was increased by decreasing taxes. Reagan's ability to adopt these and other equally incongruous mindsets provided conservatism with a coherence that evaporated once he was withdrawn from the scene. He himself never came to terms with the incongruities; that was left to his pretenders.

Those who would be Reagan overlooked the fact that Reagan had never struggled for the leadership of the movement. It had fallen to him by virtue of his luck in not being preceded by a dominating Reagan-like figure. If Reagan was the alpha, Kemp and Robertson each saw themselves as the beta. Reagan's story was the preface to theirs, which flowed as logically as their doctrines. The temporal carrier of the vision was the conservative movement, just as a religion is cradled by a church. As it turned out, though, Reagan's unyielding ideology was most mutable, made so by the startling metamorphosis of the Soviet Union, which had been presumed by conservatives to be even more immutable than Reagan. Kemp and Robertson found themselves chasing an image of Reagan and an image of the enemy receding over the horizon.

II

"Jack Kemp has been a leader for his entire life," said the voiceover on Kemp's first television commercial, an eight-minute spot produced in August 1987. Kemp in a business suit, posed before a wall of American flags, dissolved into Kemp in a football uniform. "As quarterback of both the San Diego Chargers and the Buffalo Bills, Kemp led both teams to championships." Suddenly, wearing another business suit, he appeared on a football field clutching a pigskin. "Since he has left the football field, Jack has had even greater success." Kemp and Governor Reagan, whom he was serving as an aide, stared at a football. Then it's 1980. Cheering delegates at the GOP convention carry banners reading "Reagan/Kemp" and "Jack Kemp persuaded Ronald Reagan to cut taxes." Not only was Kemp Reagan before Reagan was Reagan, but he was Reagan even when Reagan didn't stay the course. It's 1982. Reagan is "under enormous pressure to raise taxes." Reagan buckled. "One man stood up against his president and his party. . . . And Jack Kemp was vindicated for his courage and foresight." Reagan said his lapse was a "mistake." Crowds cheered Kemp. He was "the cutting edge of this revolution. . . . Now America needs a leader who can follow Ronald Reagan."

Jack Kemp was the child of optimism, raised in Los Angeles, the son of a successful entrepreneur. He entered politics at the personal behest of Richard Nixon. At the end of his football career, he had been spotted as a raw political talent by Herbert Klein, the former Nixon press secretary, who had become an executive of the Copley newspaper chain based in San Diego. Klein brought Kemp to President Nixon, who convinced him to run for the House in 1970. Klein hoped that a district could be found for Kemp where there was a Copley newspaper to support him. None materialized. So Kemp settled on a suburban, working-class district outside Buffalo, where his celebrity was still bright.

After Watergate, Kemp was an obscure backbencher of the minority party. Nixon had been disgraced; the Democrats were ascendant. One day in 1976, Jude Wanniski, a *Wall Street Journal* editorial writer, was wandering the halls of Congress, eager to explain to anyone a new theory. According to its miraculous formula, cutting taxes would foster growth and increase government revenues. That afternoon, Wanniski dropped by Kemp's office unannounced. By nightfall, Kemp was a convert.

Soon he was being featured in many *Wall Street Journal* editorials and courted by the neoconservatives, who had arranged the funding for Wanniski's research. The physical education major was happy to be hanging out with the campus intellectuals. He began to think of himself as a man of ideas. In 1979, he produced a book entitled *An American Renaissance,* in which he inscribed his motto: "Ideas rule the world." That year, Wanniski almost convinced Kemp to run for president. Reagan, however, gently dissuaded his potential rival. Kemp introduced Reagan to supply-side economics, which turned the old Republican plaint about taxes into a painless, world-historical new idea. "The election of 1980, for the first time, provided signs that a new Republican party might be emerging," wrote Irving Kristol, the neo-conservative "godfather," who helped promote Kemp's career. If Republicans like Kemp gained control of the GOP, he predicted, then 1980 "will in truth have been a critical election."

Kemp seemed like Sinclair Lewis's Babbitt reincarnated as a financial newsletter author, combining the boosterism of the Roaring Twenties with the ideologizing of the Roaring Eighties. He was delighted to display his arcane knowledge about M-1, "facing points," and why Adam Smith entitled his book *The Wealth of Nations,* not *The Wealth of Great Britain.* The more obscure the subject, the greater his enthusiasm: Little excited him more than explaining why a return to the gold standard would solve all the problems not cured by tax cuts. Kemp seemed to believe that his breathless talk about economics would unlock the mysteries of politics. "There's a Grand Old Party. And, careful about this, there's a Grand New Party," he said, which would include the minorities and the working class. "This is the ultimate struggle going on for the soul of the party."

The conservative movement, to his great disappointment, did not fall in behind his banner. Much of the old right viewed the neoconservatives as usurpers within the movement they had founded. By venting their spleen on Kemp's candidacy they believed they were settling scores with the neoconservative bounders. "I hope Kemp gets his clock cleaned," said one right winger, a writer on the *Washington Times*. Most of the neoconservatives, for their part, proved to be unreliable, obsessed with the notion that one of their own, the former U.N. ambassador Jeane Kirkpatrick, would enter the field. When she declined, after a disappointing trip to New Hampshire, Kemp announced that he would appoint her his secretary of state. She responded to the compliment by endorsing Bob Dole.

Kemp's upbeat talk about remaking the GOP aroused the simmering enmity of much of the right. "I saw that as the straw that broke the back of the conservative movement," Kemp reflected, "that it was basically portrayed to the poor, to minorities, to the blue-collar workers, as a negative movement." His exposure to the neoconservatives, former leftists turned rightists, had somewhat tempered his own conservatism, and his failure to jump off the far edge of the movement was duly punished. For his support of the union shop, Kemp earned the hostility of right-wing elements, such as the National Right to Work Committee, without gaining any labor endorsements. Other conservatives did not trust him because he called himself "a progressive conservative" and spoke about "liberal democratic capitalism." Their willingness to fight to the death over semantics was a shadow war of the factionalism within the movement. Kemp's supply-side ardor, moreover, was by no means universally shared by the right. The traditional Republican economists especially regarded it as a heresy for its lack of concern about the astronomical federal deficit, which was being partly induced by the supply-side remedy. Meanwhile, he courted the new right to little avail, even taking leaders such as Howard Phillips on a junket to observe the base camps of the Nicaraguan contras in Honduras. In Washington, many of those who should have been Kemp's shock-troops—the younger conservative policymakers and publicists attracted there by the allure of Reagan—were infatuated with Pierre S. Du Pont IV, who raced through the think tanks scooping up the white papers that Kemp had left undisturbed. On economics, Du Pont positioned himself well to the right of Kemp. "I've got to believe," Kemp hoped, "that if I stay in and fight long enough I will emerge as a consensus conservative."

Kemp discovered that although as a conservative he had stature in the pages of the *National Review* and *Commentary* magazine, as a House member he had scant name recognition with the public. That problem could only be cured by advertising. If the reiteration of the ideology had not restored the glow of Reaganism, perhaps the reiteration of images might. Phil Dusenberry, the creative spirit behind Pepsi's spots, who had crafted Reagan's "morning again in America" ads in 1984, was set to work. "Main Street" read the signpost. The paperboy was making his rounds, a storekeeper opening his shop, the firemen cleaning the engine, the farmers loading their pickups. And children on their way to school tossed a football across the grass, landing near a man in a business suit. "Jack Kemp has been the captain of every team he's played on." He hitched up his pants and threw the ball. Yes, it's morning again. "Good morning everyone, I'm Jack Kemp." The slogan: "If he wins, we all win."

Kemp's campaign was now split between the ideologues and the political operatives. From extensive research with focus groups, it was learned that the more voters listened to Kemp's nasal voice, the more they were turned off; so Kemp's soundbites in his own commercials were kept to a minimum. Jude Wanniski, who still had Kemp's ear, argued that Kemp needed to address the camera and to lay out the supply-side vision. Reagan had been Philip of Macedon, Wanniski told Kemp; he could be Alexander the Great, conquering the world through talking-head spots. "Part of Jack's problem is that he's put himself in the hands of the puppet masters," Wanniski said. "I was sure the Dusenberry spots would be worthless. You had to have ideas." But in the meetings with the candidate, the operatives urged him to forgo his lengthy perorations about the gold standard, which one adviser bluntly informed him were "lunatic."

Kemp understood that optimism was political magic, but he believed that the magic came from the theory. His optimism wasn't as fungible as it was for Reagan. Kemp demanded that reality adjust itself to his dogma. Reagan simply transferred his optimism from one thing to another, from Cold War conservatism to nuclear abolitionism. Nowhere did he project more optimism than when he was with Gorbachev.

The ebullient Kemp was an unlikely bearer of conservative resentment. But then in March 1987, the Iran-contra scandal incited the right wing to hit back at the usual enemies within, and Kemp valiantly strained to become their spokesman in Washington. "I have seen the Reagan Doctrine nearly crippled by State Department efforts," he told a crowd of more than one thousand at the Conservative Political Action Conference. A straw poll for president was held on the spot. Kemp won sixty-eight percent.

On the eve of the signing of the INF Treaty, Kemp raised his decibel level. He talked about Winston Churchill's call for more defense spending to resist the rising Nazi power, about Neville Chamberlain and the appeasement of the Nazis, about a "nuclear Munich." He insisted this was all "loving criticism" of Reagan. But to be against Reagan on the treaty was to be on the wrong side of the pessimism/ optimism equation. On December 3, Reagan said: "I think that some of the people who are objecting the most and just refusing to accede to the idea of ever getting any understanding, whether they realize it or not, those people basically down in their deepest thoughts have accepted that war is inevitable and that there must come to be a war between the superpowers." Reagan's old vision of the "evil empire" was giving way to his new one of the peaceable kingdom.

In the Iowa caucuses, Kemp finished fourth, abruptly displaced as the leading conservative by Robertson, who finished second. Instinctively, Kemp attempted to project optimism. "Well," he reflected, "I've got to say it's a positive. Robertson has brought people into the party. He has been a good influence. He really is a nice guy. You really sit down with Pat Robertson, he is a charming and delightful person." Then Kemp became less flattering. "On the other hand, Robertson has a very negative conservatism. If you heard him speak, it would sound like Reagan lost in 1980." Then, Kemp became angry. "He said I should get out of the race. It's offensive to me, a competitor and an old quarterback. It is illiberal."

Kemp was like that staple of Saturday morning cartoon shows, the character who runs off the cliff but doesn't fall until he stops and looks down. At the February 14 debate in New Hampshire, George Bush said, "Give peace a chance," in support of Reagan's position of watchful waiting on the Soviet withdrawal from Afghanistan. Kemp threw a fit. "You should be embarrassed," he admonished. "Give peace a chance," he insisted, was not anything "a Republican" should say. Kemp believed that he was still playing Ronald Reagan running against the George Bush of 1980. But Bush now had the policy position of Reagan. For it was not Bush who was giving peace a chance; it was Reagan.

Kemp held a press conference in the Manchester Holiday Inn to unveil his climactic commercial for the New Hampshire primary. It featured the endorsement of a conservative hero. It was not Ronald Reagan, Barry Goldwater, or even Oliver North. It was Adolfo Calero, the contra leader. "Jack Kemp," he testified, "is the only one who lifted a finger." But Calero could deliver neither magic nor votes. This spot was the final futile effort to glorify Reagan's "freedom fighters." Kemp, casting himself as the candidate of the contras, was resting his campaign on an image of desperation.

III

Pat Robertson's pretensions were greater than any other candidate. "I have a direct call and a leading from God to run for president," he said. Now the Republican primary voters had the opportunity to ratify God's selection. But if God had decided, why should mere mortals have a veto? What did this say about God? What was He up to?

America, according to Robertson, was in the throes of "moral death." It could be brought back to health only by the restoration of tradition, enforced by the authority of a "Christian nation." But which tradition and which form of Christianity? Robertson admixed his Pentacostalism, the speaking in tongues and laying on of hands, regarded by most fundamentalists as anathema, with even more enigmatic beliefs, from Dispensationalism (the Cold War as nuclear Armageddon) to Reconstructionism (America as ancient Judea). Since Robertson represented a unique religious creed, he stood for only one strand of the religious right.

His political emergence was a byproduct of the Republican ascendancy. Before the civil rights movement, the Republican Party in the South had been dominated by liberals and moderates, mainly residing in the border states, and almost exclusively belonging to the mainline Protestant churches. The transformation of the Southern GOP began in the Democratic Party. In 1948, Harry Truman set off a momentous chain reaction by openly courting black voters by deed and word. For the first time, the Democratic convention adopted a civil rights plank. The southern Bourbons, led by South Carolina governor Strom Thurmond, split off, forming their own party, the Dixiecrat (or States Rights) Party. Still, the black attachment to the party of Lincoln was not easily broken, even after Roosevelt and Truman. In 1960, Richard Nixon won almost one-third of the black vote. Four years later, as the debate about civil rights legislation moved toward its climax, the GOP nominated a fierce opponent, Barry Goldwater, who justified his stance with the rhetoric of minimal government, states rights and liberty.

In 1968, Richard Nixon secured his nomination by forging an alliance at the convention with Thurmond, now converted to the Republican Party. Nixon pursued what was called the "Southern Strategy," campaigning through the use of euphemisms about law-and-order that the voters viscerally understood. But the virulent reaction to civil rights was truly voiced by Alabama governor George Wallace, who railed against "bloc voting" and appealed to ordinary white folks against the "pointy headed" liberal establishment. His independent candidacy, which swept most of the South, almost threw the election into the Electoral College. In 1972, Wallace, running in the Democratic primaries, was removed from the contest by an assassin, who permanently crippled his quarry. In 1976, Wallace served history as a foil to Jimmy Carter, the born-again Christian, whose victory over Wallace was received with enormous relief and gratitude within the Democratic Party. Carter represented the South that had accepted the Second Reconstruction. His triumph was widely seen at the time as a way to put the nation's divisive past behind it.

Carter's outspokenness about his religion and about the place of morality in public life also galvanized the evangelicals, most of whom initially supported him. Then, in 1978, the Internal Revenue Service denied tax exemptions to white "Christian academies" that had emerged as the alternative to integrated public schools. The cadres of the new right saw their opening. An unknown minister from Lynchburg, Virginia, Jerry Falwell, was recruited in 1979 by Howard Phillips, who is Jewish, to head up a new organization to press the new right cause. Another new right leader, Paul Weyrich, a Catholic, had come up with its name: Moral Majority. Phillips assured Falwell, who did not want to enter a risky business, that through the miracle of computer-driven direct mail, great sums of money could be raised.

The strategy of the Republican right was to use social issues to separate the evangelicals, mostly southern Baptists, from their historic allegiance to the Democratic Party. Evangelicals believe that the world is a sinful place and that souls must be saved out of it. It was precisely on these grounds that most evangelicals kept themselves at a distance from the profane realm of politics: they saw themselves in the world, but not of it. The religious right, however, did not accept this direction; the leap of faith landed in a political position. Sin was redefined as liberalism, or "secular humanism," an antireligious religion; modernity was seen as the form of the anti-Christ. Everything that the religious right considered part of the fall from grace—from premarital sex to the separation of church and state, from divorce to crime—was attributed to the demonic power of liberalism. Redemption from modernity could come only through the intervention of another worldly force.

The leaders of the religious right did not try to reconcile their radical theology to the predominant southern Baptist faith. Instead, they took over the religion itself and changed the faith to fit the ideology, which was ultimately a justification for the grasping of power. The key take-over target of the religious right was the Southern Baptist Convention. For two decades, since the 1962 Supreme Court prohibited prayers in public schools, the SBC had endorsed the decision. With virtual unanimity, the SBC in 1971 supported the right to an abortion. But in 1979, a tightly organized and well-financed movement of the religious right seized control of the SBC. In 1980, this conservative faction elected as SBC president Bailey Smith, who declared: "God does not hear the prayer of a Jew." In 1982, the SBC condemned the right to legal abortions. The resolutions committee, which hammered out the language, was in constant touch by telephone with a new right leader, Morton Blackwell, who was at the time a presidential assistant serving in the White House.

Ronald Reagan's links to the religious right were forged in the 1980 campaign, when he appeared before a gathering of the leadership hastily organized by a new group called the Religious Roundtable. "You can't endorse me," he said, "but I endorse you." His courtship of them was part of his grand Southern Strategy. His first speech in the fall campaign was in favor of states rights, delivered in Philadelphia, Mississippi, where three civil rights workers had been brutally murdered during the "Freedom Summer" of 1964. In his bid for reelection, Reagan offered further encouragement. At the 1984 GOP convention, he attended a prayer breakfast hosted by the Reverend W. A. Criswell, a patriarch of the religious right, pastor of the First Baptist Church of Dallas, the largest in the country, who had campaigned against John F. Kennedy in 1960 because he was a Catholic, and whose church was a nerve center in the takeover of the SBC. Reagan's effort to shift the evangelicals into the Republican column seemed to be working. In 1980, 41 percent of southern Baptist ministers considered themselves Democrats and only 29 percent Republicans; in 1984, 66 percent identified themselves as Republicans and 25 percent as Democrats.

Throughout his presidency, Reagan paid lip service to the social issues of the religious right—abortion, school prayer, pornography—

while his staff and the Republican leadership of the Senate quietly prevented them from coming to a head. For Reagan, it was the best of all possible worlds. In the meantime, a galaxy of television ministries, operated by a host of right-wing charismatic stars, lit up millions of screens. As the 1988 campaign approached, the religious right had spun out of the control of the conservative movement and was orbiting in its own profitable sphere.

Marion "Pat" Robertson identified his destiny with the unfolding of an inexorable political scenario: mastery over the religious right would lead to mastery over the conservative movement which, in turn, would dominate the Republican Party and sweep the nation.

But Reagan had made no prophesy about his successor. He left that to the Republican voters. Also, Robertson's background was very different from Reagan's. If anything, it most resembled that of George Bush, another senator's son and graduate of Yale. Willis Robertson of Virginia, in fact, served in the Senate with Prescott Bush, though on the other side of the aisle. Harry McPherson, Lyndon Johnson's former assistant and an influential Washington lawyer, described him in his memoir as "a mix of bluster and manliness, who admired great figures like Churchill and Washington and used their words with a Tory bombast that should have destroyed his opposition in debate, but did not. . . . Once in the cloakroom he read aloud, with a kind of amused and astonished rage, a newspaper story of the latest peurile demands by African diplomats in the U.N. 'McPherson,' he said, 'these people have dropped out of the trees with umbrellas and attaché cases.' "

Willis Robertson was a squire of the Virginia gentry, a stalwart of the local Democratic machine and a domineering and distant father who had mapped out every detail of his son's life. Pat was sent to Washington and Lee and then Yale Law School; kept out of a combat zone in Korea while in the marines; placed on the staff of the Senate Appropriations Committee; and introduced to appropriate young women of the Tidewater elite—all in the expectation of a political career. Thus began what Hendrik Hertzberg has called Pat Robertson's "oedipal drama." He rebelled by flunking his bar exam and impregnating a working-class Catholic girl, whom he married ten weeks before the child was born. He moved his family to a poor black neighborhood in Brooklyn, where he went into business selling audio equipment. Through his mother, a reclusive evangelical, he was introduced to a preacher named Cornelius Vanderbreggen, who taught him how to commune with God by speaking in tongues. "No longer did I remember I was the son of a senator," wrote Robertson in his autobiography. "I was the son of the King."

It was then that he began to hear the voice of God and have visions. The first command he received was to leave his wife, eight months pregnant with their second child, and go to the Canadian woods to meditate. "I'm a nurse," she told him. "I recognize schizoid tendencies when I see them, and I think you're sick." Her entreaty did not stop him from obeying the voice he heard from on high, then or thereafter. Robertson's God made no demands on him. He was a benign and convenient God, who appeared whenever Robertson happened to be making a decision. He had plans for Robertson, but they always turned out to be the plans Robertson had already made. Unlike his own, God was a permissive father.

God, for example, told Robertson to buy a bankrupt UHF station in Portsmouth, Virginia, which his mother had informed him was for sale. It was this station that grew into Robertson's Christian Broadcasting Network kingdom, complete with the CBN University, a collection of red-brick colonial style buildings, right off the interstate highway. (According to Robertson, God, very precisely, said: "I want you to build a school there for My glory, as well as the headquarters building you need.") It was God who told Robertson not to fire the host of CBN's kids' puppet show, Jim Bakker, who had proved to be unreliable. It was God who told him not to pay more than $2.5 million for new electronic equipment. And God told Robertson, even though he had built up a sizeable following through CBN, not to endorse his father's bid for renomination to the Senate. "I yearned to get into the fray and start swinging," wrote Robertson, "but the Lord refused to give me the liberty. 'I have called you to my ministry,' he spoke to my heart. 'You cannot tie my eternal purposes to the success of any political candidate . . . not even your own father.'" Senator Robertson narrowly lost. With the counsel of the Father, the father was struck down.

As the host of his talk show, "The 700 Club," on CBN, Robertson spoke as if his average viewer were a small child. He chuckled, nodded his head at any remark he approved and always concluded with an ingratiating smile. He was smiling through the apocalypse. The second coming of Christ and the end of the world, he believed, would be ushered in by the battle of Armaggedon, to be fought in Israel, sometime soon. "Various people," he wrote in his 1982 book *The Secret Kingdom*, "have been viewed as Gog and Magog throughout history—the Goths, the Cretans, the Scythians—but indications are that this great power from the north may be the Soviet Union, for that nation occupies land specified by Ezekiel." On his television show, when asked if the Bible foretold the future, Robertson answered, "It sure does," and elaborated that it "specifically, clearly, unequivocally [says] . . . that Russia and other countries will enter into war and God will destroy Russia through earthquakes, volcanoes, etc."

By 1986, Robertson's visions began to sound like political scenarios. "God's plan, ladies and gentlemen, is for his people to take dominion," he announced on the May 1 edition of "The 700 Club." "The evangelicals," he said two weeks later, "[are] a force that nobody else really has been reckoning with, but they're going to be one to be reckoned with because God is establishing this." A month later, at a rally, he said: "It was no coincidence that Ronald Reagan was elected president. It was the direct act of God. . . . The Republican takeover and reversal of direction in this country is no coincidence."

God, who had instructed Robertson not to get involved in politics, not even his own father's campaign, now directed him to run for president. "Who Is This Man?" was the title of his half-hour campaign video distributed to supporters. It was a collage of images: the Statue of Liberty, the Capitol, golden farmlands. Suddenly, Robertson appeared interviewing contras. "Did they kill anybody in your family?" he asked a boy. On the background soundtrack, gunfire crackled. Then, at a rally, Robertson pledged to "decolonize the fringes of the Russian empire." Then, a surreal flood of images: naked women, the covers of pornographic magazines, the marquees of X-rated movie theaters, rock-throwing students from some foreign land and, filling the entire screen with red, simply the word "AIDS." "Moral leadership," promised Robertson.

But even before Robertson announced his candidacy, his sacred mission was tarnished by profane events. Jim Bakker's righteous empire was now collapsing due to financial chicanery and sexual hijinks. It was Armageddon for the religious right, with lurid revelations of devilish doings spilling out over a period of months, while Jimmy Swaggart (Gog?) and Jerry Falwell (Magog?) battled for control of Bakker's PTL remains. Spirituality had turned into materialism. And the community of virtue and harmony was exposed as an arena of sin and conflict.

By June 1987, the repackaging of Pat Robertson was furiously under way. A poll in the *Atlanta Journal and Constitution* in March had showed that 69 percent of southern voters would "not consider" voting for Robertson. Focus groups conducted by Robertson's campaign revealed that voters could not distinguish him from Falwell or Swaggart. The voice of God offered no advice, so Robertson turned to Madison

Avenue. Constance Snapp, former director of marketing for Wunderman, Ricotta & Kline, a division of Young and Rubicam, who was an evangelical herself and had handled the CBN account, was brought into the campaign. No longer was Robertson to identify himself as an evangelical or as a minister. According to Snapp's spin, "the Rev. Robertson" was now "Mr. Robertson" and the "television evangelist" was a "Christian broadcaster." Above all, he was to be referred to as a businessman. A new campaign flyer listed his résumé: "author, lecturer, educator, broadcaster, news commentator." In September, he quit his ministry. Religion was officially expunged from his campaign. On December 14, he announced, "I've never been an evangelist in my life."

By claiming to be a mere businessman, Robertson demoted his visions. But he had already gambled them when he decided to run. By sitting on a stage with the other contenders he was casting his visions into a lottery. After all, he was the prophet of God. Who were the other candidates? If God had selected him, why should the people decide who should have the job? The danger was especially grave for the faithful; Robertson had turned God into a party boss. Either he trivialized God or made too much of the Republican Party. And if God could not deliver, what did this say about His powers? More, if God was right, then the voters who failed to heed Him were flouting His will. Who were they the instrument of? And what did that make George Bush? What force was leading him?

To the degree that Robertson's prophetic mission was not undermined by his own contradictions, it was undone by Ronald Reagan. Robertson believed that a visionary politics on the right had been mandated by Reagan. He did not understand that only one vision was allowed at a time. And Reagan's had changed. The apocalyptic one of the religious right was underwritten by the Cold War. Falwell, for example, testified in 1983 to the "sad fact" that in a nuclear war the Soviets "would kill 135 million to 160 million Americans, and the United States would kill only three to five percent of the Soviets." Reagan stimulated such talk by his occasional conversations with evangelical visitors in which he appeared to give some credence to Armageddon theology. But with the signing of the INF Treaty, the earlier revelations of the Reagan presidency passed.

The complications raised by Robertson in setting himself against Reagan were fundamental. If Reagan was president due to a "direct act of God," then why did he make the treaty? In the edenic scene that Robertson painted, Reagan played Adam and Nancy Reagan played

Eve, seducing him to bite the apple. "My wife," Robertson told a GOP gathering on October 18, 1987, "does not like Communists. I want to set your minds at ease. She has never suggested that I make an accommodation to the Soviet Union in order to win the Nobel Peace Prize."

Robertson began to speak as if the Reagan White House were under the sway of a subversive, possibly satanic, power. In a cassette tape distributed by his campaign, entitled "What I Will Do as President," Robertson said: "I don't believe that conservatives should be a hunted and endangered species in the White House." He named the enemy within as the Council on Foreign Relations and the Trilateral Commission, who were "propping up communist tyrannies with loans and credits. . . . I make an absolute pledge that I would appoint people who are absolutely free of CFR influence."

In Iowa, Robertson's antiestablishment theme matched the political context. The caucuses were beautifully designed for small-scale organization; the anger against the Reagan administration for farm and factory failures ran high; the loss of economic control was often translated into resentment over social permissiveness. In Robertson, 25 percent of the Republican caucus participants saw their salvation. He finished second, ahead of George Bush. Even so, Robertson had not overcome the perception that he had something to do with religion. He bought two full-page ads in the *Des Moines Register*, featuring his portrait next to John F. Kennedy's, as if they were equivalent figures, hoping to dispel negative connotations of the religion issue.

Flushed with the Iowa results, Robertson promised that an "invisible army" would suddenly appear to sweep him to greater victories. The invisible worlds of Pat Robertson, seemingly banished by his new vita, now surfaced; the special effects started to get out of hand. In the New Hampshire debate, he claimed that the INF Treaty had a loophole that omitted those Soviet medium-range missiles that were now stationed in Cuba. Peacemaking was leading to war. We were teetering on the brink again. When Robertson finished with his extraordinary revelation, a prophecy of the imminence of World War III, the other candidates smiled and moved on, as if he were a street-corner evangelist. The next day the White House issued a statement calling Robertson "rash" and "wrong." At a press conference, the president described Robertson's remarks as "strange." His effort to sustain the Cold War by means of political hallucinations was short-lived.

Robertson also professed to know the location of the American hostages in Lebanon, claiming that "they could have been freed." Unfortunately, he produced no evidence.

Then Jimmy Swaggart, who had endorsed Robertson, was revealed to have regularly frequented prostitutes. Robertson accused the Bush campaign of timing this disclosure to destroy his campaign. "Knowing the quality of the people surrounding George Bush," he said in a press conference, "there is nothing that I would not believe they wouldn't do sleazy." To which Bush told reporters, "It's crazy."

In the South Carolina primary, Robertson donned another identity. He was now the southern cavalier, in the succession of Confederate leaders, unfurling the symbolism of the Lost Cause. On the edge of Columbia, on February 22, he mustered his remaining troops for his staging of Pickett's Charge into the steel of the Bush campaign. The encampment was at the brand-new Embassy Suites Hotel, a monument to the new South, an island of concrete and glass encircled by highways. In the fern-filled atrium, at the brass and marble bar, young professionals unwound after work with white wine spritzers, cracking jokes about Swaggart's sexual kinks. They seemed oblivious to the five hundred Robertson faithful dutifully filing past them into the ballroom.

"Recapturing the Greatness of America through Moral Strength" read the banner strung across the platform. Suddenly, the audience was plunged into darkness. A klieg light shone on a local beauty queen. A symphony orchestra of violins played on tape, then a humming male chorus, then bells. The beauty queen sang "The Star Spangled Banner," with curious new words added at the end: "See freedom's dream!"

The theme song from *Rocky* boomed. From the rear of the room, Robertson entered. "I was the only one born in Stonewall Jackson's birthplace," he said. "I'm the only one who went to the school where Robert E. Lee was president." He launched into a tirade against the Council on Foreign Relations and the Trilateral Commission. "I intend to preside over Uncle Sam, not Uncle Sucker!" He left to the strains of *Rocky*.

But the effort to recreate the Dixiecrat Party within the GOP languished. Robertson could not master the feat of time travel. In the end, the only base that held for Robertson was narrowly religious: the Pentacostals and Charismatics. Other evangelicals rejected him, often on religious grounds; about 70 percent voted against him. On March 5, in South Carolina, he finished third, with just 19 percent of the vote. He had failed to escape from his image. The Republicans were determined to show that the GOP was their party, not Robertson's. He was George Bush's salvation in the South.

IV

To the spoils belonged the victor. George Bush inherited a campaign that had not pursued the issues. His negative campaign against Bob Dole had succeeded. The Republican Party had rejected his challengers from the two branches of radical conservatism, whom Bush carefully avoided in debate. Meanwhile, the cooperative relationship between Reagan and Gorbachev helped Bush sidestep the issue of greatest potential damage to himself—his exact role in the Iran-contra scandal.

With the nomination assured, Bush set out to claim his legacy. Immediately after sweeping the southern primaries on Super Tuesday, he made a pilgrimage, unaccompanied by the press, to Saddle River, New Jersey, where he received the private blessing of Richard Nixon and discussed the fall campaign for hours.

Thus began the worst period for Bush in the 1988 campaign. From March until June, he had to complete the primaries without a foil. He was on the stage alone, and his popularity plummeted.

In Chicago, on March 10, Bush delivered what his aides billed to the traveling press as his "vision speech." Finally, he would explain his larger purpose and resolve his problem with "the vision thing." "They call it the Reagan Revolution because it was revolutionary," he explained. He listed a series of issues—the deficit, trade, education, ethics—without describing Reagan's positions or his own. He promised that as president he would appoint panels to come up with recommendations. On the ending of the Cold War, which rearranged the light and shadows on all the other issues, Bush said: "It's good to know Mr. Gorbachev, he's an interesting man, I've spent time with him, he has things to say." What "things" Bush did not say. He went on: "Clearly something is happening in the Soviet Union." He did not say what. "In time we'll know if it's only cosmetic." The events in Russia might have profound consequences, but for now Bush grudgingly acknowledged them only as superficial.

He moved on to his big closing: "Out there—that's the future. And as we journey there together I'll give you an image that stays with me. When I'm in a motorcade in the cities I'll look up sometimes and see the lights in the homes and the apartments. You see people waving and watching as you go by. I look for families. I look for young people. Now and then I'll see a student with his head bent down, reading something in the glow of a lamp. And I'll think, that child—that's what it's about." Bush was passing through America "in a motorcade," trying to peer in. His vision was of someone trying to have a vision.

6

The Strategies of Zeus

Gary Hart was the first major American political figure to grasp conceptually that the Cold War was ending. And he was the first to make the intellectual effort to understand the consequences. From the beginning, Hart had sailed the political seas in search of a big idea, a white whale of an idea, an embodiment of The Future. He began his career in Democratic politics sensing that the New Deal program and coalition belonged to the past. But what lay ahead? At times, he thought he spied parts of what was out there in the murk. He could not, however, see the whole. He knew that it must be large and that once it surfaced it would change everything. He believed that it was his destiny to see this change before others and to ride it.

Gary Hart had little idea what to expect as he was ushered into the Kremlin office of Mikhail Gorbachev on December 15, 1986. He had been in Moscow twice before, and each visit had marked a stage of his career. In 1975, as a freshman senator, he had sat face to face with

Leonid Brezhnev and felt he was at the waxworks. "His jaw didn't work right," Hart recalled. "He seemed to be medicated. You had a sense you were with a stodgy old governor, who hadn't had a thought in a long time—if ever."

Ten years later, in January 1985, Hart visited again. Moscow, in this season, was tuning up for another dirge. Konstantin Chernenko lay dying, and Andrei Gromyko, the master bureaucrat who had outlasted all of his masters, was now the caretaker of the state. Hart met briefly with him.

A more significant encounter occurred at the U.S.A. Institute, where he delivered a lecture. The younger experts who packed the room were especially curious about Hart, for they thought they saw in him a glimmer of their own sense of opportunity. He stood for the university-educated new class, harbored a disdain for the past, wanted to try out new ideas. "I talked about reform in America," Hart said, "how the party system was not responding to change, how our leaders needed new ideas, how both superpowers had to rethink their policies. Afterwards, the most moving thing happened. The young people came forward. About a half dozen had xeroxed copies of my book [A New Democracy] and wanted me to sign it for them."

Now, less than a year later, Hart was returning to find Gorbachev in charge. The change was immediately apparent. "My first impression was of a totally different generation—physically, chronologically, attitudinally." This was no perfunctory meeting, no photo opportunity. Gorbachev, said Hart, was "distressed." It was two months after the failed summit at Reykjavik, one month after the exposure of the Iran-contra scandal. Gorbachev needed a Reagan who was still able to play the role of leader of the Free World and who was willing to sign an arms treaty. And Reagan, whether he knew it or not, desperately needed a conciliatory Gorbachev to lift him out of the morass of scandal into which his administration had sunk. The power and reputation of both were hanging in the balance.

Gorbachev began the conversation by producing a letter, never publicly released, that he had sent President Reagan after the Geneva summit. "He said in his letter that he wasn't going to another picture-taking summit," Hart recounted. "He said he would go to a summit if we bring specific items to reduce arms. He felt our position was that Reagan was there to do that."

At Reykjavik, Reagan had proposed that he and Gorbachev meet without their staffs. "Gorbachev was surprised. He thought Reagan needed staff support. He told me that he said, 'Whatever suits you, Mr.

President.' " Once alone, Gorbachev asked Reagan to lay his agenda on the table. "Reagan said, 'I don't have one.' Gorbachev said he was disappointed. Reagan said he didn't understand. Then Gorbachev asked if they would use his agenda as the basis of discussion. Reagan said, 'Fine.' Gorbachev said that the pattern that followed was that they would take up an item for an hour and a half, break for an hour to brief their staffs and return to discuss another item. On each point, Gorbachev asked: 'Do we have an agreement?' 'Yes,' said Reagan. Then, on each point, Reagan would return and say, 'No, we don't have an agreement.' " Then, Gorbachev told Hart, he would go on to make another verbal agreement. Finally, the summit collapsed on the issue of testing Star Wars components outside of the laboratory. On Gorbachev's desk, as he spoke to Hart, was his own negotiating file, which he referred to as he told the story. "Gorbachev was very scrupulous in not characterizing Reagan's behavior." Clearly, though, he was disturbed by it.

He spoke to Hart for four hours as someone of present and potential use. First of all, he could be an emissary. "He was trying to send signals through me on his flexiblity on what was a laboratory," Hart said. Also, Hart might help to advise him how to deal with this baffling administration. "Who should we be talking to? Is there a back channel?" inquired Foreign Minister Eduard Shevardnadze of Hart in another long meeting held immediately after he left Gorbachev. "They were not sure, based on observations from Geneva and Reykjavik, who had authority," said Hart. In the Nixon years, the Soviets had relied upon Henry Kissinger as their "back channel." Now, they wondered if that model might be revived.

There was a larger, unstated question on the table in this delicate diplomatic encounter between Gorbachev and Hart. Gorbachev had taken the traditional Soviet view in his dealings with Reagan that the Republicans were more reliable partners than the Democrats. This generalization was drawn from recent history—the rise of détente under Nixon and its decline under Carter. But Gorbachev's puzzlement over Reagan led him to make an investment in the future. The Democratic frontrunner did not seem afraid of negotiating. Perhaps Hart would understand what could be achieved through arms control. Hart might be just the president Gorbachev could do business with. Unlike Reagan, he would at least arrive with negotiating positions. None of this was explicit in the meeting; it did not have to be.

"Here was a man on the fast track, and we'd have to get on the same track too if we wanted to take advantage of what his regime offered,"

Hart explained in early 1989, retracing his thinking. "We needed to match drama with drama. We may hold the key to his success. In an Aristotelian way, he may hold the key to our success. The Russians have always held the key. If we have the opportunity to end the Cold War think what it does to our priorities. Time is slipping by. One thing we cannot recover is time."

In the education of Gary Hart, this last lesson was something he had learned at a prohibitive cost.

II

In March 1970, an unglamorous senator from South Dakota, George McGovern, landed in Denver to make a round of political stops. Gary Hart was a young lawyer there, active in local Democratic circles. He had been a poor boy, raised in small-town Kansas and pushed by his mother toward a career as an evangelical preacher. But his intelligence lifted him to a wider world: Nazarene College in Bethany, Oklahoma, where he met and married his wife, Lee, the daughter of the college president, and Yale Divinity School, where he had won a scholarship. He soon decided that he did not wish to become a minister or a professor. Inspired by the example of John F. Kennedy, he wanted a career in public life. After graduating from Yale Law School, he got a job in Robert F. Kennedy's Justice Department, where he worked in the brackish backwater of Internal Security, a clerk in the Cold War, hunched over briefs about Communist front-groups. As soon as he could, Hart moved over to the Interior Department. When Richard Nixon won the presidency in 1968, Hart left Washington and established himself in Denver.

He volunteered to drive George McGovern around. McGovern told Hart he intended to run for president. Within the party establishment his hopes were dismissed as dim. The heavy favorite was Senator Edmund Muskie, who had been Humphrey's running mate. Hart, thinking of the contacts he might pull together through his political friends in Denver, proposed to McGovern a plan to organize the western states. His proposal was very specific, though Hart did not really have all the contacts. McGovern asked him if he would be his campaign manager. The 1972 campaign, in which the Democratic Party underwent a dramatic realignment and Cold War domestic politics reached its greatest refinement, was a matrix for much of what followed, including the main lines of Hart's career.

McGovern's issue was the Vietnam War. No other Democrat in the field had opposed it as early or as passionately. In domestic policy, McGovern was a midwestern progressive, heavily influenced by the Social Gospel; in foreign policy, he was an idealistic internationalist, a latter-day Wilsonian. Though close to Hubert Humphrey, McGovern never really shared Humphrey's premises about the Cold War, which had been forged in the bitter struggle to drive the Communists out of Minnesota's Democratic Farmer-Labor Party in the late 1940s. McGovern believed that the conflict between the U.S. and the Soviet Union was a conflict between great powers, not unchangeable ideological monoliths; he also believed that the arms race could be drastically curtailed.

After McGovern quickly disposed of Muskie, the power brokers within the party desperately threw their resources behind Humphrey. In primary after primary, McGovern shocked him. Their ultimate battle came in California, in a series of bitter debates. Humphrey, facing oblivion, called McGovern's proposed defense cuts "reckless," and accused him, in a television ad, of wanting to reduce the U.S. to a "second-class power in the face of the expanding Russian navy and air force." Humphrey decisively lost, but the charge of weakness still hung in the air. (Later, Humphrey confided to McGovern that he regretted what he had done.)

McGovern was undermined by the forces he had overthrown in the primaries. For the first time in memory, the AFL-CIO refused to endorse the Democratic candidate. This act in itself would have doomed McGovern, even if there had been no Tom Eagleton dilemma to gore him when his running mate was disclosed to have been treated for an emotional disorder. The principal reason for the break with organized labor was McGovern's attitude toward the Cold War—not just the Vietnam War.

George McGovern was haunted by the specter of Henry Wallace, whose 1948 nominating convention he had attended as a student. McGovern was not shunned simply because he was against the war. He may have captured the antiwar fervor more than Muskie, but Muskie's policies on the war (and much else) would not have been markedly different from McGovern's. (It is of interest on the point of McGovern's "radicalism" that he selected Lyndon Johnson's longtime aide, Harry McPherson, to run his transition team.) The presence of Wallace in McGovern's past fundamentally altered the response to him.

McGovern's political lineage ran back to George Norris and Robert La Follette, not V. I. Lenin. But to the AFL-CIO leadership, heavily influenced by disillusioned veterans of the Communist movement who had become their advisers, McGovern was on the wrong side in the Cold War: While Humphrey battled Stalinists, McGovern, in old left lexicon, was "objectively" a fellow traveler. The influential neoconservatives saw the campaign as an apocalyptic contest of Cold War metaphysics. The refusal by other key Democrats such as Senator Henry Jackson to endorse McGovern was one of the first signs that the sectarian politics of the old left would begin to play an important role in national politics in the 1970s and 1980s.[1] This factor was ignored by the press at the time, though Nixon's senior campaign operatives attempted behind the scenes to exploit it.[2] It was only after Reagan had become president that the presence of those who became known as the neoconservatives became visible in councils of state and on op-ed pages and elsewhere in the media.

For Richard Nixon, the 1972 campaign was the culmination of Cold War politics. In a tour de force of agenda-setting, he perfected the political themes of the Cold War as drawn from the past and projected into the future. Nixon's manipulation of the imagery and rhetoric of national security in 1972, as we shall see, shaped the campaign of 1988.

Nixon used the Cold War to cast himself as both a peacemaker and a warrior. The anti-communist Republican delegates cheered *Portrait of a President,* the campaign film shown to the convention, in which Nixon appeared with Mao Tse-tung and Leonid Brezhnev, then unanimously passed their platform, which claimed that McGovern was "bemused with surrender" and prepared to commit "an act of betrayal" by withdrawing from Vietnam. The war was depicted as both ongoing and concluded. "It is so easy to forget how frightful it was," read the GOP platform on the recent past, when the Democrats were in the White House. "There was Vietnam."

1. Senator Henry Jackson, a hardline cold warrior, always presented himself as a loyal party man, in spite of his disagreements with others inside the party. But according to a memo of June 14, 1972, that served as the basis of a discussion between Nixon and John Mitchell, his campaign chairman, who was later convicted of Watergate-related crimes, "Jackson told Kissinger he wanted to help in the campaign against McGovern."
2. On June 12, 1972, Charles Colson, a presidential assistant who was later convicted of Watergate-related crimes, wrote to another presidential assistant, Ken Khachigian: "Can we get the proceedings of the 1948 Wallace convention? Specifically McGovern's speech to the convention? Do you have any research in this area that we could use? I need this immediately because some of our labor friends would like to distribute it." In fact, McGovern delivered no such speech. And when he became aware of the Communist influence around Wallace, he became disillusioned and withdrew his support.

McGovern had issued a seventy-five-page paper describing in detail his proposal to cut the Pentagon budget by $30 billion over four years. His plan, he explained in early 1989, was an early attempt to shift the emphasis from military strength to economic strength. "I wanted to make the military more modern and to divert more spending into the civilian sector."

McGovern's proposal served as a bulls-eye at three feet for Nixon's media team. In one television spot, to the soundtrack of a military drumroll, an arm, representing McGovern, knocked over toy soldiers, ships and planes. Cut to Nixon standing aboard a battleship. "President Nixon doesn't believe we should play games with our national security." In another ad, Nixon was shown getting off *Air Force One*. "Moscow. May 1972. Richard Nixon becomes the first American president ever to visit the Russian capital." McGovern was thus depicted as unreliable because of the raging Cold War, which Nixon was cooling.

It was in the 1972 campaign that the social issue was melded with the national security issue. What evolved by 1988 into a Republican attack on the "L-word" was earlier formulated as an attack on "McGovernism." McGovern was maligned as weak abroad and weak at home. "Acid, amnesty and abortion"—this was the slogan hurled at him by vice president Spiro Agnew, who was assigned the role of chief hatchet man. Whatever chaos or difficulties troubled the country were attributed to "liberal permissiveness."

Within two years of his landslide victory, Nixon resigned from office. On the merits of the case and with dramatic speed, McGovern's statement that Nixon had conducted the most corrupt administration in American history was made manifestly true. Indeed, as Jonathan Schell has pointed out, McGovern ran the most effective losing campaign in American history. No other candidate saw himself lose by such a large margin and then, on the very issues he raised, see his opponent leave the White House in shame. And yet the stigma of the campaign smears stayed with McGovern and the Democratic Party. "This curious inversion of reputations," Schell wrote, "in which the disgraced president is honored and the unblemished candidate who opposed him and warned the country of his abuses of power is held in disrepute, points to one of the central mysteries of American political life in the post-Vietnam war period." But the mystery appears less enigmatic in the light of the Republicans' success in sustaining Nixonian Cold War themes. The conundrum for the Democrats was how to escape being tainted as weak and unpatriotic while the Cold War continued. This was the problem that Gary Hart tried, ultimately, to solve.

"Right from the Start," an early slogan of the McGovern campaign, was also the title of Hart's book on the campaign. Hart's main contribution was neither ideological nor strategic; it was organizational. But it implied a different brand of politics. Hart helped McGovern tap into the grassroots intensity that drove Eugene McCarthy's campaign. He was also "good as a frontman, laying out scenarios of how we were going to win," McGovern said. Hart, however, was inexperienced and McGovern often overruled him in favor of the state organizers. When it became clear that McGovern was going to be the party's nominee, the pressure on the candidate by the older politicos to replace his campaign manager was great. "I thought," McGovern explained, "that the press explosion would offset any gain we'd get." So Hart was kept in place, his office decorated with a life-size picture of Candice Bergen and a small statue of Don Quixote.

In his book, however, Hart presented himself in the light of another literary figure. " . . . one could sympathize, and occasionally identify," he wrote, "with General Kutuzov"—the commander of the Russian armies defending Moscow, one of the central figures of Leo Tolstoy's *War and Peace.* Since reading Tolstoy at Yale, Hart had accepted his view that men act as "involuntary tools of history."

When he spoke to a few colleagues in the 1972 campaign about his plans to run for the Senate from Colorado, he would often cite the maxim of General Kutuzov: "It is not difficult to capture a fortress but it is difficult to win a campaign. For that, not storming and attacking but patience and time are wanted. . . . There is nothing stronger than those two: patience and time, they will do it all."

III

Out of the conflicts of 1972, Hart also developed an anthropological theory of power:

> The old must give way to the new. . . . But it is a myth that power is passed, like a torch, from one generation to the next. If, in primitive times, the chief caveman was also the keeper of the fire, he fought to prevent younger, stronger cavemen from taking the fire, for it was not only the key and symbol of his power, but also his defense against obsolescence.

Hart's Senate campaign of 1974 was that of a "younger, stronger" man against a Republican elder in poor health, further weakened by Watergate. Hart's slogan was "They've Had Their Turn, Now It's Our

Turn." The title of his stump speech was "The End of the New Deal." As he described it, the New Deal was "bureaucracy." Hart conflated it with the Great Society and pointed only to its "failure." The New Deal, it seemed, was a period of betrayed ideals, running from November 22, 1963, to Election Day 1968. Hart warned of the "interlocking marriage of big business and big government," calling for a divorce—"cut the financial ties that bind them." And, he concluded, "we will only begin to restore real opportunity in our society when we stop thinking only in terms of New Deal solutions. . . . This nation desperately needs a new breed of thinkers and doers who will question old premises and disregard old alliances." McGovern had won only 36 percent of the vote in Colorado; two years later, Hart won his race with 59 percent.

"We're not a bunch of little Hubert Humphreys," he said upon entering the Senate. For Hart to assert that was to assert a difference of kind, not of degree. Hart was running away from something he labeled the "New Deal," by which he meant a Cold War liberalism that had gone rancid in Vietnam. McGovern, preeminent among Democratic leaders, recognized this. Yet, to Hart, even his program suffered from intellectual exhaustion. "Although McGovern himself had excellent insights into the general mood of the electorate, it was apparent throughout the campaign that the fount of specific proposals and programs was running dry," wrote Hart. "The traditional sources of invigorating, inspiring and creative ideas were dissipated. The best thinkers of the 1930s, 40s, and 50s and even the 1960s were not producing. . . . By 1972, American liberalism was near bankruptcy." But Hart believed that "a new generation of leaders" could "recapture power . . . in very little time." New ideas were the means to power.

The McGovern campaign had taught Hart the political pitfalls of appearing weak on defense. This was his motive in asking for a seat on the Armed Services Committee. The debate on the committee was an endless battle between those advocating more and those advocating less spending. Hart wanted to rethink the basic premises of military strategy. Instead of attrition warfare, he proposed maneuver warfare. Instead of a navy of big carrier groups and recommissioned World War II battleships, he proposed more smaller ships. He wanted to streamline the bureaucracy and alter the procurement practice of buying the most sophisticated weapons for their own sake. His line (developed by his brilliant aide, former Dartmouth professor Larry Smith) was: "More is not better, less is not better, better is better." Hart also cited Tolstoy on "that intangible force called the spirit of the army." The view of this new school of military thought was to be cogently elaborated by journalist James Fallows in his book *National Defense.*

In 1980 Hart, like all Democrats, was on the defensive. His Republican opponent for the Senate, Mary Estill Buchanan, began with a blast of full-page newspaper ads attacking him as weak on defense. Just like the successful assaults on McGovern and later on Dukakis, the ads listed the weapons systems Hart was against. Hart, however, had spent a lot of time explaining his military reforms to the Denver newspapers' editorial boards. Even before Hart responded to the ads, the papers published editorials critical of his rival's distortions. Then Hart counterattacked by climbing into a tank. This was the Ur-tank commercial, the first time a politician put heavy metal on video. The image made Hart appear credible, just as it would make Dukakis, following in his tank treads, appear incredible. The difference was not simply that Hart looked like a rugged film star and Dukakis, as the writer Joe Klein put it, looked like Rocky the Flying Squirrel. Hart looked in control because he was in control. His imagery was edited by Robert Squire, his media consultant. Dukakis's ride was a free media event whose imagery was edited by network producers. Dukakis looked out of control because he didn't control how he looked. More important, Hart had spent years developing policy positions about tanks. He and the tank driver carried on a spontaneous, arcane conversation about the effect of dust on various kinds of tank engines. Bits of this banter were used in the soundtrack of the ad. The ad was staged, but it was not phony. Hart knew what he was talking about. Because he had developed new ideas to reposition the issue, he was able to reposition his image. He narrowly won reelection.

On defense issues, Hart did not sound ideological at all. His language was that of the specialist. But he was using technical ideas to attack certain conservative policies. He was the only Democrat to alter the public debate on defense in the period of the Republican right's ascendance. He was trying to transcend the old categories, which he called "false choices"—both Cold War liberalism and Cold War conservatism.

IV

Ronald Reagan, according to Hart, practiced the "politics of distraction." Reagan's ideology was of, by and for the past. But he had made ideas important in politics, whatever their merit. Hart again took the political challenge to come up with alternative ideas.

Reagan's first thrust was to enact his program of supply-side economics. Hart sought to develop a similarly sweeping program that would also counter the failure of Jimmy Carter's, which had seemed to demand futile economic sacrifice in a zero-sum society, an era of limits. Once again, Hart argued that the questions posed were "false choices." He envisioned a New World, like Francis Bacon's Novum Ordum, based on science and technology.

"Over the past thirty years," he wrote in 1981, "the U.S. economy has been undergoing a transformation as significant as the Industrial Revolution of the nineteenth century. It is shifting from an economy based primarily on heavy industry and basic manufacturing to one increasingly based on advanced technology, information, communications, and services." This notion had been given seminal expression in *The Coming of Post-Industrial Society* by sociologist Daniel Bell. Though published before the advent of the microchip, Bell's book already saw that a new form of society was coming into being. "The concept 'post-industrial society,' " wrote Bell, "emphasizes the centrality of theoretical knowledge as the axis around which new technology, economic growth and the stratification of society will be organized." All of this affirmed Hart's basic political precept that ideas were the raw material of power. High technology, in this scenario, had a magic potency. In the late 1960s and early 1970s, the dominant image of technology for the new generation was of a lethal, oppressive instrument of war: napalm. By the early 1980s, the dominant image was of user-friendly, insurgent "appropriate technology": the personal computer. The spread of high technology was a shortcut to change. It was already a fast-acting social solvent that was dissolving the older class and political structures.

Hart was the first politician to seize upon what became known as industrial policy—a national strategy for coordinating resources in the postindustrial, global economy. He proposed a series of highly specific bills to retrain workers, retool industries, refinance education, and revitalize the export trade. His "new ideas" at the time were more comprehensive and concrete than any other politician's. Though he had hardly solved all the problems, he was attempting to force the debate beyond the "false choices" of either the free market or central planning, free trade or protectionism.

Almost as soon as Hart began developing the issue, he was in touch with the most advanced thinkers working on it, just as he had been with military reform and would be with Gorbachev's Soviet Union. He discovered a small group of youthful scholars, the analogue to the new generation of politicians, whose representative figure was Robert Reich, a former director of policy planning at the Federal Trade Commission and a professor at the Kennedy School of Government at Harvard. His book *The Next American Frontier,* published in 1983, drew upon ideas Reich had already made influential in liberal circles. Mixing subtle argument with an acute sense of politics, Reich summarized a view that Hart had already adopted:

> America confronts a choice. We can continue to endure a painful and slow economic transition in which industrial assets and managers are endlessly rearranged through paper entrepreneurialism, political coalitions seek and obtain shelter from foreign competitors, and a growing share of American labor becomes locked into dead-end employment. This kind of transition can lead only to a lower standard of living for many Americans. It will be coupled with political rancor and divisiveness as a steadily shrinking economic pie is divided into ever smaller slices.
>
> The alternative is a dynamic economy in which capital and labor adapt to engage the new realities of international competition. Rapid adjustment offers Americans a rising standard of living. But the politics that must underpin a dynamic economy are far more difficult to achieve. Ultimately America's capacity to respond to economic change will depend on the vitality of its political institutions.

Hart's book of the same year, *A New Democracy,* was an almanac of various policy proposals, much of it along Reichian lines. To strike a note about the current state of politics, he quoted the early twentieth-century Scottish writer John Buchan: "The old world was crumbling, and there was no unanimity about the new."

Though intended to herald his presidential campaign, his candidacy seemed stalled. He had been ridiculed as an "Atari Democrat," as if faith in high technology was a laughable whimsy with little political content. Hart's language was, in fact, often technocratic, a blizzard of esoteric policy proposals. The policy parts did not add up to a political program. Hart made it seem that he saw salvation in a piece of circuitry, that its electrical impulses could replace an outmoded culture and politics. For traditional Democrats, there was also the problem of his aloof manner. His refusal to shed an occasional rhetorical tear made it appear that he lacked sympathy for those displaced by The Future he was planning.

In 1982, in a *New York Times Magazine* article, Mondale, the prohibitive frontrunner, also had called for "new ideas." Reich sent him a copy of his book in galleys. "This should do it for the Democrats," said Mondale. But after Senator Edward Kennedy declared that he would not run, freeing the traditional constituencies within the party, Mondale adopted a different strategy. He gave up on "new ideas." Instead, assuming that the coalitions of industrial-era politics were effective, he reverted to type by practicing on a national scale the politics of the old Democratic Farmer-Labor Party of Minnesota. Mondale happily toted up the organizational endorsements. He had been Humphrey's heir, and now he believed that he was restoring the natural order of things.

Hart, campaigning in his black cowboy boots, was in the position McGovern had been in twelve years earlier. He was ideally positioned as the insurgent, in a line of tradition stretching back to 1968. Since then an epochal shift from an industrial to a postindustrial economy had reordered the work force and thus the electorate. The rising new class, educated in the universities and unmoored to the old political organizations, was not a thin elite but a mass. It was not an old-fashioned intelligentsia, though its labor demanded cerebral methods—"a new intellectual technology," according to Bell. The new class, as Bell pointed out, was "the major class of the emerging new society." It comprised four estates: the scientific, the technological, the administrative, and the cultural.

The political history of the new class is a generational history, because this class had only come on the scene with the postwar generation. The student movement of the 1960s was its earliest phase. When that movement petered out, many commentators dismissed the notion of generational politics as simple and predictable nostalgia for lost youth: The Big Chill. But the rhythms of generational politics may be intrinsic to the cycles of progress and reaction in American politics, as Arthur M. Schlesinger, Jr., has pointed out. The postwar, postindustrial generation neither occupies the mental universe of World War II nor is circumscribed by the youthful forms of the 1960s. Its political history is only at its beginning, very roughly comparable to the same stage of political development as that of the industrial working class in the late nineteenth century. How the new class—offspring of the American Century—responds to the ending of that golden age will largely shape the next major phase of American politics.

Hart himself was at least ten years older than members of the postwar generation, his political base. But he was part of the new class in Colorado, where a fresh political idiom with an emphasis on western independence was being spoken. These innovative Democrats found each other easily, and they formed a series of study groups to debate books, politics and policy. Its members became the heart of the party, including future governor Richard Lamm, congresswoman Patricia Schroeder, congressman and later senator Tim Wirth, and Gary Hart. There was no powerful establishment to block their rise.

Hart understood the battle of generational succession and had written about it after the McGovern campaign, which was an early milestone in new class politics. In 1984, Hart's call for "new ideas" was a direct appeal to those for whom "new ideas" are the tools of their trades. He was no longer calling into a misty future.

His victory in the New Hampshire primary, in which about two-thirds of the voters were under forty-five years old, was perhaps his finest political moment. When it seemed to some in the national press that Hart might win it, comparisons were drawn between Hart and Kennedy—and Mondale and Humphrey. "I've been very dicey about this Kennedy connection," Hart said, riding in a car from a rally in Concord to another rally in Manchester. "Of course, I'm not Kennedy. It's a very sensitive thing for me to talk about. Ordinary people like to talk about it. For a lot of people the world stopped in 1963 [with Kennedy's assassination], and everything since then is bad. They want someone to go back to 1963 and pick it up from there. The clock stopped on November 22, 1963; it's a question of starting it again."

Hart encouraged the comparisons indirectly by talking somewhat speciously about "two wings of the Democratic Party—the Stevenson–Humphrey wing and the other one carved out by JFK." And, trying to invoke the Kennedy–Humphrey showdown in 1960, he said: "This could be the West Virginia primary of 1984." Hart grasped that he had tapped into something deeper than a new policy initiative. "Myth," he said at the time, "is powerful. Myth is suprarational, metarational."

Hart claimed that he was establishing a new framework for American politics—a revolutionary "paradigm shift." But the press and his political enemies tried to prove that there was something missing in him. The holes revealed in Hart's background, telltale signs of his alienation from it—his name change from Gary Hartpence to Gary Hart when he was at Yale and his misrepresentation of his age by one year early in his career—were presented as proof.

"When I hear your new ideas, Gary, I'm reminded of that ad, 'Where's the beef?' " said Mondale, repeating the advertising slogan of Wendy's hamburger chain. Thus new ideas, which Mondale himself no longer pursued, were derided. Hart's arduous, decade-long effort to develop a specific program was dismissed as a campaign ploy.

In the primaries, Mondale deployed the ultimate imagery of the Cold War against Hart: an ominously blinking red phone, the hotline to the Kremlin. The blinking meant a crisis, perhaps a nuclear crisis. Could the voters, asked the voiceover, trust an "unsure, unsteady, untested" hand on the receiver? In state after state, this was the most recurrent image Mondale broadcast. Hart was especially upset by Mondale's misrepresentation of his arms control positions; for Hart had very discreetly served as the vice president's personal emissary to the arms talks in Geneva.

By his negative campaign and his support in the industrial states where the old coalition still held, Mondale managed to beat back Hart. At the critical juncture, Hart displayed an odd passivity, a shrinking will to power. Lacking strong leadership, his campaign fell into factional warfare.

The Cold War symbolism Mondale had manipulated in the primaries was ultimately turned against him in the general election. In his acceptance speech to the GOP convention, Ronald Reagan framed the election as a choice between freedom and "totalitarianism." The Republican Party, he said, was "America's party." So his landslide election proved. Whose party then was the Democratic Party?

After Mondale's debacle, Hart was positioned as the frontrunner. More than anyone else the Democratic Party might nominate in 1988, he now represented continuity. He had a sense of his place in history as heir of the party's legacy of change. He had been assailed during the campaign as a self-invented man. But Hart, the Tolstoyan, believed he was more than partly made by events. And he thought that his story was not near its end.

V

As the frontrunner, Hart believed that he could determine the character of the 1988 campaign. Before he left the Senate, in 1986, he laid out his strategy during a long conversation in the Senate dining room. He would set the context for the other candidates by creating a "threshold" that must be crossed to be credible. Mondale had made the collection of constituency group support the standard. Hart intended to establish a different criterion—new ideas. This was still at the heart of his public persona. He was driven now to demonstrate that he had "beef" by the truckloads. He would redefine issue after issue. Those who did not compete with him in this project would fall by the wayside. "I'm talking about rethinking in fairly big terms the whole postwar world."

The year before, for the first time, he became truly interested in foreign affairs, as distinguished from defense policy. In Paris, he was ushered by white-gloved guards into the velvet and gilt office of French president François Mitterand in the Élysée Palace. Mitterand startled Hart by treating him as an equal; he spoke to him as one politician to another. Mitterand had experienced many ups and downs in his career, and had endured. Hart, from his perspective, might easily rise again and be president. The curtain had rolled back to reveal an even wider and more personally promising world. Now Hart wanted to explore the possibilities of the game of nations.

A year later he was ready to deliver a series of three credolike speeches on foreign policy. "He thought the U.S.–Soviet rivalry was way out of date," said an aide. "Gary had an inchoate feeling that this 'twilight struggle' was really stupid." He wanted to reframe the basic questions. The elaborate speeches were a rough first draft of a program of redefinition. He divided U.S. foreign policy into phases: isolationism, "making the world safe for democracy" and containment. A new phase was needed. "Enlightened engagement," Hart said, "is a rejection of isolationism; and it is a rejection of traditional, bipolar containment. It is a recognition of a fundamental new truth—the diffusion of political, military, and economic power is an opportunity for America." In this postcontainment world, he argued, economic power would be more salient than military power.

The Soviet Union he depicted was an adversary that might, in some far distant future, discover "the inherent unworkability of the Soviet system." Though Gorbachev had been in power for a year and his efforts to transform his country were already apparent, neither he nor his policies were acknowledged. Hart's view of the USSR was based on his 1985 trip.

In his speeches, Hart devoted a good deal of rhetorical energy to combating the neoconservative charge that seeking "self-interested cooperation" between the superpowers on a range of areas, from arms control to global famine, was "isolationist." Yet this idea of finding grounds of mutual interest, the key innovative, post-Cold War idea in his speech, was only sketchily developed. "Some," Hart said, "will label any movement as retreat, withdrawal, isolationism."

Hart staked out a position on the Cold War that, in 1986, was at the farthest edge of acceptable discussion in American politics. His rejection of "traditional, bipolar containment" was still considered radical. The severe ideological limits of political debate were reflected in Hart's speeches. Even he felt forced to couch his position in defensive terms and preemptively respond to right-wing attacks. There was something anachronistic about the effort, though it was not apparent at the time; for even as Hart was speaking of new possibilities, the Reagan administration was engaged in the diplomacy that would bring Gorbachev to Washington for the signing of the INF Treaty just six months later. The new era Hart was promoting was already under way, and even his rhetoric lagged behind reality.

Hart's speeches generated much press attention. "In 1984," wrote the conservative columnist George Will, "he was hurt by the suspicion that he was a plastic man, skin deep all the way through. . . . His theme of 'new ideas' was more theme than achievement. But Hart knows something: American elections are about ideas. He is playing the game as it ought to be played." Hart's attempt to create a "threshold" test for the nomination was succeeding. He was getting written recognition as a statesmanlike figure. The "threshold," however, was established not by his intellectual success but by his political deftness in creating an example of conceptual ambition that other candidates would have to meet.

At the same time Hart was circling around the Cold War question, he set up a think tank, the Center for New Democracy. Conservatives, operating out of a host of think tanks, institutes and journals, had come to dominate the ideological tone of political society in the 1980s. Hart had assumed the burden of transforming political society that no liberal candidate alone could carry. By necessity, his center became a policy and speechwriting shop, in the service of his immediate political needs.

Hart also devoted much attention to constructing a large campaign apparatus, directed by seasoned pros, with clear lines of authority, which would not repeat the chaos of 1984. This organizational effort ran parallel to his intellectual effort to avoid the mistakes of 1984. He was not going to lose the last war.

In late 1986, on the eve of his visit to Moscow, he telephoned Stephen Cohen of Princeton. They had never spoken before. Just as Hart had sought out the innovative thinkers on defense and economics, he now sought out an iconoclast on the Soviet Union. Cohen's biography of Nikolai Bukharin, a Bolshevik advocate of "market socialism," who was liquidated in Stalin's first great purge, had influenced Gorbachev himself. After the 1984 election, in an article entitled "America's Missing Debate," Cohen had written:

The greatest failure of American democracy today is the absence of a real national debate on U.S. policy toward the Soviet Union. . . . The entire American political spectrum bears responsibility for this failure of the democratic process. The right is mindlessly committed to cold war, including military build-up, as an eternal virtue. The left is instinctively opposed to the arms race but has no ideas for achieving the broader political accords needed to end it. And the vaunted "bipartisan center" wishes only to stand safely somewhere between them.

Two months after Gorbachev took power, in May 1985, in an article entitled "Who's Afraid of Gorbachev?," Cohen presciently described the new Soviet leader as radically different from leaders of the past. "The United States therefore must decide whether it is a friend or foe of Soviet reform," he wrote. "A policy of cold war will almost certainly freeze any prospects of a Moscow spring."

During his four hours with Gorbachev, Hart fitted himself for the role of president. In effect, he had been temporarily appointed by the Soviet leader. It was the pinnacle of his campaign and career. Gorbachev's behavior toward him confirmed Hart's own idea of himself.

In Gorbachev, he was eye-to-eye with the kind of leader he aspired to be. Gorbachev was the world-historical man living in a world-historical moment. He had found what Hart was looking for—The Future, with himself at its forefront. Hart's image of Gorbachev was an image of his ideal self. "We were dealing," Hart said, "with a very formidable man, a true reformer, if not a revolutionary."

Hart emerged from the Kremlin possessed with the idea that the Cold War could really be made to end. He understood the dimensions of the change Gorbachev was seeking in Russia, and he began to sense how that might radically transform American policy and politics. Hart had labored at military reform and industrial policy piece by piece, like a craftsman. The idea of the Cold War's end seemed to make his positions cohere into a program and to put the present, stultifying debate in the dustbin of history. As if to commune with the idea of history, he drove with Cohen out of Moscow to Tolstoy's estate.

Two months later, Hart spoke at a fundraiser in New York: "What Gorbachev is doing is an unprecedented opportunity. I look forward to being an innovative president to meet the challenge of Gorbachev. Wouldn't it be tragic if at the moment the Soviet Union produced this leader, we had a conservative Republican administration that wasn't doing anything?"

Hart made plans to deliver a major address on U.S.–Soviet policy in which he would openly discuss the end of the Cold War. He intended to give the speech in the fall, after his campaign was in motion. Meanwhile, he diligently continued his Russian studies, reading books and articles suggested by Cohen, and reached the point where he was citing obscure articles of the Soviet constitution.

Hart's mind sped ahead to Inauguration Day. "I had been toying with ideas such as inviting Gorbachev to the inaugural and a major arms control summit in the first ninety days." He saw himself and Gorbachev standing astride history. They were in another era: The Future.

VI

On the surface, Gorbachev and Hart appeared to have parallel lives. Gorbachev grew up in a small rural town outside of Stavropol, acquired a law degree from Moscow State University, and returned to his native province to work as a party official. Hart grew up in Ottawa, Kansas, gained his law degree from Yale, and returned to the West to set up a law practice and become active in the local Democratic Party. Neither Gorbachev nor Hart served in the military. Both were military reformers who sought to foster a "new patriotism" on a less martial basis. They were of a new generation of leadership. One stressed the need for "new thinking," the other "new ideas." They were determined to upset the existing ideologies. And both encountered fierce opposition from their entrenched party establishments.

But the analogy between the two can be stretched only so far. "One must therefore be a fox to recognize traps, and a lion to frighten wolves," wrote Machiavelli. Hart was neither. Gorbachev, in the Machiavellian sense, was both a fox and a lion. He became the general secretary and Hart a lost soul. One mastered the exercise of power; the other didn't. "And," observed a Soviet diplomat, smiling sardonically, "there are other differences."

Hart had studied and organized and campaigned to get to play opposite Gorbachev. At his best, he offered the possibility of a positive, conceptual politics that looked beyond the Cold War. His strengths were exceeded only by his weaknesses.

In August 1972, Hart gave a revealing and bizarre interview to Sally Quinn of *The Washington Post.* "I don't want to do the safe things," he said. "Just as challenge and insecurity frighten most people, security and safety frighten me." He described himself as a "compulsive politician." Also: "I'm very obscure and I intend to remain that way." When asked about his marriage and his long absence from his wife, who was back in Colorado while he worked in the Washington headquarters, he said: "Let's just say I believe in reform marriage." And: "I never reveal myself or who I really am."

But Hart revealed his desires through the figures he identified with. During the McGovern campaign, Gary Warren Hart made a lasting friendship with Warren Beatty, who was raising money for McGovern by staging rock concerts. They became alter egos, reflected images of the other's desire. Hart, the child preacher, forbidden from seeing movies, discovered a world in the movie colony he did not even imagine in Ottawa, Kansas. Beatty, who lived in a theatrical trunk, discovered politics. Partly from that alliance came the establishment of modern Hollywood as a political force. And Hart, the founding father, became its favorite son. Hollywood wanted what it always wanted: a leading man who could set the deal. Then the script would make sense and all else would fall into place. Hart cast himself for the role. What was happening in Hollywood was paralleled in politics. Feudalism was collapsing in both places. The old party and the studios were being superceded by independent candidates and independent producers. Hart and Beatty, in their respective realms, were the models.

Beatty saw in Hart his serious side; Hart partly saw in Beatty a sexual role model. He noticed that Beatty's large and deserved reputation as a lover did him no harm in his own world as a star. Beatty undoubtedly thought of himself as someone who might have a political career. Hart did not understand that what made a political career impossible for Beatty was precisely his Romeo image. Hart also came to rely upon Beatty for political advice, and began to call him the name Jack Nicholson gave Beatty—"The Pro." They learned a great deal from each other and from each other's worlds, but they did not learn that neither of them could have become the other.

Though political society and movie society—Washington and Hollywood—may be roughly analogous, the differences are enormous. Washington is a cross between Winesburg, Ohio, and Paris. It is parochial and cosmopolitan, puritanical and sybaritic. And it echoes like a small tile bathroom. After his first year in Washington, knowledge of Hart's sexual life was hardly a secret, especially to the press, though it was presented later to the public, when he was the frontrunner, as a revelation. Power in Washington requires more discretion than in Los Angeles.

Hart understood cerebrally the importance that symbolism and images had assumed in the new political system. And he studied this subject like no other candidate, believing that there was a gnostic wisdom that could be plumbed and brought into politics. It was a kind of magic that would enable him to transcend the grinding political toil and the pandering of emotion. "I hate this," he whispered to an aide upon entering a room filled with his eager financial contributors.

Hart viewed the conventional political style as virtually immoral. He developed his own cool manner almost into a personal theology, a passion play in which his taciturnity was a mark of exquisite virtue. For the rest, he searched for a politics of signs that would create public emotion with little public display of it on his part.

Hart's interest in myth was rooted in his hero-worship of John F. Kennedy. To Hart, Kennedy was not a figure of ideology, or the end of ideology, but of civic virtue. His appearance enabled Hart to see how to transmute his religious enthusiasm into a political calling. Kennedy's coolness and distance also appealed to Hart. He believed that Kennedy's charisma came from the friction of his coolness with events, which produced a public frisson.

In preparation for the 1988 campaign, he and several of his advisers began to study with Sarah Russell Hankins, a professor at the University of Colorado. She was steeped in the thought of Joseph Campbell. From Campbell's *The Hero with a Thousand Faces* she derived archetypes of heroism in American popular culture and analyzed how they affected the way presidential candidates were perceived.

Hankins gave Hart an article on the structure of Reagan's mythic appeal that fascinated him. She wrote:

> The presidential choice in 1980 was an attempt to align the human with the illusion of the heroic, a person who could act the part of the leading man and who has cultivated a persona that is quintessentially American—the classic hero of the Old West. . . . The election of Reagan was a grand experiment. Could a leading man carry off a magnificent improvisation in life? Could he make us believe, if only for a time, that this was the America of the past? Could he make us believe hard enough to regain some of those old values?

Hankins suggested that one could anticipate the coming of heroic models by analyzing their prior celebration in the popular culture. In the study group with Hart, according to an adviser who attended, she submitted that Hart would have to fill another archetype. His story fit with the heroes whose origins are obscure, even enigmatic, have certain strengths of character and intelligence, are drawn to an older sage, pass through a trial of fire, and emerge better and stronger. This model seemed to apply to many recent movies, including *An Officer and a Gentleman, Top Gun* and *The Karate Kid.* Hankins's analysis of myth, however, was somewhat mechanistic. The culture throws up many archetypes at the same time; it anticipates many models, which compete with each other. What makes one archetype and not another come to life is not its ability to fascinate, but the ability of a politician who embodies it to assume power. There was another problem: Hart did not fit all the criteria Hankins designed for his myth.

Hart was never to reconcile Campbell's views of history with that of his previous mentor, Tolstoy. One stressed the impersonality of history, the other the irrational force of personalism; for Tolstoy, no man ruled events, for Campbell, great men embodied them. Hart aspired to be the "hero with a thousand faces" while believing that history was faceless.

The contradiction between these views was not just a conceptual one, but was rooted in the oscillations between Hart's self-dramatization as a man of risk-taking decisions and an entrenched passivity that had already disarmed him in the face of the Mondale campaign. "So long as histories are written about individual persons—whether Caesars, Alexanders, Luthers, or Voltaires—and are not histories of all, absolutely all those taking part in an event," Tolstoy wrote, "there is no possibility of describing the movement of humanity without the concept of a force compelling men to direct their activity toward a certain end. And the only concept of this sort known to history is that of power."

Hart's hero, John F. Kennedy, was a ruthless practitioner whose natural elegance and ease served his purposes. But he was not a Carlylean titan, an imposing personality sweeping all before him. He was borne along by the tides of the Cold War, which carried him to his rise and his crises and, ultimately, created the conditions for speculating on what might have been. Hart, finally, was a fantasist of power whose contradictions could only be resolved by a fantasy.

Hart's novel, *The Strategies of Zeus,* was an allegory of his basic conflict. (It was written before Hart's visit with Gorbachev but published a month afterward.) Its hero is a third-generation Montana rancher and the chief U.S. arms control negotiator. Frank Connaughton is "a private man in a public job. A Westerner with an Eastern education. A family man trying to create a family without its basic ingredients. A patriot in the service of a president he considered little better than a fool, or perhaps a dunce." Connaughton's wife, conveniently, is a madwoman locked in a psychiatric hospital.

The aging president is a passive nonplayer in his administration's deliberations. Into the vacuum steps the conniving but "limited" vice president, who sets in motion a military confrontation with the Russians in order to advance himself toward the presidency.

Russia, in Hart's novel, is still the evil empire. There is no hint of Gorbachev. The hardliners in the Kremlin are also moving toward confrontation. And the war-gaming on both sides is spinning out of control. Connaughton is the last, best hope for peace. His back channel in the Soviet delegation is the beautiful young translator, Ekaterina Davydova. Their discussions turn into an affair—diplomacy as an erotic escapade.

For more than one hundred pages, the lovers are staked out and chased. They elude the hunters by posing as a married couple. Part of the ruse involves Connaughton's changing his name, using his first name as his last name. Finally, they find refuge in a small inn in northern Italy, which happens to be owned by a Russian Orthodox priest named Father Tolstoi, a distant relation of the author of *War and Peace.*

Tolstoi and Connaughton ruminate on the philosophy of history. Is Connaughton being loyal to his country by betraying the machinations of a Cold War plot? Tolstoi speaks: "There are some lines of Tennyson's which sustain me:

> *Our little systems have their day;*
> *They have their day and cease to be:*
> *They are but broken lights of Thee,*
> *And Thou, O Lord, art more than they."*

Tolstoi blesses Connaughton. The lovers manage to thwart the hardliners on both sides. And the vice president who attempts to use "national security" to gain the presidency is frustrated.

In the nonfiction world, the Cold War background required a Democrat of hard mettle in order to prevail, a Tolstoyan practitioner of power on the order of a Kennedy, a Disraeli, a Gorbachev—not a Frank Connaughton. But now the able Hart was overmatched against the disabling Hart. He approached the campaign filled with forebodings and still desiring to escape crowds; he demanded to be considered only on the basis of his ideas, yet called attention to his personal life; while he continued his errant sexual conduct, he baited reporters to "put a tail on me." All of these were interrelated symptoms of his disability to assume power.

Privately, he had a portentous feeling about the campaign, that some malevolent force was out to get him. In October 1986, a month before the Iran-contra scandal broke, he stood outside the Senate Russell Office Building, reflecting on the secret designs of CIA director William Casey. The Reagan Doctrine of low-intensity warfare against communism, Hart estimated, might be fueled by $500 million; tens of thousands of armed guerrillas were in the field on three continents; perhaps hundreds of cloak-and-dagger agents were at work. Hart had experienced the Watergate scandal from the cockpit of the McGovern campaign. As a senator, he had investigated massive CIA abuses. And he believed that this gigantic clandestine buildup would infiltrate the 1988 presidential campaign. Hart suggested that he might be the ultimate target. But a month later the scandal was exposed, and a month after that Casey was felled by a cancerous brain tumor.

Hart's apprehensions were not calmed. He was now the prohibitive frontrunner for the Democratic nomination, and his feeling that enemies in politics and in the press were set on his downfall became acute. His deputy campaign manager, John Emerson, warned him of a rumor that reporters planned a Hart stakeout. But Hart did not try to deal with his fears by altering his behavior. It was almost as if he were an observer standing outside himself, watching the action.

He had a homecoming in Ottawa, Kansas, trailed by the national press corps, where he choked up speaking about his parents before a town meeting. He was making his personal story his campaign theme. On April 13, 1987, Hart announced his candidacy standing alone, atop a large rock in a national park, with his wife conspicuously posed on another rock beneath him. "Ideas have power," he said. "Ideas are what governing is all about."

Hart's campaign debt from 1984 was still enormous, about $2 million. He still despised fundraising and fundraisers, but the rounds of fundraising were endless. He was therefore especially grateful to William Broadhurst for his eagerness in soliciting money for the campaign and for making politics fun. Broadhurst, known as "Billy B," was the law partner of former Louisiana governor Edwin Edwards, who had been investigated by seven grand juries (though never convicted). Broadhurst represented oil, gas, mineral, and other interests. He established a Washington branch of his firm to be close to Hart. Broadhurst confided to a friend that when Hart was president he would have terrific access to the White House.

Broadhurst came from a netherworld of favors and sleaze that Hart knew little about. He was near-blind to the whole side of politics that involved getting power and getting near to power simply for its own sake and its material rewards. Hart associated that with the old politics. Hart was not hanging around with Billy B to get more power, but more liberty, away from the crushing constraints of the campaign and his strained marriage. Hart was seduced by Broadhurst because he did not understand that almost all the relationships of a leading presidential candidate are ultimately about power.

Aboard the airplane carrying Hart from Colorado, where he had just announced, to California, reporters continuously questioned him about his sex life. He wished he were elsewhere. Back in Washington, Billy B was arranging a cruise away from it all.

Hart turned toward the reporters. "Anybody want to talk about ideas?" he asked plaintively.

CHAPTER

7

The Vacuum

I

It had not been Michael Dukakis's idea to run for president. Seated in the governor's corner office of the gold-domed State House atop Beacon Hill, in the high-backed leather chair before the portrait of Sam Adams, he was completely content. He was in a familiar world, where he had already passed all the signposts. After his reelection in 1986, his ambition had reached the limit of his horizon.

In October 1988, when the race was already lost, a child asked Dukakis, "What gave you the idea to run for president of the United States of America?" The candidate groped for an answer: "It was a very important decision for me to make and a difficult one. This was an opportunity to run for the presidency of the United States, to hold what is probably the most important political office in the world. When you have that opportunity, as I did, to think about it. . . ." But what he had thought he could not say. He paused for a long time. "My family was very supportive," he continued. "All of my children, as well as my

133

wife, thought I should run, and that's very important. So here I am."

Perhaps no public official, at any level of government anywhere in the country, more quickly grasped the fine points of complex policies. Dukakis was voted the chairman of the National Governors' Association out of genuine respect and admiration. But he never knew why he ran for the presidency, and he resisted almost all advice that might have helped him articulate a rationale.

The great mystery about the Dukakis campaign was why, when he was seventeen points ahead of George Bush in early August 1988, he did not deflect Bush's negative thrusts and dramatize his own views. But Dukakis's failure was present in the beginning. He called the campaign a "marathon," but he had no sense of it as an intellectual marathon, as being about ideas of where the world was moving and how its movement could be shaped. Instead, his campaign was a series of intellectual failures and the consequences that flowed from them, including winning the nomination.

On the other side of the globe, in Moscow, at the U.S.A. Institute, the Soviet experts watched it all unreel with incredulity. "Was this a trick?" asked one sarcastically. If, the Russians wondered, Dukakis could not handle phony campaign issues, how would he ever have handled, well, the Russians? The irrational nature of the supremely rational Dukakis in the campaign was the most irrational spectacle some of the experts said they had seen in American politics. "Why did he run?" demanded one. "Why was he nominated at all?"

II

In September 1978, Governor Michael Dukakis was crushed in the Democratic primary by an opponent he considered so beneath him—a beefy, inarticulate businessman named Edward King—that he barely campaigned. His loss was personally devastating, and he referred to it as a "public death." Several days afterward, just after dawn, he stood at a trolley stop, as he had promised before his defeat, to campaign on behalf of a progressive tax initiative. There he met its chief organizer, a native New Jerseyan in his early thirties—John Sasso. Dukakis went through the motions of shaking commuters' hands, but he was now beginning to come back, and the street-smart and efficient Sasso was the man who would arrange it.

Dukakis was the second son in a family of relentless ambition. His father, Panos, was the first Greek immigrant to graduate from Harvard

Medical School. His mother, Euterpe, was the first immigrant from the large Greek community in Haverhill, Massachusetts, to attend college. She graduated Phi Beta Kappa from Bates College and became a teacher. When Michael was a small child, the family moved from the depressed milltown of Lowell to the leafy streetcar suburb of Brookline. It was then among the wealthiest towns in the country, overwhelmingly Republican, populated by a Brahmin Yankee elite and an Irish civil service. (After doing well as the president of a South Boston bank, Joseph Kennedy had moved his family there. It was where his son, John F. Kennedy, was born.) The town boasted the nation's first country club, with perfect discretion called The Country Club. Brookline was also a pure democracy, governed by the town meeting form of government, established in the seventeenth century. The values of good government, participation and public service were paramount. The Brookline citizenry viewed these values as a sharp contrast to the corruption, chicanery and cronyism of neighboring Boston, where the Irish had seized control. For all intents and purposes, Brookline was the matrix of Dukakis's politics.

After World War II, many of the Yankees drifted away, displaced by a rising professional middle class whose members often came from the ethnic minorities, like the Dukakises. (Panos Dukakis viewed his move to Brookline as part of his American assimilation. He himself was a staunch Republican.) The original values of the place were now tempered by a rigorous belief in meritocracy. Education, above all, determined status. And, just across the Charles River, Harvard, having dropped its quota system against Jews, became for this middle class what it had always been for the Brahmins: the ultimate House of Credentials.

The Brookline of this period produced two prominent political figures, each of whom embodied a version of the town's ethos. On the Republican side, there was Elliot Richardson, every bit of whose training conditioned him for the moment when he refused to carry out Richard Nixon's order to fire Watergate special prosecutor Archibald Cox of Harvard Law. On the Democratic side, of course, there was Michael Dukakis.

From the beginning, Dukakis was understood to be a kind of Yankee in state politics. It was not until his presidential campaign, in fact, that he ever emphasized his ethnic immigrant heritage. The dominant ethnic groups in Massachusetts were Irish, Italian and Jewish. (Blacks were not really a sizeable voting constituency until the 1970s.) To be Greek was to be panethnic and to be from Brookline defined one as assimilated into the suburban professional middle class. Dukakis was a WASP in all but name, and he lived according to the strictures of the Protestant ethic. But though he may have fit the political slot that the Yankees were vacating, he had none of the aristocratic sense of noblesse oblige, broadness and intellectual flair that was associated with the great Brahmin families like the Holmeses, the Adamses and the Lowells.

Dukakis's early career was shepherded by Allan Sidd. In his spare time, Dukakis liked to shop for generic brands in the supermarket, tend his tomato plants and read technical studies on public policy; but, above all, he liked to work hard. Sidd loved to eat, gamble and schmooze. He was raised on urban machine politics in a Jewish working-class neighborhood in Boston, and he applied the lessons he had learned on behalf of Dukakis, the quintessential suburban candidate. Together, in 1959, they took over the Brookline Democratic committee, turning it into Dukakis's political launching pad. Sidd got himself elected town treasurer, and through his influence helped Dukakis rise. Because of this background, Sidd was one of the few people Dukakis would listen to.

In 1960, Dukakis became the first Democrat elected to the Brookline town meeting. Two years later, he rose to the state legislature. Brookline was beginning its transformation from a Republican into a Democratic stronghold. Kennedy was now president, but he had imposed himself on the local political culture as a returning war hero and then flown beyond it. Dukakis, by contrast, spent every day of his public life, even as a presidential candidate, when he was a sitting governor, still guided by the Brookline criteria of good government and still immersed in local issues.

In the early 1960s, Massachusetts had fallen into what seemed like an irreversible economic and political decline. Its politics were mainly a vindictive quarrel between Yankee and Irish, as if Cromwell's occupation of Ireland had occurred yesterday. Dukakis cast himself as a small-scale Ralph Nader, even with his own cadre of graduate student "Raiders" writing investigative reports for him. Throughout the 1960s, he did not thrust himself into the antiwar and civil rights movements in a state where these causes were passionately taken up by liberals. Instead, he concentrated on procedural reforms of regulatory agencies and political bodies. This was the time-honored method used by Yankee reformers to foil the entrenched politics of favors and deals. But Dukakis was practicing it within the Democratic Party, not outside it, and from an expanding suburban base.

His goal since at least college was to be governor. In 1974, he entered the race with the presumptuous slogan: "Mike Dukakis Should Be Governor." In the primary, he assailed the party regular, Attorney General Robert Quinn, with some exaggeration, for incompetence, mudslinging and softness on corruption. In the general election, he criticized the Republican incumbent, Frank Sargent, on the same counts. Sargent, a Brahmin blueblood, was a real liberal, the last of a dying breed within the Republican Party, even in Massachusetts. Dukakis campaigned to his right, against the excesses of the welfare state and on the promise that he would not raise taxes. He won largely because he was a new species in Massachusetts politics. (Interestingly, his landslide victory by 11.6 percent was tempered by his razor-thin margin in Brookline, where his moralistic denunciation of Sargent's liberalism was greeted with considerable disgust.)

The Dukakis style was plain from the outset. He construed politics as a contest between the worthy and the unworthy. He was the most meritocratic of all. To him, a campaign was always about how the voters gradually came to recognize his virtue and therefore their own. His invariable theme was competence. While he laid out his superior résumé, he poked holes in his opponents'. They stood for corruption and ignorance; he stood for integrity and expertise. And he never had any self-doubts.

Upon taking office, he was confronted with a worst-case scenario: a devastating recession, with unemployment soaring above 15 percent, and a constricting tax base. Dukakis began slashing programs for the poor, the elderly and the handicapped. Cries from his left for compassion were met with stern, puritanical lectures about cold necessity. At the same time, he incurred the wrath of business by embarking on banking and insurance reforms. Moreover, he was systematic in his alienation of the old-style pols. To be sure, there was massive corruption to be rooted out. But, in his zeal, Dukakis often struck only himself. He humiliated the legislators, for example, by denying them the ability to hand out summer jobs to teenagers in their districts. He even refused to reappoint one of Tip O'Neill's oldest friends to his long-held state job because he did not meet Dukakis's unyielding standards. O'Neill agreed with almost all of Dukakis's positions; his son happened to be Dukakis's lieutenant governor; but his loathing of Dukakis was bottomless. The governor may have been holier than thou, but he did not understand the most venerable of political virtues: loyalty.

When Dukakis vetoed an already appropriated federal grant of $51 million for highway widening because he decided it was spendthrift, the House repudiated his veto by a 219–1 vote. Then, breaking his campaign vow, he raised taxes. He also estranged one friend after another by creating little tests of rectitude that they were doomed to fail. His campaign manager, Francis Meaney, was banished from his presence because his law firm had handled some state bonds. To Dukakis, this was proof that Meaney had taken advantage of their relationship.

The year before the reelection campaign, Allan Sidd died of a heart attack. He had smoked too many cigars and savored too many pastrami sandwiches. Now, on his own, Dukakis decided that he would dispense with television ads since the voters were already aware of his fine record. He would not insult their intelligence. Unfortunately, his principal opponent, Edward King, was delighted to do so. King was the sum of much of the animosity Dukakis had aroused. He was an Irishman who had been a football star at Boston College and played for the Baltimore Colts, and rose to become the head of MassPort, the public agency that oversaw the airport. In that capacity, he paved over much of East Boston, where he had grown up. King was hamhanded, imperious and dim. He believed that the business of Massachusetts was business. His social views had not been revised by Vatican II. And he suffered fools gladly. When Dukakis forced his removal from MassPort, King plotted a cultural war against him. His program was simple, even simplistic: tax cuts, capital punishment, mandatory sentencing for drug pushers, the drinking age raised to twenty-one, and a prohibition on state-funded abortions. In the meantime, another candidate, Barbara Ackerman, a Cambridge city councilor, chipped away at Dukakis for his betrayals of liberalism. In the debate, Dukakis froze—unsuccessfully trying to correct the misperceptions he believed King was spreading. He allowed King to set the terms. King continued with his sledgehammer approach, riding a mood of disillusionment and social resentment.

What was happening in Massachusetts seemed to be reflected on the national stage. Jimmy Carter, too, was an antipolitician, whose initial promise, based on integrity and competence, was running up against what his extraordinary pollster Patrick Caddell was to call a national "malaise." Dukakis and Carter, indeed, were quite similar in approach. "My favorite governor," Carter had said. Antipolitics, however, was now consuming the antipoliticians. At King's election night celebration, one of his campaign strategists, in high spirits, blurted out: "We put all the hate groups in one big pot and let it boil!"

The former governor conducted a dignified exile on the faculty of the Kennedy School of Government at Harvard, while John Sasso honed his skills in the 1980 presidential campaign of Senator Edward M. Kennedy. Edward King went on to preside over an administration rife with corruption and behave like a buffoon. He spent much of the operating budget of his office on take-out lobster lunches. More than anyone else, King made Dukakis's comeback possible.

Certain traits of character had defeated Dukakis in 1978. He was determined to compensate for them in 1982. Sasso was the manager's manager. He matched Dukakis in diligence and attention to detail, and he had the political instincts that the candidate lacked. If Dukakis had run as an antipolitician before, Sasso now mobilized a traditional Democratic coalition behind him. Dukakis had alienated liberals and regulars alike; now Sasso made sure that he made amends. Dukakis had neglected fundraising and media; Sasso moved these activities to the center of the campaign. Dukakis had appeared cold; Sasso tried to warm his image. When Dukakis seemed passive, Sasso prodded him. If Dukakis now took risks, Sasso smoothed the ground beforehand.

It was called "The Rematch," and it was Dukakis's kind of campaign. A huge scandal involving state construction contracts that had tainted King set the stage. Testifying under a grant of immunity before the investigating commission, political fixer William Masiello said: "I hate to give him an endorsement because, if any one man destroyed me, it was Governor Dukakis. When he came in there were no open hands. And the game was over. And you had four good years. And what did Dukakis get for it? He got kicked out. All right, the people of Massachusetts deserve what they get." Masiello was more than the witness for the prosecution; he was the witness for the campaign. Sasso had a poster printed up in the thousands, featuring a giant picture of a no-nonsense Dukakis over the slogan "Competence and Honesty."

Dukakis now assailed the mounting scandals besetting the King administration as a "corruption tax." And he inoculated himself against King's negative campaign by personalizing the crime issue. He spoke about how his older brother had been killed by a hit-and-run driver and his father mugged. Dukakis did more than sympathize with the families of crime victims; he identified with them.

The small group of strategists clustered around Sasso wanted to advance past the predictable themes. They wanted to seize the economic issue from King, who advertised himself as a "can-do" pro-business candidate—his strongest point. King was a Democrat, but he was also a supply-sider and supporter of Ronald Reagan. Dukakis was still associated with Jimmy Carter. Some of the politicos in the Dukakis operation had become familiar with the notions of industrial policy floating around Harvard, which offered a way to combine economic justice and economic growth. They understood that high technology was remaking the Massachusetts economy and the electorate. And they believed that Dukakis could present himself as the tribune of The Future. At a late-night strategy meeting, as talk around the table in Sasso's office of the new theme became incandescent, the words "White House" were first voiced. But nobody there, except perhaps for Sasso, connected "White House" with Dukakis.

Robert Reich, the industrial policy advocate at the Kennedy School who was already advising Gary Hart, was brought in for a meeting with the candidate. Dukakis's mind was one that inhabited the specific, the linear and the present. He recoiled from generalities unattached to prosaic illustrations. So he grasped the details of industrial policy—how government could stimulate cutting-edge technologies, the need for industrial research centers, why worker retraining was crucial in an increasingly unsettled global economy—but failed to see the larger political implications. He kept asking if this meant he would win blue-collar votes in the towns where he had previously lost them to King. But it would take him years before he could speak persuasively about The Future. For now, he said, over and over again, "Steady as it goes. One step at a time." In 1982, "competence and honesty" were enough to beat King.

Dukakis's defeat in 1978 entrenched his caution. After winning "The Rematch," he raised his caution to a principle. The business of government, as he saw it, was consensus. He wanted to have a consensus in place on every conceivable issue. The public/private partnership was now at the core of his view of public life. Conflict was simply a sign of the absence of a knowledgeable manager to bring the warring parties together to reach an agreement. And he was that manager. Sasso implemented the conviction politically. He deftly used the building of public/private partnerships to split business, shattering Ed King's old base and building one there for Dukakis.

During the Carter administration, Dukakis had grown close to Walter Mondale and in the 1984 Democratic race he threw his support to the former vice president. When Hart upset Mondale in New Hampshire and then in Massachusetts, Dukakis was completely baffled. He had no understanding of Hart's place in the party or of his appeal. (In the 1972 Democratic primaries, Dukakis had endorsed Edmund Muskie, not George McGovern.) Dukakis's perplexity in the face of Hart showed his incomprehension of the increasing political role of the new class, which was his own main support in Massachusetts, and of The Future theme, which his strategists were still trying to get him to adopt.

When Mondale won the nomination, Dukakis was held in reserve as a vice presidential candidate if the others refused. When Geraldine Ferraro accepted, Dukakis lent her Sasso, who ran her campaign. When it was over, the taste of national power was still in Sasso's mouth. On his second day back in the State House, Dukakis asked him why the Democrats had lost so ignominiously. Sasso replied that they lacked credibility on the economy, that Massachusetts now offered a model for the country and that Dukakis happened to be what the party was looking for. Dukakis instantly dismissed the idea.

Sasso began packaging Dukakis's various proposals as "The Miracle of Massachusetts," with the governor cast as the miracle-maker. Dukakis, in fact, had enacted an innovative industrial policy. More important, Sasso had figured out a political way for him to speak about it. Dukakis could rattle on about the specifics while a neon billboard above his head flashed "The Miracle." At the National Governors' Association and the Democratic National Committee, Dukakis finally unveiled The Future theme in a major speech.

Still recovering from the shock of his earlier defeat, Dukakis needed to prove that he could win reelection. Fortunately, the Republican Party in Massachusetts cooperated. Dukakis ran against a GOP that was the inverse of the powerful national party; in the Bay State, the Republicans had steadily shrunk to such a point of ineffectiveness that they had become a laughingstock. The first candidate they slated to run against Dukakis in 1986 was exposed as having a habit of lounging in his office with no clothes on. The second candidate turned out to have lied about his military record. Finally, the third, a millionaire blowhard with no political experience, was revealed to be running a company investigated by a slew of federal agencies. His debate with Dukakis was broadcast during the sixth game of the World Series between the Boston Red Sox and the New York Mets. Dukakis won in a landslide.

Just days after the election, Sasso mapped out Dukakis's presidential strategy over lunch at Locke-Ober, a restaurant in downtown Boston. He held up two fingers. In 1984, the party had split between Mondale and Hart. In 1988, Mario Cuomo would be the new, improved Mondale; Hart would be the new, improved Hart. Cuomo would stand for traditional Democratic values, Hart for new ideas. Dukakis, according to Sasso, combined the strengths of both. Like Cuomo, he was an ethnic, could convey a sense of party tradition, was a governor and from outside Washington. Like Hart, he had dealt with issues of high technology, but he had made new ideas work.

This scenario was to be the rationale for the campaign. Sasso knew from the day he met him that Dukakis was unable to sustain an emotional connection with voters. Sasso avoided wasted motion. It was easier to take Michael Dukakis through a political opening than to wait for him to get political passion. But even so, Dukakis had taken years to adjust to The Future theme. Here Sasso took an enormous leap. If Dukakis were successful in winning the Democratic nomination, he might just be changed enough by the experience to go on to win the White House.

Dukakis had learned a number of self-protective devices; but Duke II, as he was called after 1982, happened only because Duke I had failed. Underneath the plaster, Duke I was still present. He had realized the limitations of that political persona only by experiencing defeat. The problem was that there was no similar event to teach him the limits of Duke II except the campaign itself. Though he now felt secure in Massachusetts, he had not learned to compensate for his flaws in a national race, even with John Sasso at his side.

"A transitional man for a transitional time," said Sasso, meaning that Dukakis could represent The Future as the manager of the Massachusetts economy, which had made the transition to postindustrialism.

But Ralph Whitehead, a professor at the University of Massachusetts and a member of Sasso's kitchen cabinet, warned him that "Andrew Johnson was a transitional figure. William Jennings Bryan was a transitional figure. Woodrow Wilson in 1919 was a transitional figure. Al Smith was a transitional figure." Whitehead reflected, "Sasso made the assumption that being a transitional figure per se was an advantage. His concept was plausible in theory, but tough to develop in practice. He didn't realize how perilous it was."

Nonetheless, this was the case Sasso made for Dukakis. And just as Sasso was attempting to draw him into the race, the Iran-contra scandal broke. Late 1986–early 1987 was an opportune time for the emergence of Michael Dukakis, a period in which a campaign for "competence and honesty" appeared compelling. In February, the Tower Commission blamed President Reagan's "personal management style" for the scandal. It could be taken as a clarion call for a hands-on manager who would not tolerate wildmen in the Situation Room. "The scandal really bothered him," said Sasso. "He said: 'I want to take a look at this [the campaign.]' " That same month Mario Cuomo declined to run, widening the opening for Dukakis. By then, Sasso had been spending months trying to convince him to run. His wife, Kitty, who had been made excited by the idea of a presidential run by Sasso, joined in the campaign of persuasion. Various state officials and politicos whom Dukakis trusted were recruited by Sasso, and told the governor what he wished to hear, that in running for president he would not be taking a risk, that he could always go home again. Almost from the instant that Dukakis made his decision to run, Sasso demonstrated his prowess as a political manager by fielding the biggest, wealthiest and best-staffed organization of any candidate. On this basis alone, Dukakis was immediately seen as a formidable contender.

In a memo Sasso gave to Dukakis on April 4, entitled "Getting Off to a Good Start (April–June)," he laid out the candidate's theme, which he ran on until he fell far behind George Bush a year and a half later: the promise of economic opportunity, which Dukakis could deliver because of his proven executive ability in making Massachusetts a model of the future.

"There is very little question in my mind," wrote Sasso, "that at this stage your fundamental theme should be the goal of providing economic opportunity to every citizen in every industry in every state in every region of America. . . . When all is said and done, decent jobs and the economic future of America will be the most cutting issue of the 1988 primary season."

Sasso presented the campaign as a job search. He described the qualities Dukakis appreciated in himself and projected them as the desires of the electorate. It followed that they wanted what Dukakis had. He did not have to change; once they understood who he was and his theme of "opportunity," they would vote for him. "This theme," Sasso told him, "is not only useful in defining the issues and agenda for the race but can also help the American people know you as a person. . . . Your immigrant roots, your background, your reasons for entering politics, are the reasons you feel strongly about striving for economic opportunity for every citizen."

Sasso cautioned Dukakis about being seen as a liberal. "It will be important for us to define what you mean when you speak of opportunity for all. There is a danger that the concept can be misunderstood and viewed as simply classic liberal rhetoric. We must evoke the image of the expanding pie where everyone does better when we all do better. We must define the proper role of government as a catalyst, bringing people together, combining public resources and private initiative. . . . To reinforce these themes we have to use examples from our experience in Massachusetts. . . . These are the ideas and solutions which point the way to a brighter future."

So Dukakis set off to win the presidency on the basis of his state industrial policies, which had been quite successful, complicated and limited. Massachusetts, he was to argue, would serve as a microcosm of the rest of the country. In early 1988, he published a campaign book, *Creating the Future: The Massachusetts Comeback and Its Promise for America* (co-authored with Rosabeth Moss Kanter, a business professor at Harvard), whose conclusion was that "we must make sure that growing and durable regional economies—with good jobs, good wages, and hope for the future—take root everywhere." But he was never to appreciate that "The Miracle of Massachusetts" was only a metaphor. To Dukakis, the future economy was not a place that existed at some distance, to be reached through political struggle. He had been persuaded that the future was to be found in his own recent record.

Sasso pointed out only one intellectual challenge to the candidate: competence in foreign affairs:

> We have to start to demonstrate that you have an understanding and an approach on international matters. We should continue to do the briefings on arms control such that you start to develop an approach and become familiar with the language. The Fletcher School speech is a good start on the trade issue, however, we need one overseas trip, to either Moscow, Europe or Central America, to help develop credibility in this area. We probably need a major speech in June which demonstrates your understanding of the world and maybe even a bold proposal on arms control.

This was all that appeared on the subject in the memo. Dukakis's global reach did not even extend to the bottom of the page.

Dukakis entered this arena as a novice. As a politician, he had gone abroad only once, to Greece. He had not studied the game of nations and showed little interest in doing so. He resisted or put off the seminars and tutoring sessions his advisers set up; their feeling was that he did not like to be the less knowledgeable person in the room. Even so, Dukakis might have understood the ending of the Cold War and articulated its meaning. After all, he had never been a cold warrior.

Dukakis belonged to the generation of the fifties. He was not silent, but unlike the civil rights activists of the sixties the thought of staging something like a sit-in never occurred to him. Nor was he engaged by the antiwar movement. He accepted the conventions of politics. Though Dukakis was later entranced by the glamorous Kennedy, the dominant political figure of his formative period was Adlai Stevenson.

Dukakis was an admirer of his intellectualism and shared his beliefs in civil liberties, arms control and the United Nations.

To the extent that Dukakis had views on foreign affairs, they were shaped by two experiences as a student in the early 1950s. He spent a year studying abroad, living with a family in Peru, where a military dictatorship was in power. While there, he paid close attention to the CIA-sponsored overthrow of an elected reform government in Guatemala. (A book on this episode of imperialism that impressed Dukakis was *Bitter Fruit*, by Stephen C. Schlesinger and Stephen Kinzer, published in 1982. Kinzer, a fellow Brookliner and an adviser to Dukakis during his first term, became the *New York Times* correspondent reporting on the contra war in Nicaragua.) From his Latin sojourn, Dukakis learned Spanish and developed a suspicion of right-wing dictatorships justifying themselves by anticommunism.

The second experience was his brush with McCarthyism on campus. Even at Quaker-sponsored, liberal Swarthmore, left-wing speakers were forbidden from lecturing. As a leader in the local chapter of Students for Democratic Action (the affiliate of Americans for Democratic Action, the national liberal organization), Dukakis attempted to break the ban by inviting I. F. Stone to speak. He saw his role as a negotiator with the administration, appealing to reason. The effort failed, but Dukakis got satisfaction from watching McCarthy self-destruct on televised hearings, with the coup de grace delivered by a Brahmin Boston attorney, Joseph Welch: "Have you, sir, at long last, no sense of decency?" Dukakis believed that McCarthyism was an aberration of the early Cold War, an expression of militant ignorance that had been dispelled and could not recur.

Dukakis was a Stevensonian without his hero's eloquence, irony and a sense of history. History, to him, was the linear march of progress, temporarily detained by roadblocks of irrationalism, such as McCarthy. In Massachusetts, Dukakis had seen his view confirmed by the shriveling of the Republican Party and his own vindication.

But he never fully articulated or applied the political lessons he learned in the 1950s. His anti-interventionism, drawn from his Peruvian experience, did not make him outspoken about the Vietnam War. Though he opposed it, he repeatedly refused entreaties from liberals to make a strong statement in the legislature—hardly a risky gesture since it had passed a resolution condemning the war and challenging the legitimacy of the draft.

Whatever he believed, he filtered through the language of the law. Dukakis had the traits of a good lawyer, able to penetrate a case but blinkered. He discussed foreign affairs as if it were a branch of the law. Time and again, he reduced political questions to legal semantics. The key to settling the Nicaragua imbroglio, he insisted, was the Rio Treaty, a pact pledging multilateral action signed by North and South American countries. His argument in favor of international law and pressures was not misplaced—in fact, these forces were precisely what brought about a democratic election in Nicaragua—but Dukakis presented his solution as a narrow, abstract logic, which he assumed should be persuasion enough.

Dukakis did not see the ideological dimension of issues. The important distinction to him was whether one was right or wrong, which reflected whether they were smart or dumb, not left or right. He did not even understand his own liberalism as liberalism, but as rationalism. Ideology, as he understood it, was an expression of passion and thus irrational. The intellectual problem that arose from Dukakis's approach was that it was incapable of explaining the central question in foreign policy, rooted in ideological conflict: the Cold War. Because he didn't understand it, Dukakis could neither wage it nor end it. His conventionality led him to accept the deeply ingrained shibboleths that had kept the Democrats on the defensive for decades. He wound up operating on the premise that the Cold War was not over and that he needed to demonstrate his bona fides as a cold warrior. So he climbed into a tank. Almost everyone around him told him that this was smart.

In his early campaign speeches, Dukakis said that his first name and Mikhail Gorbachev's, if pronounced in Greek and Russian, sounded alike. What he was implying, if anything, he did not say. To him, Gorbachev might have been the mayor of a big Lowell, a depressed industrial town that was coming back as a result of economic restructuring; perestroika might be similar to the "miracle" of turning the old satanic mills into condos and software labs. But Dukakis did not even articulate this much. He was not only without a worldview, but without an idea of what a worldview might be.

Thus it was that the Tower Commission report was a perfectly misleading trap. It communicated to Dukakis a message, almost hand-tooled for him, about the need for competence, honesty and the rule-of-law. The Reagan he was campaigning to replace was the Reagan of late 1986. Sasso bolstered Dukakis's self-image. "In my opinion, and based on available survey data to date," he wrote in his early strategy memo, "Americans will elect a president in 1988 of hands-on competence, integrity, intelligence . . . who can manage orderly economic change in what they know is a changing world." But as Dukakis was shrinking the campaign to the scale of a state, a new global order was emerging with the end of the Cold War. Between "The Miracle of Massachusetts" and the miracle of Red Square, where Gorbachev and Reagan were declaring peace, there was no contest about which was the overshadowing event. But Dukakis still did not realize that an era, not just an administration, was passing.

Less than two weeks after Dukakis announced his candidacy, Gary Hart dropped out. This was, at best, a mixed blessing. "We're not ready," said Sasso. Hart's withdrawal radically altered the magnetism of the field. There was no longer a frontrunner against whom the other candidates could define themselves; they were now like random, colliding atoms.

One of Dukakis's advisers suggested that he could pick up Hart's generational appeal and bend it to his own purposes. Hart and Dukakis were roughly the same age, both in their early fifties, elected to office as members of the post-Watergate class of 1974. But Dukakis dismissed the idea out of hand. He didn't want to do anything that might identify him with Gary Hart. Moreover, he didn't believe in the idea of generational succession. He made no connection to the rise of Daniel Bell's "new class," the first mass university-trained generation, as indispensable to the postindustrial society as factory workers were to the industrial one whose nineteenth-century crucible was also Massachusetts. Instead, he regarded what Hart had to say about generational politics as nonsense. Dukakis didn't even believe that he was part of a generation, which placed him with many others in the post-Depression, pre-Vietnam generation.

After Hart's fall, only a model of abstemiousness—defined not by what he expressed but what he repressed—could fit the new implicit job description of a presidential candidate. For twenty years, the qualifications for a Democrat had become a lengthening list of don'ts: don't be too liberal; don't be too passionate; don't be too closely identified with the poorer or more militant constituency groups; don't be too negative; and especially don't challenge Cold War conservatism too much. Dukakis's great strength was that he wasn't like Hart, who wasn't like Mondale, who wasn't like Carter, who wasn't like McGovern, who wasn't like Humphrey, who was unfortunately Lyndon Johnson's underling.

Dukakis's allure to the Democrats was his surety. He was not going to make a mistake; he was not going to wander off into the night; he was not going to have a skeleton in his closet. The one skeleton, his wife, Kitty, was trotted out early by Sasso to confess to former addiction to diet pills.

Dukakis was the candidate for the age of safe sex—stable and steady, no peaks or valleys. If, as a famous wisecrack had it, George Bush reminded every woman of her first husband, Dukakis was like the second husband a woman marries if her first husband had been a cad rather than a bore. (Indeed, Dukakis *was* a second husband.) The lack of excitement was the saving grace; the thrill was gone, thank God.

In early August, David Dreyer, who had been Hart's issues director, was interviewed for almost an hour by Dukakis himself for an important job in the campaign. The governor shot about thirty rapid-fire questions on policy at Dreyer in no particular order, demanding instant, succinct answers. "It was jumbled, disembodied," said Dreyer. Then Dukakis asked him if he had anything to say. "I tried to have a discussion with him," Dreyer recalled. "I said: 'Developing the issues eighteen months before an election is very important, the only way to shape a mandate. I hope that the campaign will be very issue-oriented. So what are you doing in August 1987 to bring a mandate into office in January 1989?' "

"David," Dukakis said tartly, "you're missing the point. I've been traveling around the country for four months. I've just been to the governors' conference. I've just finished reading the next fiscal year's budget. All the indications are that the preconditions for change are out there. The real thing that's plaguing me is how to get the Congress and the executive branch working on the same wavelength, especially on foreign policy. That's the only stumbling block."

Dukakis's response seemed to Dreyer to be without any political context. Was he envisioning himself like Reagan, who had been at odds with the Congress over the contras? Dreyer tried to draw him out. He asked if Dukakis was worried about the right wing that had embedded itself in Washington. Dukakis brushed the question aside. "All the people are looking for is their leaders to cooperate," he said.

Dreyer had not held a job since Hart dropped out and his wife was pregnant. But after meeting with Dukakis he immediately took himself out of consideration for work on the campaign. "I walked out thinking that I may not be a master of politics, but he really doesn't get it."

Dukakis saw his presidency as a continuation of the managerial Duke II; his anxiety was the possibility of a recurrence of the divisive Duke I. For the rest, Dukakis was a man for all vacuums. He was going to have enough money so that simply by putting one black wingtip in front of the other he would arrive at the nomination, while everyone else self-destructed or fell by the wayside. So he made no mistake, because he did not risk making one. And that was the mistake.

"The country is tired of polarization and division," Dukakis said in August 1987, serenely anticipating the Democratic primaries. "I think that's a reason the administration is crumbling." Reagan, he said, had tried to exploit "all those devils out there. I don't think people are particularly looking for devils when what they're looking for is a president."

Such statements lacked conviction. Conviction, after all, is one side of an argument; Dukakis wanted his positions to arouse no contrary response, and he did not expect that his comfortable assumptions would be fundamentally challenged in the general election. The Democratic-controlled Congress, he believed, was simply waiting for a president like him to arrive.

But what of the criticism that his politics were too instrumental, too technocratic? "Where does that come from?" Dukakis wondered. "I'm kind of baffled. Out on the road I never hear it. I think I had some of that in my first term. Since coming back, my shop has been better run. I run a good solid shop."

III

In early August, a Gallup poll revealed that the frontrunning Democrat by a two-to-one margin was . . . Gary Hart. Since his withdrawal four months earlier, no other candidate had filled the vacuum. But Sasso noticed a blip in his polls from Iowa: Joe Biden was beginning to move.

Senator Biden of Delaware loved to campaign; he loved the crowds, the touching, but most of all the talking. His campaign was really based on one speech, brought to a high pitch that invariably moved Democratic audiences, particularly of his generation (he was 44), to tears and ovations. He invoked John F. Kennedy, Martin Luther King and Robert F. Kennedy, and then went on:

> The cynics believe that my generation has forgotten. They believe that the ideals and compassion and conviction to change the world that marked our youth are now nothing but a long-faded wisp of adolescence. They believe that having reached the conservative age of mortgage payments, pediatricians' bills and concern for our children's education, that we have forgotten. But I'm here to tell you, ladies and gentlemen, they have misjudged us. Just because our heroes were murdered does not

mean that the dream does not still live, buried deep in the broken hearts
of tens of thousands of Americans. For I can still hear those dreamers,
and so can you, speaking to us from across the wilderness divide.

Biden believed that he was more authentic than Gary Hart. The day
after Hart dropped out, Biden, in his Senate office, said that Hart did
not "get it," referring to generational message. He described how Hart,
in the Senate gym, had asked him to explain certain cultural phenom-
ena. But Biden had hardly been an activist in the 1960s. His feeling
at the time, he once admitted, was that antiwar protestors were "jerks."
He was the son of a car dealer, a fraternity member interested in good
times, with mediocre grades, who married young. He was elected to the
Senate when he was twenty-nine. His early dramatic rise contributed
to his insecurity about his social and intellectual background, which he
attempted to cover with displays of rhetorical self-confidence.

To listen to his patented speech was to enter a wind tunnel filled
with flying shards of rhetoric. He had difficulty filling in his generalities
with specifics. He was straining to make a political connection with his
generation and to say something original without establishing strong
positions. The evening before the first Democratic debate on July 1,
1987, closeted in a hotel room with a small group of advisers, Biden
at one point, as a way of asserting himself, assumed a batting stance,
gazing out at an imaginary pitcher. He said that other kids imitated
Willie Mays's or Mickey Mantle's stance, but that he was always
looking for his own way of hitting.

Biden had a coach. His name was Patrick Caddell, a pollster in his
mid-thirties who was a combination of Mark Hanna and John Belushi,
political kingmaker and bad boy. He had been recruited by Gary Hart
for the McGovern campaign as a senior out of Harvard. More than a
precocious math nerd, he did not simply measure public opinion, add
up his numbers and report it to the campaign strategists. Caddell
invented hypothetical categories, even hypothetical candidates, and
then applied the most sophisticated computer-driven, multiple-regres-
sion analysis to reveal each constituency's potential and liability. With
an uncanny sixth sense, and by targeting issues and voters, he located
vacuums that candidates could race through.

Caddell was the Democratic Party's most effective politico in modern times. Of the four elections since he had achieved voting age, he
had been a key player in the inner circle of the Democratic candidate
every time. His polling was essential in guiding Carter through the
hazards of the 1976 primaries and the general election. When the

Carter administration had virtually collapsed in 1979, it was Caddell's idea that the president should retreat to Camp David for two weeks of rethinking. The so-called malaise speech, attributing the nation's problems to a "crisis of confidence," was the consequence. In 1984, after unsuccessfully attempting to lure Biden into the campaign by polling for a hypothetical candidate named "Smith" (who had roughly Biden's characteristics), Caddell joined up with Hart. He took a candidate in the single digits, just as he had taken McGovern and Carter, and helped bring him to the point where he nearly seized the nomination away from the all-but-certain frontrunner. Having won the nomination, Mondale faltered and turned to Caddell for advice, thereby succeeding in his first debate with Reagan.

Caddell worked in cycles of cyclonic energy and lassitude. When possessed by a political idea, he raged and sputtered until it was accepted or he was locked out of the room. Initially, he was mistrusted only by the old-fashioned politicos, whom he out-generaled time and again in presidential primaries. "Stop him before he kills again" became their rallying cry. But his temper gradually alienated him from almost every friend he had in Washington.

At last, for the 1988 campaign, Caddell's model of "Smith" was in the field. Caddell and Biden were indeed close. "Sometimes it's hard to know where Pat's thinking stops and mine begins," Biden said. Caddell had the intellectual authority and generational sense that Biden craved. They even spent vacations together. On Martha's Vineyard, at Caddell's summer house, the pollster played old tapes of Robert Kennedy's speeches for him. They lamented the loss of what might have been and hoped for what might yet be. On January 1, 1987, Caddell produced one of his famously mammoth strategic memos. It was an exceedingly grim and acute diagnosis of the crisis facing the Democratic Party—"in its worst straits since the post–Civil War period." Though the Democrats may continue to control the Congress, on the presidential level the party "has no electoral base. Further, it is suffering from an internal statistical cancer that seems to be inexorably spreading." The Democrats, he wrote, were now "a minority party." It had lost its edge in party preference, especially among white males and younger voters. "We fear," he wrote, "that the crisis with white males extends beyond the issue of economics. What damage has been wrought by the perception that the Democrats are 'soft' on defense? Finally, we must face the sensitive question—is the Democratic Party perceived as a 'feminine' party—and the GOP a 'masculine' party—not only on policy issues but rather on characteristics such as 'strong,' 'tough,' 'forceful,' and 'leadership?' "

It was "a myth," Caddell warned, that the Iran-contra scandal had created the conditions for victory, because "it does not solve the public's problem with the Democratic Party." It was another "myth" that "what we need is a moderate, centrist, etc. . . . To a great degree, the party's problem is relevance, as much or more than ideology. . . . The larger truth is this: The road to victory is enhanced by the party's historical principles—the task is not to abandon those principles but to adapt them to the demands of our present and future." Finally, according to Caddell, the "very worst group" for the Democrats, which was the one until 1984 that had been the "very best group":

> . . . any careful sorting and stripping away of the landslide debris leads to one overwhelming conclusion—The crisis of the Democratic Party is first and foremost a crisis of generation. It supersedes and is fundamental to analysis of other subgroups, men, white Southerners, middle class, etc. In 1988 no factor will be more crucial than the politics of the baby boom generation. . . . Disastrously, this massive generation appears to be turning its back on the Democratic Party. One is tempted to conclude that the most significant political change in the 1980s is this generational rejection of the Democratic Party.

To counteract this massive defection of the young, Biden acted as if charisma was all that was needed. "There's never been a specific answer [offered by] the people who've moved us," he said. "John Kennedy: Name me the specific answers he offered. Give me the specific programs that Franklin Roosevelt offered while he was running." While Biden was developing his leadership act, New York governor Mario Cuomo referred to him as a "dumb blond."

The irony of Biden's effort to rise on imitation alone was that he was actually grounded in issues of enormous political significance. He had been a leader in the effort to secure ratification of the SALT I arms control treaty in 1979. And, in early 1987, he initiated and chaired a joint hearing of the Foreign Relations and Judiciary committees to prevent the Reagan administration from undermining the Anti-Ballistic Missile Treaty of 1972, the cornerstone of modern arms control. As the Judiciary Committee chairman, he was preparing for yet another signal issue: the confirmation hearings of Robert Bork to the Supreme Court. With these issues, Biden had the basis for presenting himself as an authority on arms control and hence the fate of the earth—and as a protector of constitutional rights and liberties. Like the purloined letter, these credentials lay on his desk while he madly searched for credibility.

He was impatient to give another self-dramatizing speech. Just such a speech was called to his attention by Caddell. It was on a tape of a television spot produced by the Labor Party in Britain's recent election. It featured Neil Kinnock, the party's leader, delivering an impassioned autobiographical peroration about his working-class heritage. "Why am I the first Kinnock in a thousand generations to be able to get to university?" he asked. Soon, Biden was giving a new speech: "Why is it that Joe Biden is the first in his family ever to go to a university?" And so on. The first few times he delivered it he cited Kinnock. Then, the attribution disappeared. He was doing the same with phrases he borrowed from Robert Kennedy, John Kennedy, Jimmy Carter, and Hubert Humphrey. On the eve of the Bork hearings, on September 16, the *New York Times* on its front page reported Biden's appropriation of Kinnock's life story. The following day, Biden held a press conference where he admitted that he had failed a course as a first-year law student because of plagiarism. Within days, he withdrew from the race. The irony of it all continued: While Biden's impersonation act dominated political discussion, the U.S. and the Soviet Union announced the agreement on the INF Treaty. (Shortly after his withdrawal, Biden suffered an aneurysm, underwent operations for almost a year and received, when he returned to the Senate, an outpouring of sympathy. On the Foreign Relations Committee, he became a serious student of the issues.) In Washington, the long knives were now out for Biden's handler; it was time to settle longstanding scores with Caddell. Like Hart, though for a different reason, Caddell was disgraced, his name turned into a byword for political failure. He had indeed been a bad politician in terms of his own career and relations with his peers, and his prescient thinking about the Democratic Party was dismissed along with him.

With the demise of Hart and Caddell the very idea of generational politics was now ridiculed. Editorials and news stories assailed it as nothing more than a nostalgia trip down Penny Lane. An article in the *Wall Street Journal* called it "a political bust." Once the generation's experience was no longer engaged by the politicians, it seemed mysteriously to evaporate. For the most part, it cut across the conventional constituency groups: hence, it could be reached only through the media. Yet there it was, relentlessly courted as a market by ads for almost every product.

A new generational politics implied a different ideology to square with the shift in experience. With Hart, this change was explicit. The prevailing concepts of Cold War politics—appeasement, containment, falling dominoes—were rooted in the understanding of the generation that had fought World War II. Mikhail Gorbachev was the first leader in either the Soviet Union or the United States who was a member of the successor generation. Hart saw himself as the American counterpart to Gorbachev. And at the core of his politics was an idea of ending the Cold War. Though Hart and Biden had fallen for purely personal reasons, the Democrats abandoned their generational strategy as well. In the absence of an alternative politics based on this revised vision of the world and the electorate, the Republicans filled the void with a vengeance. The Cold War thus remained as the template of American politics. For the Democrats, the failure to grasp the political significance of a generational succession was catastrophic. In 1988, they repeated their unprecedented loss of younger voters in 1984. A year after the campaign, fewer voters among this group—especially those under thirty—favored the Democrats than ever had.

With Biden's removal, Caddell was self-exiled to Los Angeles, and the nominating campaign began its descent into ever narrower self-promotion. Meanwhile, the hunt continued for the perpetrator of the exposé: Who had called attention to Biden's plagiarism?

John Sasso, frustrated that he could not get any reporter to look into the source of Biden's speech, had produced a videotape containing both it and Kinnock's, and sent it to the *Times*. After the story broke, Michael Dukakis announced that he would fire anyone on his staff who was involved and asked Sasso about the incident. Sasso said he was investigating. He had already been lying to senior operatives in the Biden campaign. But Dukakis's self-righteous persistence made it impossible for him to continue his pose as bystander.

On the surface, Biden and Dukakis appeared to be opposites. While Biden picked up political themes quickly, too quickly as it happened, Dukakis took seemingly forever to say the most obvious things. But Dukakis was as dependent upon his political alter ego as Biden. As much as possible, Dukakis was to be kept away from the tactics of the campaign. Dukakis's impulse in dealing with differences over issues was to dismiss his opponents and to trumpet his own superior morality. Sasso's skill was to clear the field a step ahead of Dukakis, whose plodding progress could then continue unimpeded. The so-called attack video was no more illegitimate than two newspaper clippings stapled together; entirely composed of materials in the public domain, it discredited Biden's oratorical eloquence and his character. Because

Dukakis's "Brookline" style placed him above the rough-and-tumble of politics, his campaign could not be seen as part of it. By fostering this sterile image, Dukakis forced Sasso to act as if his sharp point about Biden, which was deadly accurate, was as shameful as a lie. Thus Sasso was prompted to lie.

Now he told Dukakis of his culpability in making the "attack video" and said he had to quit. Dukakis sadly agreed. He could not bear the criticism of Sasso, which he saw as tainting his own image, though it was never made clear whether Sasso had to resign because he had made the video or because he lied. On September 30, he left Dukakis to campaign by himself. This incident was the prologue to Dukakis's incapacity to handle the thrust and parry of politics, which would ultimately prove to be fatal. It is unimaginable that, under similar circumstances, George Bush would have allowed the indispensable James Baker to leave him.

With the exit of Sasso, Dukakis impaired three of his senses: sight, sound and speech. Sasso had structured what he saw, what he heard and what he said. "People say I lost a friend. It's worse than that. I lost a brother," said Dukakis. He actually had lost his older brother, Stelian, who was mentally ill and got killed by a speeding car one night while riding his bicycle.

His campaign was fundamentally altered. The circumstances of Sasso's departure prepared the groundwork for Dukakis's failure to respond to Bush's negative assault. A decade earlier, Dukakis had been a self-destructive politician who understood that he could not resolve his flaws himself. So he bonded himself to Sasso, whose job was to minimize risk. The aide, however, was more ambitious than the politician. His greater political talent enabled him to maneuver Dukakis into running for president. With Sasso departed, Dukakis redoubled his caution. What he learned from the affair, he said, was the "very hard and very tragic lesson" that "negative campaign efforts to hurt other candidates should have no part in my campaign [or in] American politics." He was afraid of having his permanent record further tarnished; he was desperate to rise above controversy; the avoidance of intellectual risk became his strategic imperative.

IV

Gary Hart had been interred like a barrel of toxic waste, but the disturbing events in the campaign shook loose the cover of his crypt.

On December 15, he was back in the race. The date explained his motive. It was a week after the Washington summit, a year to the day after his meeting with Mikhail Gorbachev.

In September, Hart had already begun to stir. He delivered the speech on the ending of the Cold War he had been contemplating before he withdrew from the campaign. Gorbachev, he said, was "a modern man," who stood for "the possibility of historic change in the Soviet Union" that would "redefine the superpower relationship." The U.S. needed "new political thinking" that sought "deep reductions in existing arsenals" and "more cooperative ventures in our mutual self-interest." If the U.S. continued down the "blind alley of excessive nuclear armament," it would become "militarily musclebound, uncompetitive and broke." In the absence of American leadership, Gorbachev would show himself "more farsighted and insightful than we are" and the Soviet Union could become "a more relevant superpower than ours in the twenty-first century."

Only one candidate felt prompted to respond to Hart's speech: Bruce Babbitt, the former governor of Arizona, who was campaigning with little money or organization. The exchange between a politician beyond the fringe and another without a chance marked the high point in the campaign as far as coming to terms with the new world reality.

"I want to say this very plainly," said Babbitt. "In the postwar competition, they have lost and we have won. . . . The bottom line is that Soviet Marxism has long since stopped making converts. As an evangelical movement, it is dead." He elaborated:

> In *The Brothers Karamazov,* Dostoyevsky's Grand Inquisitor said that "freedom and bread enough for all are inconceivable together." In this century Dostoyevsky's countrymen have been the leading exponents of that belief. They were wrong—exactly wrong—because liberty and prosperity advance fastest and farthest together. The world has come increasingly to understand that. To me, the ultimate significance of Gorbachev's remedial agenda—of glasnost and perestroika—is to show that even the Soviets can no longer pretend otherwise.

Babbitt then dismissed "the Ollie North view of the world, which sees an America besieged: not only locked in a bitter twilight struggle with hostile forces, but constantly in danger of losing." Ronald Reagan, he said, was "in spirit . . . still back in 1949."

Yet he sought to separate himself from Hart: "I am not saying—as

Gary Hart said recently—that cooperation might soon replace competition as the dominant feature of relations between the superpowers." But his emphasis on their difference was more rhetorical than real. "I believe," said Babbitt, "that it is fundamentally in the American national interest to embrace a new kind of competition with the Soviets, based upon economic power and political appeal as a substitute for an arms race that threatens the very survival of this planet. . . . It is time to transform our competition from one in which there can be no winners to one in which the contest itself does some good."

Babbitt's speech, the most advanced position of any candidate, was ignored by all the other candidates and by the press, except in a terse Associated Press dispatch: "Democratic Contender Says Cold War Could Be Ended."

Though it was still five months before the Iowa caucuses, Babbitt was considered out of the running, even though his potential appeal to Democrats was immense. He came from a prominent family in Arizona, graduated from Notre Dame, and went to the University of Newcastle in Britain on a Marshall scholarship and Harvard Law School. He had been trained as a geologist and was an active environmentalist. In the early 1960s, he worked for Acción, a Peace Corps–like volunteer agency, in a Caracas barrio. In 1965, he marched in the historic civil rights demonstration at Selma, Alabama. He met his wife, Hattie, while working in a federal antipoverty program in Texas. She became a trial lawyer, and their marriage was a marriage of equals. As attorney general of Arizona, he was a scourge of organized crime, even marked for murder at one point. No one could accuse him of softness. As a Democratic governor in a Republican-dominated state, he enacted an innovative and progressive program—and was reelected in 1982 by 63 percent. He was also an utterly modern, yet committed post–Vatican II Catholic. Babbitt was a man of ideas, witty, self-confident enough to know when to be self-deprecating, and stable.

Unfortunately, he came across badly on television. In the first Democratic debate in July, his eyes popped, his facial muscles twitched, his deep voice droned, and his money instantly evaporated. In addition, Babbitt had made the deficit his top issue—an issue that had not worked for fifty years for the Republicans and was a proven failure for Mondale in 1984. Even after his speech on the end of the Cold War, Babbitt continued to stress austerity—budget cuts and higher taxes. He did not connect his statement about the Cold War with the effect its ending might have on the budget. "Stand up!" he urged audiences that remained seated.

By the beginning of November, none of the candidates, with the exception of Jesse Jackson, who had secured his natural but limited base, was receiving the support of more than 10 percent of the Democratic electorate. This was a consequence of more than their failure to assert any compelling public philosophy; it revealed almost a total lack of interest in their personalities. To the voters, the Democratic field was a row of talking heads.

"If a dominant or more dominant personality had gotten in and occupied part of a vacuum, it would have changed my thinking," said Gary Hart. "But they didn't." He compared himself to the others and found them all too small. "It's not just a difference of point of view. It's a difference of dimension, scope, depth, and size." They "cannot match" Gorbachev. "I can do it best."

Overnight, he was the frontrunner again. "I have the power of ideas," he proclaimed. He was conducting a campaign that had already died; now he had nothing left to lose. "I can't be hurt and I know no fear." In short, he was a ghost. And he could be exorcised only by the voters. "We decided to take it to the street," he said. "Let the people decide."

"What's your sense of the race?" asked an adviser. "I don't know," Hart answered. "You're crossing the Nietzchean void," said the adviser, referring to the campaign's vacuum. Hart laughed.

Before he could meet Gorbachev again, he had to debate with the other candidates in Des Moines. He wanted to show that his thinking was larger than theirs, that they were not equal to Gorbachev. But Hart was immediately asked about the "character" question, and he plunged into an irrelevant apologia: "I am a sinner. My religion teaches me that all of us are sinners." His self-defensiveness made him stiffen. And every time he raised the question of Gorbachev, the others evaded him. He was minimized and diminished; his support rapidly began to disappear until, when the people began deciding in Iowa, it was almost nonexistent. He was dead again.

Out of the klieg lights, Hart traveled frequently to the Soviet Union, meeting with high officials and arranging joint venture deals as an international lawyer. He made plans to write a book on the Russian events, "like John Reed," he said. The author of *Ten Days That Shook the World*, of course, had been depicted in the movie *Reds*, played by Hart's friend Warren Beatty. By mid-1989, months before the Central European revolution, he was trying to put together a conference on converting the economy that would begin to address the question of what to do when the military budget was slashed at the Cold War's end. Gary Hart was intellectually still leagues ahead of the political pack, though nobody was listening.

Hart's brief second coming in the campaign had not succeeded in placing the end of the Cold War at its center. Indeed, his lack of credibility worked to obscure the issue he wished to raise. His ultimate political effect was to underline Dukakis's dreary virtues.

V

Dukakis now entered Iowa without Sasso around to guide him. All that was left of Sasso was his incomplete game plan. Its themes had been based on the political climate of late 1986–early 1987. A year later, after the Washington summit, a new reality was emerging that did not cry out for competence and honesty as an alternative. Dukakis, however, tightly clung to the game plan. And he refused to leave Boston for more than four days a week. His justification was that he had to continue to demonstrate his efficiency as governor. But he was also fortifying himself against change, including the change in his organization, in a cloister of familiar surroundings.

His new manager was Susan Estrich, a thirty-five-year-old Harvard Law School professor, who had served in the Mondale and Kennedy campaigns. She had never managed a political campaign before. Estrich was hired because of her qualities and discounted by Dukakis because of them. She had a driven personality, with a quick, lawyerly mind that assumed arguments prevailed on their merits. Unlike Allan Sidd and John Sasso, she did not complement him but instead reflected and reinforced his credentialism. She could never deal with his flaws because she could not counteract them. Her efforts at correction were too close to his own style, which he resisted from a junior. Almost from the beginning, she was made a nervous wreck.

One of the first people Estrich called upon to help deal with Dukakis's paralysis was Marco Trbovich. He came from a working-class Chicago background, became a political consultant in Boston and then set up a practice in Los Angeles. He had originally been hired for the campaign by Sasso. In his first memo to Sasso, of May 1987, Trbovich argued that Dukakis's "moral character" and "executive record" would be weakened as themes unless they were joined to an "insurgent populism." As a populist, he suggested, Dukakis would be "the kind of man who wants to stop lobbyists and corporate raiders from running amok in Washington and on Wall Street; stop special interests from pollut-

ing the environment and ripping off our defense dollars; stop our
trading partners from taking unfair advantage of American good will;
and start investing in the education, training and public services that
will create economic and social independence for every individual—
and especially for the American working family." Trbovich warned that
running as a "quasi-incumbent serves no advantage and may in fact
prove disastrous to projecting a compelling image—in either the primary or the general election."

In July, Sasso had put Trbovich on the plane to Iowa with Dukakis and placed him in charge of focus group research with Iowa voters. Based on his findings, he wrote Sasso: "The perspective of our
electorate is global, not local. They are looking for a statesman who
can restore America to world class leadership." The Iowans were
asked: "Which of these men can you envision sitting across from
Gorbachev?" It was still too early to tell, but in the absence of
someone who could fill that role Representative Richard Gephardt's
tough talk on international trade appealed to voters' "anger, resentment and partisanship."

When Sasso got caught in the feedback loop of the Biden tape
incident, Dukakis froze. He refused to move beyond his initial pat
phrases: "opportunity . . . good jobs at good wages . . . competence."
The only new issue he added seemed a self-parody of his sanctimonious-
ness and instrumentalism: how the deficit could be reduced by more
stringent IRS enforcement.

In October, Estrich asked Trbovich to travel with Dukakis in California and to help work on a new "theme speech." Trbovich wrote her
a memo in which he stressed that Dukakis could dramatize his values
by using "the values of Washington and Wall Street" as a "counterpoint." Estrich gave the memo to Dukakis to read. He drew an arrow
pointing to the word "counterpoint." "I don't like this," he wrote in
the margin. "Forget the strawmen!!"

Trbovich wrote Estrich another memo, noting that the "overriding
focus on Massachusetts and managerial prowess . . . lacks emotional
and, therefore, motive force." But Dukakis did more than reject all
such advice. He disputed with Trbovich over poll numbers that pointed
to any trend he did not approve of.

By early December, Estrich privately characterized the Dukakis
strategy as "a disaster" to New York political consultants David Sawyer
and Mandy Grunwald. But Estrich believed that a solution at last was at
hand. After intense pleading Dukakis had agreed to deliver a new
speech, written by Estrich's husband, Martin Kaplan, chief speech-

writer for Mondale in the 1984 campaign and now an executive at Walt Disney studios. The speech was billed as "The Next American Frontier," a title taken from Robert Reich's book but bearing no other resemblance to it. Heavily edited by Dukakis, the speech was a reinvention of boilerplate: "We must not let that Republican deficit crimp our plans or crab our dreams. . . . The next American frontier is a vibrant and growing economy that provides good jobs at good wages for every citizen in the land. . . . We cannot turn back the clock. . . . The end of the next decade will mark the beginning of a new century. . . . We must have a president . . . who believes in the American dream. . . ." The speech had the same effect as if it had not been delivered.

Even before a single ballot was cast in a primary, Dukakis had frustrated almost all the politicos who dealt with him. "Guys," said Dukakis, time and again to his handlers, "just give me the lines. What are the lines?" So they'd give him the lines. And then he would reject them.

It was all in his voice, a voice that closed discussion, brisk and often abrupt, on the edge of snappishness, a voice filled with barely suppressed exasperation that whomever it was addressing had to have the most simple, obvious things explained, that anyone who was intelligent already knew. And as the voice rose in inflection, reflecting the foregoneness of his conclusions, his head slowly began to shake side to side as if to say that any other view was simply inadmissible and that, if you were thinking it, don't.

In mid-December, Estrich called for a meeting of the inner circle of the campaign with Dukakis in his State House office to discuss the "theme problem." Dan Payne, the campaign's chief media consultant, had brought a list of at least twenty ideas—"some I agreed with, some I didn't"—that had been recently presented to Dukakis and rejected.

Payne had been at the heart of the political transformation of Massachusetts, involved in almost every important liberal campaign for almost twenty years. It was Payne who had invented the slogan of "The Rematch" in 1982. At his first meeting with Dukakis to talk about the presidential campaign in February 1987, the governor asked Payne what he thought his message should be. "I was taken aback," said Payne. "I figured he knew why he wanted to be president."

Estrich now beseeched Payne not to show his list to Dukakis. "She prevailed on me because she was nervous about his views on themes," Payne said.

The governor's agenda at the strategy meeting was singleminded. He demanded to know why a rationale for his candidacy had not been created by advertising. The ads, he complained, were not up to Payne's "usual standards," and he was "disappointed."

This discussion, Payne replied, was not "very helpful." It would be more helpful, he suggested, to talk about how the campaign had gotten to this point.

"I don't understand why things aren't done right," insisted Dukakis. He demanded a new ad, a man-in-the-street ad, in which ordinary people attested to his competence and honesty.

Payne explained that this was a hackneyed technique, not useful in establishing a presidential candidacy. "It's used," he said, "to sell a product that's struggling."

"I don't think the work is right," said Dukakis.

"If you can tell me what it's all about, what you're trying to say, I'll try to present it," said Payne. "I resent being blamed for what's going on."

"I don't think the work is right. I don't know why the fuck we can't get this right." The room was still. Dukakis had said "fuck." "It was the first time I ever heard him say 'fuck,'" said Payne.

Payne started to leave. "I don't need to take this shit," he muttered.

Paul Brountas suddenly intervened. He was Dukakis's oldest and closest friend. They had roomed together at Harvard Law School and shared the same lawyerly perspective. Brountas was the campaign's chief counsel, and he had urged Dukakis to fire Sasso. "Stay," he now said to Payne. Dukakis stood up, closed his office door and took his seat again. Payne stayed; tempers cooled. And the meeting limped along to no conclusion.

Payne produced the man-in-the-street ad, but it had no impact. A month before the Iowa caucuses, he wrote a script for another spot. It would feature clips of Gorbachev and Reagan signing the INF Treaty. "New leaders, new challenges, new problems. A world where it is becoming harder and harder to tell friend from foe . . . where cheap labor can be just as damaging to us as the most sophisticated rocket. . . . Isn't it about time we had a new leader who knows how to make change work for us?" Cut to slogan: "Mike Dukakis . . . A president for the nineties." Payne submitted it to the campaign and he received no reaction to it whatsoever. The campaign, he felt, was "a façade, an illusion."

As the Dukakis campaign poised for an ascent to the nomination, it refused to take off, lumbering down an endless runway, mile after mile.

CHAPTER

8

Born in the U.S.A.

I

The Iowa victor landed in Manchester, New Hampshire, with a blast: *"Born down in a dead man's town . . ."* To the thunderous strains of Bruce Springsteen, enter Dick Gephardt, who did not look like the saxophonist in the E Street Band.

A week before, in an unheated railroad shed, in a small town about an hour's drive north of Des Moines, Gephardt had mounted a platform to speak. Behind him was a gigantic yellow diesel locomotive, draped with two American flags, a monument of industry at a standstill. "What this election is all about is fundamental, basic change." His words formed a vaporous cloud. It was zero degrees. "We're losing our standard of living. The middle class is starting to shrink. Those just interested in paper profits don't want change." Then: "It's your fight, too!" The huddled crowd of about a hundred rural folk—in overalls, heavy wool coats and baseball caps featuring the logos of feed companies—looked as though they had been drawn by Central Casting for a black-and-white, Depression-era movie—or a music video. But they were quite real, and so were their hard times. "It's your fight, too!" they began to chant. "It's your fight, too!"

Now, in Manchester, in his suite in the Holiday Inn, Gephardt reached for a phrase that would strike the right note. "I'm talking about an American rejuvenation, a renaissance—an American *perestroika.*"

For more than a year, Gephardt had spent almost all his time in Iowa, campaigning as if it were a huge congressional district. He was ambitious and earnest, echt midwestern in his middleness, from neighboring Missouri, an Eagle Scout known early in his political career as "Little Dickie Do Right." As the joke went, he was Dick, his wife was Jane, they had two kids and were missing only a dog named Spot. In Iowa, he shook tens of thousands of hands, patted the snouts of animals at county fairs and cooked pancakes at church socials. He even rented an apartment and moved his elderly mother in. His speeches were about how hard he was campaigning. By December 1987, he had exhausted the appeal of his state-of-the-art ordinariness and was in last place.

On the day after Christmas, Gephardt flooded the airwaves with a new message: "They work their hearts out every day trying to turn out a good product at a decent price. Then the Korean government slaps on nine separate taxes and tariffs. And when that government's done a $10,000 Chrysler K car costs $48,000. It's not their fault we can't sell our cars in a market like that—and I'm tired of hearing American workers blamed for it." If Gephardt were president, the Koreans would "be left asking themselves: How many Americans are going to pay $48,000 for one of their Hyundais? It's your fight, too."

Gephardt flourished none of the self-congratulatory rhetoric declaring the Cold War over and America victorious. He did not grasp the ending of the Cold War as such; it existed in his cosmology mostly as a cause of American decline. The new threat was a product of mishandling the old threat; the specter of the hammer-and-sickle was replaced with the specter of the Rising Sun. "The United States and the Soviet Union," he said in a speech, "are having an arms race and the Japanese are going to win."

The American Century had come full circle. It began with Japan's defeat and ended with Japan's ascendance. Its success was emphatically not an American success story. Japan contradicted a central tenet of conservatism that markets unfettered by government work most efficiently. "In Japan and many other modern industrial nations," Gephardt told the voters, "government and industry and labor have produced a new model of cooperative enterprise. . . . We're eating their economic dust."

Reagan's economic policies, intended to demonstrate the "magic of the marketplace," had in fact empowered Japan. Their first phase produced the worst recession since the 1930s and destroyed much of the U.S. manufacturing base. Their second phase produced the high dollar which priced U.S. producers out of the world market, enabling Japan to secure its gains and expand. The third phase produced the cheap dollar which turned the American market into a firesale for the now cash-rich Japanese. "The global economic order has rapidly and radically changed," warned Gephardt, "and unless we change and adapt our thinking toward the competition, America could become a modern-day Great Britain."

The Cold War had been essential to the rise of the Japanese trading state. According to Cold War strategy, Japan was our ally, situated on the Asian flank facing the USSR, dependent for its defense upon us. "Free trade" was a euphemism for American dominance. The center of U.S. economic planning, as it were, was located in the Pentagon and concerned with the development of technology only as it applied to weapons. In the meantime, the center of Japanese planning, MITI, was devoted to developing technology for commercial uses. By the late 1980s, Japan seemed to be recreating on a new basis the Greater Asian Co-Prosperity Sphere, the dream of empire that World War II had thwarted. Befitting its new status as a great power, Japan was even building its own weapons industries to extend its mercantile dominance; it was unclear that the U.S. advantage in even that area could long be maintained. "All the new missiles, the bombs and the throw-weight will prove to be nothing more than grim adornments on a nuclear Maginot Line—if behind them there is a weakened economy and the trends are moving against America," Gephardt said in Iowa.

It was not Soviet competition that had reduced American industry after industry to ruins. It was not Soviet bankers who had gained supremacy in the world's financial markets. It was not Soviet interests buying up American corporations and large chunks of American real estate. It was not the Soviet lobby that was unfolding the long green to the wise men of both parties in Washington.

Since the dropping of the atomic bomb on Hiroshima, American insecurity had been expressed in politics mainly as a military issue: Kennedy's missile gap, Reagan's window of vulnerability. Gephardt recast the theme from a military comparison with the Soviets to an economic comparison with our trading partners. "It's the economic gap," he said. "The real competition of the next twenty or thirty years is economic and not military."

The theme of The Future that had seemed golden to Gary Hart just four years earlier had dimmed. Postindustrial society was not, after all, paradise. It was a place of new inequalities and difficulties. And it was not somewhere over the horizon, but in front of our eyes. "The transition can go on for years," said Gephardt. "Takeover attempts, trashing companies—it's killing us." He saw the Wall Street rentiers as red-suspendered vampires, "making money out of the decline of the American economy." Though Gephardt railed against "the establishment," his morality play was only in part a class conflict. It was also a sector conflict between those who speculate and those who produce. His iconography featured hard hats and overalls, but the sector conflict was not necessarily between high-tech and low-tech industries, because even high-tech industries were falling before the Japanese onslaught. Thus Gephardt introduced economic nationalism into American politics.

He began far from thoughts of an American perestroika. Gephardt grew up in the "Scrubby Dutch" section of St. Louis, so called because of the custom of its ethnic German residents of washing their sidewalks. Gephardt's father had lost a family farm and a job as a milkman before he became a real estate agent; his mother was a schoolteacher. He attended Big Ten schools: Northwestern and the University of Michigan Law School. After graduation, he joined a downtown St. Louis law firm and promptly plunged into local politics. In 1971, he was elected alderman; in 1976, he was elected to the Congress. His career path was straight and narrow.

There have been politicians like Gephardt in every generation, who have climbed the rungs of the ladder, mastering the conventions as they rose. Gephardt was of the postwar generation, but untouched by the transcendant if somewhat delusional movements of the 1960s; no one ever accused him, *pace* Springsteen, of being a "cool rocking daddy in the U.S.A." It was inconceivable to him to challenge the authority of his elders. Hart's James Dean-like rebellion against becoming a "little Hubert Humphrey" was beyond the younger Gephardt, who in 1968 supported Hubert Humphrey—not Robert Kennedy. Gephardt was on the lookout for mentors, not lodestars. Once in the House, Gephardt was taken under the wing of Richard Bolling, the most influential member of the Missouri delegation. For his protégé, Bolling secured a coveted seat on the Ways and Means Committee—another rung.

On issue after issue, Gephardt followed the prejudices of his district. He cosponsored amendments to outlaw abortion and busing—and to mandate prayers in public schools. He assailed President Carter for granting amnesty to Vietnam War draft resisters; he voted for the neutron bomb; and he adroitly positioned himself to catch the wave of the business reaction of the late 1970s, teaming up with an ambitious young congressman across the aisle, David Stockman, to draft a bill countering Carter's effort at hospital cost containment. When Reagan became president, Gephardt voted for the regressive supply-side tax program. More, he criticized Reagan from the right, calling him "a disappointment to those in the Congress who represent constituencies for whom . . . social issues represent the government's resolve to reverse the misguided social trends of the '60 and '70s."

Gephardt had plodded upward by the most traditional means while casting himself as a representative of the new breed, beyond the ideological disputes of the past. His "centrism" was carefully calibrated between a fading liberalism and a rising conservatism. It tended to follow the direction set by the right but was presented as an alternative for Democrats. It was less an ideological position itself than a constantly shifting effort at positioning.

Then, caught in the crossfire between the White House and the House, which was the only Democratic stronghold throughout most of the 1980s, Gephardt began to evolve and to rise. In 1982, he was chosen by the leadership as a key member of the task force that advocated an industrial policy. But after Mondale's defeat, Gephardt retreated behind the label of "terminal centrist." He became the first chairman of the Democratic Leadership Council, a newly organized group of mostly southern Democrats who tended to blame liberalism for the Democrats' failure to gain the White House. The "centrists" were chasing a middle ground that existed only in abstraction. They believed that the Democratic Party needed to suppress its liberalism and that reining in entitlement programs that benefited Democratic constituencies would allow them to escape Mondale's fate. By seizing upon domestic budget-cutting as the homeopathic cure for the Democratic malaise, they cast their own party's base as the problem. But this was not all the medicine they prescribed. The "centrists" also believed that Democrats could overcome their image of weakness only by demonstrating their bona fides as Cold War conservatives. For all their counseling of strength, the "centrists" were the Democrats most intimidated by Reaganism.

Just as in the political drift immediately after Reagan's reelection

Gephardt seemed to emerge as a leading representative of "centrism," he was caught by another tide: the battering that basic industry in his district was taking at the hands of foreign competition. In 1985, he proposed the Gephardt Amendment, which would automatically trigger negotiations and retaliation, left unspecified, against U.S. trading partners that were running a surplus. It was this measure, a congressman's hastily drawn response to a local crisis, that became the foundation of his presidential platform.

Among Gephardt's greatest political qualities were his ability to listen and his tenacity. He listened so well to his colleagues that they elected him chairman of the House Democratic Caucus. As the leader of a group whose center of gravity was liberal, Gephardt made a number of new adjustments. Gephardt's "centrism" was not entrenched after all, much less "terminal." On issue after issue—abortion, prayer in school, arms control—his position moved leftward. And he never voted for contra aid—the centrists' litmus test. He was becoming a national Democrat. Above all, he was concerned with the trade issue. The more he worked on it, the more he believed in it. In Iowa, Gephardt's campaign honed his message into effective thirty- and sixty-second spots. His victory in the primary seemed to lift him into orbit, but his moment dissipated almost as swiftly as it had appeared. In New Hampshire, Michael Dukakis was the favorite son of the local Democratic Party, largely because of proximity and his opposition to the Seabrook nuclear reactor. John Sasso was a practiced poker player, known for winning with low hands. And New Hampshire was always the trump card. No matter what happened, even Sasso's removal from the campaign, New Hampshire was there for Dukakis. Gephardt was now attempting to defy gravity.

He also found himself in the white-hot spotlight of ideological controversy. His challenge to the myth of free trade aroused a ferocious opposition that saw in this polite, boyish figure a barbarian at the gate. Editorials in almost every major newspaper, conservative and liberal alike, denounced him. A slight tremor of anxiety swept through Wall Street. In Washington, the lawyer-lobbyists whose client lists bulged with Japanese firms vigorously campaigned against him at dinner parties.

All of Gephardt's switches on the issues were dredged up by the press. Was he adjusting his positions only to the exigencies of the moment? What did he really believe? He excoriated "the establishment," but he was a ranking member of the congressional leadership. How could he be an outsider when he was an insider? The press, reflecting the Washington opinion-making elites, refused to accept his candidacy as genuine.

Gephardt was a model of rectitude in his financial affairs. But how could a congressman compete for president? If he were a governor, he could draw upon the resources of his state. If he were a senator, his face familiar on national television, he could call on Manhattan and Los Angeles, Chicago and Houston. But Gephardt's claim to a national base was through his House colleagues. Throughout the 1980s, the congressional Democrats, led by Tony Coelho, had tried to reach financial parity with the well-heeled Republicans by using their incumbency to tap the political action committees and corporate lobbyists. The Gephardt campaign was perforce dependent on these methods. One planeload of congressmen journeying to Iowa to stump for Gephardt was subsidized by the corporate PAC-men, some of whom came along for the ride. "It's our flight, too," said one of them, riffing on Gephardt's class struggle slogan.

His campaign in Iowa was ingeniously but narrowly conceived, spun out of the Gephardt Amendment and his consultants' scripts. Both had their merits, but they lacked conceptual depth and political breadth. What worked in Iowa did not necessarily apply elsewhere. And the pace and stress of the campaign were hardly conducive to intellectual growth and deliberation.

Gephardt's campaign decided that the only way he could finish second in New Hampshire and preserve his candidacy was to act as the magnet for the anti-Dukakis, antitax vote. Gephardt took the age-old tack of campaigning in New Hampshire against high taxes in Massachusetts. Instead of downplaying his vote for Reagan's economic program, Gephardt emphasized it. He was now campaigning both against the consequences of Reaganism and, in effect, as one of the early supporters of Reaganomics. This had the effect of reinforcing the image of inconsistency he was trying to avoid.

Senator Paul Simon of Illinois, edged out by Gephardt in Iowa, scraped together his remaining funds and launched a television salvo aimed directly at Gephardt's changes of positions, or "conversions," as Simon called them. The helium rapidly began to escape from Gephardt's balloon. In the Highway Hotel, a mammoth wooden structure in Concord, Gephardt called an impromptu press conference in the crowded lobby after the New Hampshire Democratic dinner. He mounted a staircase to speak and take questions from the press. His face was flushed and he had an air of embattlement. "Enough is enough on these negative ads," he said. "To put it very straight: enough is enough!" Simon immediately convened his own press conference in the same lobby, about ten yards away. "Last week, he stressed his opposition to Reagan's tax bill," the senator observed. At the same time, "Saturday Night Live" veteran Al Franken, noted for his uncannily accurate Simon impression, was holding another press conference in Simon's shadow. Amid the din, Gephardt was saying, "I'd like to know where Governor Dukakis's policy on trade is." Dukakis, as it happened, was not absent. He was winding his way along the perimeter of the crowd, fleeing the scene. "Excuse me," he said quietly. "Excuse me."

Gephardt finished second, with 20 percent, and returned to his populist theme in the next primary state, South Dakota—which resembled Iowa in its economic troubles. He also put a negative ad on the air attacking Dukakis for once suggesting that hard-hit farmers should grow Belgian endive. Dukakis had been ahead in South Dakota before the ad ran; after several days of play, Gephardt emerged the victor.

Super Tuesday loomed; Gephardt was still roaming the countryside; and Dukakis was bruised. He responded to attacks only after losing, and he had lost again. Before South Dakota, he had been hesitant about going negative, but after the loss his handlers showed him the Gephardt ad. "Wow!" he said. "This is tough." They had already prepared a double-barreled response: an ad listing Gephardt's PAC contributors and another by Dan Payne featuring a Dick Gephardt lookalike flip-flopping across the screen.

To Dukakis, Gephardt's campaign had become unworthy. The governor, in a conversation with David Nyhan of the *Boston Globe,* noted that Gephardt's pollster happened to be Ed Reilly, the very same pollster who had worked for the nefarious Ed King. This was not merely a campaign for president. It was something more. It was the continuation of "The Rematch." "Go ahead," said Dukakis. Soon, the negative ads were unreeling.

Gephardt's funds were low, his ads few. Senator Albert Gore of Tennessee criticized him for inconsistency while borrowing his tough trade talk. And the Dukakis campaign blanketed the flip-flop ad over five states where Gephardt couldn't afford a single ad of his own.

Iowa had been a false start for the campaign. In Washington, there was smugness about Gephardt's fall. Economic nationalism was dismissed as only the manipulative gimmick of a shallow candidate. There was little sense that the issue was simply in its nascent stage.

Gephardt had wanted to define the post-Cold War world. What he lacked was an analysis of the Cold War. He could partly describe the symptoms of America in decline, but his amendment, which aroused such wrath, was simply a mechanism to negotiate trade surpluses among nations overridden by corporations whose branches extended across all borders. The Gephardt Amendment was a small thing to have provoked such a big reaction, but the reaction showed that he had touched a sensitive nerve.

The controversy he had started over international affairs was circumscribed by the trade issue. Gephardt spoke to issues of global economics, but not to broad topics of global politics. To the extent that he understood the Cold War, he saw it as a matter of military hardware. Early in the campaign, in August 1987, he jabbed at Dukakis: "We can't be against every weapons system and win the presidency. I don't know what he is for." As the campaign heated up, Gephardt also became a critic of the "arms race." Both of Gephardt's positions reflected the debate within the Democratic Party since the Vietnam War more than the actual state of U.S.–Soviet relations. One had to have a deeper grasp of world politics and ideology to know why and when the American Century and the Cold War were over. His ambition was limited by its narrow character, which had brought him high on the political ladder but had not prepared him for the ideological debate he aroused.

For two generations, an attractive, ambitious politician did not have to invent first principles. The framework was already in place. The hero of most of the candidates, John F. Kennedy, had appeared heroic only against the ground of the Cold War, which was a given. Now that the sharp lines and primary colors of that were fading, the man in the arena had to create another play.

After the campaign, Gephardt became the House majority leader, replacing Coelho, and was in line to become the next Speaker of the House. The most powerful Democratic politician to have run in 1988, he defined his agenda in 1990 precisely as connecting the ending of the Cold War to "a world in which economic competition will take precedence over military conflict."

II

Dick Gephardt had been Michael Dukakis's strongest opponent, but on Super Tuesday he won only his home state. Dukakis's victories in seven out of the nineteen primaries on that day, more than any other Democrat, were made possible by his money, his negative ads and his careful targeting of dozens of media markets—not by any particular message. Gephardt's campaign reinforced in Dukakis, according to his advisers, his sense that having an emotional message was dangerous. He believed that his organization in the field had made his victories possible, that this proved his competence. He thought he now had only to walk across the room and open the door to the nomination.

Illinois was next. Behind the door stood Paul Simon, who had already acknowledged his defeat after New Hampshire. Resting in a Chicago hotel room, Simon saw the future as a dreary contest between Dukakis and Bush—"two kind of gray figures," he said, "people who are not going to do any great harm, but aren't going to do much great good either."

In his home state, Simon offered himself as an alternative to Dukakis and the other Illinois favorite son—Jesse Jackson. Simon's candidacy was positioned early in the campaign against "The Candidate"—the archetype from the Robert Redford film of the modern, ambitious young man in a hurry. With his bowtie and floppy ears, Simon was a character actor as the leading man. He ran the purest generational campaign of all, surrounding himself with evocations of the past. "I'm not a neo-anything," he proclaimed. His slogan: "Isn't it time to believe again?"

He was the son of a minister, a fervent believer in the Social Gospel, who settled in a small town in downstate Illinois, where he had edited a newspaper. Simon was the candidate from the age of the manual typewriter. His god was Lincoln. While serving in the Illinois legislature, he composed a book on the Great Emancipator's years in the same body, *Lincoln's Preparation for Greatness.*

Simon believed that if Reagan and Mondale had somehow exchanged personalities Mondale would have won the 1984 election. "The American people didn't reject Fritz Mondale's ideas," he said. In his stump speech, Simon denounced the Reagan era as the time of the "free lunch." Fracturing the keynote of Kennedy's inaugural, he declared, "let the word go forth that the lunch period is over." In his deep rumbling voice, he delivered his orations like an itinerant Shakespearean actor of the Victorian era: "We need [long pause] a government [pause] that [*fortissimo*] cares ." At his final rally in Des Moines, in the packed ballroom of the Savery Hotel, Simon called for "heart and soul . . . a government that has a heart that really cares." That "heart" had a name and Simon called it out like a train stop: "Huuuu-berrrrt Hummmmm-phreeeey!" Humphrey's death scene was recalled and the audience informed it had the power to resurrect his brand of liberalism. "He knew he was dying, and we knew he was dying . . . tears running down my cheeks . . . peace, freedom, opportunity . . . build it brick by brick." It was a wonderful example of the Social Gospel as political rhetoric. Alas, only Humphrey's legacy of domestic reform could be mentioned; his tragic captivity to Lyndon Johnson and his enthusiasm for the Vietnam War were passed over. For Democrats to have voted for Simon on a recollection of Humphrey would have been an act not of memory but of amnesia.

Simon advertised his consistency of beliefs as his strength. But he did not adequately explain his paradoxical support for massive public works projects and a balanced budget. He was running as if he believed in the economic programs of both the candidates of 1936: Franklin Roosevelt and Alf Landon. These dichotomies reflected the tensions within Simon himself—the strong government liberal and the Main Street tightwad. This seeming contradiction might have been partly bridged by a post-Cold War program that explained how to shift money spent on the military to domestic uses. But when the contradiction was pointed out by Simon's opponents during a debate in December 1987, he had no ready answer. Instead, he seemed befuddled. His falling star helped make possible Gephardt's brief rise.

In Illinois, the Democratic Party had long ago devised a formula for deflecting charges of hackdom and corruption bred by the Cook County machine: the Blue Ribbon ticket. At the top of the ticket, it slated impeccably clean reformers such as Adlai Stevenson and Paul Douglas. But Simon's political career was inconceivable without both the local liberal mythology and the machine.

The liberals and the regulars in the land of Lincoln were unimpressed with Michael Dukakis. His advertising in Illinois featured a crusty Boston bricklayers' union official who testified that Dukakis might not be someone to hoist a beer with but that he could get things done. One had to be there not to hear Dukakis's message; otherwise, there might be the presumption that something was said and that one had just missed it. To the Democrats of Illinois, Dukakis was of virtually no interest whatsoever. They were convinced that the convention could still be brokered. If so, they wanted to be the brokers. A familiar and honorable method was at hand: the Blue Ribbon ticket. Paul Simon, once again, was their man. So Dukakis came to Illinois at seventeen points in the polls, spent a large sum of money and left at seventeen points.

The huge "Unity '88" Illinois state Democratic dinner provided Simon with the occasion for a valedictory and a premonition: "If we listen to the siren song of those who want us to abandon our traditions, we lose more than the election. We will lose our soul."

Simon's victory tolled his defeat. But Illinois also showed that Dukakis lacked the stature to claim a big state, even in the wake of his win on Super Tuesday. The primary was held as if it were about local politics. Dukakis continued to believe he had only to present himself to win; by acting as if he were inevitable he would become so, if not in Illinois then in Michigan.

His campaign was fixed on the goal of finally finishing off Gephardt, who had skipped Illinois for a last stand in the Michigan caucuses. But, impoverished, Gephardt's campaign was gasping for breath. Dukakis, still flush, was now accumulating the big endorsements. With Gephardt blocked at every turn, Dukakis felt assured of victory in Michigan and a straight path to the nomination.

In the vacuum of his inevitability, huge crowds, unexpected crowds, electrified crowds, suddenly materialized. But they were not gathering for Michael Dukakis.

"I am!" called the speaker.

"I am!" the crowd responded.

"Somebody!"

"Somebody!"

This speaker, too, was looking ahead to the Michigan results.

9

The Cat in the Hat

I

Within sight of the White House, at the elegant Jefferson Hotel on Sixteenth Street, the establishment of the Democratic Party gathered for a private breakfast with the winner of the Michigan caucuses. Those present had tried to alter the rules of nomination to reduce the chances of an insurgent. But now they paid homage to the one who had upended Michael Dukakis and would clearly challenge him until the last ballot at the convention.

"I don't claim to be speaking for everyone here, but I have been moved by your message," said John White, the former chairman of the Democratic National Committee. "I've been waiting for years for a candidate who wasn't so surrounded by polltakers and advisers. In this campaign, it's just you and your very strong message."

All eyes then turned to Clark Clifford, the ultimate Wise Man of the party, who had been the chief strategist of Harry Truman's 1948 victory and as the White House counsel had been very much "present at the creation" of the postwar order. Now eighty-one years old and silver-haired, the image of Romanlike gravity, he rose from his seat and led a standing ovation.

The guest of sudden honor, the illegitimate son of a black teenaged mother from a small town in South Carolina, born under the sign of Jim Crow, Jesse Louis Jackson ("That's my third name—I wasn't born 'Jesse Jackson' "), grinned from ear to ear.

Perhaps no other political figure, black or white, was more desperate to be visible than Jesse Jackson. He spoke of his fear of being made an "invisible man"—a reference to Ralph Ellison's classic novel of black identity. In fact, since he first brought himself to the attention of Martin Luther King, Jr. and his associates in Selma, Alabama, in 1965, he had become impossible to ignore. He could be seen at King's funeral and unseating Mayor Richard J. Daley of Chicago as a delegate at the 1972 Democratic convention, negotiating with the executives of major corporations and the commissioner of baseball, speaking before a special session of the Alabama legislature, featured on "60 Minutes," "Nightline," and every evening news show, praying with the Pope, marching at the head of a thousand demonstrations, and meeting with presidents of the United States and dozens of potentates. "I've met more world leaders live than George Bush has dead," said Jackson.

Jackson had more than one vision; he had many. But, above all, he had a portable sense of his relevance. He was willing to go places and do things that would never occur to others. His mind had a remarkable facility for synthesizing the most disparate elements and transforming them into even more remarkable happenings. "You need Action Jackson!" he told campaign crowds, presenting himself as a black Rambo. The presidential campaign of 1988 gave him a series of almost unending backdrops. "Drama, that's what it's all about," he told his press secretary.

Jackson did not distinguish between himself and the masses of the dispossessed because he believed he had a special destiny. He compared himself to many heroes in representing "the emotions and self-respect and inner security of the whole race." Black America was Jesse Jackson and Jesse Jackson was black America. This conviction lay at the heart of his political identity. His power drew upon his almost mystical sense of self, which many blacks understood as the vessel of their hopes, seeing him as the deliverer from all that afflicted them.

Jackson's sense of urgency transformed itself into enormous energy. His physical stamina and ability to function without sleep were extraordinary. He tired everyone around him. As advisers nodded off, he grew stronger. He had a gift for language—for the witty turn of phrase and the cadenced epithet, unrivaled in eloquence by anyone in public life, except Mario Cuomo. Jackson also was able to make complex issues accessible to the ordinary person. He countered Reagan's image of the poor—a "welfare queen" in her Cadillac—with an equally vivid and truer line: "They take the early bus." His eloquence, especially in contrast to the other candidates' banality, made him seem as though he were the only one speaking to the issues.

He was a nonstop talker who called friends at all hours to spin out his latest notions. Then he would call someone else, one of his hundreds of confidants, from famous black comedians to the editors of major newspapers, soliciting advice, trying out ideas, probing, ruminating. He exhausted anyone who let him. He called before dawn and after midnight; he had more time than anyone because he slept less. Jackson was not a reader of books, though he did read the memos given him by aides. When asked by a reporter why he did not read books, he explained that he learned by talking—endless, constant talking.

The memoirs and recollections of some of his former aides are tales of physical and mental depletion, descriptions of feeling drained—"Jacksonian abuse," according to Elizabeth O. Colton, his former press secretary. In these accounts, the man of history is invariably depicted as impatient, thoughtless, selfish, petty and rude. History as told by valets may be trivial, but these portraits of Jackson were not completely unimportant. He had come from afar and seemed to be going far. But he was in such a rush that he was tearing past those around him, even those helping him on his way. His abrupt manners were another aspect of his sense of destiny.

Many Democrats cursed his existence and believed that their difficulties would be lessened to the degree that he could somehow be made less visible. But he was the shadow of their own failures. In the 1988 campaign, he had had his moment only because of the other candidates' inability to close on the nomination. The vacuum existed independently of Jackson. He merely entered an empty space. If he mocked, mimicked, haunted and threatened them, it was because of what they were not doing. No matter how often or nicely the pillars of the establishment asked him to *please* behave, he always found a way to torment them with a disturbance of the peace. The social critic Gerald Early has described the psychological needs that drove Jackson to become a very visible man:

> His compulsion is to have what white men have: complete and relentless control over his own fate and everyone else's. It is a kind of remorseless and single-minded envy that drives him. This is what he

preaches to the "locked out": Act, don't react; make deals, not compromises. Jackson is our real-life Cat in the Hat. . . . He strolls into the lives
of some middle-class white kids, invades a white middle-class home, and
wreaks havoc for a time while the parents (Mother's absence is particularly emphasized) are away. . . . Everyone as a child has read this
subversive stuff that, in effect, predicts the coming of, to borrow a title
from an old Art Ensemble of Chicago album, *A Jackson in Your House.*
. . . And so like the Cat in the Hat, Jackson brings his chaos and his
VOOM! and his pinko cat ring, as well as his aching ambition and his
hatred of inadvertence, into our house.

"If they had my budget, they could not compete," Jackson said of
the other candidates, campaigning in Michigan. "If I had their budget,
they would have to surrender." Certainly, the first half of that statement was unassailable.

Jackson's pulpit was the television camera lens, filling the space that
was once held by stable political parties. His movement was like a
religion of the oppressed, inseparable from its messianic leader. It was
large enough to hold him up, but too small to raise him to the top.
Jackson overwhelmed his movement, but he could never capture or
supplant the Democratic Party, which itself was too small to hold him
down and too large to let him rise to the top.

"The party of the Democrats has always been the party of innova-
tion," Clark Clifford said at the press conference in the lobby of the
Jefferson Hotel, with Jackson standing at his side. "It is possible that
Jesse Jackson may be the one bringing the innovation."

Thus the establishment hoped that Jackson could speak even for
them. They, too, wanted to be somebody again. They were willing to
let this cat in the hat into the house, if he could perform miracles as
he claimed. Perhaps, if he could inspire the vast party of the nonvoters,
nearly half the potential electorate, mostly of lower income, enough of
them might be brought into the Democratic Party to tip the scales
against the GOP. But the establishment saw Jackson's role differently
than he did. What the establishment saw as a way to gain a partisan
advantage, Jackson saw as part of a cosmic revolution. His nonnegotia-
ble demand was for a willing suspension of disbelief about his bid for
the presidency, an office he had only the remotest chance of winning.
They would allow him in their house to juggle fishbowls on broomsticks
so long as they were still in control at the end of the day. But he
unleashed the chaos for his own reasons.

The reality was that for decades Jackson had been running an "endless campaign," as he put it, for an office for which there is no election—president of black America. Becoming president of the United States makes someone the leader of the Free World. But becoming president of black America would confer the leadership of the Third World, the vast majority of the people on the planet—"the real world," as Jackson called it in his speech to the 1988 Democratic convention, in contrast to both the first and second worlds. More than any other candidate, his conception of domestic politics was shaped by his international perspective.

What made it possible for Jackson to present himself as a global statesman also defined his limitations. He was boxed in by his Third World vision. Jackson urged recognition of the Cold War's end, but failed to account for the centrality of U.S.–Soviet relations, or the importance of Europe generally, except as neocolonial overseer. Only the Third World, at whose head stood black America, was, as he put it, "real."

Jackson presented himself as the spokesman for the oppressed, beseeching the powers that be. His imagery of both the powerless and the powerful was vivid, but he had no effective image of, much less rapport with, the majority. He was limited by the very affinities that gave him his political magnetism. He identified with the farmer who was foreclosed, not the one who wasn't; the worker who was unemployed or underemployed, not the one bringing home the adequate paycheck; the homeless begging for spare change at a train station, not the homeowners returning to the boroughs and the suburbs.

His restless, expansive ego, which had carried him from obscurity into the forefront of a presidential campaign, also encapsulated him. Whenever his ambitions were blocked by the political process, he attempted to turn the tensions within himself into the central issue of the Democratic Party. He demanded that everyone share his crisis.

Jackson charged every setback he suffered as a further slight against the wretched of the earth. Like Caliban in *The Tempest*, he believed: "For I am all the subjects that you have." But he was a Caliban in a brave new world that was missing a Prospero.

For an instant, though, as Jackson rushed out of the Jefferson Hotel into the bright sunlight of early spring to catch a campaign plane to Wisconsin, the site of the next primary, he seemed to have surrendered himself to the illusion that he might win it all, that Caliban could become Prospero.

II

To locate Jackson's motivation one need look no farther than the circumstance of his birth. "You are God's child," he told crowds. "I was born out of wedlock. . . . I only slept in my daddy's house one night. . . . You are somebody. . . . Call me illegitimate, call me bastard. . . . You are somebody. . . . You are God's child."

He was born in 1941 to Helen Burns, a teenager, in Greenville, South Carolina. His father, Noah Robinson, was a high school junior, already married, who lived next door. After Jesse was born, his mother was voted out of the Springfield Baptist Church by the congregation, her story a southern black version of *The Scarlet Letter.* Two years later, she married Charles Henry Jackson, who adopted her son. Jesse Jackson later claimed that his stepfather was a janitor and his mother a maid, and that "I had to steal to survive." In fact, Charles Jackson was a post office worker, Helen a beautician, and Jesse earned extra money collecting tickets at the movie theater and caddying at the country club. "We were never poor," said Charles Jackson. "We never wanted for anything." If Jesse felt a special mark of rejection it was because of his illegitimacy, compounded by segregation. From his background, Jackson brought an intense identification with all those branded as outcasts and underdogs. He felt that identification so strongly that he exaggerated his own disadvantages. As "God's child," he felt he had an uncommon, even a divinely inspired, destiny. Jesse, of course, is another name for Jesus. And Jackson told many of his aides that Jesus, like himself, had been born illegitimate.

Jackson excelled in high school and won a scholarship to the University of Illinois, where he discovered that as a black he could not join a fraternity or play quarterback for the football team. He transferred to the North Carolina Agricultural and Technical State College, where he became the student body president and the star quarterback. He also became a leader of the local sit-in movement to end segregation.

He decided to become a minister and was accepted at the Chicago Theological Seminary. But he refused to write papers for his classes, demanding instead to present them as oral reports. One of his professors remembered him as "a tremendous con artist." (Jackson never received his degree in theology. Later, the seminary's granting him an honorary degree sparked a faculty revolt.)

In 1965, Jackson led twenty seminary students, all white, to Selma, Alabama, after Bloody Sunday, when hundreds of civil rights marchers were tear-gassed and beaten by Alabama Governor George Wallace's state troopers at the Edmund Pettus Bridge, and King issued a call to the nation's clergy for support. The new contingents gathered on the grounds of Brown's Chapel African Methodist Episcopal Church, where Jackson spontaneously mounted the steps to bark orders and, during an all-night vigil, delivered a speech. King's lieutenants were somewhat startled and annoyed by his audacity. Jackson implored Ralph Abernathy, King's second in command, to hire him for the staff of a new chapter of the Southern Christian Leadership Conference in Chicago. What little King had seen of the showboating Jackson he had not much liked. He agreed to the request only as a personal favor to Abernathy. Jackson left Selma before the march on Montgomery. Back in Chicago, he dropped out of the seminary. The civil rights movement, up until then, had been fought only on southern battlefields, winning impressive victories, creating the momentum that would end state-supported segregation and assure legal equality. Now King brought the Second Reconstruction to the next front, wheeling his forces to face de facto segregation in housing and education, and economic inequality in the North.

When King landed at Chicago's O'Hare airport, he was met by a black limousine provided courtesy of the local Baptist Ministers Conference. His chauffeur was Jesse Jackson. King was entering a world he did not know. In Chicago, Mayor Daley, who was no George Wallace, and black leaders, who were part of the local political machine, resented his intrusion. Marching on the neighborhoods of working-class white ethnics lacked the moral authority of the marches on the southern citadels of legal segregation.

Young Jackson was a minor player on King's Action Committee who occasionally took it upon himself to make policy statements to the press without prior approval. When Jackson was given the opportunity to introduce King at one event, he delivered a long speech preempting him. After a march on a blue-collar neighborhood in which King was hit in the head by a rock, Jackson announced that King would next lead a march into Cicero, a very tough white working-class town adjoining Chicago that had once been the headquarters of Al Capone. "If we don't go to Cicero, we can't go back to Mississippi," he said. "Some of us live in Mississippi, so by virtue of that logic, we're going into Cicero." Without warning, Jackson had laid King's credibility and prestige on the line. King felt he had little choice but to announce the next day that he would indeed march on Cicero. He was rescued from certain disaster only by Daley, who brought him into City Hall to announce a symbolic agreement on open housing, thereby rendering moot Jackson's "logic" and the reason for the march. Shortly afterwards King left Chicago, dejected and defeated.

Back in Atlanta, in his first meeting with the new executive director of the Southern Christian Leadership Conference, William Rutherford, a black Chicago businessman, King charged him with getting Jackson to shape up. "Dr. King was a very gentle person and a very patient person," Rutherford said, "and if he reached the point when he told me to either get rid of Jesse or to get him to toe the line, he was very seriously exercised by a number of things."

"He was always leery of Jesse," said Bernard Lee, who had been an adviser to King. "Martin used to say, 'He just simply does not know how to love.'"

On March 30, 1968, at an SCLC staff meeting at the Ebenezer Baptist Church, King asked for full support for a Poor People's Campaign. But Jackson argued with him. "If you are so interested in doing your own thing that you can't do what the organization is structured to do, go ahead," King told him. "If you want to carve out your own niche in society, go ahead, but for God's sake don't bother me."

The next week, on April 4, standing on the balcony of the Lorraine Motel, while Jackson stood below him, King's last words to him were that he should change his clothes and wear a tie to dinner. This was among the last conversations King was to have.

After the shot rang out and King crumpled, Jackson claimed that he rushed to his side and cradled his head, but his account has been disputed by others who were on the scene. Jackson told two members of King's entourage not to give press interviews. That night, an emergency meeting of King's disciples was convened. Jackson said he could not attend because he felt sick. Within hours, Jackson began giving interviews, saying he had been with King on the balcony when he was shot. The next morning, King's disciples were astonished to see Jackson live from Chicago on NBC's "Today Show," wearing a turtleneck that he said was caked with the martyr's blood. Hours later, still wearing the bloodstained shirt, Jackson addressed the Chicago City Council. "I come here with a heavy heart because on my chest is the stain of blood from Dr. King's head," he said. "He went through, literally, a crucifixion. I was there. And I'll be there for the resurrection."

Jackson sought the transfer of charismatic power by the medium of blood—and publicity. Two days before King's funeral, Jackson met with Don Rose, a Chicago public relations specialist who had helped King, to plot his press strategy. Jackson used all the events and ceremoniès surrounding King's death to vault himself to national prominence. In this blaze of attention, he made his claim on the apostolic succession.

III

A month after King's death, a Poor People's caravan of thousands wound its way across the country, led by a mule train, ending in Washington at a tent-site on Independence Mall called Resurrection City. Jesse Jackson, whose opposition to the event had provoked a lashing from King, tried to upstage Ralph Abernathy, King's successor as the head of the SCLC, by anointing himself the "mayor" of Resurrection City. Rain soon turned the encampment into a sea of mud. It had no unifying purpose and its poverty-stricken residents began to reproduce the squalor from which they had sought to escape. On June 22, they were routed by tear gas after rocks and bottles were thrown at passing cars. At 2:20 A.M., Jackson ordered them to disperse. "Nobody has been killed!" he shouted into the night.

After Resurrection City collapsed in a shambles, Jackson returned to Chicago, which was to be his base for the following twenty years. It was there he sought his "own niche." He now had himself introduced at his speeches as the "Black Messiah." At his organization's dinner he appeared onstage to the strains of "Jesus Christ Superstar." In his headquarters he displayed two portraits of himself and King. One had King in a dim background with Jackson in the bright foreground. The other featured black silhouettes of King's and Jackson's heads, side by side. What Jackson gained from King was more than Gandhian strategies and tactics, more than the application of theology in a fallen world. His politics were now built on a symbolic christology, with King representing the crucifixion, Jackson the resurrection. Even before King's murder, he had had this idea in mind; he had issued a leaflet, under the imprimatur of the SCLC, advertising a King speech, that showed a series of steps with King at the bottom, Jackson higher up, and then the cross. "At least," said King to an aide who had shown him the circular, "he put the good Lord over him."

When Jackson's biographer, Barbara Reynolds, told him that she had called him a demagogue, he retorted: "Don't you realize Jesus was a demagogue?"

In the period of disillusionment following King's death integrationism was eclipsed by Black Power. Since the Civil War, the pendulum for blacks had swung between these two poles. "There faces the American Negro therefore an intricate and subtle problem of combining into one object two difficult sets of facts," wrote W.E.B. Du Bois. The tension he described was that between being black and being American. When the quest for equality has stalled, black nationalism has been the reaction.

Jesse Jackson put on a dashiki and grew an afro, but his black nationalism was always a matter of ambiguous signals. He never descended into the romance of black leather jackets and shotguns. At most, he led crowds in a new chant: "What time is it? Nationtime!" But what did "nationtime" mean?

When King had departed Chicago he left behind a local chapter of an organization called Operation Breadbasket, which Jackson turned into a vehicle of economic black power. He demanded that corporations sign "covenants" to increase their number of black contractors and franchisers or else face boycotts. Unlike affirmative action, which had the force of federal law and was building a black new class, these concessions had little impact on the black community beyond the businessmen who profited. Wringing "covenants" from corporations afraid of bad publicity was not a self-sustaining enterprise but gave scope to a charismatic leader. The black businessmen, in the meantime, became a financial source of Jackson's activities. In a way, it was a mimickry of the Daley machine.

Jackson the cultural nationalist devised two "Buy Black" holidays: a Black Christmas, featuring a "Black Soul Saint" who replaced Santa Claus, and a Black Easter. In 1970 he organized Black Expo, a fair of black businesses and artists whose theme was "Rhythm Ain't All We Got" and which attracted hundreds of thousands of people. The next year, however, large sums of money from the event were found to be unaccounted for. Operation Breadbasket's parent organization, the SCLC, received a paltry share and was blocked from seeing the records. Jackson was suspended and then resigned. He founded his own group, PUSH, or People United to Save Humanity, which continued its demands for "covenants."

In 1973, when PUSH's coffers ran low, Jackson created a spinoff called PUSH for Excellence, devoted to motivating black high school students. His approach emphasized a pledge to study two hours every night. "Nobody can save us from us but us," he told cheering assemblies. Jackson raised millions from foundations, the city of Los Angeles and the federal government. The program was widely hailed and featured on "60 Minutes," but then a federal audit revealed that more than $1 million was unaccounted for and that many of its planned activities had never gotten off the ground.

Jackson seemed now to be fashioning himself as a modern Booker T. Washington, stressing the themes of self-sufficiency and self-help. He also resembled Washington in his effort to become the nation's number one black leader by dominating the means of publicity and philanthropy. But in his private correspondence and then his public statements Jackson was beginning to cite occasionally the authority of a very different predecessor from either King or Washington—Malcolm X.

Malcolm X was a black separatist, the heir apparent to the Honorable Elijah Muhammad, the Prophet of Allah Himself and spiritual leader of the Nation of Islam, who preached that the only reason Allah had not yet destroyed America was the existence of the "so-called American Negro." Malcolm advocated the achievement of his goals "by any means necessary," though his violence was confined to a rhetoric which expressed what many blacks, in their anger and frustration, wanted to say but feared to. "I am for violence if non-violence means we continue postponing a solution to the American black man's problem—just to avoid violence," he said. He was their channel, in James Baldwin's phrase, for "fantasy revenge."

Malcolm's pilgrimages to Arab countries led to his breaking with the Black Muslims. He transformed the race war between blacks and the Devil White Man he formerly believed inevitable into an apocalyptic battle between the Third World and the West. "It is incorrect to classify the revolt of the Negro as simply a racial conflict of black against white, or as a purely American problem," he said. "Rather, we are today seeing a global rebellion of the oppressed against the oppressor, the exploited against the exploiter."

The idea of the Third World had its roots in anticolonialism, but depended on the first and second worlds being locked in conflict. The Third World was the offspring of the Cold War. It was officially proclaimed in Bandung, Indonesia, at the 1955 conference of "nonaligned" nations, recently emerged from colonialism. It superseded an older pan-Africanism. The new constellation conveyed a common, even universal, mission of state-building that masked the enormous differences among the states being built. Nonalignment, in truth, was an opportunistic strategy of underdeveloped countries for playing off one superpower against the other.

The idea of the Third World also evolved into political myth of national liberation movements that was partly a response to revolutionary prophesy in the industrial countries. In the Cold War, the god that failed was alive and well in places like Vietnam and Cuba which Karl Marx had dismissed as hopeless backwaters. The countryside (the Third World) would surround the metropole (the West), according to Mao's comrade, Lin Piao. According to Frantz Fanon, the Algerian theorist of revolutionary violence, " 'The last shall be first and the first last.' Decolonialization is the putting into practice of this sentence." "Two, three, many Vietnams," pledged Ché Guevara.

After splitting from the Muslims, Malcolm recreated himself as a Third World revolutionary leader. But at home he called now for registering black voters—ballots as well as bullets. He had a grandiose vision of entering "the mainstream of the political structure" with his Organization of Afro-American Unity as a "nonaligned" force. But this, too, was rhetoric rather than a viable politics—fantasy power laid over fantasy revenge. His plans were never to be developed. In February 1965, he was assassinated by Black Muslims for his crime of heresy.

Malcolm's influence fed on the despair following King's death, and his images of fantasy revenge took on greater and greater emotional force until he attained a stature among blacks second only to King. His fusion of black nationalism with Third Worldism provided the ideology for the militant wing of the black movement in the late 1960s and early 1970s, taken up by Stokely Carmichael, LeRoi Jones, and the Black Panther Party's Huey P. Newton and Eldridge Cleaver. Malcolm's views, however, remained fundamentally irreconcilable with King's. Nowhere was that plainer than on the issue on which they had reached their closest point.

In 1967, after much agonizing, King delivered one of his most powerful speeches—against the Vietnam War—declaring himself on the side of "shirtless and barefoot people" rising up against "old systems of exploitation and oppression" in a "world revolution." Unlike Malcolm, King's opposition to violence was absolute. Nor did he believe America was a thoroughly corrupt, damned country. On the contrary, he argued that America could lead the global "revolution of values," overcoming "a negative anti-communism" with "a positive thrust for democracy, realizing that our greatest defense against communism is to take offensive action in behalf of justice."

King connected his opposition to the war to the politics and morality of the civil rights movement. He noted that the slogan of his organization, the SCLC, was: "To save the soul of America." King did not think of American blacks as a Third World people in the enemy camp. To him, they were nothing less than full American citizens. "Now," said

King, "it should be incandescently clear that no one who has any concern for the integrity and life of America today can ignore the present war. . . . So it is that those of us who are yet determined that America *will* be are led down the path of protest and dissent. . . ."

Thus the radical differences between King and Malcolm were a reflection of Du Bois's "two difficult sets of facts." The highly problematic task of squaring them was taken up by Jesse Jackson. In 1970, he addressed the founding convention of a group called the Congress of African People that was conceived as a successor to Malcolm's Organization of Afro-American Unity: "Why [were] Martin and Malcolm shaking hands and smiling while some were still trying to make a decision as to which one of them we wanted when both of them belonged to us? Why? Why?" He would now try to become the leader of both camps, the heir of both the warrior and the preacher.

IV

The Congress of African People was the brainchild of LeRoi Jones—poet and playwright, spokesman of Third World revolution and, on occasion, an exponent of black anti-Semitism. "I got something for you . . . I got the extermination blues, jew boy." He had moved from Harlem to Newark (or "New Ark"), where, under his new African name, Amiri Baraka, he worked for the election of Kenneth Gibson, the city's first black mayor, using the rainbow as the symbol of racial unity. His plans for a successor group to the Congress—a National Black Political Convention—provoked broad discussion among black leaders.

Jackson, who had played a role at the Congress and had campaigned for Gibson's election at Baraka's behest, started to promote the need for a "third force" and for a black presidential candidacy. "We must have enough of a collective ego to seize the levers of power," he wrote in his syndicated column, "Country Preacher."

In March 1972, about eight thousand blacks flocked to Gary, Indiana, for the Baraka-inspired convention. Speaking to the delegates, Jackson called for a "Black Liberation Party." "Without the option of a black political party," he said, "we are doomed to remain in the hip pocket of the Democratic Party and the rumble seat of the Republican Party." He was booed by many black Democrats. The effort to forge a united front collapsed, even before the nationalists produced their provocative "Black Agenda," which, among other abrasive points, condemned school busing and Israel.

Unlike most other black leaders, Jackson did not endorse any of the Democratic candidates for president. He was much more involved in Chicago politics than in the national scene. While a student at the University of Illinois, Jackson had been granted an audience with Mayor Daley, who suggested that he perform political work in his ward in exchange for a good-paying job, such as toll collector. Daley treated the young man as he would any other young supplicant, but Jackson felt insulted and demeaned. A decade later, in opposing Daley, whom he took to calling "Pharaoh Daley," Jackson was also defining himself as the Mosaic deliverer of his people, carrying on where King had left off.

In 1971, Jackson tried to launch the Bread 'n' Butter Party, which would then nominate him for mayor. His idea was to graft the protest politics of the civil rights movement to the Chicago model. But his education in Chicago politics and his understanding of Daley's role were incomplete. Jackson conceived of his "party" as the exclusive vehicle of blacks and the poor. The evangelical preacher made no appeal to the mostly white Catholic majority. He did not see himself as a coalition leader, transacting business and thrashing out compromises among ethnic groups, neighborhoods and classes. In any case, Jackson failed to collect enough signatures to qualify for the ballot and received only thirty-five write-in votes. His ambition was not deterred. His abortive race for mayor prompted him to think about running for president. Briefly, he toyed with reviving his stillborn party in 1972 as a means to the candidacy. He dropped the idea when Representative Shirley Chisholm, without consulting him, plunged into the campaign, becoming the first black to run for president. But she did not run a protest or racial candidacy, which was contrary to Jackson's notions.

At the Democratic convention, Jackson gained some revenge against Daley. He joined with leading Chicago reformer alderman William Singer in unseating the Daley-led Illinois delegation, which had neglected to follow the new rules stipulating minority and female representation. Jackson then testified to an incredulous credentials committee that he was not a registered voter, though he was able to remain a delegate. (Singer and Jackson later fell out, Jackson referring to him as "the little Jew," and Singer regarding him as anti-Semitic.)

When George McGovern named the liberal Thomas Eagleton as his running mate, Jackson attained a momentary preeminence among black leaders at the convention by being the only one to denounce the choice because they were not consulted: "I want black people to know that their leadership has been humiliated and violated, but I am not too embarrassed to tell the truth. Let the others act as if they were in on the decision, but I say McGovern has been dishonest." His attack on McGovern had all the elements of the strategy he would deploy against subsequent Democratic nominees.

Afterwards, Jackson tried to get McGovern to acknowledge him and not Daley as *the* power broker in Chicago. When McGovern attempted to get Daley to work for the ticket, Jackson contended that McGovern's campaign was implicitly racist. Finally, in a fit of pique, Jackson announced that he would not campaign for McGovern. He threw himself into local elections, endorsing Republicans for four offices, including candidates for senator and governor. Jackson, in fact, had a previous political arrangement with GOP governor Richard Ogilvie. In exchange for Jackson's support and making trouble for the Democrats, Ogilvie made sure that the state dispensed contracts to black entrepreneurs who supported Jackson.

But Jackson's influence on the local scene was minor. He was really a national character with a Chicago address. He was far more rooted in Chicago-based media—Hugh Hefner's *Playboy*, John H. Johnson's *Ebony* and *Jet*, and the "Phil Donahue Show," which had been crucial in creating his national image—than in Chicago politics.

In the 1970s, Jackson's flights of rhetorical fancy into black nationalism dovetailed with his Republican flirtation. The party of Lincoln was looking for a few good blacks. And his calls for black self-reliance harmonized with Republican efforts to limit the commitment of government to black advancement.

In 1974, two days before the twentieth anniversary of the Supreme Court's *Brown v. Topeka Board of Education* decision, which struck down Jim Crow, Jackson gave credence to the crassest arguments against integration in a statement to the *Chicago Tribune:* "White people don't like to relate to it because of strong sexual overtones. . . . A lot of blacks have a hangup, too, because integration suggests we are inferior and only by sitting next to white people, having white teachers, can we be somebody."

The election of Jimmy Carter empowered the black leadership from Atlanta, who had distrusted Jackson and expelled him from the SCLC. His courtship of the Republicans, which had previously been confined to anti-Daley machine efforts in Chicago, went national. He became a well-received speaker at GOP functions. "Mutual need is the basis of an alliance," he told the Republican National Committee in a 1978 speech. He called black adherence to the Democratic Party "blind loyalty." "We've got to diversify our game plan," he said. "We are growing up now. We are maturing. We know how to split our tickets."

Soon, Jackson thrust himself into a controversy that fostered a bitter rift between blacks and Jews, the most loyal groups within the Democratic coalition. In January 1979, United Nations ambassador Andrew Young admitted that he had met with a representative of the Palestinian Liberation Organization, an act contrary to official U.S. policy. Unlike Jackson, Young had been an intimate of King's. Like King, he was suspicious of Jackson's motives. When Jimmy Carter ran for president, Young had been his most prominent black supporter and he had been rewarded with the U.N. post. At first, he claimed the meeting was accidental. Then he confessed he had not told "the whole truth." Within days, under pressure from Secretary of State Cyrus Vance, who viewed Young's action as insubordinate, he resigned.

Many black leaders interpreted Young's departure as a martyrdom for the greater cause: The highest-ranking black in the administration had been punished for dealing with a Third World liberation movement that was being suppressed by white imperialists. The complex rights and wrong of Mideast history were simplified into a black-and-white passion play. And Jews in general were cast in the role of "oppressor." "When there wasn't much decency in society Jews were willing to share decency," said Jackson, who was among the first to protest Young's resignation. "The conflict began when we started our quest for power. Jews were willing to share decency, but not power." Jackson's willingness to scapegoat the Jews for a decision that arose out of an internal administration dispute was the first public sign of a reflexive anti-Semitism that would later plague Jackson's political campaigns. It also showed that he made an unreflective connection between Third Worldism and the inchoate antagonism he felt toward American Jews.

The Young episode was only one of the many crises afflicting the Carter administration. In July 1979, the president summoned a parade of eminent leaders and intellectuals to Camp David to advise him on how to dispel the national "malaise." Jackson was among those invited. He was assigned to share a cabin with Sol Linowitz, the former ambassador to the Organization of American States, who had a detailed and profound knowledge of the problems of underdeveloped countries. The cabin had two bedrooms, one larger than the other. The winner of a coin toss would get it. "Heads," called Jackson. It came up tails. "Well, looks like I win," said Linowitz. "Yeah," replied Jackson, "you Jews nearly always do."

Two months later, a delegation of ten black leaders sponsored by the SCLC revived the Young affair by traveling to the Mideast, where they awarded Muammar Khadafy the newly created "Decoration of Martin Luther King," met with Yasir Arafat in Beirut and embraced him and his position.

Since King's death, Jackson had regarded the SCLC as a rival. Now it had seized the stage. But within weeks, Jackson had the spotlight back. He visited with Arafat, who threw his arms around him. Arafat smiled as Jackson advised him to respect "Israel's right to exist." Jackson then allowed hundreds of PLO supporters to carry him on their shoulders, chanting: "Jackson! Arafat!" He advised them to avoid terrorism and emulate the civil rights movement. His principal motive, however, was not located in the Mideast, but in black politics at home.

On this trip Jackson visited Israel's Yad Vashem memorial to the six million Jews who perished in the Holocaust. He had earlier complained about Jewish obsession with the Nazi genocide. Now he said he grasped "the persecution complex of many Jewish people that almost invariably makes them overreact to their own suffering, because it is so great." Then he flew to meet with Hafez al-Assad, the dictator of Syria, a contact that would later yield an important photo opportunity.

Jackson's sojourn in the Holy Land was not without its tangible rewards, for his preachments were followed by the passing of the collection plate. There will be "no black leader left" who would be willing to come to the aid of the Palestinian cause if there were no contributions from Arab states, he told a group of Arab-American businessmen. "We will all learn to recite the alphabet without three letters, P-L-O."

This sermon led Jackson to the pot of gold at the end of the crescent. His various organizations had already received an infusion of funds and more was forthcoming—$200,000 from the Arab League and $10,000 from Libya's chief diplomat in the U.S.

V

"Really, we're saying the same things," Jesse Jackson told Ronald Reagan about the latter's rhetoric of self-reliance as governor of California. When he was elected president, everything changed. Reagan's domestic policies of studied neglect fostered an increase of poverty and a broadening of the underclass, as well as a growth of hopelessness and rage among blacks. The defeat of Carter, who was seen as having a special sympathy, was taken as a direct rebuke of black interests. Jackson now had a national cause and purpose to make him a plausible politician.

The president battled against the extension of the Voting Rights Act, purged the U.S. Civil Rights Commission and rendered it impotent, argued for federal aid to segregated schools and colleges, stopped incentives for integrated housing, opposed affirmative action and slashed programs that benefited poor blacks. Millions of dollars in federal grants to civil rights groups suddenly dried up and their staffs were drastically cut. None of the old civil rights strategies worked and new ones were in short supply. A huge leadership vacuum among blacks opened up.

In Chicago, in the meantime, the Democratic machine had fallen on hard times since the death of Mayor Daley. The flight of whites from the city had increased and the black population approached 50 percent. In the 1983 Democratic primary for mayor, two white candidates split the white vote and Harold Washington, a black congressman who had been a Daley ally, narrowly emerged the victor. At his victory celebration, Jackson leaped on the stage into the spotlight. "We want it all! Super Bowl! Super Bowl!" he shouted. And he led the crowd in chants—"It's our turn now!"—making ethnic spoils the campaign's theme. But Washington needed 20 percent of the white vote in the general election to win. Jackson was a liability even before his unrestrained performance on primary night. Now he had to be kept under wraps for the rest of the race.

Still, Jackson took the Chicago experience as a personal sign of encouragement. In early 1983, he explored the possibility of running as an independent candidate for president. He even considered trying to take over the moribund organization of John Anderson, the moderate Republican who had run for president as an independent in 1980. But the difficulties of operating a third party, he discovered, were too great, and the openness of the Democratic primaries too alluring. Even before Washington's November victory, Jackson had become a candidate.

"From the outhouse to the statehouse to the White House!" He campaigned by mounting a series of tableaux vivants. In late December 1983, he took off for Syria to ask Assad to release a U.S. pilot, Robert Goodman, who had been shot down while bombing Syrian-held territory in Lebanon. Goodman happened to be black. At first, Assad gave no indication of what he might do. Jackson visited Goodman and then a Palestinian refugee camp. He tried to lead them in chants: "I am somebody!" And: "You may have been born in a slum, but the slum was not born in you!" They were bewildered. Finally, Assad released his prisoner into Jackson's care, undoubtedly to embarrass President Reagan. When they came home, however, Reagan invited Goodman and Jackson to the Rose Garden, where he congratulated the rescuer. Elevating Jackson increased the Democrats' potential disorder in an election year. "It is poetic justice that Lieutenant Goodman is from Portsmouth, New Hampshire," said Jackson. "There are political consequences in every moral act." In Syria, he saw himself as the central dynamic actor, Jackson of Arabia, though he had been made use of by calculating world leaders. Nevertheless, the event had the effect of making him a national figure at the beginning of the presidential campaign.

Jackson's campaign rhetoric took the form of a jeremiad. He cast the blacks in the same role the Puritans saw themselves playing as the Israelites on a mission in the wilderness. Blacks, according to Jackson, were the key to America's becoming Zion. Their progress measured the progress toward the promised land. If they failed, America had failed; if blacks were not equal, then America was not free. Jackson's purpose was to point out the path of true democracy and to make the country true to that path. The way to keep the Democrats true to themselves was to make them identify with the dispossessed and racially branded who, since the beginning of America, had been the index of the truth of our creed. Jackson claimed that he could once again turn the spiritual into a political revelation. He offered to make the Democrats into what the Republicans claimed to be, the arbiters of Americanism. In his announcement speech, he railed against the fall from grace under Reagan: "anti-black, anti-Hispanic, anti-civil rights, anti-human rights, anti-poor." He called for "new covenants."

These new covenants would be made underneath the rainbow, God's sign pledging that there will not be another flood. No matter what its race, class or religion, any group could belong to the Rainbow Coalition if it saw itself as oppressed like blacks or opposed to this oppression. This was hardly a Marxist notion, owing far more to the early Christian idea that an admission of earthly weakness led to an investment with heavenly power. The Rainbow Coalition was a political version of the ideal of integration. But Jackson's civil religion was intertwined with his Third Worldism. If he were triumphant, the Rainbow Coalition would stand at the head of more than America.

"My basic sensitivity to the Arabs is that I'm a Third World person," Jackson explained to *The Washington Post*. "I grew up in an occupied zone, Greenville, South Carolina, and had to negotiate with the superpower, really the colonial power, for the right to vote, for open housing, equal pay." Through metaphor, he assimilated American blacks into the Third World.

His slogan—"Our time has come!"—had been the slogan for the National Black Political Convention twelve years earlier. But few black elected officials supported Jackson. They did not want him to usurp their roles. The more he became a black Somebody, the more they would be diminished. Andrew Young, Mickey Leland, and most others endorsed Walter Mondale.

Almost as soon as the campaign began in earnest, Jackson's fusion of Third Worldism, anti-Semitism and black nationalism threw his candidacy into crisis—a crisis that has sharply limited his political possibilities ever since.

"Let's talk black talk," Jackson told a black *Washington Post* reporter in late January, in the cafeteria of the National Airport. He began to talk about "Hymie" and "Hymietown." The newspaper published his remarks, followed, after a brief pause, by an uproar. Jackson held a press conference at which he stood mute, as if dumbfounded. The one who did all the talking was Louis Farrakhan, who issued a warning to Jews: "If you harm this brother, it will be the last one you harm." The next day Jackson flew to a synagogue in New Hampshire to say that his talk about "Hymie" had been "innocent" and "wrong."

Farrakhan promptly issued a death threat against the *Post* reporter, then a few weeks later described Hitler as a "very great man" and several months after that called Judaism a "dirty" religion. Fantasy revenge was his specialty. He issued the terrifying warnings that Jackson did not want to make. But these threats were not about what would happen if God withdrew the sign of the rainbow. The peril of Farrakhan was not the fire next time; it was something even more extreme: complete and irrevocable separation of blacks from America. In the campaign, the real damage was to Jackson's message. If blacks were separate, they were out of the picture; they conceded their moral claim. By demanding secession, they abandoned the mission of equality. Still, it took weeks before Jackson was willing to distance himself from Farrakhan.

Farrakhan's presence in the Jackson campaign was not some bizarre happenstance but testimony to Jackson's ambition to represent the entire spectrum of black America.

Louis Farrakhan was born Louis Walcott in Boston. He first sought his fortune as a singer under the names "Calypso Gene" and "The

Charmer." Songs such as "A White Man's Heaven Is a Black Man's Hell" earned him some notoriety. Malcolm X personally recruited him into the Black Muslims, and he became one of his closest workers until Malcolm left the sect. Farrakhan then declared him "worthy of death." In spite of the conviction of Muslims for the murder, Farrakhan claimed that Malcolm was killed by the federal government. Afterwards, Farrakhan assumed Malcolm's place in the Muslim hierarchy. When Elijah Muhammad died, the group divided, with some following his subdued son and others following the fiery Farrakhan, who moved to Chicago's South Side, the home of the movement.

Jackson had known Farrakhan for a long time, since at least the 1972 National Black Political Convention, which they both addressed. A month later, Jackson flew to Harlem to express his solidarity with Farrakhan after a riot broke out and a policeman was killed on the street in front of his Muslim Temple No. 7. Farrakhan was important to Jackson's notion of himself as the national black leader and the unifying point for the black masses, transcending all differences. His alliance with Farrakhan was the manifestation of his belief that the ideas of Malcolm and King were compatible because the two men were both black. This was racial mysticism, thinking with the blood.

On Thanksgiving night 1983, Jackson had Farrakhan to his home. The would-be successor of King (and Malcolm) and the would-be successor of Malcolm (and Elijah Muhammad) cut a deal. Farrakhan agreed to provide Jackson with glowering members of his Fruits of Islam as security guards before the Secret Service was assigned, in exchange for becoming an officially designated "surrogate." He accompanied Jackson on his travels, warming up crowds before the candidate spoke. He also joined Jackson on his trip to Syria. Jackson had not made a mere alliance of convenience with Farrakhan to protect himself from the fanatical members of "Jews Against Jackson," led by extremist rabbi Meier Kahane, the Jewish counterimage to Farrakhan. His and Farrakhan's union was, said Jackson, "historic . . . an important coming-together." As he later explained to *Ebony* magazine: "You see, before, historically, we did not spiritually unify blacks of different ideological persuasions. This time we've involved the nationalists, whether it's Herb Daughtry (a preacher known for his resentful remarks about 'the Jews') or Farrakhan."

Jackson won most of the black votes in the primaries and hardly any white ones: a demonstration of the despair blacks felt during the Reagan era and their pride in having an articulate champion on the ballot for president. After his third-place showing in the New York primary,

Jackson employed the same symbolism he had after King's martyrdom. "What was a crucifixion in April of 1968," he said, "[became] a resurrection in April of 1984." Christ, in this metaphor, had two bodies: King's and Jackson's. When his campaign sagged toward the end, Jackson seized the network cameras by journeying to Cuba, where he embraced Fidel Castro. Speaking to a crowd at the University of Havana, Jackson made clear his Third World dream with a series of chants: "Long live Castro! Long live Martin Luther King! Long live Ché Guevara! Long live our cry of freedom! Our time has come!" Castro gave Jackson a cigar to smoke and forty-eight prisoners to take back to the U.S. Jackson then swooped down on Managua for a few hours, where he praised the Sandinistas. He was asked if these often authoritarian Third World revolutionaries were true to the principles of the revolution. "We had a revolution of our own," replied Jackson. "It was thirteen years from General Washington to President Washington. It has been only five years in Nicaragua." Thus Jackson turned Reagan's cracked analogy calling the contras the "moral equivalent of the founding fathers" on its head, making it refer to the Sandinistas.

Jackson approached the Democratic convention by strewing the ground ahead of him with demands. "What does Jesse want?" became the question of the day. But this was hard to answer because, even a month before the convention, his program kept shifting. He also issued threats that blacks would boycott the Democrats in the fall if he were not treated well. But Jackson dropped all his demands when Mondale agreed to give him an hour of prime time for a speech. It appeared that what Jesse had wanted was for everyone to wonder: What does Jesse want?

On the eve of the convention in San Francisco, Jackson declined to endorse a resolution condemning anti-Semitism. Tim Hagen, the blunt Irish-Italian Cuyahoga County (Cleveland, Ohio) commissioner, who is not Jewish, lobbied Jackson in his hotel room to no avail. "You should derive no pleasure whatsoever from this meeting," he told Hagen. Jackson then patted his arm. "You Jews are much too sensitive," he said.

When the convention began, in spite of endless negotiations with Mondale, Jackson had still not made it clear that he would support the Democratic ticket. His stance of alienation from the party helped incite his more militant delegates to boo and hoot Coretta Scott King and Andrew Young when they appeared before them to make a conciliatory case for Mondale. (Mrs. King and Young represented both the national and Atlanta black leadership that had always mistrusted Jackson and his motives.) This incident prompted Jackson and Mondale to compromise on a question involving delegation representation so that Jackson would appear to have won something. And yet he still tried to rouse all the black delegates, almost half of whom were committed to Mondale, to vote for him and embarrass Mondale by denying him a first ballot victory. When that gesture misfired, the only weapon he had left was his speech and whether he would endorse the ticket or bolt. "You're either going to become a chump, a chimp, or a champ, and you'll find out tomorrow night," he told Mondale's campaign manager, Bob Beckel.

Standing before the convention, Jackson revealed his Christological vision of death and resurrection, describing the death scenes of both King and Hubert Humphrey, and proclaiming his mission to "the desperate, the damned, the disinherited, the disrespected, and the despised." He asked for forgiveness for his "low moments." To the relief of the entire party, he declared for Mondale. His electrifying performance momentarily lifted much of the bad feeling that had preceded it.

"Be patient," he said. "God is not finished with me yet."

VI

Immediately after his first meeting with President Reagan at the Geneva summit, Mikhail Gorbachev went to the lobby of the Soviet mission to the United Nations, where he surprised a group of fifty American peace activists who were there to present a petition signed by one million people urging a nuclear test ban. At the head of this delegation stood Jesse Jackson.

Face to face with Gorbachev, he asked that the Soviet leader discuss the "plight of Soviet Jews." But Gorbachev brushed the question aside and talked instead about arms control. After forty-five minutes, he wrapped his scarf around his neck and departed. Jackson told reporters, who had heard everything, that Gorbachev "made it clear that his business is disarmament."

Jackson's business was less clear. By questioning Gorbachev's policy about Soviet Jews, he was still dealing with his troubles of a year earlier in the presidential campaign. By recasting himself as champion of the Jews and making anti-Semitism Gorbachev's problem, Jackson was playing to several audiences simultaneously: Jewish leaders, liberals who were sympathetic to him but could not bring themselves to vote for him and opinion-making elites. The audience most distant from him was the man standing three feet in front of him.

On Jackson's map of the world, the Soviet Union was a large blank space. His understanding was at best rudimentary. For all his global talk, he simply failed to account for the Soviet Union. Was it a new nation that was a model for and backer of the masses of the Third World? Or was it part of the exploiting West? Was it a superpower exactly like the U.S.? Where did Russian nationalism, which is strongly anti-Western, fit in? What of pan-Slavism and the problem of Central Europe? What of the nationalities within the Soviet Union? When he later traveled to Soviet Armenia, trying to rouse earthquake victims with chants of "Keep hope alive!," he believed he was in a corner of the Third World, according to an adviser. But were the Armenians Third World, or Western, or both, or something even more complicated? Jackson never addressed any of these questions, or any like them.

He had materialized in Geneva just as Gorbachev was about to move the Cold War out of the Third World. To Gorbachev, it was a tragic arena. He would soon tell the Sandinistas that they would not be subsidized and should agree to elections, pressure the Angolans to settle their civil war, work for settlements in Namibia and Cambodia and withdraw from Afghanistan. He would also demote Cuba from international vanguard to a small, isolated Stalinist island.

The ideological consequence of Gorbachev's historic shift was that it made much right-wing and left-wing thinking passé. In the romantic left-wing view, the exploited Third World possessed a moral superiority and political strength against the neocolonial West. Gorbachev, however, had punctured the political myth of the Third World as the model of global change. Jackson understood the economic importance of the underdeveloped nations as trading partners, but he did not come to terms with the political role of the Third World, altered by Gorbachev. The idea of the Third World, after all, was no more immutable than the Cold War.

VII

Within days of Jackson's meeting with Gorbachev, Harold Washington suddenly dropped dead. The City Council would pick the new mayor. Almost instantly, the Washington bloc split into two factions, both led by black aldermen who had risen within the regular party organization. Jackson now descended upon Chicago, conducting five separate meetings with factotums of one faction at the airport. After gathering an entourage he made his way to City Hall, singing "We Shall Overcome" as he entered. But he had no real organization in the city, even though PUSH, which was a church manqué, had been operating for nearly two decades. Jackson's political effect, to the extent that he had any, was to undermine the alderman he was supporting. At an all-night meeting, the other black candidate and his allies combined with most of the white aldermen to seize the mayoralty.

The succession to Harold Washington demonstrated Jackson's political impotence in Chicago. But this was a much tougher arena than national politics. As he stood on the eve of another presidential run, Jackson's standing with the black leadership class was higher than it had been in 1984. There was no white candidate like Walter Mondale who had a prior claim on their allegiance. It was clear that in this field Jackson would at least equal his 1984 vote among blacks. Black politicians also calculated that he might help increase black turnout, which could ultimately benefit them. Few saw any compelling reason not to endorse him, even if they had misgivings about him.

This time Jackson was determined to run a more credible campaign. He took advice from experienced politicos (Bert Lance, Carter's former budget director, and Ann Lewis, the former chairman of Americans for Democratic Action, who happened to be Jewish), allowed a role for a manager (Gerald Austin, also Jewish, who was pushed aside toward the end of the primaries) and, in the most important departure from 1984, devised a specific platform with the consultation of policy experts. Dozens of post–new left intellectuals were mobilized.

Chief among them were Roger Wilkins, the former assistant attorney general in the Johnson administration ("You are the civil rights movement inside the government," King had told him), and Robert Borosage, the former director of the Institute for Policy Studies, the most significant left-wing institution in Washington, which had languished since Nixon's resignation, the dramatic conclusion of the 1960s era. Jackson turned these intellectuals into players inside the Democratic Party. Wilkins, who had previously distanced himself from Jackson, now changed his view. He saw him as a powerful fullback, breaking the tackles of those opposing black progress. Borosage, for his part, saw the Jackson campaign as a catalyst for a new progressive majority. But this scenario was dependent on a mercurial personality, who was mistrusted by much of the black leadership, the Democratic Party regulars and most white voters.

Jackson's central theme in 1988 was formed in reaction to his last

campaign. He overlaid his jeremiads with a rhetoric of reconciliation—
"common ground." His campaign was presented as a grand thauma-
turgy, a magic healing from the wounds of Reaganism—and, implicitly,
the divisive Jackson of 1984. "America," he said, "is like a quilt, many
patches, many pieces, many colors, many sizes, all woven and held
together by a common thread." His leitmotif was "economic violence,"
the corporate transfer of jobs from the U.S. to the Third World to
exploit "slave labor." The "slave" metaphor also turned up in his
discussion of the "drug scourge."

Drugs was the issue Jackson used to stress his self-help theme and
to prove implicitly to whites that he was socially responsible. "Drug
lords are the masters and drug users are slaves," he said. Drugs were
one of the chains holding blacks in poverty. He insisted that it was a
greater threat than the Russians. "This enemy," he said, "is more
devastating than the enemy in the other uniform with the other ideology."

Jackson's talk about the blacks' "cycle of pain" suggested their
drastic condition twenty years after the Kerner Report, commissioned
by President Johnson to uncover the causes of black urban riots and
to recommend remedies. Its ominous predictions of the consequences
of racial inequality had all been borne out; it stood as a monumental
historic rebuke to the turn the political cycle had taken a generation
ago. As it had warned, in the absence of effective policy the black
underclass had become more "separate and unequal" than ever. And
the postindustrial revolution had deepened the problems; it had made
the old civil rights agenda an artifact of a bygone era, like a Stone Age
implement in the Bronze Age.

No one made this clearer than William Julius Wilson, a social
scientist at the University of Chicago, who emerged as the country's
leading diagnostician of a growing tangle of pathologies—"lawlessness,
illegitimacy, and unemployment." The title of his early book on the
subject, *The Declining Significance of Race*, told much of the story.
"Race specific" policies, such as affirmative action, while they lifted the
"talented tenth" of blacks into knowledge-intensive jobs in the postindustrial economy, left the black underclass untouched. Its intractable
existence, Wilson wrote, "is due far more to historic discrimination and
to broad demographic and economic trends than it is to racial discrimination in the present day."

Since the Kerner Report, he observed, "there has been a movement
from an institutional ghetto—which fully duplicates the structure and
activities of the larger society . . . back to a physical ghetto, which is

incapable of providing basic services, resources, and opportunities." In 1970, nearly half of all black urban males were employed in blue-collar jobs. They were the special victims of deindustrialization. Many of the jobs they used to fill simply no longer existed. During the 1970s, Chicago lost 200,000 manufacturing jobs and New York City lost 600,000. In the 1980s, the process accelerated. What was needed, Wilson argued, was nothing less than *fundamental* economic reform." The meaning of Wilson's scholarship for politics (not to mention policy) was profound; his analysis revealed the inadequacy of leadership and rhetoric that was solely based on race.

The Booker T. Washington model of self-help, however much it instilled a sense of self-discipline, was an anachronism. "Finding work now requires more than a willing spirit and a strong back," wrote Wilson. The Martin Luther King model of Mosaic inspiration, however much it upheld the principle of hope, was, as King himself recognized in his final days, incapable by itself of guiding black folks to the outskirts of the Promised Land. And the model of ethnic big-city politics—call it the Adam Clayton Powell model—could not cope with "structural changes in the economy and the soaring rates of inner-city joblessness and labor-market exclusion," as Wilson put it. The cities no longer had the resources or the opportunities they possessed in the industrial era when the immigrant working classes had streamed in; the rising black urban politicians were succeeding in a diminished orbit. As Jackson strove to become the number one black leader, he attempted to encompass all these models, which, even by addition, were not enough to match the crisis. Only the whole nation, represented by the national government and mobilized by the executive, had the ability to mount the essential effort.

But in any sober calculation, Jackson could never be nominated for president, much less elected. Through his campaigns, he had convincingly made himself into a representative of blacks, but despite his claims for the Rainbow Coalition, he had failed to convince more than a minuscule number of whites that he could represent them. It was not just that he had held no previous public office and had been accountable only to himself. He was still too much the movement leader—the crusader, the protester, the man with a special cause—to be persuasive to them as a politician. It was unclear whether he himself wanted to make that transition. The whites who voted for him, mainly young professionals concentrated in university towns or neighborhoods, saw his candidacy in the same light: as a protest vehicle to send a general antiestablishment message.

Jackson, moreover, could never be nominated for vice president: any black candidate would likely doom the ticket; Jackson also delivered the burden of the "Hymietown" incident and his association with Farrakhan. His Jewish problem had become a vexing problem for the Democratic Party. Jews, along with blacks, were its most loyal adherents. To most of them, Jackson was anathema. His profuse apologies and meetings with Jewish leaders to soothe hurt feelings did not change many opinions. They would never trust him. From the point of view of an overwhelming majority of Jews (and many others within the Democratic Party), his anti-Semitic remarks, which he publicly regretted, were not slips but a deeply held and threatening hostility. It was as unacceptable to them to reward Jackson with the second place on the ticket as it would be to give the slot to someone who had made racist remarks about blacks.

Given the tension that he had produced within the party, Jackson's campaign had to be a precarious act. He had to mobilize the hopes of his constituency by getting them to identify with him. "I stood with you," he told black audiences, recalling his service in the civil rights movement. "Now you must stand with me." Yet if he completely equated his political chances with their needs they were bound to be disappointed. He had to push and prod the party without acting out a drama of disillusionment. While expanding the boundaries of the possible, he had to be the model of the realism and restraint he urged upon black youth. If he lost his balance, he would make it more unlikely for a Democrat to become president and thus undermine the achievement of his own stated goals. For his politics to be successful, he had to keep his eyes on the prize, not just on himself.

VIII

"All politics is local," said Tip O'Neill. This was especially true for the governor of Massachusetts. Blacks in Massachusetts were not much of a force to be reckoned with; their numbers were too small. Until the growth of a sizeable ghetto in Boston after World War II, they had been overwhelmingly Republican and were seen by Irish Democrats as pawns of the Yankees. The tumultuous busing crisis of the mid-1970s was generally understood by everyone involved as an episode in the age-old feud between the Irish and the Yankees, with blacks caught in the middle. As Boston turned into Belfast, Dukakis stood so far above the fray that he was not even an unseen presence.

The Yankees in the past had dealt with a black upper class assimilated to Emersonian virtues such as self-reliance and higher education.
Senator Edward Brooke, a transplanted Washingtonian, was the last
representative of this kind. Dukakis, the heir of the Yankee tradition
of good government, maintained a similar arrangement. His few political connections in Boston with blacks were with the senior partners of
State Street law firms, professors, Episcopal ministers, and social workers.

The most significant black politician he encountered was Mel King,
a towering, soft-spoken man with a shaved head, goatee and dashiki
who was also a state legislator and a professor of urban studies at MIT.
During Dukakis's first term, King led demonstrations at the State
House to protest the governor's harsh budget cuts. But his militance
always took the form of reasoned arguments; he never threatened the
fire the next time. "I was the first person to go in to tell him he was
making a mistake by saying he wouldn't have to raise taxes," said King.
But Dukakis did not heed him. And King went on to run a strong
campaign for mayor of Boston as the candidate of what he called the
Rainbow Coalition.

Dukakis was utterly free of racial prejudice. When his advisers
showed him polls indicating that a certain small percentage of racist
votes was accruing to him because he was seen as an alternative to
Jackson, he refused to believe that anyone who was biased would ever
support him. In the early 1950s, before the Supreme Court had issued
its decision, in *Brown v. Board of Education*, that segregation was
unconstitutional, black students at Swarthmore could not find a barber-
shop to serve them. Michael Dukakis, class of '55, set up shop in his
dormitory, charging sixty cents a cut. He also unsuccessfully campaigned to throw local chapters of fraternities that discriminated
against blacks off campus. These actions were typical of Dukakis, reflecting his decency, insistence that others adhere to his scrupulous
standards and enterprising character.

The style of black politics that had become common in every big
northern city in the post-civil rights era, however, remained foreign to
him. He did not really know when he was being mau-maued, or when
he wasn't; he did not know when to push back and when simply to
smile. In Jesse Jackson he faced the unknown.

Throughout his campaign, Dukakis had struggled for a rationale. In
Michigan, he believed that he didn't need one. He thought that he no
longer faced a strong challenger, that the other candidates had exhausted themselves and their treasuries. He still had more money than

anyone else, and began to parade his endorsements by prominent Democrats before the voters. His private poll showed him comfortably beating Jackson by more than ten points. His confidence was so great that he even stopped campaigning and returned to Boston, where he immersed himself in minor state business. But the polls were wrong—wildly wrong—because they did not measure the intensity of Jackson's support; nor did they account for the fact that this contest was a caucus, not a primary, and was being conducted on a Saturday. Dukakis's potential supporters had no compelling motive to spend a good part of a weekend day shuffling to one side of a room in an elementary school or firehouse to be slowly counted, because he had given them none. For Jackson's parishioners, however, going to the caucuses was like going to church on Easter Sunday.

Jackson's victory by a two-to-one margin was a shock to Dukakis's campaign and to the national press. Overnight, Jackson's face was on the cover of the newsweeklies and filling the network news programs. "Jesse Jackson has become the frontrunner," announced Dan Rather on the CBS "Evening News" of March 28. To the extent that Jackson's chances were inflated, Dukakis's nomination was assured. From the moment of Jackson's victory in Michigan, Dukakis's nomination was guaranteed, even though it appeared that Jackson was just beginning to have his chance. In fact, his chance was over. All along Dukakis's appeal had been the absence of certain qualities. He wasn't Hart, or Mondale, or McGovern. Now he wasn't somebody who was actually in the race. He wasn't Jackson.

Dukakis's campaign decided that the candidate should always avoid engaging Jackson's ideas. Dukakis did not have to do anything to make clear his obvious difference. He just had to exist. In the race with Jackson, he was always in the center. His strategists believed that having Jackson as a foil helped position him for the fall. They also feared that if he disputed with Jackson over issues he might alienate black voters, and Dukakis was obsessed with the avoidance of political risk. The convulsions that had plagued his candidacy from the start now ceased. His campaign at last had a reason to stop hunting for its cause. But the very vacuousness of the Dukakis campaign induced Jackson to press on, no matter what the results of the rest of the primaries.

There was much that Dukakis and Jackson could have debated that might have forced Dukakis to explain himself, better preparing him for the fall campaign. Dukakis's and Jackson's conceptions of postindustrialism were poles apart. Where Dukakis saw a "miracle," Jackson saw "economic violence." Jackson's program was more ambitious than

Dukakis's; Dukakis's had been tested in Massachusetts. But this was a debate that was studiously and successfully avoided by Dukakis.

In a series of detailed speeches, Jackson spoke of the Cold War's end. He talked of the "resources freed from military spending [that] can be invested in rebuilding America." He demonstrated the abstract point about the importance of economic over military strength with a brilliant display of his ability to captivate crowds. First, he asked for a show of hands of those who owned MX missiles and then those who owned Japanese VCRs. He also enumerated the points of a Jackson Doctrine. Though none of them laid out a policy for a changed U.S.–Soviet relationship, they did detail a noninterventionist, nonexploitive U.S. approach toward the Third World.

"People often ask why I put such emphasis on the Third World. I suggest to you that we must recognize the new order that is coming into being," he told the World Affairs Council of Los Angeles. "When Reagan and Gorbachev meet in Moscow, they will represent the two most powerful nations of the world. But they will represent only one-eighth of the world's population. Seven-eighths will not be at the table." But foreign policy, too, was a debate that was not joined by Dukakis.

In Wisconsin, Dukakis's chief rhetorical adjustment was to drop "hell" and "damn" into his speeches, as in "Hell, they're paying $6 an hour at McDonald's in my state." This was his concession to his advisers, who urged him to sound more populist, more like a man of the people. He also indirectly slighted Jackson by slighting Reagan: "After seven years of charisma in the White House, maybe it's time for a little competence." To him, Jackson and Reagan were alike, both embodying passion and ideology, the danger of moving beyond lawyerly logic.

In the vacuum, Jackson presented himself as the tribune of the Democratic tradition. "I'd rather have Roosevelt in a wheelchair than Reagan on a horse," he said, in a line he had used to great effect since 1984. Of all the Democratic candidates, Jackson had the spottiest record as a Democrat. None of the others, however, had hidden histories of alliances with Republicans in their home states; nor had they engaged in a courtship ritual with the Republican National Committee. Despite this past, Jackson was simply taking the liberal tradition that Dukakis would not claim.

In the midst of the Wisconsin primary, however, Jackson nearly careened into the orchestra pit by attempting to insert himself into the drama surrounding Panamanian dictator Manuel Noriega. The U.S.

had imposed economic sanctions in an effort to force the drug lord's overthrow, and Noriega was defiant. Jackson decided that the imbroglio required his presence, so he offered himself as mediator. In Syria, his personal diplomacy had worked only because it served the purposes of others. In Panama, he was dismissed by all parties because he was seen as serving only his own purposes, and the affair swiftly disappeared from view as the sight of Jackson gathering huge crowds of white voters in Wisconsin seized public attention. Indeed, though he did better than expected, far better than he had in 1984, he lost by twenty points.

The pattern for the rest of the primaries was now set. Jackson's tenacity permitted Dukakis to roll up big margins in state after state. But in each place Jackson proved his flair and imagination by staging ever more arresting tableaux—spending the night in a crime-ridden housing project with a welfare mother and her children, lecturing drug gangs, embracing AIDS patients at a rally of gays, leading a march of cancer victims afflicted by toxic waste.

Running against an opponent who would not engage him or the electorate, Jackson came to believe that he was being denied what was rightfully his. Dukakis, for his part, believed that he was capturing the national imagination. On the sidewalks of New York those illusions were set in cement.

10

Gotham

I

The resonant voice of New York politics has wildly contrasting parts but is all of a piece: combative and compassionate, unillusioned and idealistic. In 1988, this is what that voice, the distilled essence of its "varied carols," sounded like discussing the campaign:

"So far, through no fault of the candidates, we have heard phrases. We haven't even gotten to paragraphs, even sentences. . . . Interconnectedness with the Soviets? You can't discuss immense ideas in twenty-eight seconds. You wouldn't be able to do it in a debate for the presidency. You are not going to do it in the campaign. You should think of the world as a constant set of emergencies. Can we talk about them in the campaign? . . . I'm against debates. You don't govern that way. It's the last ability I want to see in a president sitting down with Gorbachev. I would call in the media, all of you, as many as I could get in the room. Today, we're going to do the media. What we'll do, you are going to ask questions on the economy. It may take five hours, six hours, twelve hours. Every question you can think of. . . . A candidate says the same one minute's worth of intelligence for six months. One hundred debates, it's the same one hundred times. You never get beyond it. I don't want that anymore. I want to get beyond that first minute. . . . Nothing has been said that's real. A lot of it has to do with false values interpolated into the process. These are artificial values. We made celebrity important. We said there were stars that were not playing. . . .

"Mario Cuomo? That's the biggest myth of all."

Mario Cuomo was the man who stood up destiny. If he had a rendezvous, it was up to destiny to prove it. He was the ultimate unconventional candidate: the candidate who wouldn't run. Cuomo foreswore the role of hero, instead taking the part of the chorus. But the more he declined to enter, the more the feebleness of the drama cast his offstage shadow even larger.

Cuomo's life story was present in his every movement and every expression. He combined an intense, personal feeling for community with a cool, detached skill for nuanced maneuver. He was southern Italian in his sense of family (his closest adviser was his son Andrew, and the Empire State was "the family of New York") and northern Italian in his sense of politics. With his painterly strokes of indirection, Cuomo was like the Florentine who described an artful approach to power.

Cuomo liked to portray himself as everybody's uncle who lived around the corner. On the surface, he was a familiar figure to New Yorkers. His claim to ordinariness, however, masked his utter originality. He was a man of the people who was also an introspective intellectual; he read deeply and widely, and wrote in his diary every day. He was a serious Catholic who had studied theology and was steeped in the Church's tradition of social reform. Jacqueline Kennedy said of her husband that it was unfair to hold his Catholicism against him because he was such a bad Catholic. In this respect, Mario Cuomo was no Jack Kennedy.

His experiences were not stages he had passed through and left behind. They were constantly available to him. He was a Jesuit-trained former prosecuting attorney who relentlessly employed the Socratic style of the courtroom to leave his opponents sputtering. He had been a professional baseball player with a Pittsburgh Pirates minor league club, a ferocious player who quit for St. John's law school after a fastball to the skull gave him dizzy spells. "I think Cuomo has the tools to go all the way if the best can be brought out in him," wrote a baseball scout about the minor league prospect. "If he lacks anything, it is a realization on his own part of the fine potential he has. Sometimes, I think he has a slight inferiority complex and needs to be told frequently that he has the goods. Like all bright fellows, he is sometimes moody and different than the ordinary person. It takes some time to get his confidence and to know the warmth that is in him. . . . He is aggressive and plays hard. . . . Will run you over if you get in his way."

Cuomo brought a physical audacity to politics. During a debate in the 1982 race for governor against Republican millionaire Lewis Lehrman, Cuomo reached for Lehrman's wrist, around which was wrapped a gold watch. "That's a very expensive watch, Lew," he said. Cuomo evoked an almost palpable, animal fear in his opponents. Even when he was being cautious, he placed himself in the action. His remarks from the wings usually stung more than the rehearsed thrusts of the candidates on stage. In 1984, for example, he said that his mother had referred to Walter Mondale as "polenta," an Italian cornmeal mush. And poor Mondale happened to be the candidate Cuomo was supporting.

His critics said he was sometimes too tough, even vengeful. This criticism was exacerbated by his thin-skinned practice of regularly telephoning reporters and arguing with them about their stories, thus violating the press's belief in its sacrosanct self-importance. But just when the stereotype appeared to ring true, when his gamesmanship appeared too transparent and self-serving, Cuomo would shatter the image with an unexpected act that transcended the banality of the immediate political moment.

Even since his evocative keynote address to the 1984 Democratic convention, he had loomed over the national party. He was compared to Ronald Reagan because of his charismatic speechmaking, his ability to articulate the basic values of his party. But Cuomo's conception of power bore little resemblance to Reagan's. Though Cuomo had played on many fields of dreams, he had never been an actor who learned to relinquish control by second nature to directors and scriptwriters. Cuomo did not have a view of himself as an element in a studio system, or, as he put it, the "presidential campaign industry."

Cuomo, of course, occupied the same office as Franklin D. Roosevelt, a fact that he did not neglect to mention frequently. His background—he was born to immigrant parents in a room above the family grocery store in Queens, an urban log cabin—could not have been more different from Roosevelt's, born on the family estate at Hyde Park. FDR, after graduating Harvard and Columbia Law School with an indifferent record, easily gained, through family connections, a job in a Wall Street law firm. Cuomo, after graduating at the top of his law class and holding a clerkship in the state's highest court, applied to dozens of the finest law firms and was granted an interview at only one, where he was rejected.

Cuomo spoke admiringly about the New Deal, but he did not consider its programs a catechism or Roosevelt infallible for all time. He did not confuse the party with the church. Cuomo was called an old-style New Dealer, wedded to the past, as if the New Deal were a term of oppobrium. He was guilty, above all, of having a sense of history. Indeed, he thought a lot about Lincoln and his relevance. Cuomo was more systematic and philosophical in his thinking than virtually any other politician, certainly more so than FDR or JFK. Yet his mind was anything but brittle; in fact, it was restless and open. In this he was genuinely liberal.

Cuomo's principles were unshakeable. In 1985, a year after the Democratic debacle, he delivered an affirmation of the liberal credo at Yale. *"E pur si muove,"* he said, repeating the words spoken by Galileo when the Church demanded that he deny that the earth revolves around the sun: *And yet it does move.* Cuomo did not make this speech because he identified with Galileo the heretic-martyr but because he believed that American politics was not static and that the conservative age that was at its noontide would run its course. He acted as if a Second New Deal could only be made by a child of the First New Deal.

Roosevelt's immense self-confidence came from his social position; he relished being a traitor to his class. Cuomo's self-confidence came from being completely self-made; still, he retained an undercurrent of insecurity that was inextricable from his motivation: he was driven by a hunger for recognition and justice. But neither the self-made man nor the patrician felt they owed anyone anything.

Cuomo never shrank from power. It was not just that he believed that a strong government was indispensable in redressing economic and social inequities. It was that he could act as a lion and a fox. He was loved and feared like nobody else in the Democratic Party—and he understood the political uses of both sentiments. Unlike Gary Hart, he did not have a passive view of himself or history. Unlike Jesse Jackson, he did not have a Ptolemaic view of history with himself as the sun. Unlike Michael Dukakis, he had a view of history.

"A second-class intellect. But a first-class temperament!" Such was the judgment of Oliver Wendell Holmes, Jr. on Franklin Roosevelt. Cuomo, for his part, had a first-class intellect. The ruling on his temperament would have to be withheld until its exercise on the national stage, where Cuomo was unwilling to venture.

But it was not as if Cuomo wasn't preparing himself for something greater than Albany. In 1979, when he was lieutenant governor, Cuomo charted the cycles of liberalism and conservatism in New York state politics in a study he composed for his own use. He may have been inspired by Arthur Schlesinger's idea of the cycles in American history. (Stephen Schlesinger, Arthur's son, worked as a political aide to the governor.) In any case, Cuomo seriously contemplated how he might be carried by its currents.

In 1987, he read a book that he extensively marked up and sent around to some of his advisers. *Mortal Splendor: The American Empire in Transition*, written by a young, independent scholar, Walter Russell Mead, was a sweeping analysis of the decline from the "Periclean" age of the American Century to the present. Mead was not a gloomy prophet of an inevitable fall; rather, he saw possibilities for another turn in the cycle.

> We are still too close to Franklin Roosevelt to appreciate the magnitude of his accomplishment. . . . But of all his accomplishments this was not the least: to take the battered and backward old Democratic Party and forge it into a political instrument that could reorganize first the American Republic and then the whole Western world. . . .
>
> Modern Democratic strength has always found its source in this union of the good and the useful. When the party can synthesize the moral and the economic yearnings of the masses of the people into a line of pragmatic policy, then it is invincible. When it fails, it loses.
>
> The current debate over the future of the party reflects the difficulties inherent in recreating Roosevelt's political achievement.

What was needed, wrote Mead, was a "new social contract" on a global scale to accommodate the globalization of the economy. The pattern that Keynes discovered, that economic growth could be stimulated by increased consumption and higher wages, should be applied on a worldwide scale. Just as austerity was not the answer to the Depression, so it was not the answer to modern stagnation. More consumption and higher wages abroad could begin to solve the problems of the underdeveloped and advanced industrial countries at the same time. Mead called for a global Keynesianism, a policy for a Second New Deal.

Cuomo appointed Mead to a state commission he had assembled to

come up with just such a plan. On it were labor and business leaders,
economists and lawyers—a good slice of the leadership of New York.
The result was not especially coherent, and included dissenting opinions from various commission members. It was a case study in the
difficulty of making a "new social contract." Cuomo broadly endorsed
the approach of the global Keynesians, stressing the theme of "interconnectedness." The "American system," he wrote in his introduction
to the commission's report, "has reached a critical point in its history"
on the order of the watershed of the Civil War and the New Deal.
What was needed was a response equal to the situation.

Cuomo's willingness to go through the exercise of the commission
was a sign of his larger intention. In September 1987, there was an even
bigger sign: Cuomo flew to Moscow, where he met with a range of
Soviet officials, including the conscience of perestroika, Andrei Sakharov. A month after his return, Cuomo presented his thinking to the
Council on Foreign Relations in Washington. He did not, he said,
agree with the skeptics who argued that Gorbachev was "insincere."
"This is the alternative I prefer," he said. "We are standing at a
possible turning point in the history of both nations and the modern
world. . . ." He minced no words. "We should seize this moment in
history—and try to begin to negotiate the end of the Cold War."
Cuomo may have been the first prominent politician to use these words
in public: "the end of the Cold War." He concluded by urging the
candidates for president to take up the issue. "I hope that in the end,
they will all agree, as I do, with the recent observation of the Institute
for East-West Security Studies that 'new political thinking in the East
requires new policy thinking in the West.' "

Cuomo then took questions. The audience included more than the
pinstriped internationalists of the old school. Some of the Cold War
conservatives were also present. Richard Perle, former assistant secretary of defense, who had made a career out of putting obstacles in the
way of arms control and had fine-tuned the practice of intimidating
political opponents, began to parry. He was joined in his attack by
Elliott Abrams, assistant secretary of state for Latin American affairs,
whose ideological fervor had carried him into the netherworld of the
Iran-contra scandal.

Cuomo, according to several accounts, forcefully answered their
arguments. The confrontation with the foreign policy elite revealed
that his broad and highly informed conception of power enabled him
to move in many fields. "A tour de force," said Charles William
Maynes, the editor of *Foreign Policy* magazine. "It was a marriage of

confidence and intelligence. He made a big impression on everyone in the audience. He will not allow himself to be pushed around by people trying to intellectually bully him." Almost everyone in the room felt themselves in the presence of a presidential candidate. But Cuomo had already ruled himself out.

Unlike many people with large egos, Cuomo could envision his own failure. He knew his weaknesses; he had lost a race, experiencing a "public death," as it were. In 1977, he had been unsure about running for mayor but allowed himself to be pulled into the arena and lost. He never forgave himself; his vanity had betrayed him. In 1982, he felt ready to run for governor and won. The product of these two campaigns was a highly developed cunning and an even more developed sense of self.

As 1988 approached, he felt himself being pulled, but he resisted the tug of the vacuum. Some of his closest advisers had implored him for two years to run. But, unlike Dukakis, Cuomo believed that he could not govern and campaign at the same time. He was sure that everything that went wrong in New York would be held against him. His will to power was undeniable, but he told these advisers that he did not feel that he could master the entire process this time. The last thing he wanted was to be embarrassed. He knew that things could go drastically wrong, that he could be humbled. Nothing was more important to him than his pride. Thus Cuomo refused to play the games of what he called the "presidential campaign industry." If he ever sought the presidency, it would be, as much as possible, on his own terms. Until then, Mario Cuomo was the wayward noncandidate of an aimless party.

In his speech to the Council on Foreign Relations, with Gorbachev and a future American president in mind, Cuomo gave a hint of his idea of power. "Historians and philosophers have always quarreled about how much influence individuals have on events," he said. "But for the leaders of nations there can be only one working principle: events will be what they make them." Yet Cuomo himself had relinquished this role. His withdrawal to his study, where he continued to fill his diaries, left the field to others. His absence considerably widened the vacuum—and Michael Dukakis's opportunity. It also created an enormous opportunity for mischief by Cuomo's longtime archrival, the mayor of New York, Edward I. Koch.

Koch's three main interests were me, myself and I. These subjects never failed to fascinate him. Whatever was happening he believed it was about himself. "I want to come back as me," he said, giving his opinion on reincarnation. He never let an incident pass by without attempting to throw himself into the middle of it. "How'm I doing?" he shouted as he paraded down the street.

Koch was a tall, bald, pear-shaped bachelor who wore baggy suits and held on to a small rent-controlled Greenwich Village apartment. He had no interests outside his political career—not history, international relations or any other of those that enriched Mario Cuomo's mind.

He had a bad word for almost everybody, and he filled two autobiographies with insults. The word "idiot" came to his lips with no more hesitation than another person would demonstrate before extending his arm to hail a taxi. Koch did not restrict his abuse to rivals, real or imagined. He assailed the weak, too: the homeless, street vendors and beggars. His abuse was flaunted with a kind of abandon; he took an almost childish delight in the offense he gave. His rantings ("Do you want to know what I think!?") ranged from Borscht Belt monologues to operatic arias. "He's a kind of 'Evita,' " wrote Cuomo in his *Diaries*.

No white politician in New York had done more to try to calm its racial tensions than Mario Cuomo; none had done more to exacerbate them than Ed Koch. In 1971, when a low-income housing project was proposed in the middle-class Jewish neighborhood of Forest Hills, Koch, positioning himself for his first race for mayor, stoked the primal racial fears of the residents, talking ceaselessly about the lurid crimes that were about to be visited on them. Cuomo served as the mediator between the community and the housing authorities, and guided them to a compromise settlement that wound up a success.

In their classic work on ethnic politics, *Beyond the Melting Pot*, Nathan Glazer and Daniel Patrick Moynihan contrasted the southern pattern of race relations with the northern pattern of ethnic group relations—a pattern of rhetorical extremism, racial appeals, violence, and fear of the other versus a pattern of competition, bargaining, coalition-building, and accommodation. The northern model, they wrote, was "perhaps best realized in New York City." But as the southern style was fading in the South itself, it was resurging in the North. Demagogues who manipulated the rhetoric of black nationalism played some role. More important, though, was the ascension of politicians riding "white backlash" for political gain. In New York, Koch was the most successful example of this type.

Koch later called his maneuvers around Forest Hills "my Rubicon." But his passage from liberal reformer to neoconservative antireformer was not the result of any personal or political crisis. Nearly all tales of the journey from left to right fit a mold: belief in high ideals, followed by feelings of betrayal and disillusionment and a lurch in the opposite direction. Koch had started out as one of the leaders of the Village Independent Democrats who were trying to oust the De Sapio machine. Koch's conversion, which appeared to be motivated solely by ambition, made some of those who had been his closest friends speculate on whether he had had any beliefs in the first place. They had known him for decades but wondered who he really was.

In 1977, Koch and Cuomo ran against each other in the Democratic primary for mayor. "I'm for capital punishment, are you?" said Koch, buttonholing voters on street corners. Capital punishment was not, nor would it ever be, an issue for the mayor to decide. The clubhouse bosses whom Koch once denounced were now working the precincts for him. They were shrewd judges of character with keen instincts for self-preservation. Cuomo inspired their fear, Koch their relief.

After Koch's election, he did not turn reformer again. While he pranced before the cameras, calling many black leaders "poverty pimps" and most blacks anti-Semitic, the clubhouse politicians battened on the public treasury. In Koch's third term, more than one hundred officials were convicted of crimes of corruption, from bribery to extortion. His defense was that he hadn't been paying attention, but in fact he had paid a lot of attention to real estate interests.

Koch claimed that he was a "mainstream" Democrat battling the "wackos." But he had little party loyalty or, for that matter, loyalty of any kind. Without proferring a formal endorsement, he supported Ronald Reagan in 1980. Twice he supported Alfonse D'Amato, the right-wing Republican candidate for the Senate, in the same way. Koch also heatedly denounced the Democrats running against them.

By 1982, it appeared that his influence was beginning to recede. His primary race against Cuomo for governor turned into low comedy when he gave an interview to *Playboy* magazine in which he freely insulted everyone who did not live in New York City. "Have you ever lived in the suburbs?" he said. "I haven't but I've talked to people who have, and it's sterile. It's nothing. It's wasting your life." What was worse, he went on, was being "out in the country, wasting time in a pickup truck when you have to drive twenty miles to buy a gingham dress or a Sears Roebuck suit." He was the biggest city's biggest provincial. Beyond the last subway stop, he was a political misfit.

When the 1988 presidential campaign pulled into town, Koch was as gleeful as if it were the circus. He awaited the slightest summons to the center ring. *Ring!* On the front stoop of Gracie Mansion stood an earnest young man seeking a guide in the big city.

III

Al Gore was the boy on horseback. It was 1970, in Tennessee. His father, Senator Albert Gore, who served in the most exclusive club in the world with Prescott Bush and Willis Robertson, was fighting for his political life. He was the antithesis of the Gothic southern politicians, who mixed their populism with racial appeals, just as they mixed their bourbon with branch water. Gore was of the first wave of the postwar new South, one of only three southern senators not to affix his signature to the segregationist Southern Manifesto and subsequently to vote for every civil rights bill. Unlike the Bourbons, he did not wave the flag while currying favors with the military-industrial complex. During the Vietnam War, he refused to march in lockstep, according to the orders of the commander-in-chief. At the electrifying Foreign Relations Committee hearings in 1965 on Vietnam policy, chaired by Senator J. William Fulbright, Gore directed sharp questions at high government officials. The war had not brought on the apotheosis of the Great Society, as Lyndon Johnson dreamed, but the liberal crackup.

In 1970, President Nixon planned a purge. During his presidential campaign he strongly implied that he had a blueprint to end the war, but the war widened and intensified. Now, he directed the Republicans to discredit his critics by mixing themes of social resentment and national security—a position that had gelled in Nixon's first campaign in 1946 and had served him thereafter. As part of the latest offensive, Spiro Agnew, Nixon's hatchet man, labeled Gore the "Southern regional chairman of the Eastern liberal Establishment." Gore's Republican opponent applied the time-honored campaign techniques of Cold War conservatism, accusing him of betrayal and appeasement. His antiwar speeches, the Republican charged, were being used by the North Vietnamese to brainwash American POWs: Gore was aiding and abetting the enemy; he was the enemy within.

Gore's response was a television commercial. In it, he appeared on a white horse, accompanied by his son on a brown horse, wearing an army uniform. "Son," said the senator, as they rode toward the sunset, "always love your country." Patriotic Gore.

Gore, however, could not deflect the Republican fusillade. He was a longtime incumbent, a veritable Washington fixture. Even though the Republicans held the executive branch, they blamed all problems on the shortcomings of government, which they identified with the Democrats. Gore had been an opponent of vested interests in his state, but the Republicans associated his liberalism with being a member of "the establishment," distant from the concerns of Nixon's "Silent Majority." The senator was slow to answer the attack and defensive when he did. He went down in a hail of negative campaigning. "Someday, and someday soon," he said in his concession speech, with his eyes fixed on his son, "I know that the truth shall rise again in Tennessee!"

Al Gore, Jr.'s whole life seemed an education for a higher destiny. When school was in session at St. Alban's, the exclusive prep school, he lived in the old Fairfax Hotel (now the Ritz Carlton) on Embassy Row, watching the diplomats come and go. In the summers, he was at the family farm in Carthage, Tennessee. Then on to Harvard and marriage to his high school sweetheart. Even though he opposed the Vietnam War, he volunteered to go; once there, he was assigned as an army journalist. And then a job as a reporter on the *Nashville Tennessean;* election to Congress, where he compiled a record as a consumer and environmental advocate; election to the Senate—finally succeeding his father. It had come very quickly and easily. Gore had the perfect upbringing, the attractive wife, the perfect résumé, the influential mentors, the careful selection of issues, the studied answers. What he did not have, once he began campaigning for the presidency, was a clear political identity.

On the shuttle from Washington to New York, he reflected on his ordeal in Vietnam. Before he went, he said, "I saw it in black and white terms." Upon returning, he saw it "in terms of complexity and subtlety." He had learned that "a lot of people there hated communism. The antiwar movement of which I was a part wouldn't admit that. I had to admit it." Still, the war was "wrong." Gore tried to sum up: "In the words of the old Judy Collins song, I've looked at the Vietnam War 'from both sides now.' " Gore's description, however, was not a complex discussion but a simplification of the arguments over the war. Being anti-communist and believing the war wrong, for example, were not mutually exclusive positions and hardly obscure. Gore's view of the war may have been no more than a politician's effort to have it both ways: "both sides now." In general, he appeared to be standing above his experience. At thirty-nine, Gore was the youngest candidate in the race. He attempted to convey that he was more capable and masterful than his elders by suppressing his youthfulness with a dour tone and stolid appearance. His image as a generational figure was also clouded by his wife, Tipper. She had once been a member of an all-female rock and roll band, but at the dawning of the age of Reagan devoted her energies to a crusade against smutty rock lyrics. Gore helped arrange a congressional hearing at which she held forth. When he launched his presidential campaign, however, they rushed to Los Angeles for a private meeting with rock music executives, who had been critical of Mrs. Gore, explaining that the hearing had been an awful "mistake" and that the senator had never been in favor of it. These Hollywood producers, promoters and agents specialized in creating "acts" and public personas. They came away from the Gores' performance impressed with its calculation but also convinced that it would wear thin very quickly.

Gore's candidacy began in the oldest possible way: in a closed room of cigar-smoking kingmakers. After Walter Mondale's defeat, his chief financial backers formed themselves into a political action committee. As the 1988 contest was about to begin, most of these political jockeys found themselves without a horse. Gore was summoned. He seemed to fill the vacuum as they understood it. He was, as he put it, "a raging moderate" who might use the Super Tuesday southern primary as a gigantic lever to pry open the nomination. Seventeen members of the group pledged cash on the line.

Gore spent a lot of time at town meetings in Tennessee, but his understanding of power was based on a notion of "the center." Washington, as he saw it, was the center of opinion-making; from there, ideas radiated out to the country, and the blocs of power negotiated through their brokers. Gore assumed that the party was filled with such blocs and that the money men who had encouraged him to run were one of them. He measured political geography on a linear scale from left to right. The party, he argued, needed to move to the ideological center, where it would be closer to the voters. But "the center" was as changeable as the political tides.

In April 1987, a month after his decision to run, Gore made the rounds of the press, discussing the greenhouse effect and other futuristic problems. George Will ridiculed him for his interest in issues that are "not even peripheral." Some of Gore's advisers had suggested that it would appear natural for the most youthful candidate to seize the theme of The Future. But Gore was more responsive to the Will column. He was so Washington-tropic, so sensitive to the prevailing opinion-making elites, having grown up among them, that he backed off from his own prescience about the issue, which had been a sign of his originality.

In his announcement speech, Gore described himself as an American version of Mikhail Gorbachev: "For the first time in at least a generation, the Soviet Union has a leader who combines youthful energy and innovation with experience. And the free world urgently needs a leader who can match him, bargain with him, and make the most of this possibly historic opportunity for a safer, saner world."

A month later, as Oliver North testified before the Iran-contra hearings, Gore had a new motif. "This is the principal theme I'm emphasizing in my campaign—a pledge to restore the rule of law to the White House," he said. "I'm really emphasizing it heavily." But that theme evaporated as quickly as Olliemania.

After the summer vacation, Gore delivered a full-dress speech with trumpets blaring at the National Press Club. Now he presented himself as a stalwart cold warrior against the weaklings of his own party. "The politics of retreat, complacency and doubt may appeal to others, but it will not do for me or for my country." He attacked all the other candidates as being "on the edge of the mainstream." (It was this characterization that was picked up by the Bush campaign and ruthlessly used against Dukakis.) Gore had seen a niche that he believed he could fill, and it was in the center. He presumed to be the rightful heir to the Henry Jackson wing of the party, which had never been sufficient to sustain the late senator's own higher ambitions and whose cadres had mostly drifted over to the Republican camp. Gore had miscalculated where the center lay within the Democratic Party. He was partly misled by the sound and fury of the neoconservatives, omnipresent in Reagan's Washington. Gore did not fully appreciate their compulsive sectarianism or their marginality. (At the moment Gore was attacking his fellow Democrats for their weakness in the Cold War, Joshua Muravchik, a neoconservative polemicist and one-time staffer to Senator Jackson, wrote an op-ed piece in the *Wall Street Journal* assailing Gore's generally "dovish record" and calling his Cold War talk "another campaign maneuver.")

Gore downplayed the ideas that demonstrated his grasp of the future, such as the greenhouse effect, while highlighting ossified ideas, such as Cold War resolve, as if they would make him appear mature. He was positioning himself as a political anachronism. It was also more than a little ironic that he was employing Cold War themes that had been used to end his father's political career.

Far behind in Iowa, barely visible in the low single digits, he traveled to the Democratic dinner there in November to attack the state for distorting the process. The "small state of Iowa," he said, demanded "ideological purity" that ruled out a winner in the general election. Iowa was not in the center; Iowa was not concerned enough about the Cold War. Gore would skip the Iowa caucuses entirely—and New Hampshire for good measure.

After the Washington summit, he stepped up his attack on the Democrats for their Cold War softness. But Gore did not seem to grasp the motives driving Gorbachev in his effort to transform the Soviet Union. In order to further distinguish himself from the field of Democrats, he credited Gorbachev's signing of the INF Treaty to Reagan's strength. "I find this difficult to believe. Do you really think the Soviets just said to themselves, 'We're feeling some economic pressure: Let's remove our SS20s'?"

In spite of his rhetoric, Gore did not provoke a great debate on the Cold War. Since he had already exempted himself from the early contests, there was no reason for the other candidates to pay any attention to him. It was as if he were in a separate campaign, all his own, occupying an echo chamber. With nobody responding to him, he kept responding to his lack of effect. His themes changed constantly; his oscillations made for a wavering image that never came into focus. Gore's image-making was perversely projecting a picture far worse than his reality.

Now the early primaries were over and the campaign headed South. All along, Gore had claimed that only a certain southern favorite son could make a credible national candidate because he was the only one in the center. But he never gave a speech on the new South, or explained his understanding of the region's special place in the nation. When asked about the different waves of new South politicians, from his father's generation to his own, he said, "I've haven't really thought about it." He acted on a caricature of the South as the bastion of flag-waving and the military-industrial complex. For Gore, it was almost as if the southern people, imbued with an ancient sense of loyalty, honor and patriotism, were the natural supporters of the Cold War and he was their cavalier. Gore missed the opportunity to address how the winding down of the Cold War—once a seemingly "irrepressible conflict"—might affect the mind and economy of the South. He was uniquely endowed to become a leader of this newest new South, but he was facing the past: the Cold War as a kind of antebellum ideal.

Gore's first television ad unreeled, featuring still photos of the handsome candidate in various poses as though he were in a *GQ* spread. Above these pictures appeared big block letters: "Stronger . . . Smarter . . . Character." No issue was mentioned.

Gore had earlier disdained the populist theme raised by Gephardt as defying "common sense." Though Gephardt had proven its potency, he was stumbling badly. Gore now pushed him aside and outfitted himself as the populist. He put on a plaid shirt over his blue suit, promising "to put the White House back on the side of the working man."

On Super Tuesday, Gore won six states, one less than Dukakis and one more than Jackson. According to an analysis in the *Congressional Quarterly,* he won four of six communities with large military facilities and every county where the presidential campaign of George Wallace had done well in 1972 and 1976. It was a peculiar regional mixture of Cold War vested interests and Dixiecrat remnants.

Gore had taken the southern primary as a blank check made out to him. Unfortunately, it was written in invisible ink and backed by the full authority of the Confederate government. In the North, he didn't seem to know where he was and few seemed to know or, worse, care that he was there. He entered New York with his last million dollars in his pocket.

IV

Michael Dukakis had expected an early endorsement from Mario Cuomo. A ceremony was finally arranged to take place after the Michigan primary. But Jesse Jackson trounced him and Cuomo took a long step backward.

The two men had never been especially close. On the surface, they seemed to be similar: liberal, ethnic, northeastern governors. But there was less here than met the eye. If they had a common trait it was their pride, which made their relationship prickly. Cuomo, in private, viewed Dukakis as something of a case of mistaken self-identity. The austere New Englander, the son of a Harvard-educated doctor who grew up in suburban Brookline and had never before this campaign bothered to mention the immigrant saga, was now running as Mario Cuomo. The contrasts in their seemingly similar roots went far in explaining the differences between them. Dukakis never spontaneously mentioned class; it was simply foreign to him. Cuomo's feelings about the injustices of a class-ridden society, however, were never far from the surface. Class, in fact, was a major theme of his keynote address to the Democrats.

Cuomo held back his endorsement partly because Dukakis failed to create the kind of momentum that would make Cuomo look wise in his choice. It was not as if Cuomo didn't give Dukakis his chance. In November 1987, Cuomo held a special luncheon for the most active New York Democrats to hear the Massachusetts governor. He presented the campaign up to that point as a false start. "We didn't know how many distractions there would be . . . irrelevant things," he said. "People cribbing in school. . . . We're asked to concentrate on people smoking a cigarette fifteen years ago. . . . We're asked to think about it as relevant because it was illicit. . . . We're asked to think about people who misplace affections when we have spent millions and trillions on weapons of destruction." But now we could focus on reality. We could hear Michael Dukakis.

The crowd had elevated itself on that special brand of New York adrenalin that can be felt at much-heralded Broadway openings. For these movers and shakers, this was the beginning of the campaign; they smelled victory; here was the likely candidate. But by the time Dukakis elaborated his proposal for cutting the deficit through improved tax collection, the audience was looking for the exits. "You can applaud if you would like," he offered in conclusion. In the car taking him to the airport after his speech, Dukakis expressed his irritation that people kept questioning his tax proposal. It made perfect sense; it had worked in Massachusetts; it was all in the data.

A week before the New York primary, Dukakis appeared at a candidates' forum at Town Hall. The crowd consisted of liberals who had mostly made up their minds to vote for him and simply wanted to feel good about it. But the applause when he finished was considerably less than when he started. He had lost no votes, just enthusiasm. Seated off to the side of the stage as Dukakis droned on about "good jobs at good wages" was his constant traveling companion, his Sancho Panza, Nick Mitropoulis. Is Dukakis thinking about saying something more than this? he was asked. "He thinks he *is* saying something," replied Mitropoulis.

Dukakis really wanted Cuomo's endorsement now. He was more annoyed than ever that he had not gotten it. On April 15, he flew to Albany, where he was ushered into Cuomo's large office. He seemed dwarfed by the surroundings, according to one of his aides, and put his hands in his belt to give him some swagger. Cuomo, powerfully built and a full head taller than Dukakis, sensed his unease. He escorted Dukakis to a special place in the room and pressed a button. A riser appeared. That, said Cuomo, was where a short governor of New York used to stand to make him seem taller. Then Cuomo opened his door, pronounced Dukakis "superb" and "excellent" to the jostling reporters, but declined to endorse him.

Dukakis also sought Ed Koch's endorsement, paying court at Gracie Mansion, listening politely as the mayor went through his shtick, hoping for the best. As it happened, he was in luck. Koch threw his arm around Al Gore. "Have shoes and mouth and will travel," Koch said.

Gore was already foredoomed. In a contest between Jackson and Dukakis, he was the odd man out. But the exact nature of his fate was now sealed. Even before Koch's endorsement, Gore had been relieved of his wallet by Koch's media consultant, David Garth. Garth was tough-talking, vulgar, clever, and skillful. He often dominated his clients, even putting them on physical regimens as he toughened up their images. In the early 1970s, at the zenith of the age of Nixon, Garth began to use the word "tough" in many of his commercials to armor his clients. "He's young, he's tough and nobody owns him" was his best slogan of that period. How did he see Gore? "He's young, he's tough and nobody owns him," he said.

Koch, however, did not wait for the candidates to arrive before he began the campaign. He had already seized the stage with a soliloquy on the Jews and Jackson: "And he thinks maybe Jews and other supporters of Israel should vote for him? They have got to be crazy!" But very few Jews were "crazy" enough to consider voting for Jackson. Koch was employing his usual tactic of exploiting racial and ethnic tensions for his own political advantage. "I'm the Paul Revere," he said.

For the first time, Al Gore, who had risen in the post–civil rights South, was dragged into the racial politics of the North. He had little idea how to respond. His initial instinct was to seek protective covering behind his consultant. "My contract with David Garth prohibits me from commenting," he said, upon being asked about Koch's outbursts. Yet Gore soon joined in the spirit of Koch's wisecracks. "We're electing a president, not a preacher," he said. He also accused Dukakis of being too "scared" to criticize Jackson.

Trying to force an opening for himself, in search of the middle, Gore continued to polarize. After meeting with the Israeli leader Yitzhak Shamir, he praised his irredentist position on the occupied territories. (Garth happened to be a consultant to Shamir's right-wing Likud

Party.) "The means are not important; it's the ends that matter," said Gore, in defense of Shamir. Then he denounced thirty of his Senate colleagues, all longtime supporters of Israel, for sending a letter to Shamir urging him to accept the idea of land-for-peace. "I'm not pandering," Gore said.

He had been accusing Dukakis of weakness for months. In February, he claimed that Dukakis had said he would accept a Soviet client state in Nicaragua, which was untrue. In New York, Gore distorted Dukakis's accurate restatement of NATO nuclear doctrine to make him seem unreliable and dangerous. On April 12, in a debate, Gore resorted to a new issue to make Dukakis appear weak. Some years ago, a convicted murderer in Massachusetts named Willie Horton had been furloughed by prison authorities and committed a rape. The furlough policy had begun under the administration of Dukakis's Republican predecessor. The governor, in any case, does not review the furloughs of individual prisoners, a process handled by a board. Most states have similar policies, and so does the federal government. When Dukakis first learned about the Horton incident he hesitated to change the policy. The penal experts assured him that, in spite of this unfortunate exception, it was working. Furloughs, they explained, were an essential instrument in a rewards-and-punishment system to control the prison population; doing away with the furlough program would have no effect on the crime rate. Nevertheless, a crusade by a local newspaper, the *Lawrence Eagle Tribune*, stirred up public opinion. And Dukakis, under pressure, finally agreed to tighten up the policy on first-degree murderers. One more fact: Willie Horton was a fearsome-looking black man.

In the debate, Gore mentioned neither Willie Horton's name nor his race. He depicted Dukakis as weak, handing out "weekend passes for convicted criminals." Dukakis, responding indirectly, shot back that his "experience" as an executive was superior to Gore's. Gore shrank from his attack, never alluding to the issue again. But James Pinkerton, the Bush campaign's director of opposition research, was monitoring the New York debate. It was the first time anyone in the Bush group had ever heard of Willie Horton. "The more people who know who Willie Horton is, the better off we'll be," he told Lee Atwater.

Gore's million dollars were spent. Garth explained that another million was needed. Koch, who prided himself on never having gone unmentioned in a twenty-four-hour news cycle in New York in more than a decade, raised his profile. At the entrance of a subway stop, Koch drowned Gore out shouting to the crowd, then grabbed him, pushed him and pulled him back. Gore recoiled, but Koch snared him again. Gore had become his complete captive.

Koch's unceasing derision of Jackson gave his object of scorn the moral upper hand and the dramatic advantage, for Koch's antics coincided with Jackson's idea of the storyline. Koch made possible the occasion to which Jackson might rise. By refusing to answer Koch's talk in kind, he presented himself as the successor to the martyrs of the civil rights movement. Because of the attacks, he attained a transforming quality that he would not match later in the campaign. Thus Koch brought about what he was inveighing against: the legitimation of Jesse Jackson, in "Hymietown" no less.

At last, Gore attempted to separate himself from Koch. The mayor, he said, was speaking for himself, which was something that had never been in doubt. What was in question was Gore's larger purpose. He appeared superfluous to his own campaign. He was engulfed by New York.

Throughout the 1980s, Gore had adroitly maneuvered in Washington—the center—by the profession of centrism. Yet his search for the middle in the campaign, similar to the middle he had found in the capital, had been in vain. Presidential politics within the Democratic Party was not Reagan's Washington writ large. Where Gore had located himself was not in the center but in a vacuum. Koch, for his part, had damaged not only Gore but himself. His exhibition in the primary offended and embarrassed many New Yorkers who had tolerated him until then. A year later, with voters wearied of his long-running act and flourishing city corruption, he was defeated in the Democratic mayoral primary by David Dinkins, a progressive black of a generation older than Jackson, who put enormous stress on civility.

Amid the hounds of hell, Dukakis had been calm and collected. He skirted invective, appearing a model of self-control. Without any change in his manner, he rose above the clamor. The Democrats began to invest him with a presidential air because of his indifference to the barking and baying. It was in New York that Dukakis's campaign style, or rather his nonstyle, was stamped and certified once and for all. He still had no real message. But the New York primary seemed to him to have solved the problem that had embroiled his campaign since its beginning. New York had proven to him that his minimalism was more than enough. He saw the results there as a personal triumph, dismissing his aides when they attempted to explain the racial undertow and the role of Jackson.

For the rest of the primaries, Dukakis's schedule assumed a clocklike efficiency. Three days a week he was in Boston, four days on the road. He claimed that managing the state demanded his time. But, in truth, he did not really want to leave home. If he were going to win anyway, he saw no good reason for being in unfamiliar places. He commuted to the campaign.

Jackson flew out of New York in a rage. The composure he maintained there began to crack. After convincing himself that he had been on the verge of a breakthrough, Jackson could not scale back his expectations. But Dukakis won all the primaries after New York, except in the District of Columbia. He pretended that Jackson was not even there, as if he were an invisible man. Jackson campaigned harder, slept less and lost every Tuesday. The bitterness that he had carried away from New York would have to be served at the convention.

Dukakis's natural self-restraint in New York seemed, at the time, to augur well for a happy ending. The less Dukakis was doing or saying, the more Bush sank in the polls. Dukakis did not even bother to use the remaining primaries as a forum to develop a message for the fall campaign. During the California primary, hardly anyone was aware when he was in the state.

Michael Dukakis had been an announced candidate for president for more than a year. In his odyssey, he had passed through personal traumas—his wife had publicly confessed to drug addiction; his closest associate was banished from his presence—and yet he had triumphed. He had spent sleepless months in every region in the country, delivering hundreds of speeches before every kind of audience. He had suffered setbacks, but had vanquished a large field of experienced opponents. He was the toast of his fellow Greek-Americans, who hailed him as a modern Achilles, and of the Commonwealth of Massachusetts. He was the prospective nominee of his party in a year that seemed to belong to the Democrats. He had every expectation of occupying the Oval Office six months hence.

Back in his office in the State House, he telephoned his former press secretary, Patricia O'Brien. "I'm sitting here at my desk staring out the window and wondering how it all happened," he said. "It's still hard to believe. I keep asking myself, 'What happened to the other guys?' "

11

The End of Ideology

The earliest drafts of Michael Dukakis's acceptance speech contained no references to Mikhail Gorbachev or the Soviet Union. They did, however, deal with the question of whether he was tough on crime; already Willie Horton was stalking him. "Crime," he was scripted to say, "is when a seventy-year-old man is attacked and beaten. Crime is when a young man is killed by a hit-and-run driver who may have been drunk or on drugs. Crime is *real*. I know, because that seventy-year-old man was my father. That young man was my brother. And don't let anyone tell you that the chief executive you're looking at right now is soft on crime."

These horrific stories happened to be true. Dukakis, unlike George Bush, had been deeply touched by crime. And this rendering of his experiences had been used to great political effect before. In 1982, in "The Rematch" with tough-guy Ed King, Dukakis's campaign staff had spent considerable effort turning the candidate's story, which he didn't like to talk about, into emotional rhetoric. When Dukakis used it, the crime issue was neutralized in the campaign. But most of this draft, including the true-crime story, was tossed aside and with it the preemptive reply on Willie Horton.

In the next draft, Gorbachev made an appearance. Dukakis was to say that he would "take the lead" from him "with an *agenda for action*: . . . We will challenge him to a new era of peaceful competition. Technological competition. . . . The kind of competition that we Americans can win." But this was cheerleading more than policymaking; it failed to recognize the uniqueness of Gorbachev, or that U.S.– Soviet relations were in a sea change. The "agenda for action" prescribed no specific action. Along the way, the crime issue had vanished from the speech. Now the "agenda for action" did too.

"Why are we doing something radically different?" Dukakis asked testily of his advisers. "Why don't we do something we've done all along?" He claimed to have no taint of ideology in his bloodstream. He was eager to declare a war against ideology. To him, the end of ideology was the reign of virtue. Ideology was a form of corruption—a corruption of reason. In spite of his disavowals, however, Dukakis did have an ideology—a worldview—which even had an address. It was located on the corner of Memorial Drive and Kennedy Street in Cambridge, Massachusetts, at Harvard's Kennedy School of Government—"my State Department," he said. Dukakis's principal experience of the Cold War took place within the confines of its red brick walls.

After his defeat in 1978, he exiled himself to the banks of the Charles River, ten minutes away from the State House on the Red Line. As Dukakis instructed students in the State and Local Government Program, he himself assimilated what was known as the "twenty bromides of effective public management." ("Cooperate, don't capitulate; in the end, we're all in this together.")

The world according to the Kennedy School was fragmented into case studies of discrete situations to be discretely solved. Dukakis's favorite case was of an economic development project in Mount Olive, New Jersey, thwarted by political cross-pressures. What was missing in the equation was the disinterested manager to keep the politics under control. This was Dukakis's ultimate ideal of leadership. It was what he meant by competence.

The Kennedy School was in the business of competence. Professors joked that the school was "exactly halfway between left and wrong," as one put it. The approach manufactured at the Kennedy School was sold as neutrality. Those who were passionate were suspect. Being above it all assured integrity; disengagement was the true sign of professionalism. The questions asked were not: Who benefits? What do you stand for? What kind of society do you want? Conflict existed to be resolved. In the Kennedy School lexicon, the word "conflict" never stood by itself. It always appeared as "conflict resolution," or "partnership," as Dukakis preferred to call it. Instability was the greatest evil; it was worse than injustice. Politics was a technical task, a matter of problem-solving.

The Kennedy School came into being in 1966, just as Camelot was collapsing in Vietnam. The war had been formulated by the "best and the brightest," many of them trained at Harvard, who tried to reduce the Cold War flashpoint to a series of managerial assignments: "kill ratios," "strategic hamlets" and "urban relocations" (i.e., bombing the countryside). The Kennedy School was not based on a critique of this mindset. Instead, it sought to routinize and rationalize it.

The school became a huge credentialing operation for the administrative class of the modern state. For some of its founders, the model was France's École Nationale d'Administration—ENA—set up after World War II to ensure that France produced the top civil servants in Europe. The énaques, as the graduates of ENA were known, were technocrats par excellence who not only came to rule the bureaucracies of the French state but also left government service to head powerful French corporations. Graduation from ENA, in short, assured France of a highly polished cadre who enjoyed unparalleled prestige and power.

Management, of course, is inevitable and necessary in any society. But management for what? The Kennedy School tried to armor its students against the ebb and flow of ideologies so that they could survive with long careers of public service. To be protected against the cycles of American history, they had to be made intellectually asexual. They were told that the higher cause of "good government" required it. The ideological lobe of their brains was gently burned away with the penetrating ray of case studies. Many of them became politically color-blind, tone-deaf and sterile. No superior could suspect them of political deviance because they were void in the suit of ideology. Thus the Kennedy School created a contradiction in terms: the person purporting to make policy—which is always driven by interests, ideas and values—purports to have no interests, ideas or values. What then will drive the wheel of policy? *The data*! And that was why the students at the Kennedy School were called "the quants." Quantification was the lifeblood of efficiency, which was the essence of "good government." The bias in favor of problem-solving led Richard Neustadt and

Ernest May, two of the senior professors at the school with a deep sense of history and politics, to write a counterbook, *Thinking in Time: The Uses of History for Decision Makers.*

"I don't understand why people use this word 'technocrat.' I don't know what it means," said an annoyed Dukakis. What it meant was someone who defined himself in terms of technique and procedure. But Dukakis regarded the word as a false label, like "liberal." He did not see himself as the outstanding representative in American politics of that segment of the new class for whom managerialism is an ideology.

The Kennedy School was not a community of scholars. In spite of their "value-free" teachings, many of the professors were no less political than any establishment in the past. The great post-Camelot example was Henry Kissinger, a Harvard professor of government who had made his reputation with a clinically written book on policy options in nuclear warfare, *Nuclear Weapons and Foreign Policy.* Kissinger was elevated from the faculty club as a traditional brain-truster. He was supposed to provide the ideas that would serve the Wise Men of the old establishment. Under the patronage of Nelson Rockefeller, Kissinger rose to his initial prominence writing his study on nuclear strategy for the Council on Foreign Relations. Rockefeller, first Nelson, then David, envisioned Kissinger as the preeminent intellectual in their retinue.

The old and new establishments had completely different sources of their notions of public service. Both believed they were disinterested. But the old establishment, resting on piles of old money, was deeply aware of the power of wealth. Indeed, it believed that its personal security enabled it to transcend all venal interests and represent the national interest. The new men of power, technocratic in disposition, dealt with the nitty-gritty world of interests by reducing them to scientistic categories in case studies. This special knowledge was the equivalent of old money; it was what enabled the technocrats to transcend the material.

The old establishment could always fall back on the power base of its own class. The new establishment, however, had to find a base. The professors were political entrepreneurs; the game theory they taught was an abstract form of what they practiced. For these players, the base had to be a candidate.

The closest thing Michael Dukakis had to a spiritual identity was as a Harvardian. Though he had not gone to Harvard College and lacked the characteristic jokey cynicism of his generation that had, it was as inevitable that he would turn for advice to his technocratic soulmates in the House of Credentials as it was that he would buy his next suit in Filene's basement. The Kennedy School had saved him during his "public death." It had given him a renewed meaning. Now it provided him with a shadow government.

Both Dukakis and his Kennedy School colleagues were victims of the recent history of the Democratic Party. They were driven by the need to replay their political defeats and overcome them. In the mid-1970s, they emerged as precocious and promising. Dukakis had been elected governor, Carter president. Carter called many of the Kennedy School professors to Washington. Suddenly, they found themselves being routed by an ideological movement they could not grasp and considered irrational. The Dukakis retreat and the Carter retreat converged at the Kennedy School. They had been partly undone by their own technocratic fixations. But the lesson they learned was not that they had been too blind to larger ideas; it was, essentially, that they hadn't been clever enough. Inside the citadel of technocracy, they refined their craft and plotted their restorations. Dukakis was their instrument for correcting the errors of the past. The new world of the 1990s was already dawning, but they were still litigating a case they had lost in 1980. With Dukakis, they hoped to refight their last war and win it. Then they could prove that they were truly the expert managers of national security.

Within the Kennedy School, the State and Local Government Program was just across the atrium from the international affairs department. But in taking that walk Dukakis wasn't traveling from the particular to the universal, from the local to the global. Every office had the same phones, the same chairs, the same desks, the same furniture of the mind. To the technocrat for whom means were ends, a case study of industrial policy in a milltown existed on the same plane as a case study of the Cuban missile crisis. He did not understand that these two cases, however similar they might be in their bindings and typefaces, were radically different. The gulf between what he knew and didn't know was flattened and narrowed by the floor plan of the Kennedy School.

Dukakis felt especially indebted to the dean of the Kennedy School, Graham Allison, for making it possible for him to come there after his defeat. Allison was an empire builder. During his ten-year reign, he tripled the size of the faculty and increased the budget more than sixteenfold. His methods, however, aroused controversy. He promised to make a wealthy Texas businessman and his wife officers of the school in exchange for a hefty gift. He arranged for the bestowal of a special

award on then-Attorney General Edwin Meese, who had approved
large government contracts to the school for seminars for Reagan
administration officials. The crassness of the Meese arrangement incited general outrage at Harvard and Allison was forced abruptly to
cancel it. In the meantime, he was being paid as a part-time counselor
to Defense Secretary Caspar Weinberger. Allison also approved a
$250,000 grant from the Arms Control and Disarmament Agency for
a study that showed arms control as a failure, thereby lending the seal
of Harvard to conservative views. While he was on Weinberger's payroll, Allison was advising Dukakis, which gave a new meaning to the
value-free ideal of the Kennedy School. How the puritanical Dukakis
overlooked this glaring conflict of interest remains a mystery. Eventually, Allison emerged as Dukakis's chief adviser on Gorbachev and in
the circles around Dukakis was mentioned as the next CIA director or
national security adviser.

There was also talk that another high official in the Dukakis administration was bound to be Joseph S. Nye, Jr., a deputy undersecretary of
state during the Carter years and the director of the Center for Science
and International Affairs at the Kennedy School. He edited, with
Allison, a book on foreign policy entitled *Hawks, Doves, and Owls.*
Owls had the wisdom to glide above the ideological factionalists. Nye's
most recent work was *Nuclear Ethics,* a careful essay on the morality
of deterrence. His conclusion, calling for a "managed balance of
power," was a composition in the mandarin bureaucratic style prized
at the Kennedy School: "Where there is a degree of common interest
in stability, the balance of power can become a positive situation in
which both sides win."

Madeleine Albright, a deputy on the National Security Council
under Carter and a professor at the Georgetown University School of
Foreign Service, was placed in charge of his task force on national
security. Daughter of a liberal Czech diplomat and a former foreign
policy aide to Senator Edmund Muskie, she tried her best in the
campaign to act as an honest broker among the policy advisers, the
political strategists and the candidate. She discovered that it was a
frequently thankless and frustrating task.

The first meeting of members of the foreign policy team was an
informal gathering in December 1987 at the Harvard Faculty Club.
Later that month, near Christmas, Allison and Nye met with the
governor at the State House. The main outcome of that meeting was
perhaps the most important intellectual decision of the campaign. Nye
had read parts of a book about to be published by Paul Kennedy, a Yale

University professor, entitled *The Rise and Fall of the Great Powers*. Kennedy's sweeping history from 1500 to the present was a long illustration of Walter Lippmann's maxim (cited by Kennedy) that "the nation's commitments and the nation's power" had to be brought "into balance." Kennedy called the imbalance between means and ends "imperial overstretch," and charted how overseas commitment led to massive military spending and then to economic decay. His argument was not a Procrustean bed, but quite subtle and varied. In the American case, "relative decline" was due partly to the natural recovery of Western Europe and Japan from the devastation of World War II. But it was also due to self-destruction and self-indulgence that were producing an increasingly insolvent foreign policy. " . . . decision-makers in Washington," he wrote, "must face the awkward and enduring fact that the sum total of the United States' global interests and obligations is nowadays far larger than the country's power to defend them all simultaneously." The price of continued "overstretch," the historian predicted, would be continued decline.

At issue was the decline not simply of America but of the entire postwar order. Kennedy had assimilated the Cold War into an older historical perspective about the rise and fall of empires. In so doing he debunked the Cold War's permanence. As he explained, it had had a beginning and a middle and it would have an end. It did not have a destiny of its own; it was just a chapter in world history. Thus Kennedy was speaking the unspeakable.

"My argument," recalled Nye about his conversation with Dukakis, "was that it [Kennedy's idea] was analytically not correct and also probably a political loser. It was a misrepresentation of the nature of the problems we faced, a series of problems created by foolish decisions in the 1980s."

The roots of America's predicament, according to Nye, were not deep; they ran only to the irrational decisionmaking of the Reagan era. In an article in *Foreign Policy,* Nye explained his position. At its center, though, was a logical contradiction, because Nye accepted and denied Kennedy's analysis at the same time. "The United States," he wrote, "will be the leading state in an era when, in contrast to the 1800s or the 1950s, the conditions for economic hegemony no longer obtain." In short, he accepted the essence of Kennedy's analysis but rejected his conclusion. "Although the next decade will require Americans to cope with Reagan's debts," he wrote, "there is no reason why the world's wealthiest country cannot pay for both its international commitments and its domestic investments." In short, we could still afford everything. Technically, Nye might be right. All that was lacking was a political consensus willing to sustain his point. But he never considered that this monumental task would entail a drastic upheaval. And he neglected to factor in the cataclysm in the Soviet Union that had already made many of our "international commitments" anachronisms. Nye prescribed better management of a world that was rapidly fading.

Dukakis was predisposed to accept Nye's arguments even before he heard them. "He agreed," said Nye. "He had a natural optimism about the country. He said something to the effect that 'I don't think this is a country in decline.' " Kennedy's ideas were instantly discarded. "It was never a temptation," said Nye. "It wasn't these advisers holding him back. It was kicking open an open door."

Their meeting took place before Kennedy's book was published, and there is no evidence that Dukakis read it then or later. He was willing to dismiss what he had not pondered. Dukakis saw the theme of decline only as a threat to himself. He did not want to be broadcasting bad news. Acknowledging difficulties, much less decline, was the third rail of American politics. Jimmy Carter had touched it with his talk of a "crisis of confidence" and his eyeballs had melted. Survival dictated an upbeat message and extreme caution about the rest.

Dukakis, therefore, sharply narrowed the issues at the beginning of the campaign. The intellectual scaffolding was partly in place for constructing a picture of the Republicans as the party of decline and insolvency, incapable of coping with a radically different world. But the rejection of Kennedy reflected an inclination to act as if nothing was fundamentally wrong—or new. In an interview with Robert Scheer of the Los Angeles Times in late May, Dukakis said, "When you say 'an end to the Cold War,' I'm not sure I understand what that means."

It was not until the primaries were over that Dukakis delivered a major foreign policy speech. In June, he chose the Atlantic Council, an old-line organization devoted to the care and preservation of NATO, as his forum. "According to his aides," wrote Don Oberdorfer in The Washington Post, "Dukakis' main aim was to persuade the audience of foreign and defense policy experts and U.S. allies that he is 'not another George McGovern' promising drastic changes in U.S. foreign policy as did the 1972 Democratic nominee." Dukakis pledged that his approach to Gorbachev would be "steady, step-by-step," nothing immoderate. He balanced his opposition to certain nuclear weapons systems—the MX and Midgetman missiles—with what he called a "Conventional Defense Initiative." Beefing up conventional forces in Europe to raise the nuclear threshold was one of the oldest theories hatched in the laboratories of the nuclear strategists. Dukakis unveiled it just as the threat of Soviet tanks crashing through the Fulda Gap in Germany, which was a principal rationale for NATO, was disappearing. On the spindle of Cold War history, Dukakis would scrupulously sum up the old thinking with a slightly different pattern.

Immediately after Dukakis's speech, Nye flew to Paris, where he reassured a diplomatic audience at the French Institute for International Relations that as president Dukakis would be a circumspect manager of the Cold War. It was "silly," Nye said, to compare him to McGovern. Nor was he "running as an outsider" like Carter. And he wouldn't do anything as rash as Reagan had, such as proposing the elimination of all nuclear weapons. "No more Reykjaviks," pledged Nye. "No more loose talk about getting rid of nuclear weapons." Dukakis was a man who could "see the big picture." With him in the Oval Office, there would be "no free gift" for Gorbachev. Nye understood the Dukakis strategy by defining him by who he wasn't. In Nye's account, he wasn't McGovern, Carter or Reagan. But who was he in the period in which the Cold War was ending? That identity could only be provided by redefining the questions, not by giving the old answers.

At the very beginning of the campaign, Madeleine Albright attempted to bring the candidate into contact with specialists on the Soviet Union. The first meeting of what was supposed to have become a regular group was scheduled for July 1987 at her Georgetown townhouse. But Dukakis cancelled the session in order to prepare for a debate. It was a year later, on the eve of the Democratic convention, before the meeting finally took place in his State House office—the first and only meeting of its kind. "We were told before we went in that he was impatient, that he wasn't interested in long analysis or explanations," said Robert Legvold, the director of the W. Averell Harriman Institute for the Advanced Study of the Soviet Union at Columbia University. "The discussion would begin; he'd cut it off. He'd ask a series of staccato questions that would prevent him from learning about the fundamental issues at stake. I came away convinced that he was condemned to chaos on foreign policy. He didn't have a depth to orient himself. He wasn't building a foundation for dealing with East–West issues. It seemed to be a kind of chaotic, almost incoherent approach. All of that was discouraging. He wanted to prove he was in charge of the discussion at the expense of learning."

Afterward, Legvold suggested to Christopher Edley, the campaign's issues director, that the governor needed a series of individual sessions with Joe Nye. Edley thought it was a good idea, but nothing ever came of it. The policy experts were constantly held in check by the political strategists. From the moment that the first poll arrived showing public perception of Dukakis as weaker in foreign policy than Bush, the campaign high command decided to downplay the subject as much as possible. Albright argued that the public's view could be changed, but she was overruled. By avoiding foreign policy, the campaign implicitly accepted the definition of Dukakis's credentials as inferior and his image as weaker. Early on, Edmund Muskie suggested to Albright how Dukakis's image could be strengthened. He and the other former secretaries of state from Democratic administrations, Dean Rusk and Cyrus Vance, would have a session with the candidate. Then they might emerge at a press conference, where they would pronounce him informed and fit. Albright liked the idea and conveyed it to the strategists, who tossed it aside. They feared guilt by association: if Dukakis appeared with Muskie he would be thought of as another Carter. And it was crucial to protect the idea of who Dukakis wasn't.

The tension between the policy and political sides of the campaign was partly relieved by a rhetorical gambit. The dramatic events in the Soviet Union were reduced to a formula: "testing Gorbachev." (Allison scaled up the concept into an article in *Foreign Affairs* entitled "Testing Gorbachev," which Dukakis used as his Cliff Notes on Soviet policy.) According to this line of reasoning, the burden of action was put on the Soviet leader. It was up to Gorbachev to prove that he was real. Dukakis, in the meantime, demonstrated his toughness and knowledge by his skepticism. There was no need for him to go into too many details. Bush, too, talked about "testing" and "challenging"; Dukakis's caution reduced his actual differences with Bush to a series of nuances that were virtually impossible to discern. It was this approach that prompted Robert Legvold to write:

> As the new Soviet leadership has begun to stir interest in the West, the closest thing we have had to statesmanship is the urging that we "test" Gorbachev, by which was meant that we take him seriously and probe to see how far he is willing to alter Soviet policy. It seems increasingly irrelevant advice, as Gorbachev meets more and more tests we have not yet collected ourselves to pose. Increasingly the test is for the West: Do we have the imagination, creativity, and brave courage to respond to the very revolution in Soviet foreign policy we have waited half a century for?

The culmination of evasiveness was reached in the Democratic platform, a 2,500-word document, shorter than most magazine articles, written in orotund, vague phrases, intended to avoid the sort of ideological disputes that had rended the party in the past. It was entitled "The Restoration of Competence and the Revival of Hope"—Michael Dukakis spliced with Jesse Jackson. In it, Gorbachev appeared as fundamentally no different from other Soviet leaders. The Cold War was still very much on. "We believe in an America, neither gun-shy nor trigger-happy, that will promote peace and prevent war . . . not by relaxing our vigilance on the assumption that long-range Soviet interests have permanently changed . . . but . . . by testing the intentions of the new Soviet leaders. . . ."

If the word "vigilance" recalled the "long twilight struggle," it might be because the author of the platform was Theodore Sorensen, John F. Kennedy's intellectual amanuensis, who had helped craft his inaugural address. That speech was the rhetorical high point of the Cold War, delivered at its zenith. This platform, produced at its end, was as fatuous as Kennedy's speech was stirring. Nevertheless, the Dukakis campaign was delighted with the effort to keep dangerous new thinking to a minimum. "Brevity is the soul of victory," said Sorensen.

II

There was no Kennedy School case study to prepare Michael Dukakis for Jesse Jackson. For a moment, Jackson had believed that he might win the New York primary and go on to win the nomination. He was scourged and flailed there, and he took it as a kind of martyrdom. As he suffered loss after loss, his feeling of glorified victimhood grew. He considered his defeat an injustice and the process illegitimate. Once he thought of things in this way, the chaotic cosmos made sense again. The millennialist civil rights protest rhetoric was unfurled. Jackson got back on the cross.

By staying the course after he had been decisively beaten, Jackson created the illusion of momentum for Dukakis. "Keep hope alive!" Jackson shouted. He kept the drama alive by casting himself as the spoiler. As soon as he had lost in New York, he raised the quadrennial question: What does Jesse want?

Since 1972, he had been using the selection of the vice presidential candidate as an occasion for denouncing the nominee. His complaint of exclusion was consistent for sixteen years. In 1984, he was aggrieved that Walter Mondale had not considered him as his running mate. When asked to join Mondale and Gary Hart at a fundraiser to retire George McGovern's campaign debt, he wrote, in a fit of pique, "I have no intention of being one more false prophet for my people. . . . I will not be one more snake oil salesman telling them to get out there and vote, and everything will be okay." Upon Mondale's selection of Geraldine Ferraro, members of Jackson's immediate entourage donned buttons: "Ferraro, Thank Jesse Jackson." Jackson played out his drama with Mondale into the fall, even appearing at a joint press conference at which he was supposed to endorse Mondale but failed to do so, thereby humiliating the candidate as the network cameras whirred.

The day after the 1988 New York primary Jackson resumed his long game with an opening bid for the vice presidency. "I need his support base to win. He needs my support base to win. Together we can win." Early in May, he started protesting the convention rules, just as he had in 1984. The week before the California primary, he claimed he had "earned" consideration. "If I were to win the nomination, with the kind of campaign that Dukakis has run, he would deserve consideration and he would get it." Jackson then defined the qualifications for vice president as "Third World experience and sensitivity."

Dukakis never had any intention of naming Jackson. Unfortunately, he didn't bother to tell him. Instead, he tried to smooth things over by treating him with false deference. Jackson, he said, was under "very serious consideration." It was "still a very open process." He met with Jackson at his Brookline home on July 4th, disingenuously asked him if he wished to be considered and then dropped the subject. Dukakis did not ventilate his principled differences with Jackson or explain on practical grounds why picking him would doom the ticket. Jackson, for his part, insisted on being treated more equal than others. He was late in submitting financial records, which were incomplete, and refused to answer questions about his health. By postponing the inevitable rejection, Dukakis was building the pressure for a massive explosion. He believed that with his calm manner and the inexpressive, lawyerly conduct of his counselor, Paul Brountas, who interviewed Jackson about the vice presidency, he was laying the groundwork for conciliation. But Dukakis's idea of respect was Jackson's idea of disrespect. He thought that Dukakis was making him an invisible man. By stringing Jackson along, Dukakis inflamed him. He never understood that what Jesse wanted was to dominate the stage.

There were many rational reasons for picking Lloyd Bentsen. The chairman of the Senate Finance Committee, deeply knowledgeable about the ways of Washington, Bentsen looked like an elder statesman. He conveyed an aura of prudence and stability. He was a native Texan, born to wealth, who had won his Senate seat by defeating a Republican carpetbagger, George Bush. While Bentsen was a Tory Democrat, congenial to big business, he had always maintained his partisan loyalty, unlike John Connally, who had defected to the Republicans. It was also of great importance that he had always supported civil rights. When his name came to Dukakis's attention, he was so far ahead of Bush that he was even leading him in Texas. Choosing Bentsen would not only reassure the conservative elements in the party but send a message that Dukakis would contest Bush everywhere, even in his home state. It was an aggressive, calculated and ultimately safe move.

But there was also an irrational reason for choosing Bentsen. Without it, Dukakis might not have picked him, according to several of his advisers. The man who didn't seem to dream was in the throes of a fantasy. It was that the 1988 election would be a replay of 1960, with himself in the role of the Brookline native—John F. Kennedy. Kennedy had chosen Lyndon Johnson as his running mate. By picking Bentsen, the Boston–Austin axis was reconstituted. (While Dukakis pondered his choice, Brountas, his law school classmate, who had driven across the country with him in 1960 to see Kennedy accept the Democratic nomination in Los Angeles, handed him a black binder containing a copy of *Washington Post* publisher Philip Graham's memo to Kennedy urging him to select Johnson.) The myth was literal in Dukakis's translation. He acted as if, seeing his team, the country would respond with a shock of recognition. Time and again, during the campaign, he returned to the theme. "They said the same thing about Jack Kennedy in 1960—all that gloom and doom. And what was he saying? 'We can do better.' . . . Cite these facts and George Bush will tell you that you're downgrading America, the same thing Richard Nixon did in 1960 when John Kennedy was telling us to look to a new frontier." But Kennedy, who was completely unlike the dreamer, could only be worshiped in a dream. Dukakis was Kennedy School, not Kennedy. In his wishful thinking, he passed over the history since Kennedy in which the Democratic Party lost power and fractured over the Vietnam War. Dukakis had no sense of the formidable task of redefining the party at the end of the Cold War. His story was not the climax of an heroic epic—the return of the king—but the triumph of the clerk. His insistence on the Kennedy motif underlined the final pathos of his campaign.

Two hours after Bentsen told Dukakis he would accept his offer, the campaign tried to reach Jackson in his hotel room in Cincinnati. He had already left to take a plane to Washington. Upon his arrival, a swarm of reporters broke the news. "I'm too controlled!" he said. "I'm too clear! I'm too *mature* to be angry!" That night he brought the NAACP convention to its feet. "I may not be on the ticket, but I am qualified. *Qualified! Qualified!*"

All of Dukakis's superficial attempts to gloss over the tension with Jackson had made matters worse. Now they reversed roles, with Dukakis as the supplicant. Jackson's position rested on his claim to be the gatekeeper to the black vote. It had been argued that there was a hole in the electorate—a space that ought to be filled by those who did not vote. Most of them were of lower income and many of minority background. If these natural Democrats ever showed up at the polls they would transform politics. Jackson, therefore, had to be handled with care. But the missed telephone call had ignited his wrath; it was the fire this time. "It is too much to expect," he said, "that I will go out in the field and be the champion vote-picker and bale them up and bring them back to the big house and get a reward of thanks, while people who do not pick nearly as much votes, who don't carry the same amount of weight among the people, sit in the big house and make the decision." The man he privately called "that little Greek" was now a slave driver.

By his miscue Dukakis had provided Jackson with the opportunity to stage his drama of neglect and disillusionment and make himself the center of attention. He threatened a floor fight, saying, "There's room for it in the rules." Cameras. He went into a sulk in Chicago, canceling all his appointments. More cameras. He asked former president Carter to mediate, as if only the master negotiator of the Camp David accords could bring the two sides together. Even more cameras. He boarded the "Rainbow Express" bus caravan, a slow train of protest across the country to Atlanta. Cameras in every city. He arrived at a rally of tens of thousands in Piedmont Park, calling for "shared victory and shared responsibility." The next night, speaking to three thousand at the Fox Theater, he was defiant: "I will never surrender!" By now, the entire national press corps was in attendance at Jackson's performance: The Cat in the Hat Comes Back.

Dukakis may have won the nomination, but Jackson had seized the convention. It revolved all the more now around the question of what did Jesse want and how to bring him on board. Dukakis granted most of Jackson's demands to keep him from making further trouble that week. "I feel my role would be less if I had a job, a salary, a title,"

Jackson said at a peacemaking press conference with Dukakis and Bentsen.

Jackson's histrionic grievance was to have its effect. Black turnout in 1988 fell 4.3 percentage points from 1984, from 55.8 to 51.5, according to the U.S. Census Bureau. (Curtis Gans, the director of the nonpartisan Committee for the Study of the American Electorate, estimates that because of overreporting of black turnout by exit pollsters the true number is closer to 44 percent.) The major burden for black apathy must rest with Dukakis. It can also be attributed to Bush's appearance as a much less threatening figure than Reagan. But Jackson made a contribution with his play on the themes of deceit, discrimination and disenchantment. "There's no question in my mind that Jackson helped depress black voting," said a key Dukakis adviser, expressing a belief widely shared within the campaign. "It was his whole attitude and what it conveyed. We never recovered."[1]

On the night of Jackson's speech to the convention, Dukakis agreed to let his followers control the floor. Jackson delivered a powerful reading of excerpts from his collected speeches. He called the Third World "the real world." When Reagan and Gorbachev met, he said, "Seven-eighths of the human race was locked out of that room." He urged his listeners to see their fate in him: "When my name goes in nomination, your name goes in nomination." He envisioned his martyrdom: "I'd rather go down in a stirring fight than drown to death in a

1. After the election, the idea that a bigger turnout by nonvoters, especially blacks and Hispanics, would have brought Dukakis victory was challenged by an established scholar on the subject, Ruy A. Teixeira. Dukakis, he pointed out, lost the election by slightly more than 6.9 million votes. "If black turnout had matched turnout in the general population, the Democrats would have netted about 610,000 additional votes. If black turnout had matched that of whites, the net Democratic gain would have been about 862,000 votes. And if black turnout had somehow been ten points higher than whites, the Democratic gain would have amounted to about 2,349,000 votes." However, Bush won fourteen states by a margin of less than 5.5 percent, most of them by margins less than that. These states, with the exception of Louisiana, were located in the Northeast, the Midwest and the West. Together they accounted for 200 votes in the Electoral College, more than enough to have changed the outcome of the election. In these states, Bush won by slightly more than 1,115,000 votes. If black turnout in states such as Maryland, Pennsylvania, Ohio, Michigan, Illinois and California had been greater, the final result might very well have been much closer. Teixeira shrewdly observed that "increased turnout cannot by itself be [a] winning strategy," but his model was static, neglecting political factors. A different candidate and different issues—in short, a different political dynamic—might in the future increase turnout, as it has in the past. The arguments about nonvoters were not conclusively proved one way or another by the 1988 campaign. The question was particularly muddled by Jesse Jackson, whose actions helped curdle the strategy of mobilizing nonvoters.

sheltered shore." And he foresaw the resurrection: "It gets dark sometimes, but the morning comes. Don't you surrender. . . . Keep hope
alive! Keep hope alive! Keep hope alive!"

For more than a month, Jackson had consumed most of the time
and energy of the Dukakis campaign, which had not yet developed a
strategy for the fall. During the week in which Dukakis was supposed
to have the public's undivided attention, he had been overshadowed
by Jackson. Jackson, who had once tried to exhaust an audience's
emotions before it could be addressed by Martin Luther King, Jr., had
succeeded in depleting the Democrats before Dukakis uttered a word.
His acceptance speech now had to achieve what he had failed to do
in the entire campaign preceding it.

III

Dukakis had become the standard-bearer of the oldest political party
on earth by saying as little as possible. His blankness had served him
well, but it had also caused his troubles. John Sasso knocked Joe Biden
down because Dukakis was not being propelled forward by his own
energy. Jesse Jackson rose in Michigan because Dukakis could not grasp
what was already in his hand. Having elevated Jackson, Dukakis went
on to win because he could not lose. He was careful not to upset himself
by saying anything new.

Now Michael Dukakis wasn't George Bush. Most of Dukakis's advisers regarded Bush as a gag put on for their benefit. Just mentioning his
name made them smirk. They laughed at his mangled syntax and his
latest absurd charges about furloughs and the flag. Bush was mercilessly
ridiculed by the convention speakers: "He was born with a silver foot
in his mouth"; "Where was George?"; "He was born on third base and
thinks he hit a triple." The class undercurrent of the rhetoric, in fact,
was highly effective and aroused considerable anxiety among Bush's
handlers. But this line of attack did not last beyond the convention.
Dukakis disliked the class angle. He considered it emotional and thus
false. More important, he paid Bush little mind. Asked about Bush, as
he drove from the State House to Logan Airport, Dukakis said dismis-
sively, "Is he from New England?" That was all. It was a kind of joke
because Bush, of course, was originally from New England but had
moved away. This was Dukakis's way of ending discussion before there
had been any. What he didn't understand must be unreal. "Is he from
New England?" The unspoken answer was: He fell off the edge of the

earth. It never occurred to Dukakis to run against Bush as if he were a wealthy Yankee Republican from New England, which he was. Dukakis did not even draw upon the strength of his parochialism. It did, however, occur to Bush to run an old-fashioned Yankee Republican campaign against Dukakis as an un-Americanized immigrant.

When Dukakis entered the convention hall, Neil Diamond's song about immigrants, "Coming to America," was turned up so loud on the sound system that the floor boards rumbled and vibrated. The intention was to generate the crowd excitement that the candidate hadn't ever done by himself. Dukakis's first words were to thank his first cousin, the actress Olympia Dukakis, for introducing him. She had won an Oscar for her performance in *Moonstruck* as a long-suffering Italian wife and mother, living in an ethnic enclave of Brooklyn, whose forbearance keeps the family together. In her shadow, Dukakis was a member of the extended family of *Moonstruck*, "a son of immigrants," as he put it, one who has crossed over the bridge for white-collar work in the city "as a proud public servant."

Seven times at the beginning of his speech Dukakis referred to a "dream." It was a dream that had brought his parents to America, "carried me to this platform" and would enable Democrats to win. Michael Dukakis, the dreamer, promised to make one dream in particular come true. It was a dream of restoration—"to recapture the spirit of energy and of confidence and of idealism that John Kennedy and Lyndon Johnson inspired a generation ago." This was a vision of progress as the repetition of the past, with Dukakis in the role of Kennedy. As if to emphasize the literal-mindedness of his self-mythologizing, he dubbed his forthcoming administration "the next American frontier." Of course, he had used this phrase before as the blurry theme of a forgotten speech in December 1987 that was supposed to fill out the thinness of his message. Now he defined the "next frontier" with a numbing phrase he had uttered thousands of times: "good jobs at good wages." He was not headed toward some unexplored, sweeping frontier but to a smaller and familiar place. This speech was not a summons to blaze trails but a promise of material security.

Dukakis went on to list the several things he would do to make the middle class feel safer. His speech mostly consisted of lists of things to do, broken up by bursts of forced eloquence. Dukakis's favorite literary genre was the list. (Almost every page of his campaign book, *Creating the Future,* was filled with lists of what his policies had accomplished and would do.) On its face, the list seems to be efficient, brisk, orderly. But a set of points is the antithesis of narrative.

Dukakis presented no storyline about how the American people had arrived at this moment. He assumed their hopes and thus avoided the sticky subject. "I don't think I have to tell any of you how much we Americans expect of ourselves," he said. With this line, he began to dismiss the need for a larger purpose.

In his speech accepting the Democratic nomination for governor at the 1982 convention in Springfield, Massachusetts, Dukakis strained so hard for the Kennedy effect that he achieved unintentional parody: "Let the word go forth from Springfield. . . ." But in his attempt to emulate Kennedy in Atlanta Dukakis denied the essence of Kennedyism—the politics of high expectations. The man who would be Kennedy offered a rhetoric that could not have been more directly contradictory of Kennedy's 1960 acceptance speech, in which he sighted the New Frontier: "But the New Frontier of which I speak is not a set of promises—it is a set of challenges. It sums up, not what I intend to offer the American people, but what I intend to ask of them. It appeals to their pride, not their pocketbook—it holds out the promise of more sacrifice instead of more security. . . ."

After telling us that he would not tell us what we needed to do, Dukakis explained why he would not explain. "Because," he said, "this election is not about ideology. It's about competence."

A few weeks before the convention, a group of Dukakis's advisers met in a conference room in Boston's World Trade Center to develop thoughts for the acceptance speech. The chief guideline for the coming campaign was explicitly stated here: if the election were held on ideology, Bush would win; but if it were held on competence, Dukakis would win. From the beginning, the Dukakis campaign assumed its ideological weakness and rehearsed a defensive crouch. The offstage premise about ideology was so strongly felt that almost all of Dukakis's advisers encouraged him to insert it into his speech.

But not everybody within the campaign concurred. Tom Herman, deputy issues director and a former state official, who had known Dukakis for a long time, reviewed the speech with him. Herman said that he didn't believe that the line was true. He thought the campaign was about ideology. "Does this mean we're running only on making the trains run on time?" he asked. Dukakis grunted and moved on. He did not stop for even a moment to discuss the criticism. Dukakis really believed in the line. To him, ideology was irrational extremism. In 1978, he had lost to an ideological conservative; four years later, he won on the theme of competence. The line perfectly expressed his conceptions of public service and professional policymaking. It affirmed the technocratic sensibility as taught at the Kennedy School—an ideology of managerialism.[2]

Dukakis did not want a grand debate about national purpose. He hoped to avoid that. At his crowning moment he demonstrated in any case that he did not know how to make a larger argument. It was his notion that we would elect a president on bloodless, instrumental grounds, precisely where he believed that he was strongest. His line was a call for us to dream about his efficiency, which was virtue itself. But consider the line restated: This campaign is not about ideas, it is about techniques. Half of the line was prescient. Dukakis was done in by Bush's campaign techniques. But half of the line was blind.

In his speech, Dukakis tried to leap over the ideology question by putting himself in a time machine and setting the date at 1962. " . . . the courage that looked Khrushchev in the eye during the Cuban missile crisis is as strong and as vibrant today as it has ever been. We must be—we are—and we will be—militarily strong." Then Dukakis set the date at the present. "President Reagan has set the stage for deep cuts in nuclear arms—and I salute him for that. He has said that we should judge the Soviet Union not by what it says, but by what it does—and I agree with that."

Thus Dukakis presented himself as resolute as Kennedy was standing on the brink of the single most dangerous moment in the Cold War. Dukakis described a Soviet Union fundamentally unchanged since then. He was skeptical of Gorbachev's revolution. Dukakis's support for arms control was under the foolproof authority of the gold-plated cold warrior Ronald Reagan. Dukakis showed his toughness by clinging to the past. He did not take his cue from Kennedy's acceptance speech: "The old era is ending. The old ways will not do."

Dukakis was hiding under political camouflage. He hoped that the witnesses he called—Kennedy and Reagan—would make his case for him. Yet he was making no case for himself that their names might be useful in proving. Once he had failed to acknowledge the reality of

2. Dukakis's disavowal of ideology could not have been farther from the temper of Kennedy's acceptance speech. Kennedy presented the 1960 presidential campaign as a contest to determine who would be the champion of the American spirit in the Cold War. "Can a nation organized and governed such as ours endure? That is the real question," he said. " . . . Can we carry through in an age where we will witness not only new breakthroughs in weapons of destruction—but also a race for mastery of the sky and the rain, the ocean and the tides, the far side of space and the inside of men's minds." "A race for mastery of the . . . inside of men's minds"—this was a definition of ideological struggle. At the end of the Cold War, Dukakis acted as though it was still at its height, but dismissed its substance—ideology.

Gorbachev's epochal transformations, he forfeited his greatest opportunity to define the historical moment. Dukakis's positioning was driven by fear—not of the Soviets, but of the Republicans.

By calling Reagan to the stand, Dukakis undercut his main theme. His line about ideology and competence was an oblique reference to the president. But the Reagan he was pushing aside was the Reagan of late 1986 and early 1987—the Reagan of the Iran-contra scandal. In the meantime, Dukakis was embracing the Reagan of the summits. The problem was that the inflexible ideologue had been replaced by the statesman. Dukakis was running against one Reagan and concealing himself behind the other. He was afraid to go beyond him, into a new frontier, as it were.

Dukakis closed by taking an ancient Athenian oath pledging good government, a gesture that evoked his immigrant background, devotion to public service and the Periclean atmospherics of the Kennedy period. " . . . We will revere and obey the law. We will strive to quicken our sense of civic duty. . . ."

The Democrats had been starved for victory for years. They had felt so defeated by Reagan that they abandoned criticizing him by name for fear of arousing a reaction against themselves. But Reagan was departing, and they were not frightened of Bush. Early in his speech, Dukakis said what they most wanted to hear: "We're going to win this race, we're going to win this race." The Democrats hungrily devoured these words and let out a ferocious roar. By the end of Dukakis's performance they had persuaded themselves that for the first time in a long time it might be true.

His speech had seemingly accomplished what he needed to do. In the afterglow, he appeared vital; the party delegates were filled with energy; and he was leading George Bush by seventeen points.

At the Kennedy School, "controlled euphoria" reigned, according to a professor there. The candidate's advisers began to envision their new jobs and offices in the capital. Some began scanning *The Washington Post*'s real estate section. One professor told his graduate students to hurry up and finish their work because they would be going to Washington in a matter of months.

For Dukakis, the convention speech was the climax of his career. Ten years before, he had experienced his "public death." In 1982, he had to overcome the man who had beaten him in order to return to life. In 1986, he had to exorcise the ghost of defeat by proving that he could win reelection. Winning the Democratic nomination was his final vindication. But the nature of the general election campaign to come had not really occurred to him. It didn't figure in the personal scenario. Thus his acceptance speech was at once an act of catharsis and hubris.

As Dukakis concluded his speech, one of Bush's handlers, who had been watching on television, phoned another. "It's a godsend," he said. Dukakis had fallen into the trap laid by the Pledge of Allegiance issue. "He just took a foreign oath."

12

The Birth of a Kinder, Gentler Nation

I

For his entire political career, Ronald Reagan had played the hero against Soviet Russia—"the very heart of darkness," he called it. But, on a sunny June day in 1988, he leisurely strolled across the cobblestones of Red Square arm in arm with Mikhail Gorbachev, who introduced him to children along the way as "Grandfather Reagan." The Cold War, Reagan decided, was over. "I was talking about another time, another era," he said.

On his journey home, the president stopped in London, where he delivered a speech explaining his mission to Moscow. "To those of us who remember the postwar era, all of this is cause for shaking the head in wonder," he said. But the "postwar era" was just ending. And the astonishment he referred to had to do with the reaction to his own role. If we remembered the Reagan who said that "the bombing begins in five minutes," this Reagan might appear out of character. Now the Cold War seemed so distant to him that he reminded his audience that he remembered it. "Quite possibly," he said, "we are beginning to take down the barriers of the postwar era." Gorbachev was "a serious man seeking serious reform. We must do all that we can to assist it. And this means openly acknowledging positive change—and crediting it."

Reagan's abandonment of Cold War nostalgia was a giant ideological step. On the right, the brief against him was lengthy. He was charged with being naïve and foolish, unduly influenced by his personal encounters with the seductive Gorbachev, guilty of fostering a false euphoria that betrayed the rationale of his military buildup, and creating breathing space for the unchanging enemy. "For conservatives," wrote George Will, acting as their proxy, "Ronald Reagan's foreign policy has produced much surprise but little delight. His fourth and, one prays, final summit is a suitable occasion for conservatives to look back with bewilderment and ahead with trepidation. . . . Reagan's rhetoric has accelerated the nation's intellectual disarmament. In his seventh and eighth years, he has declared the Cold War over."

Many prominent conservatives, from Robert Bork to Norman Podhoretz, signed their names to a full-page cartoon in the *New York Times* on June 23. It depicted a glowering bear, with sharp fangs, clawing a helpless man in a business suit. "Have We Forgotten That Every Time We've Hugged the Bear Somebody Else Has Suffered?" read the caption. "Now the bear is tired, wounded, and asking for our help. And our country is euphoric about giving it, forgetting that a wounded bear can be very dangerous. . . . We cannot be sure who will suffer next. But the United States can ill afford to assume that the bear has been tamed."

With the divergence of the right wing and Reagan over the central organizing principle of conservatism, George Bush was placed in an awkward position. The vice president was the impeccable loyalist and had altered every one of his beliefs, such as they were, that conflicted with the president's. By adopting Reagan's popular stance on the INF Treaty, Bush had outmaneuvered all of his opponents, whose hesitation or resistance had inflicted damage only on themselves. However, since his entrance into politics in Texas, Bush had always tried to accommodate the right wing. He feared what they might do to upset his ambition. For most of the 1980s, he pacified the right by simply echoing Reagan. But now if he mimicked the president he would roil it, harming himself most of all.

There was another figure in the fray, whom Bush admired more than Reagan and feared perhaps as much as he did the right. In the period when Bush earned his much-vaunted foreign policy credentials, he was in thrall to the colossus of foreign policy—Henry Kissinger. When Kissinger landed in China, where Bush was the U.S. envoy, his attitude was "adoring," according to a source who observed him at first hand. He loved to quote Kissingerisms, getting as much pleasure from repeating them as if he had thought them up himself. But Bush's personal opinion of Kissinger was not unalloyed. He had been furious at him when he discovered, after making a valiant defense of Taiwan's membership in the U.N., that he had unwittingly served as a cover for the opening to China. Still, to Bush, Kissinger was a giant. To Kissinger, however, Bush was a spear carrier. "Bush, following instructions . . ." reads a typical entry in Kissinger's voluminous memoirs.

Like his great inspiration, Bismarck, Kissinger had no unbendable principles, and was given to sudden reversals and lightning moves. Yet stability, or the balance of power, was his most important objective. His conception of stability differed from the one taught in the "conflict resolution" classes at the Kennedy School, where obeisance was paid to human rights. To Kissinger, the child of Weimar, stability was the be-all and end all. His fabled mastery of *Realpolitik* was required by the Cold War. He could not imagine another cockpit for his brand of diplomacy, which raced between personal deal-making and constant confrontations to demonstrate "credibility." The end of the Cold War meant chaos.

Like Bush, Kissinger had spent much of his time since the Ford administration trying to placate the right, which despised him as an architect of détente. Behind his increasingly rightward-tilted arguments lay the still-burning dream of power.

When Gorbachev and Reagan agreed to the terms of the INF Treaty, Kissinger interpreted it as a major rupture in the global system that he and Nixon had constructed. As he saw it, the Soviets were breaking out of their isolation and bidding to split the Western alliance, which would upset the balance of power. After the Washington summit, at which the treaty was signed, Kissinger described his mood as "melancholy" in a long piece in *Newsweek*. "This most conservative of postwar presidents," he wrote, "seemed bent on ending his term by dismantling the concepts and practices that have shaped Western strategy for four decades." Kissinger deplored the "euphoria sweeping Washington," which had led "business leaders and public figures" to become "nearly abject in their eagerness to celebrate a new era. . . ." It was, he warned, not "realistic" to think that Gorbachev was moving in a radically new direction. "He has never wavered from basic communist doctrine."

A month later, Kissinger delivered a speech, attended by many of the leading conservatives in the capital, at the Heritage Foundation. Gorbachev, he said, was nothing new. "This idea that we are dealing with a problem not of foreign policy, but of conversion of a system, is not new at all—the Soviets abolish their claim to world revolution every decade." Kissinger presented himself as immune to the latest "charm offensive": "I was not swept away by the Gorbachev euphoria." Only two approaches were possible—*Realpolitik* or a war of ideology. Kissinger observed that "my friend Norman Podhoretz never tires of raising with me" his view that *Realpolitik* is "not sustainable by the American people—that the U.S. needs an ideological mission. There is a lot of merit in what he is saying. But we now have proved to ourselves that we cannot maintain an ideological foreign policy for eight years, and therefore we may be left without an anchor."

Thus it was time for *Realpolitik* and the return of its foremost practitioner. Kissinger laid down a new line. He was willing to support the ratification of the INF Treaty, "not because I see any merit in it, but because I think the damage of not ratifying it would be greater." But he opposed reaching agreement on a new Strategic Arms Reduction (START) Treaty on strategic missiles unless an agreement to reduce Soviet conventional forces in Central Europe was reached at the same time. Using this favorite Kissinger device—linkage—he was trying to stall the next phase of arms control. Few analysts expected that negotiations on conventional forces in Europe (CFE) would achieve success, particularly any time soon. Linking CFE to START would defer another arms treaty indefinitely, or at least until the dangerously utopian Reagan was out of office. Nobody anticipated that Gorbachev would render the Kissinger line obsolete in less than a year by his dramatic announcement at the United Nations of unilateral conventional cuts.

Kissinger believed that those who were discarding Cold War assumptions were incapable of understanding the U.S.–Soviet relationship. They were self-deluded and would inevitably come to grief. Kissinger, at the Heritage Foundation, held up an enduring standard—Richard Nixon. "And in all his writings," he said, "I defy anybody to find any statement of President Nixon concerning fundamental conversions of the Soviet system, changes of the Soviet attitude." Kissinger's *Realpolitik* was now an exercise in nostalgia. In effect, he was seeking a world restored.

Like Kissinger, Bush was not an ideologue. He was born to serve, but he could not explain why. His agenda was to get the job. But Bush wished to see himself as part of the Kissinger circle. The most able foreign policy operatives, he believed, were those who, like himself, had worked for Henry: Brent Scowcroft and Lawrence Eagleburger (Kissinger's partners in Kissinger Associates), and William Hyland (the editor of the Council on Foreign Relations' magazine, *Foreign Affairs*). Bush relied heavily upon them for advice, especially Scowcroft. "Before we say that, check with Brent," he often told his campaign handlers. And Scowcroft, following the latest Kissinger ukase, was openly critical of the INF Treaty and of a START agreement without conventional arms linkage. Bush did not want to ruffle the Kissingerians, who were after all his own advisers. He did not want them to say that he did not know what he was doing. By a process of mental osmosis, he accepted their positions as his own.

On May 25, the day Reagan left Washington for the Moscow summit, Bush made an effort to explain his view of the recent history of U.S. foreign policy. In a speech at the U.S. Military Academy at West Point, he hailed "the great bipartisan consensus" of the early Cold War, framing it with the formula recommended to every candidate by every pollster: peace through strength. Strength, according to Bush, meant "military strength." He elaborated: "The day Kennedy was inaugurated, Theodore H. White said of the new president and his aides: These are the junior officers of World War II come to power." By this invocation of the hero and his Homeric chronicler, Bush attempted to associate himself with the romance, for he, too, was a junior officer in World War II.

"By the seventies," Bush continued, "the consensus had fractured— splintered—the center did not hold." He was drawing upon William Butler Yeats's famous line, but not a line that follows it: "The worst are full of passionate intensity." In the 1970s, in fact, it was the ascendant right wing that was full of passionate intensity. Circling around the heart of the matter, the causes of the crackup, Bush said: "The death of Kennedy, Vietnam, the lure of the old desire to once again leave the world and turn inward." It was unclear what Bush meant by stringing together these words in a sentence fragment. Was he saying that the death of Kennedy was connected to the escalation of the Vietnam War? Did the "old desire" refer to, as he had said elsewhere, "the post–Vietnam thing?" The connection of these disconnected allusions to the fate of the postwar consensus could only be murky. "The reasons," he said about its shattering, "would take another speech." But "another speech" on the subject was never delivered.

Bush plunged ahead. After his Yeatsian remark on the collapse of the consensus, he pretended he had not said it. There were "changes," but "the great bipartisan consensus endured. The logic still applies." This abrupt resurrection of the consensus occurred with as little explanation as its collapse. As it turned out, according to Bush, there was only one group outside the consensus: "The liberal elite do not understand—they never understood—the common sense behind the consensus." This was, of course, historically wrong. It was the liberal elite, for better or worse, that forged the consensus. It was the Republicans who had to be convinced of its "common sense." It was the Republican right, virtually from the beginning, that sought to upset the consensus by calling for a "rollback" of communism and a "liberation" of Central Europe and by impugning the liberals' patriotism. It was Ronald Reagan who openly cast aside the principles of internationalism. Bush himself had played a minor and mostly passive role in the undermining of the consensus as CIA director by approving the right-wing B-Team's scarifying report on the Soviet military, which encouraged Cold War conservatism and was a rationale for the Pentagon buildup. It was his major contribution to American politics before his presidential campaign.

Bush's lessons for the West Point cadets avoided discussion of the actual events and personages of the 1970s, when he had gained his foreign policy experience in Kissinger's shadow. The consensus, in fact, had not endured; for Nixon and Kissinger never repaired it. These partners in *Realpolitik* failed mainly because of their methods. They were obsessed with credibility, and the Vietnam War was prolonged and widened in the effort to sustain it. When they felt that the occasion demanded, they consciously acted out the "madman theory" of diplomacy, seeming to be irrational in order to attain their ends. Kissinger was also obsessed with farfetched geopolitical connections, justifying his actions from Cyprus to Chile to the Mideast by stretching Cold War logic. Nixon and Kissinger also preferred not to explain the underpinning of their policies to the public. They hid their purposes by the Bismarckian tactics of secrecy and surprise. Bush himself was familiar with the technique, having played the fool in defense of Taiwan at the U.N. Far from gaining a consensus, Nixon and Kissinger continued to divide the nation, opening the way to Carter and Reagan, both of whom promised a return to morality.

After Reagan returned from the Moscow summit in a glow of triumph, George Bush, the loyalist, broke with him on the salient question of foreign policy, Bush's most important departure as number two from a presidential position. Bush had reached his decision without prodding from his campaign team. Unlike virtually on every other issue raised in the race that followed, the source of the decision was the candidate himself—not his consultants. (The political press uniformly treated this as a minor development, illustrating only Bush's awkward efforts to establish his independence.) "I don't agree," Bush said, contradicting the president, "that we know enough to say that there is that kind of fundamental change, a turning inward, à la China, on the part of the Soviet Union. I don't feel that way." Would a reduced threat lead to defense cuts? he was asked. "First," Bush replied, "I don't agree with the premise." The threat, he contended, existed as it had in the past; nothing significant had changed. "The Cold War is not over," he said throughout June and July in several speeches. "Let's not," he said on the eve of the Democratic convention, "because we've made some progress, adopt a euphoric, naïvely optimistic view about what comes next." Once again, he was repeating Kissingerisms, this time obliquely directed against Ronald Reagan.

Bush carefully staked out a position that enabled him to have it all ways. He was in favor of a START treaty, "for the rest of this adminis-tration," which he acknowledged was an unlikely prospect. Failing that, he announced that he favored "two tracks": START linked to conven-tional arms talks—in short, the Kissinger line. For Bush, it was a safe line that required him to do nothing at the moment. He kept the Reagan mantle, satisfied the Kissingerians and mollified the right.

Reagan's abandonment of Cold War conservatism had given his presidency, moribund since the Iran-contra scandal, a new purpose for its last act. But Bush's split was a sign that he considered the Nixon legacy more instructive. It was also an indication that, after all these years, Kissinger's influence was still strong.

Kissinger had provided an intellectual foundation for opposing the end of the Cold War. The Kissingerians in Bush's camp acted as his interpreters. But Kissinger's *Realpolitik,* which was both autocratic and constantly shifting to reflect the permutations of power, was difficult to translate into the idiom of a democratic system. It was too obscure, in any case, to serve as the basis of a presidential campaign. Bush had to offer something more promotable than Kissinger's sinuous argu-ments.

In 1984, the Reagan campaign deftly portrayed the Soviet threat in a purely symbolic television commercial as a bear in the woods. The USSR was not even mentioned. In 1988, the fading of the Cold War provoked the search for its replacement. These might not be the same woods and we might be lost, but the demand was not for a new map. It was for a new bear.

II

George Bush's general election campaign began with his collapse—"his worst hour," according to a senior adviser. He had just emerged from the Republican primaries as his party's nominee; all his foes were vanquished; the field before him was clear. But, on June 9, on ABC's "Nightline," Ted Koppel dragged out the skeletons that were clanking in his closet: the Iran-contra scandal and Manuel Noriega, the drug-running Panamanian dictator who had been on the CIA's payroll when Bush was director. In response to Koppel's questions, the vice president was barely able to form a coherent sentence. Time and again, he called him "Dan," obviously thinking of Dan Rather.

"I'll tell you what," said Koppel. "If you stop calling me Dan try calling me Peter or Tom or—"

"Did I do it again?"

"Well, that's all right. You can call me anything you like, but, you know, it's—"

"It's Freudian. Hey, listen, it's Freudian."

"It's getting a little bit repetitious."

"I am not trying to be clever. I'm, I'm—"

"No, no, I know you're not."

"I promise you, it is Freudian."

At the show's conclusion, Bush signed off: "Ted, I apologize for calling you Dan. I wasn't being smart—"

"That's—"

"I can't see you, I'm in Houston, Texas, and I was not trying to be provocative or amusing."

"No, not at all, and I didn't take it that way. Next time, call me Barbara."

Bush seemed trapped within himself. He was a paradoxical combination of a man without many firm beliefs, opening him to most suggestions, and a man with a narrow image, seemingly closing off most possibilities. Therein lay the dilemma for his handlers. They could make him say almost anything, but he was the one who had to say it. To the extent that he had succeeded in public life it had been through a courtier strategy of appointments and personal alliances. Since his election to a congressional seat in a safe Republican district more than

twenty years earlier, he had failed at presenting himself to the electorate. His winning of the GOP primaries in 1988 had turned on a
weekend of going negative against Bob Dole in New Hampshire. Since
then, his image had waned in the public mind. And no displays of his
mastery of protocol, which had served him so well in the court life of
Washington, could elevate him further. He needed a different approach quickly. His name was even entering the popular culture as a
byword for haplessness. During the NBA championship series, after the
Los Angeles Lakers suffered a humiliating loss to the Detroit Pistons,
their coach, Pat Riley, in a locker-room talk, berated his players as
"George Bush clones." If they did not get tough, he warned, they
would lose.

Even before the end of the primaries in California, as Reagan was
starring in Moscow, the candidate had retired from the hustings to his
family estate on Walker's Point, a promontory off the coast of Maine
at Kennebunkport. Bush had a special feeling for what he called "this
sacred place," where generations of Bushes had lived. He even composed a poem about it that concluded:

Just relax and watch the sea

Treasure the strength God's given you.

His handlers, who followed him there, had another plan. They
encompassed much of the experience of the Republican Party since
1968. It was then, with Richard Nixon's victory, that the permanent
campaign system, rooted in postindustrial technology, specifically com-
puters and telecommunications, supplanted the old party system. In
the permanent campaign, the consultants replaced the bosses as the
enduring figures in politics, regardless of who was elected. The means
of campaigning—control over the images projected by the media—
became the means of governing. Governing itself became a permanent
campaign.

Nixon's basic strategy—and the Republican strategy thereafter—
had been to cripple the Democratic coalition, already hobbled by the
insurgencies of George Wallace and the antiwar movement. Nixon
sought to redefine it on Republican terms as a Silent Majority, Middle
America, a New Republican Majority. The method in the campaign
was to control the media environment, engaging in a form of electoral
warfare in which the candidate's image was zealously protected, while
strikes were launched against the opponent.

In the 1968 campaign, a series of packaged thirty-minute panel
shows, dubbed "Man in the Arena," presented a fresh, spontaneous,
open politician—a "new Nixon." Roger Ailes, the former producer of

the "Mike Douglas Show," a daytime variety show, where he had met Nixon when he appeared as a guest, was the producer of these commercials. "Now you put him on television, you've got a problem right away," Ailes told Joe McGinniss in *The Selling of the President 1968.* "He's a funny-looking guy. He looks like somebody hung him in a closet overnight and he jumps out in the morning with his suit all bunched up and starts running around saying, 'I want to be President.' I mean this is how he strikes some people. That's why these shows are important. To make them forget all that."

Ailes came from a blue-collar background and was given to emotional outbursts and threats of violence. "Violence never solves anything," he said, "but the threat of violence can be very useful." He was an expert in voice levels, camera angles and cutaways. He also specialized in exploiting a visceral politics of resentment. "You know what I'd like?" he said, as he planned the composition of an audience for one of Nixon's "Man in the Arena" shows. " . . . A good mean, Wallaceite cab driver. Wouldn't that be great. Some guy to sit there and say, 'Awright, mac, what about these niggers?' "

In 1984, he crafted a totally controlled environment around Ronald Reagan that was broken only during his first debate with Walter Mondale, in which he appeared old and confused. Ailes always instructed his candidates to invade the mental and, if possible, the physical space of their opponents. For a half-hour before their second debate, he coached Reagan, raising his morale and getting him to come up with a preemptive response on the age issue. "I got it," said Reagan. In the debate, Reagan delivered the one-liner he had rehearsed with Ailes—"I am not going to exploit for political purposes my opponent's youth and inexperience"—and his one moment of insecurity in the campaign passed. But Reagan was a professional in the way he took direction. Bush was an amateur. During his disastrous interview with Ted Koppel, Ailes hung a sign above the camera Bush was facing. It read "TED." "From there on, I behaved," said Bush.

Bush was an unlikely tribune of resentment. But the only kind of campaign that Lee Atwater, his manager, had run had capitalized on social grievances and hostilities. Atwater had entered politics in South Carolina in the early 1970s, after the Democratic Party in the South had splintered under the force of the civil rights struggles. What was once the bastion of segregation was now seen as the party of the blacks, and southern whites in great numbers abandoned it for the GOP. But while race was the fundamental realigning issue in southern politics, explicit racial appeals in the post–civil rights atmosphere were out of bounds. The race-baiting, tobacco-spitting Dixiecrat populists were truly gone with the wind. They were replaced by cunning consultants, like Atwater, who knew how to operate the technologies of media and polling to the same effect. He had even written an incomplete graduate thesis on the White House Office of Political Affairs in the early Reagan years as "the first institutionalized 'permanent campaign' operation to be located within the White House structure." "I know how to play it," he said, twanging the strings of an air guitar.

His campaigns were of a piece. He specialized in what he called "wedge issues"—issues that could be driven into the Democratic Party to divide it. He had little interest in policy and an obsession with tactics, particularly negative ones. In 1980, he managed Ronald Reagan's presidential primary campaign in South Carolina, setting the rival campaigns of George Bush and John Connally at each other's throats by circulating false charges that Connally was "buying the black vote." Atwater became a presidential assistant and, in 1984, ran the campaign in the South for Reagan–Bush. By then, he was already ingratiating himself with the vice president in anticipation of his presidential campaign. Atwater labeled himself a "populist," but he was intensely ambitious about being accepted by the establishment, despite his "antiestablishment" posturing against the Democrats, which endeared him to the rising GOP establishment.

Atwater prided himself on his innate grasp of the politics of the baby boom, which he saw as critical to a Republican realignment. He had played backup rhythm-and-blues guitar for the Percy Sledge band ("When a man loves a woman . . .") and he made much of watching MTV. Atwater also presented himself as an intellectual, occasionally quoting from Machiavelli and Sun Tzu. His political philosophy, upon which he based his version of generational politics, was a kind of heavy-metal nihilism not usually noted in the Woodstock anniversary commemorations. "Bullshit has permeated our society at every level," he said. "Bush and his whole campaign were full of bullshit. They were a bunch of elitists sitting around who didn't have any idea of what was going on, who felt they had the answers. . . . With Republicans it is wearing tuxedos, limousines." Atwater did not think that his negative campaigning was particularly bad because everything, after all, was false. Why get indignant? The important question was who won. In his theory of power, winning determined status. "Status is bullshit, and status is a new value. Bullshit permeates everything." Power, therefore, was the only measure of value in a meaningless world.

The measures of public opinion, the guideposts to power, were gauged by Robert Teeter, the leading Republican pollster. He knew all the tricks of his trade, but he had also devoted years of serious study to issue trends. In 1976, he helped bring Gerald Ford to the edge of victory from a deficit of 30 points. Teeter was initially associated with the moderate wing of the party, whose spokesmen were mostly the Republican governors. But the shift of the party to the right in the Reagan years did not leave Teeter adrift. Since the Ford campaign he had remained at the center of the GOP permanent campaign. Teeter was the pollster most trusted by James Baker, Reagan chief of staff in the first term and the de facto chairman of the permanent campaign. Teeter, who did not live in Washington but in the university town of Ann Arbor, Michigan, was detached and almost impersonal. Ailes had his flashes of inspiration; Atwater had his talent for quick maneuver; but Teeter was the more considered strategist, tempering the tone and content of resentment to make it more acceptable to the moderate electorate.

The Bush campaign was the extension of the permanent campaign that had been an ongoing project of two decades. Now, its chief practitioners were to be tested under extreme conditions. The magnitude of Bush's problem was encapsulated in two numbers: His negative rating was at the near-lethal level of 41, while Dukakis's was at 15. If these numbers were not radically altered, Bush would be doomed. It was their luck that Dukakis was still largely undefined in the public mind. He would either fill in the blanks himself, which he had spent most of his campaign resisting, or allow the Bush team to do a "paint job" on him, as Ailes phrased it. Feeling that in Bush they had little to work with, their task was simplified. They had only one choice—to raise Dukakis's negatives. In order to create a greater drama, they needed a greater enemy. So the modest Dukakis had to be inflated into a menace.

Atwater commissioned James Pinkerton, director of opposition research, to excavate any political liability buried in Dukakis's past. Atwater then placed what Pinkerton had dug up on a single index card. It read: "1. High tax, high spending. . . . 2. To the left of Carter–Mondale in opposing every defense program. . . . 3. Social issues. McGovern/ Kennedy/Jackson liberal: prison furloughs . . . 'card-carrying member of the ACLU' . . . vetoed Pledge of Allegiance."

A week before gathering at Walker's Point, Atwater, Ailes and Teeter traveled to a shopping mall in Paramus, New Jersey, where they assembled about a dozen white Catholic Democrats, who had voted for Reagan but were leaning to Dukakis, to test the issues on Atwater's index card. As the handlers observed through a one-way mirror, more than half of the Dukakis-leaners shifted to Bush. It was a campaign—a negative campaign—in microcosm. The handlers were ecstatic.

In Bush's living room, they painted a gloomy picture for him of his prospects unless he followed their strategy. But he was uncertain. So they gave him videotapes of the New Jersey group and told him to watch them. The next morning, he acquiesced without giving his formal assent.

Bush understood politics as a realm apart from policy. Policy was a gentrified realm for men of his class and the professionals—"the best people," as he once called them. Politics was dirty and unfair, a game without rules, overrun with miscreants and Democrats. One needed an Atwater, an Ailes to do business here. But they were never to be permitted to track their muddy shoes into the councils of state. Bush hesitated to adopt their strategy because of his sense of himself as a statesman, but he accepted it because of his sense of inadequacy as a candidate.

Bush had spent much of his life as a son, first to his actual father, Senator Prescott Bush, then as a political son to Richard Nixon and Ronald Reagan. Now he acted the dependent with his own consultants. He was willing to embrace their version of a "new Bush" because he had failed to establish himself on his own, even in winning the Republican nomination. Thus he threw himself upon the political furies. For the duration of the campaign, Bush looked most in control when he was most in the control of his handlers. He assumed an image of strength from attacking his old image of the wimp in the form of Dukakis.

Bush's campaign against Dukakis was an experiment in demonology. It was performed in the "paranoid style" of the "pseudo-conservative revolt" as described by the historian Richard Hofstadter twenty-five years earlier, but executed on a rational, calculated basis, aided by all the tools of modern political technology. Dukakis was half-right, after all; this election was about technique, though a different one than governing.

But it was also about ideology. "The American people need to know that ideology is important," said Bush, who had searched high and low for the "vision thing." Those who inserted the symbols of ideology into his television commercials and rhetoric were the consultants, not the ideologues. Unlike Reagan, Bush kept the conservative intellectuals at arm's length. The conservative movement that had been such a large part of the Reagan years was played out, for all intents and purposes.

But it was still emitting gales of black smoke, and Bush's campaign found valuable uses for the exhaust fumes of resentment.

Though there was an inevitability to Bush's negative campaign, his handlers did not prevent him from running a different race. It was inevitable neither that his negative campaign dominate the discussion nor that it triumph. Modern political technology may have a bias toward messages that can be reduced to thirty-second television commercials, but the process of campaigning in 1988 did not dictate the content of the campaign. Attributing its meaning to its means is a technological fallacy; such causal reasoning is determinist and ahistorical, not the least about the permanent campaign. Since its advent, all manner of messages have been broadcast through its modalities. There are as many possible permutations of the permanent campaign as there were of the system it replaced. Its forms no more define the substance than did those in the supposed golden age of political parties. Ronald Reagan's Cold War conservatism in 1980, expressed through the modes of the permanent campaign, had fundamentally the same content as that offered by the Republican right in 1948 and 1952, the first campaigns of the Cold War, waged before television became a common household appliance.[1]

The helter-skelter quality of the 1988 campaign was a sign of a deeper disorder. The operating assumptions of American politics in the Cold War were already seriously eroded, even though that erosion went unacknowledged. The old order was decaying, but a new order was not being created. In such a period, as Italian philosopher Antonio Gramsci once observed, a great number of "morbid symptoms" make their appearance.[2]

1. The single-factor argument, assigning the source of the campaign's content to the campaign's mechanics, achieved the status of conventional wisdom so quickly in Washington after the 1988 campaign that its authorship is unknown. The argument is succinctly, though not originally, made by Peter Goldman, Tom Mathews and the *Newsweek* Special Election Team, in their chronicle of the campaign, which is less a book than a corporate product—Teddy White as an assembly line. As such, it does not have a point of view. But it does present the safe thesis that 1988 was the "year of the handler" and that "attack advertising" was "the most cost-effective way to move public opinion."

2. Walter Dean Burnham, the preeminent American political scientist, in his analysis of the 1988 campaign, notes that the race was part of a "radical recomposition of the American political system" into the permanent campaign system, as first named and analyzed by the author of this book. Burnham posits a concept of the "interregnum state" as a complementary phenomenon of this change. "The emergence of the 'permanent campaign,' " he writes, "also appears chronologically linked to the end of American ascendancy in the world economy in the 1969–73 period and the beginning of a 'time of troubles' in that domain that very likely is still with us. 'The permanent

Michael Dukakis did not know or think it was his job to lay the foundation for a new order. At best, he thought his mission was to complete the congressional agenda. George Bush was unprepared and unwilling to address the new realities. He believed it was his duty to man the watchtowers of a wall, though it was about to come tumbling down. Both sides in American politics were incapable of thinking in terms of grand strategy, or even of opening their eyes to the changes that were already stirring and shaking Europe. In the land of the blind candidate, the one-eyed consultant was king.

The permanent campaign at the end of the Cold War was conducted in the crawl space between eras. It was possible to take up residence there only during the campaign, when neither of the candidates had the responsibility of dealing with Gorbachev.

Bush's campaign was the continuation of the Cold War by metaphor. What was slipping away—the monolithic dualities, the easy moral rivalry—was what he sought to sustain. So Bush's pollster, Bob Teeter, devoted his energies to researching the issues of fear and anxiety. He came up with the ideas of portraying Dukakis as "out of the mainstream" and as a "risk." Nearly every stump speech delivered by Bush called Dukakis "out of the mainstream"; nearly every television ad called him a "risk." Fear of the unknown was evoked by making one of the least mysterious men ever to run for the presidency into the personification of the unknown—"invisible," "the Stealth guy," according to Bush.

Each of the issues Bush raised was trivial by itself, but together they composed a big theme. It would be wrong to dismiss his efforts as simply a spur-of-the-moment improvisation, a disposable, nihilistic campaign signifying nothing. George Bush ran the last campaign of the Cold War. He attempted to revive its earlier draconian atmosphere through repetition of certain themes that had occurred since even before the Cold War's beginning. His campaign, of course, failed to sustain the Cold War, but, for a few months, he succeeded in creating its illusory equivalent.

"Should public school teachers be required to lead our children in the Pledge of Allegiance?" asked Bush. "My opponent says no—and

campaign' is the chief electoral dimension of the interregnum state that emerged from the cosmic smash-ups of the late 1960s. The interregnum state that has emerged on the ruins of the older political order is, in policy terms, an uneasy, incoherent mixture of interest-group liberalism and free-market (and, increasingly, social-issue) conservatism. It is also deeply blocked and deadlocked as a political regime."

I say yes." As it happened, Governor Dukakis had vetoed a bill passed by the state legislature that ordered teachers to lead mandatory pledges—after being advised by the Massachusetts Supreme Judicial Court and the attorney general that the bill was unconstitutional and unenforceable. The Pledge of Allegiance is a piece of patriotism with a curious past. It was written in 1892 for *Youth's Companion* magazine by the Rev. Francis Bellamy, vice president of the Society of Christian Socialists, who conceived it as a socialist credo: " . . . with liberty and justice for all." Its practice took root, however, only during the Red Scare following World War I. The crusade for the pledge was spearheaded in the 1920s by the Ku Klux Klan. Jehovah's Witnesses, a tiny religious sect, regarded this secular liturgy as blasphemous and refused to allow their children to pledge. As World War II approached, riots broke out against the Witnesses. In 1940, in Kennebunk, Maine, near young George Bush's family summer place, a mob of 2,500 burned a Witness church. Three years later, the Supreme Court ruled that students could not be compelled to say the pledge; since then federal courts have always rejected mandatory pledge laws. But, as the historian John Higham wrote in his study of American nativism: " . . . the new equation between national loyalty and a large measure of political and social conformity would long outlive the generation that established it."

Bush used the pledge, a symbolic issue about a symbolic gesture, as proof of which candidate was the one hundred percent American. It was a rite of conformity that protected the country from alien influences. The pledge meant unity, conformity, obedience—patriotism. But what seemed to be an objective test, a willingness to make everyone take the pledge, tapped into the collective nativist unconscious, a wellspring of intolerance. By his refusal to submit to this naturalization test, Dukakis was defined as the other; the ethnic, who was seen like a Yankee in Massachusetts politics, was not assimilated, after all. He was conspicuously different, strange, "out of the mainstream," even hostile to the nation. His physical attributes unconsciously fit the criteria: he was swarthy, short and beetle-browed. Bush's consultants deliberately played upon his appearance by presenting him in their television commercials in shadows, always frowning, with a heavy beard, while Bush was always lit from behind with a golden glow. None of this was an accident, and none of the implications escaped Bush's image-makers. ("How gloomy he is," said Bush.) Dukakis's explanation of his veto, a legalistic defense of religious minorities, helped turn him into one of the persecuted. His logic was not the logic of symbolism. He seemed blind and deaf to the power of the flag and the pledge, which only underlined the case against him as the other. And the instinctive response to the other is aversion.

Just as the Pledge of Allegiance was turned into a version of the loyalty oath of the late 1940s and early 1950s, Bush in his attack on Dukakis as a "card-carrying member" of the American Civil Liberties Union made it sound like Dukakis was a card-carrying member of the Communist Party, another legacy of that era of fear and suspicion. "I am not a card-carrying member of the ACLU. I am for the people," said Bush, as if he were testifying before the House Un-American Activities Committee.

The ACLU was founded during the Red Scare after World War I to defend civil liberties. Dukakis had become an ardent civil libertarian during the later Red Scare, when Prescott Bush was pressing for the censure of Joseph McCarthy in the Senate. Dukakis had, indeed, joined the ACLU. As governor, however, he did not agree with all of its positions, and the local chapter sued him on more than one occasion. Still, he proudly spoke of his membership as a token of his belief in the Bill of Rights. Dukakis's belated, diffident responses to the "card-carrying member" line only helped seal the image. They were contemptuously depicted by the Bush campaign as the equivalent of Dukakis's taking the Fifth Amendment, entering a guilty plea by other means— "long-winded legalism," Dan Quayle mocked.

Then the Bush campaign virtually nominated Willie Horton as Michael Dukakis's running mate. The furloughing of Horton by a prison board was turned from a weak spot in Dukakis's criminal justice record to weakness in dealing with black pressure, from incompetence as a manager to ideological extremism, from cerebral arrogance to lacking compassion for the victims of crime, and, finally, to lacking feeling per se. Dukakis, according to Bush, was a "know nothing, believe nothing, feel nothing" candidate, "the ice man."

"There is a story about a fellow named Willie Horton who, for all I know, may end up being Dukakis' running mate," Lee Atwater told a group of southern Republicans in Atlanta just prior to the Democratic convention there. "The guy [Dukakis] was on tv about a month ago, and he said, 'You'll never see me standing in the driveway of my house talking to these [vice presidential] candidates.' And guess what? Monday, I saw in his driveway of his home Jesse Jackson. So anyway, maybe he [Dukakis] will put this Willie Horton on the ticket after all is said and done."

Atwater and other senior advisers later claimed that race had been extraneous to their decision to raise the Horton issue. But a member of the Bush campaign team who was helping to produce the negative spots said: "Willie Horton has star quality. Willie's going to be politically furloughed to terrorize again. It's a wonderful mix of liberalism and a big black rapist."

The first Willie Horton video was produced in 1915. It was directed by D.W. Griffith and called *The Birth of a Nation.* The film, based on Thomas Dixon's popular novel *The Clansman,* depicted venal, lustful blacks, under the sway of northern carpetbaggers, violating traditional values, as it were. In its stirring climax, the heroine was rescued from a black rapist by the Ku Klux Klan. The "Southern rape complex," as W. J. Cash described it in his classic *The Mind of the South,* derived from "the fact that this Southern woman's place in the Southern mind proceeded primarily from the natural tendency of the great basic pattern of pride in superiority of race to center upon her as the perpetuator of that superiority in legitimate line, and attached itself precisely, and before everything else, to her enormous remoteness from the males of the inferior group, to the absolute taboo on any sexual approach to her by the Negro." The Willie Horton videos of 1988 played upon such atavistic racial feelings with even greater consequence than did *The Birth of a Nation.*

Teeter discovered that other feelings were also evoked by the Willie Horton issue. Being perceived as soft on criminals was on the same continuum as being perceived as soft on communism; public safety was seen in the same dimension as national security. Even Willie Horton was about the Cold War. The implicit issue that tied together crime and communism was toughness. The answer to both was peace through strength. So George Bush assumed the role of Dirty Harry: "Clint Eastwood's answer to crime is 'Go ahead: Make my day.' My opponent's answer is slightly different. His answer is 'Go ahead: Have a nice weekend.'" Dukakis, he added, had given prisoners "a Club Med vacation someplace."

Just as Dukakis had let criminals loose, he would let the Russians loose. "I'd like to know what he means when he wants to freeze in Soviet superiority," said Bush. Dukakis had a "blind, negative ideology against weapons." His weakness might lead to war. "That will not keep the peace. The Soviets don't understand that." And: "I wouldn't be surprised if he thinks a naval exercise is something you find in Jane Fonda's workout book." This rhetorical swipe not only ridiculed Dukakis as an ignorant wimp but attempted to smear him by association with the leftist actress.

Bush summarized all of his attacks on Dukakis in one word—liberalism. He called it "the L-word," as if it were the analogue to the C-word of Cold War days past. Bush attacked "the liberal governor" and "L-people" and the "L-crowd." He attacked Harvard, where Dukakis had taught, as a "philosophical cult normally identified with extremely liberal causes." And: "I'll leave the Left Bank to the others."

Bush's positive campaign had the same source as his negative one. Teeter's polls found a desire for change, and he prompted Bush to issue white papers on the issues where he was hurting—the environment, day care and education. But the positive and the negative were often conflated by the candidate. On the stump, he extolled the country as "a kind and gentle nation with opportunities limited only by our dreams. And we refuse to let criminals snuff out those dreams."

Bush had conjured up a diabolical foe and was running against him. He promised to insulate us from the threat. The citizenry was depicted as passive, innocent victims of wild forces out there. We were made to be frightened so that Bush could reassure us. He himself was a new containment policy. His campaign recalled the ambience of the early Cold War—the insistence on political and social conformity, the dread of dissolution, the warnings against enemies within and without.

The "vision thing" had at last made an appearance to Bush as political kitsch—"the Norman Rockwell vision of America—the vision of kids and dogs and apple pie and flags on parade," he said. Stalinist kitsch was nostalgia for a utopian future that never happened. American conservative kitsch was nostalgia for an ideal past that never existed.

"Ideology matters," Bush explained.

III

In the French Quarter of New Orleans, on Dumaine Street, in a small decrepit storefront, the Museum of Voodoo solicited business from the Republican delegates. "What does the word voodoo mean? The word voodoo means Spirit World," read a sign in a back room, where the artifacts of voodoo were on display. "What is a zombie? A zombie—he or she looks like a normal person." But a zombie wakes the dead. "It is an honor." Various potions for enhancing prosperity, psychic powers and lovemaking were on sale. For this week only, a special voodoo doll could be purchased. Usually, the dolls were faceless, so that they could represent any object of hostility. But pasted on these voodoo dolls was a tiny, recognizable face—the face of Michael Dukakis.

In the Superdome, the Republicans carried on their own voodoo, paying obeisance to the totems and taboos of Cold War conservatism, and casting spells. Even before the convention, they had been sticking long pins into Dukakis.

The first impalement was accomplished in late April. One of the most undeniable aspects of Michael Dukakis was his Greek background, which had inspired euphoria among Greek-Americans, who contributed millions of dollars to his campaign. But the authenticity of his Hellenic identity was challenged by calling into question his status within the Greek Orthodox church. A handful of isolated right-wing priests charged that Dukakis was not part of the church because of his marriage to a Jewish woman, their failure to baptize their children and his pro-choice position on abortion. The underlying point was hardly subtle. By assailing Dukakis's religion, the issue of his wife's was raised.

These "charges" were circulated by conservative publications— "Dukakis' Religious Status Emerging as Controversial Issue" headlined the weekly *Human Events*—and publicized by a host of conservative columnists, most prominently (and predictably) by Rowland Evans and Robert Novak. "Is he truly a bona fide member of the church?" they asked rhetorically. It was "a question that could undermine the core constituency of his presidential campaign."

The chief organizer of this crusade was James Jatras, a staff member of the Senate Republican Policy Committee. "An apostate is someone who has abandoned the faith. That's literally what Dukakis has done," said Jatras. "The church is the body of Christ, a mystical organism. When he attacks what the church is, he is attacking Christ."

The next skewer was aimed at Dukakis's head. On the street corners of downtown Atlanta, as the Democrats met in convention, a band of true believers in the cult of the conspiracy-mongering Lyndon LaRouche, erstwhile world leader cum federal prisoner convicted of credit card fraud, handed out leaflets charging that Dukakis suffered "from a deep-seated mental instability." Shortly afterward, a reporter from the right-wing *Boston Herald* asked him if the reports about his psychiatric treatment were true. Dukakis declined to answer what he considered a disrespectful and absurd question. The conservative *Detroit News* sent him (and Bush, for balance) a questionnaire demanding to know his psychiatric history. Then the paper printed stories about his refusal to respond. The *Washington Times,* the Moonie daily, the first and perhaps the only newspaper read by the president every day, ran a huge banner headline: "Dukakis Psychiatric Rumor Denied." The *Boston Globe* reported the back-and-forth about the LaRouche-inspired fantasy as if it were documenting an objective event.

Bush's campaign operatives, in the meantime, labored hard over their telephones trying to convince journalists to pick up the story. (The author of this book was among those approached. Bush later said that if anyone from his organization had attempted to spread the rumors about Dukakis he would fire him. No one was fired.) At a presidential news conference on August 3, a writer for the LaRouche newspaper asked Reagan if he believed candidates like Dukakis should release their medical records. "Look, I don't want to pick on an invalid," he answered. Now, all the networks and major newspapers felt obliged to report on the issue. The *Washington Times* published a new story—"Dukakis Kin Hints at Sessions"—suggesting that it possessed evidence of Dukakis's clinical depression. But there was no such evidence, and two *Washington Times* reporters, in a sudden fit of professionalism, quit over the willful lie.

Facts or no facts, in the period leading up to the Republican convention, this was the dominant issue: Is Dukakis secretly insane? A lunatic sect, led by a lunatic, had set itself up as the arbiter of sanity. Its hallucination was promoted by an eager right-wing press and the Bush campaign, and given credence by the president. First there was the rumor, then the punishment, then the trial by press.

The only hint of eccentricity on Dukakis's part was his complete regularity in all things. If he had any mental problem it was his lack of imagination. But by the time he got around to releasing his doctor's affidavit, proving that he had never been treated for madness, or even mild depression, his lead over Bush had been cut in half. "Mental Issue Ravages Dukakis" read the headline in the exultant LaRouche paper.

On the first night of the convention, the Republican right packed the New Orleans Museum of Art for its first big party. The event was sponsored by the Eagle Forum, a group led by Phyllis Schlafly, author of many tracts decrying the Rockefellers' conspiratorial hold on the GOP. A pantheon of conservative heroes made cameo appearances. Jack Kemp hailed "peace through strength ideas." Senator Phil Gramm of Texas called for the liberation of the Soviet Union: "No other goal is worthy of the American people." Secretary of Education William Bennett instructed: "What this election is all about is right and wrong. On all the issues, the Republicans are right and the Democrats are wrong." Robert Bork appeared to a huge ovation. "I certainly wish this was the audience I was talking to in the Senate hearings," he chuckled. But, on a more portentous note, he warned: "What we are seeing in the Democratic Party is a resurgence of the ideology of the 1960s." "We're all former Democrats," said Jeane Kirkpatrick. Before Reagan, "nobody was representing the United States."

As the conservatives departed, they were handed leaflets advertising a new film, *Justice on Furlough: The true story of how Massachusetts discovered that convicted killers were roaming their streets . . .* A large butcher's knife was the only illustration. "Breathtaking. Devastates Dukakis," read an unattributed endorsement. ("Video cassettes available. Send $19.95 plus $2 shipping & handling.")

The convention was like a trade show of negative campaigning. Especially eyecatching among the flood of materials being displayed was a comic book, *Magical Mike: The Real Story of Michael Dukakis*, produced by members of the religious right and published by Jerry Falwell's son, which claimed Dukakis favored "bestiality" and "homosexual privilege." A naked man was shown chasing a terrified elephant, giraffe, horse and dog. ("I want to shoot the guy's legs out from under him. I want to expose him," said Falwell, exhorting his followers to distribute *Magical Mike.*)

Also noteworthy was a "Get out of jail free" card, looking exactly like one from a Monopoly game, distributed by the College National Republican Committee. On its back, it read: "Mike Dukakis is the killer's best friend, and the decent, honest citizen's [sic] worst enemy."

In New Orleans that week, one could even order ideology on the rocks. The same night as the Eagle Forum event, the *National Review,* the leading conservative magazine, edited by William Buckley, Jr., hosted a cocktail party. At the bar were neatly printed cards: "Glasnost or no glasnost, *National Review* does not serve communist vodka."

The Republican platform was as skeptical of glasnost as the *National Review;* the plank on the Soviets was entirely framed in negative terms about the Democrats: "Americans cannot afford a future administration that attempts eagerly to embrace perceived—but as yet unproven—changes in Soviet policy, nor can we indulge naïve inexperience, or an overly enthusiastic endorsement of current Soviet rhetoric." After eight years of Reagan, the Republicans cautioned that perception was not reality, but only in the case of Gorbachev.

Every speaker at the convention assailed the opposition as soft on communism and unpatriotic. The keynote speaker, Tom Kean, was the governor of New Jersey, a future hope of what was left of the moderate wing. Kean had organized against Goldwater in 1964 and promised "the politics of inclusion." But he used his chance in the national spotlight to rail at the Democrats for the colors with which they had decorated their convention's podium—off-white, salmon and powder blue—calling the scheme "pastel patriotism." "The liberal Democrats," he said, "are trying to hide more than the colors in our flag— they are trying to hide their true colors. . . . They want to weaken America. But they won't admit it." According to Kean, this weakening would not be the result of well-intentioned, if misguided, policies. A weak America was precisely the Democrats' goal. By design, they were anti-American and un-American; they were deceitful in their refusal to "admit it."

Senator John McCain of Arizona, a former prisoner of war in a North Vietnamese camp, elaborated on the theme in a version of Douglas MacArthur's famous farewell address to the cadets at West Point, but without the cadence, rhythm or sense of occasion. Most of it expressed McCain's outrage at Dukakis's position on the Pledge of Allegiance. He told, at great length, a story about a fellow prisoner who had been beaten for making a small American flag. "He was making that flag because he knew how important it was for us to be able to pledge our allegiance to our flag and country. Duty, Honor, Country." In his Manichean division of the universe, McCain put Dukakis on the same dark side as the brutal prison guards. "We must not forget. We must not retreat. Ronald Reagan, George Bush, Republicans. Duty, Honor, Country."

Alexander Haig continued the beat to quarters. Dukakis, he said, "does not believe in peace through strength"; he will "weaken America." After pounding on this boilerplate for a while, Haig then offered the most striking phrase-making of the entire convention. The Democrats, he said, were like a bat "flying erratically for brief periods at low levels and hanging upside down for extended periods in dark, damp caves up to its navel in guano." This was an absolutely original formulation of conservative ideology as scatology.

The Republicans seemed sure about everything, but were filled with deep-seated anxieties. For them, political time had started with Reagan. Not a single speaker at the convention was allowed to say the name "Richard Nixon," three times nominated for president, more than any man in the party's history—and twice for vice president. He had been the central Republican figure in the politics of the Cold War but was now airbrushed out of the picture. The Republicans had about as much difficulty acknowledging his seminal role in shaping their politics as the Soviet Communists had in acknowledging Trotsky's contributions to the Bolshevik Revolution. But Reagan's sway over the Republicans had been partly induced by the wound they suffered over Nixon.

Bush was Reagan's anointed heir, and the Republicans worried whether he could step into Reagan's image of strength. What was the future of an illusion? Bush, for his part, could never publicly explain his private misgivings about Reagan's leadership or that his own sense of the presidency drew far more on the Nixon and Ford years.

The problem of change and continuity was central not only to the transfer of power within the Republican Party but to the election itself. Though Reagan was popular again, with the Iran-contra scandal receding into the distance, the public, by a large margin, still wanted to change the direction of the country. No other polling number, except for Bush's unfavorability rating, so worried his handlers. Then, suddenly, on the eve of the convention, the numbers on change and continuity dramatically reversed. The current of public opinion had been jolted by the June summit in Moscow. Teeter's research showed that the public's perception of a new relationship between the U.S. and the former "evil empire" was the single, overriding factor in the shift. The public now wanted to continue this change.

Bush trailed in popularity among American voters behind Gorbachev, who was not on the ballot. "Change" was associated with Dukakis, but he had not decisively associated himself with it because he did not really know what this change was and, in any case, had been advised to be wary of it. The opening was still available for Bush. He could rise in the polls by his identification with Reagan, just as the president had been restored by his association with Gorbachev.

The Bush campaigners had initially attempted to deal with the "change" issue by turning it into "risk." But the new numbers allowed them to maintain the negative line while trying to claim "change" as something positive for themselves. The task of communicating this theme was assigned to the Great Communicator himself. The president had been annoyed by the Democrats' calls for change. "We *were* the change," he kept insisting to a White House aide. But he was thinking of himself in the past tense. His speechwriters put him on fast forward.

Reagan's convention speech did not begin auspiciously. He read through pages of a creaky litany of complaint against the Carter administration as if he had been put on reverse. At the close of every paragraph, replete with numbing economic statistics, he said, "Facts are stubborn things." But his mind glazed over as he kept repeating the phrase, and he blurted: "Facts are stupid things." It seemed to be an inadvertent admission of his method at last. But he soon arrived at his theme: "Now, we hear talk that it's time for a change. Well, ladies and gentlemen, another friendly reminder: We *are* the change." He talked about how U.S.–Soviet relations had become "the best they've been since World War II" and that negotiating with "Mr. Gorbachev" was essential to the job of president. "The work," he said, "must continue."

Thus the political circle was squared: change and continuity were one and the same; by supporting change, things could stay as they were. Once again, amid uncertainty, Reagan had performed the indispensable act of reassurance.

IV

The appearance of James A. Baker III as Bush's new campaign manager also had a calming effect. Baker was the one politico who was a social peer of Bush. His family was one of the oldest and wealthiest in Houston. And he had been sent east for his education, at the Hill School and Princeton. Baker, both a patrician and a Texan, naturally fused the two elements. Bush, making his career in an alien environment, trying to be something he wasn't, could not succeed as well as Baker in achieving the fusion. Bush saw himself as a player in the Washington game. But in the Reagan administration Baker, who had been Bush's campaign manager in 1980, emerged first as chief of staff and then as secretary of the treasury, exercising more influence than the vice president. Baker's reputation was high with Congress, and his ability to influence the media was unmatched. Bush felt comfortable with Baker, whom he had known longer and better than anyone else in his campaign. Baker was an equal who could teach him how to play political hardball. Nonetheless, Baker distanced himself from the first big decision made since he had come on board: the one that Bush said would "tell all" about himself.

The *Delta Queen* swooped down the Mississippi River past the levee where thousands of Republicans were awaiting the arrival of the nominee. Bush suddenly appeared on deck, flapping his arms. The huge white paddleboat swung around and docked, and he stepped before a bank of microphones to introduce "a man of the future," his candidate for vice president. Senator Dan Quayle bounded forward like a puppy let off his leash. "Let's go get 'em!" he shouted.

Dan Quayle's grandfather, Eugene Pulliam, was a midwestern Citizen Kane—the leading conservative in one of the most conservative states, dominating it with his newspapers. Pulliam owned the two papers in Indianapolis and three others in medium-sized cities. He also transplanted his ideology to the desert, helping to cultivate a Sunbelt conservatism through his ownership of the largest newspapers in Arizona, the *Arizona Republic* and the *Phoenix Gazette*. He was virulently anti-New Deal, an isolationist American Firster and, in the postwar period, used his publications as an echo chamber for Joseph McCarthy—all in the name of old-fashioned American values. In the crunch, however, he went with power. In 1952, he abandoned the standard-bearer of the party's right wing, Robert Taft, for Dwight Eisenhower, the candidate put up by the Dewey operation, the GOP's eastern establishment. Afterwards, Pulliam promoted and patronized the early conservative movement. But, in 1964, when the Republicans nominated Barry Goldwater, whose career the Pulliam papers had advanced every step of the way, the press lord shocked his friends by endorsing Lyndon Johnson, who represented everything he had railed against his whole life. By this time, Pulliam was very, very rich. When he died he left a fortune of close to a billion dollars.

James Quayle, a former marine, married Eugene's daughter, Corinne, and was given a succession of jobs within the family business but never one at the big newspaper in Indianapolis. He never showed an inclination to strike out on his own. When he was sent to Arizona, where he was made the public relations director for the family properties, he and his wife enlisted in the John Birch Society to crusade against the Communist conspiracy. He described meeting the group's founder, Robert Welch, who had accused Eisenhower of being a Communist, as "like meeting the president of the United States."

Dan Quayle was the oldest son, born in 1947 and reared with the reasonable expectation of a life without struggle. His grandfather was a serious golfer who built his estate next to a golf course. When his parents relocated to Arizona they built their home by the eleventh tee of the Paradise Valley golf course. By the age of twelve, Quayle had won his first tournament. His grandfather often brought him to Indianapolis to be his partner as he drove around the course with his old associates, casually talking business and politics.

Quayle's grades were low, but he was readily accepted at DePauw University, which his parents, his uncle and grandfather had attended and munificently endowed. He was a "D" student, even in his major, political science; an active member of his fraternity, Delta Kappa Epsilon, the Dekes, known as the local Animal House; and the star of the golf team. He failed his final exam in political science, required for graduation, but passed a special makeup test.

With the Vietnam War raging, the former commanding general of the Indiana National Guard, who also happened to be the managing editor of the *Indianapolis News,* placed a telephone call on young Dan's behalf. In an instant, he was accepted into the guard, ahead of a waiting list of about forty. Six months later, in spite of his awful grades, he was accepted at the Indiana University Law School under an experimental program for disadvantaged minority students. He also got a job in the office of the attorney general through the influence of his father and M. Stanton Evans, a movement conservative, then the editor of the *Indianapolis News.* At law school Quayle met his wife, Marilyn Tucker, whose family had deep roots in Indiana Republican politics. They were married ten weeks after they met. Her first child was born by induced labor so that she could arrange her schedule to take a bar exam.

Marilyn was a fervent believer in creationism, as opposed to evolution, and, like her parents, a follower of a cultish evangelical minister, Colonel Robert Thieme of Houston, whose taped sermons she faithfully made her children and husband listen to at least once a week. She also converted his parents, who became avid devotees. Thieme preaches a doomsday anti-Communist theology, with quirky critiques of Catholicism and Judaism. Even quirkier, he preaches a "right man–right woman" doctrine of predestined marriage, involving exactly fitted spirits and sex organs. (But, as Marilyn Quayle once observed, "Anybody who knows Dan Quayle knows he is more interested in golf than in sex any day.") Thieme's books include *Scar Tissue of the Soul* and *Satanic Plot No. 1.* His résumé is marked by notable fabrications (Rhodes Scholar) and, as Garry Wills writes, "His claims of intellectual achievement will not bear scrutiny." Nevertheless, Marilyn Quayle drew inspiration from his teachings. By all accounts, she regards the world as a hostile place constantly organizing against her and hers, and Thieme apparently helps her sustain and point to this paranoid vision.

After law school, while Dan worked with his father on the family-owned *Huntington Herald Press,* Marilyn set up a law office, Quayle & Quayle, upstairs in the newspaper building. In 1976, Orvas E. Beers, the Allen County Republican chairman, a golfing partner of Quayle's, needed a candidate to run for Congress against the incumbent Democrat. "Danny," he said, "how would you like to run for Congress?" "You mean now?" "Yes, I mean now." "I'll have to check with my dad." "Go ahead," his father told him. "You won't win."

At the party to celebrate Quayle's victory in the GOP primary, Marilyn dressed down the campaign manager in front of a large crowd:

"Your buttons are terrible! Before you do anything, you clear it with me first!" As she later explained, she was her husband's ultimate handler: "We decided to divide the roles. Dan's role was to spend nineteen hours a day literally shaking hands with every person in the district. My role was to make sure the decisions made were the correct decisions."

In Congress, Quayle distinguished himself among his colleagues as a "wethead," one of a group of young congressmen known for charging from the gym to the House floor with wet hair. While mastering his new job, he still found time to play golf about four times a week. Running against a longtime incumbent, Birch Bayh, he was elected to the Senate in a big Republican year—1980, Year One of the Reagan Era. He owed his victory to more than fortuitous circumstances. He was also aided by right-wing groups that, independent of his campaign, spent hundreds of thousands of dollars disseminating unanswerable smears about his opponent.

Quayle received his early campaign training from a professional handler, a media consultant named Don Ringe. He was brought to Ringe's studio in Washington to be drilled in the art of eloquence. The tape of those training sessions was turned over to a transcription service to keep a record, and it is a rare document, revealing not only the unvarnished exchanges between a handler and his subject, worthy of *Pygmalion,* but the tentative effort of a future vice president to locate his own motivations and beliefs.

The tape began with a voice exercise: "I'm Dan Quayle. I'm Dan Quayle. I'm Dan Quayle. I am Dan Quayle. The real Dan Quayle. The real Dan Quayle stand up. I'm Dan Quayle. I'm Dan Quayle."

"All right," said Ringe, "and what are you running for? I'm Dan Quayle—and what?"

"I'm Dan Quayle. I'm running for the U.S. Senate."

"Sounds to me like you're not sure."

"Why are we getting into this?" asked Quayle. "Okay," he agreed. "Because I believe in public service. I want to have the opportunity to serve."

"Got you, I've got you, I've got you."

"What?" asked Quayle.

"Relax."

"Oh."

Ringe asked him again "why you're running."

"I think I'm part of that new generation of leadership and I want to be part of that new generation of leadership."

"Tell me about, tell me about your past."

Quayle explained that he had been a political science major at DePauw.

"Why?"

"Because I've always had a deep interest in government. . . . And political science was a natural for somebody like myself."

"Why? Why was it a natural for somebody like yourself? What, what is your motivation coming from?"

"I think," suggested Quayle, "my mother and father had always talked to me about public service."

"You know, it sounds to me like you're giving a speech. You're not talking to me."

"Oh."

"You should tell me why it is. Just tell me."

"Okay, just talk to you." Quayle paused and then tried again. "All right. First of all, I've always had a general interest in government. Secondly, I really always wanted to go to law school ever since I was a little kid."

"Why?"

"I've always wanted to have a law background. Thought maybe a lawyer, interested in laws. Laws affect people. And it's a good background for anything, whether you become a full-time lawyer or become a businessman or whether you get into government or whatever you're going to do. I've always wanted to be a lawyer, to have a law background. And political science, political science is the, ah, the best type of major most people say for going into law."

"What was it about people that so intrigued you to want to become involved in policy or government. What is it?" Ringe demanded.

"If you take the political science background plus going to law school, I wanted it for background for my own information. . . . I would be able to use that background and whatever I decided to do in my career. . . . But I was never a full-time practicing attorney. I left that up to my wife."

"What was it about consumer advocacy that interested you?" asked Ringe, referring to Quayle's first job, in the consumer protection division of the attorney general's office.

"Actually it was a job. It wasn't any special interest in the consumer affairs." Quayle laughed, according to the transcription notes. "I'm sure you don't want . . ."

"Now tell me what was it that turned you on about consumer affairs."

"I needed a paycheck and the attorney general said that I would be

the best to go down there because he knew that I was anti-consumer."
Quayle laughed again.

"You were anti-consumer?"

"I figured you liked that one anyway," said Quayle, trying to please.

"I'm going to have this tape bronzed," Ringe replied. He asked
about details of Quayle's early days. "You said something about having
attended all those public schools . . ."

"Because there were no private schools around."

"No," said Ringe, "I meant how many, how come you went to.
. . . Why [so] many different [ones]?"

Quayle explained the various moves made by his family while he
grew up.

"Tell me about your dad," asked Ringe.

" . . . He's a fine person. Somebody that's been a great influence on
me. And, ah. . . . Well, I think that the most, ah, telling thing he said:
Don't ever let the guys grind you down. He'd always say: What you're
going to have ups and downs in life but there'll be more ups than downs
and when you get down just remember there's another day. And I think
that was actually his statement to me when we had difficult times. He'd
always say: The sun will shine another day."

It was at this point that the tape transcription ended. "He dramatically improved. He was a quick study," said Ringe, in retrospect.

Senator Quayle was assigned to the Armed Services Committee and
was quickly captured by a new species of handlers—the circle of neoconservative operatives whose leader was Richard Perle, assistant secretary of defense, a specialist in frustrating arms control. The senator
staffed himself with neoconservative experts of the second echelon who
guided him through the arcana of nuclear theory. By 1983, Quayle had
proven himself so reliable that he was inducted into the neoconservatives' monthly strategy group, held in the office of Kenneth Adelman,
a Perle acolyte and the director of the Arms Control and Disarmament
Agency. Even at the height of Reaganism, before the Gorbachev summits, Quayle stood to the right of Reagan. He personally lobbied the
president to junk U.S. adherence to the provisions of the SALT II
Treaty, telling him that if he continued he would be seen as weak, like
Jimmy Carter. And when the INF Treaty came before the Senate for
ratification, Quayle voted for a "killer amendment" that would have
destroyed Reagan's single effort at arms control. "I don't think he's any
different from Brezhnev or anybody else," Quayle said about Gorbachev in 1988. "Perestroika is nothing more than refined Stalinism.
. . . It's not changing the system."

Senator Quayle was a contented man. He had prestige and power, which he concluded derived from his intellectual leadership. "The best mind to have," he explained, "is one that not only can create these things but to get the facts and to be the creator. The second best one is maybe if you're not the creator, but to get the facts and be able to lead. . . . I'm somewhere in between that first and second tier in *The Prince.*" Unfortunately, there are no such "tiers" in *The Prince* or anywhere else in Machiavelli's writings. Quayle was a prince of a different kind. Quayle had the face Nixon always wanted, unblemished by worry, self-pity or complication, without a hint of five o'clock shadow, sweat on the upper lip, or darting eyes. Nothing had ever gone against him. He was a prince of conservatism without any cause for resentment. "Danny's only sadness is that he can't get his children interested in golf," said his mother.

The rational political reasons for picking this golden boy seemed obvious: his age, region and ideology. But no explanation made more manifest sense for his presence on the *Delta Queen* than the psychological. In selecting a vice president, Bush, in effect, was choosing someone to play himself. His choice of Quayle revealed his view of the vice presidency and how he had spent his last eight years. Quayle was plastic and indecisive, a figure who could be completely dominated. He radiated physical energy but was intellectually and emotionally submissive. Bush had spent his career as a political son, and now he appointed his own political son. His idea of authority required that he have this sort of running mate. "I think that the one I'd like to pattern myself after is George Bush," said Quayle, when asked about role models. His press secretary, one of the many guardians named by the Bush campaign to watch over him, beamed at his response.

Quayle was touted as the first member of the baby boom generation to be on a national ticket. But he was an avatar of the complacent and compliant Reagan generation of the 1980s, not the generation to which he belonged by chronological age. Quayle had been untouched by the 1960s; he had never rebelled against anything. Like Reagan himself, Quayle was genial, lucky, self-regarding and lazy, a man of dogmatic beliefs with a weak grasp of the facts. But where Reagan conveyed the strength of conviction, Quayle looked like he did not know the answer. "I did not know in 1969 that I would be in this room today, I confess," he said at his first press conference. Quayle was then led from anchor booth to anchor booth suspended above the convention floor. After interviewing him, one anchorman remarked: "When I looked into his eyes I could see to the back of his head."

Quayle was in trouble, much to his astonishment. The press was relentless in demanding the details of how he gained entrance into the National Guard—that is, how he had evaded the overriding political and moral crisis of his generation. But the problem was deeper even than that. The facts of Quayle's life were at odds with what he had been raised to believe, a family credo of self-reliance that the coddling by his family made impossible to fulfill. His conservatism and his passivity peacefully coexisted until Bush lifted him onto the national stage for precisely both traits. Now that contradiction threatened to blow apart both of their careers.

Bush's acceptance speech to the convention, already heavily burdened, was now weighted with high explosives he had placed there himself.

V

Peggy Noonan was hired by the Bush campaign to provide a coherence to his biography that he could not provide himself. She was a specialist in crafting visions. As a young girl she had been infatuated with John F. Kennedy, and later she transferred this devotion to Ronald Reagan. She was hired as a White House speechwriter after working as a scriptwriter for Dan Rather. She had hardly any personal contact with the president, but he delivered her emotion- and metaphor-laden speeches practically verbatim. Some of his most memorable sound bites came from Noonan's word processor—his speech on the 40th anniversary of D-Day on Normandy ("These are the champions who helped free a continent"), after the *Challenger* tragedy ("slipped the surly bonds of Earth to touch the face of God") and on the contras ("moral equivalent of the founding fathers"). She went on to write George Bush's announcement speech. And when he faltered after his defeat in the Iowa caucuses, she was rushed into the emergency room to operate on his rhetoric. A "new," humanized Bush emerged to say: "I may not articulate much, but I feel." Now Noonan was brought in to help him articulate what he told her would be the "biggest speech of his life."

"With Reagan," she recalled, "the themes of his life were so clear. With Bush, it was less clear." It was hard to think of him as a Kennedy-like figure. "I don't remember him explicitly referring to patterns. He doesn't say, 'There is a consistent theme in my life.'" Noonan, however, had some ideas about themes. One of them was "a theme of

America as wide open, full of mobility of all kinds," she said. But, no, "he never said it to me." Bush's experience in World War II, she decided, was also a good theme, "important to him." But, no, "he never said it." She does remember that Bush told her a war story. "He talked about being on a aircraft carrier, a pilot came in, the plane tipped over, the prop on another plane hit the pilot, cut him up. Bush waved his hand. 'I'm telling you, this guy got filleted.' " Did Bush ever mention his father, the senator who had been his first model of public service? "No," said Noonan, "he never talked about his father." Noonan recalled that Bush talked about Texas, "how tough it was for him. It was very nervous-making for him." For an earlier speech, she had written a few lines about Bush's ulcer during his early Texas days. "I know I wrote that in," said Noonan. But the acknowledgment of how stressful it was for him to cope was excised. "He perceived himself as a man of guts," she said, raising another theme. But, no, "he never said that."

"We had the experience but missed the meaning," wrote T. S. Eliot. Peggy Noonan missed the experience but filled in the meaning.

By the night of his acceptance speech, the mood of Bush's handlers had greatly improved from what it had been just a few weeks earlier. Their skepticism about a problematic candidate had been replaced by an optimism about having begun to find the way. Bush's speech presented him with not only the right occasion for the rite of passage but also with clear themes, tailored as closely as possible to his own sense of himself. Up until that moment, there had been a split for Bush between the political father to whom he owed loyalty and the paterfamilias, the role he played at the family estate in Maine every summer, where he presided as "Dad." At this moment, he moved from being the political son to being the political father for the first time.

"And so," said Bush, standing at last before a Republican convention as its presidential nominee, "tonight is for big things." He was there to unveil his long-awaited vision. His appearance on the podium had been preceded by a biographical film, produced by Ailes, a kind of coming attractions. It featured grainy black-and-white footage of George Bush's actual rescue in World War II by a submarine after his plane had been knocked out of the sky. "I am a man who sees life in terms of missions—missions defined and missions completed," said Bush. "When I was a torpedo bomber pilot they defined the mission for us. . . . But I am here tonight—and I am your candidate—because the most important work of my life is to complete the mission we started in 1980."

Bush's ultimate rationale was continuity, a theme that played on several levels. By continuing Reagan's work as it was defined in Year One, the Bush presidency would simply be the next chapter in the Reagan era, whose lineaments were well-grooved. Bush assured the Republicans that they would not be thrown back on their former anxieties. He calmed them by inhabiting the myth of an unchanging world that would not surprise or disturb them if they only clung to the familiar. Bush was riding on the coattails of an illusion, not a president or an ideology. By denying its fragility, he held off time itself. Anxiety about the unknown was projected onto the opponent, who was equated with "risk." But the continuity that Bush was promising ran deeper than the tie between himself and Ronald Reagan, between this political moment and 1980. The narrative pulse of Bush's speech began with the flickering pictures of the young crewcut pilot being fished out of the Pacific in 1942. The story of George Bush was the story of the American Century.

"This has been called the American Century because in it we were the dominant force for good in the world. We saved Europe, cured polio, we went to the moon, and lit the world with our culture. Now we are on the verge of a new century, and what country's name will it bear? I say it will be another American Century."

The missions of the pilot and the candidate were on a continuous line. His earliest experience in the larger world and his latest were of a piece. He staked his campaign on it. The American Century was not over. The postwar order that had followed the surrender on the U.S.S. *Missouri* would last through the millennium.

Given the formative power of the war experience, one can hardly blame the World War II generation for attempting to recapture its feeling. It was "the good war," a realization of America's ideals against an evil empire. For the generation that fought it, it was the great moral parable of our time. When Bush evoked this parable as a way to explain his own life, he was evoking America's best idea of itself.

For Bush's generation, the Cold War was the moral equivalent of World War II. It was the underlying structure that allowed that generation to sustain its purpose after the war and to organize the world along rational lines. The Cold War was waged by the veterans of World War II. But the Cold War was not World War II, and it became less and less similar with each passing year. Certainly, the efforts by Democratic and Republican administrations alike to justify the Vietnam War by reference to the Munich Pact of appeasement with the Nazis did not make time stand still. After Vietnam, the Cold War had a different meaning for the younger generation than it did for their fathers who had experienced World War II. But, in Reagan's mind, as well as Bush's, the premises of the American Century were still being validated by a war whose era was radically unlike the forty years that followed it. For the World War II generation, there seemed to be a greater continuity between 1945 and 1988 than the younger generation experienced between 1968 and 1988. With Reagan still as president and another World War II veteran running as his successor, the continuity appeared unbroken.

Bush's theme about the American Century was a reprise of that of his fellow Yale alumnus, Connecticut Yankee and China hand, Henry Luce. But none of the versions of the American Century—not Luce's sermonizing Chamber of Commerce version, Dean Acheson's liberal realist version, James Burnham's right-wing apocalyptic version, or Henry Kissinger's Bismarckian version—were holding in the face of the rapidly ending Cold War. And under Reagan, who himself had promised to restore the American Century, the U.S. deficit, which propped up the Pentagon budget and the regressive tax system, was being financed by the countries we had once lifted up from the rubble of World War II. In part, their ascendance was due to the success of the postwar system led by the U.S.; however, it was also due to the failure of American policy. Early in the century, at the beginning of World War I, America had become the world's leading creditor nation and thus a preeminent power. In the 1980s, we had become the world's leading debtor nation. The period Bush wanted to preside over was no longer the American Century. But, for the moment, the myth endured; nostalgia remained a political force to be reckoned with.

And yet Bush spoke of "a new relationship with the Soviet Union," which he claimed was forged by the administration's design. "It is no accident," he said. The policy that had misjudged the direction of the Soviet Union was, according to Bush, responsible for the changes. "Strength stops them," he said. "I will not allow this country to be made weak again." He warned that "the tremors in the Soviet world continue"—tremors he did not describe. "Perhaps what is happening will change our world forever. Perhaps not." Either everything would change, or nothing. "A prudent skepticism is in order." Whichever was the case, Bush promised watchful waiting. Whatever the outcome, it would be the American Century.

He returned to his personal narrative, still drawing connections of continuity. "We moved to west Texas forty years ago. The war was over, and we wanted to get out and make it on our own. . . . Lived the dream—high school football on Friday night, Little League, neighbor-hood barbecue. People don't see their experience as symbolic of an era—but of course we were." George Bush was the living symbol of the World War II generation.

The election, he said, was "also about philosophy. And I have one." In this rendering of "the vision thing," he described America as "a thousand points of light" and vowed "a kinder, gentler nation."[3]

Bush's effort against Dukakis appeared to belie this promise, for it was neither kind nor gentle. But Bush had an affirmative message, after all; it was the flipside of his negative message, an evocation of the atmospherics of the past. The once and future American Century was the Cold War in a positive key.

Bush's campaign was an act of historic preservation—"for an endless enduring dream and a thousand points of light. That is my mission. And I will complete it." Then, before the balloons dropped, the bands played and the crowd roared, George Bush put his hand over his heart. He asked the Republicans to stand, and they did.

"I pledge allegiance . . ."

3. "Why a thousand? I don't know," explained Peggy Noonan. "A thousand clowns, a thousand days—a hundred wasn't enough and a million is too many."

13

The Dead Democrats

Michael Dukakis began his campaign against George Bush by calling himself a "conservative." "This crowd in the White House isn't conservative," he told an ABC affiliates' forum in early June. "I was always taught that a conservative paid his bills, that you didn't run up these massive amounts of red ink." He turned to his questioner, the conservative pundit George Will. "I think you're that kind of person and I happen to be that kind of person. . . . Who's the conservative and who's the liberal?"

A phantom haunted the campaign. One ran against it, the other ran from it; one tried to make everyone believe it was there, the other tried to make everyone think it wasn't. This ogre was an object of fear, anxiety and contempt. Merely uttering its name was enough to make one candidate feel strong and the other weak. Saying its first letter was enough to evoke its dreadedness: the L-word.

The phobic aura of the term pointed up the gravity of the crisis facing the Democratic Party. But that there even was a crisis was not apparent to its stalwarts. They believed that this must be their hour, even though their candidate did not know what historical hour it was. Dukakis's very inability to offer any definition of liberalism was taken as perhaps his most encouraging trait. It was seen as enormous shrewdness, a form of wisdom. Dukakis's politics of lowered expectations, his career of slashing budgets and tax cuts, made him seem a new kind of Democrat, a man of his time. His emotional flatness made him appear unflappable; his unsentimental, no-nonsense approach conveyed the 1980s mode of decisiveness. He was representative of that generation of Democrats whose formative years were the 1950s and who had begun to come into their own with the post-Watergate election of 1974. The approach of the new men was a curious regression to a pre-New Deal liberalism, a Yankee reformism whose energy was drawn from moral outrage at corruption and whose god was efficiency. Dukakis was an extreme, but by no means atypical, case in whom all vestiges of evangelical Progressive language had been replaced by the metallic language of problem-solving.

He had the notion that he could win the presidency on his own terms. If it seemed that he lacked a larger purpose, it was because that purpose was disconnected from social goals. But Dukakis did indeed have a larger purpose in mind. It was grandiose to the point of being utopian. His ambition was to fulfill the hopes and dreams of generations of good government crusaders. He proposed nothing less than to purge politics of politics; in its place he would substitute the managerial science of "conflict resolution" and "consensus-building"—the end of ideology with a vengeance. In this he appealed to the party's deep-seated fear of conflict, hatched by the confusion and defeat of the past two decades.

Shunning controversy was more than an aspect of Dukakis's tactics. It was a first principle of his antipolitics, of his belief that this election was not about ideology. Without reading the book himself, for example, Dukakis had followed his Kennedy School advisers in rejecting the ideas contained in Paul Kennedy's *The Rise and Fall of the Great Powers*, which suggested how the Republicans had managed the decline of the United States at the end of the Cold War. Dukakis also skirted any identification with Democratic presidential candidates of the recent past, afraid that their defeats would rub off. By a strategy of avoidance, he thought he could elude all supposedly negative connotations of the L-word. He acted as though the liberal tradition were so tarnished it could not be reclaimed. Some of his advisers especially went out of their way to slight George McGovern, as if his diminishment would make Dukakis bigger. In spite of his caution and because of his belief that the campaign was nonideological, he was completely unprepared for the onslaught.

George Bush paid no attention to the careful, little campaign Dukakis was constructing. The distinctions Dukakis was trying to draw simply didn't matter to him. "My opponent's view of the world sees a long slow decline for our country, an inevitable fall mandated by impersonal historical forces," he told the Republican convention, implicitly equating Michael Dukakis with a caricature of Paul Kennedy. "I'm not running against Jimmy Carter, I'm running against George McGovern," Bush crowed.

Dan Payne, Dukakis's early media adviser, who had been banished to the outer reaches of the campaign for questioning the candidate's lack of a message before the primaries had begun, had seen what was coming. On May 18, nearly a month before Bush launched his first attack, Payne predicted, "They have only one choice—savage Dukakis. This is going to be as ugly as anything he has ever faced. They'll do it as George Bush standing tall for America, while Dukakis is turning rapists and murderers loose on our streets. They will run a brutally negative campaign. They are going to throw everything that the right has thrown at the Democrats. They have no choice. They have nothing to lose."

Payne gave his premonition to the campaign strategists and it was promptly dismissed. So he went to the State House to alert Dukakis. "He was absolutely on cloud nine," Payne recalled. "He couldn't help grinning. There was still a quality of I-can't-believe-we've-come-this-far. I asked him how it was going to go in the general. He started to preach about organizational politics, going door to door. I was astonished. I said, 'We should talk about what the message is going to be.' He thought it was a staffing problem." "We have to staff it up," he said. In short, it was a problem of management. Payne then warned him about the coming negative campaign. "As far as the definition of this, we'll have to wait until other people get involved in the campaign," said Dukakis, brushing him off. But no "definition" was ever prepared.

Dukakis was a man of technique who mostly spurned his political technicians. During the weeks after the Democratic convention, Dukakis dismissed nearly every one of their ideas as not what he had in mind, though he could not explain what that might be. But there was one suggestion, urged on him by almost all of his advisers, that he took to heart. Whatever he did, they said, he should not call himself a "liberal." The poll numbers were bad on this.

Dukakis had a compulsive sense of order that was being violated by the messiness and unpredictability of the campaign. As the disorder grew, he came to view his own helpers as the agents of anarchy. Only John Sasso had known how to manipulate Dukakis's psyche, and he was in exile. Dukakis would allow no one else to temper his impulses, especially Sasso's replacement, Susan Estrich, against whom Dukakis waged a war of passive aggression almost from the day he hired her. She had spent almost a year battling the candidate and was now beyond the point of exhaustion; for every idea he grudgingly agreed to, twelve were rejected. Both lawyers, both former Harvard professors, they were most alike in rendering political points in legal reasoning.

On July 1, Estrich presented Dukakis with a strategy memo for the campaign against Bush. It was written by Tom Kiley, a former seminarian turned pollster who had come to Massachusetts two decades earlier and been in the forefront of the crucial campaigns that transformed the state's political character. (Dan Payne was his former partner and still a good friend.) Kiley, who had been part of the Dukakis campaign from the beginning, combined conviction with statistical finesse. His memo, based on the first national poll conducted by the staff, was the most comprehensive strategic plan produced for the candidate in anticipation of the fall campaign.

In it, Kiley noted that Dukakis's lead had been chipped away during June by Bush's negative thrusts but argued that Dukakis could defend his character by making his own case. "When we 'weigh in' more aggressively with our middle-class economic issues, we will broaden our advantage on this dimension once again," Kiley wrote. Bush, he pointed out, was still extremely vulnerable. His unfavorability rating, in spite of his assaults on Dukakis, was still much higher. "The reason Bush has closed the gap is he has successfully activated latent MSD [Michael S. Dukakis] vulnerabilities, while we have not the same in reverse." Kiley urged that Dukakis make "taking control of America's economic destiny and building a future of opportunity" his "central thematic message." Dukakis had to do this, Kiley wrote, by "continually" stressing that Bush "is a product of privilege, and the personification of an elite Republican philosophy that protects the interests of the wealthy few, often at the expense of the needs of middle and working class Americans." The "issue environment," as Kiley put it, was "very congenial to MSD," regardless of the Bush attempt to smear him with the L-word. To be sure, "MSD must eventually pass a threshold of credibility on the whole issue of US/USSR relations. . . ." But a graph filling a half-page showed that by a margin of 58 to 28 percent the voters felt that Japan "threatens economic security" more than Russia "threatens military security." "With a concerted effort in July," Kiley concluded, "there is every reason to believe we can widen our lead back to double digits by August 1."

Dukakis, however, did not accept this strategy. He did not even talk to Kiley about it. Nor did he offer an alternative. Instead, he suppressed discussion about strategy within his campaign. Kiley believed that Dukakis could win the presidency only by winning the northern and Pacific coast states. If the candidate thought he could run well in all parts of the country, he was deluded. Winning the South, Kiley believed, was an illusion. He pointd out in his memo that, even with Dukakis ahead nationally, "among white voters in the South, MSD is losing by 21%." By chasing after southern votes, Dukakis would be diffusing his energy and diluting his message to no end. He had to concentrate on where he could win. But the suggestion that he might lose a state was a forbidden thought. Dukakis believed that he could win everywhere by presenting himself as he wished to be seen. All discussion about the Electoral College was considered offensive to the candidate. Kiley's concerns and ideas were never permitted to have an airing, even though he was in the inner circle. The others caved in to Dukakis. Thus there was no real discussion about basic strategy because Dukakis had ruled it out of order. Dukakis had a fifty-state strategy, which meant that he had no strategy at all.

In July, Kirk O'Donnell was brought into the campaign as the communications director. He was among the most experienced and shrewdest of the Democratic politicos—the former top aide to Mayor Kevin White of Boston, Speaker Tip O'Neill, and the president of the Center for National Policy, a Democratic-oriented think tank that sought to develop ideas for a winning strategy. In the 1986 midterm elections, O'Donnell was part of the informal Democratic political directorate that had helped the Democrats win back the Senate. He had high hopes that the Republicans could be thoroughly routed from Washington in 1988. He was given Kiley's memo to read by Estrich, and he assumed that it was the essential strategic document. O'Donnell told Dukakis that he was well positioned to present an agenda for change but that he had to prepare to defend himself because the Republicans would be sure to try to make him appear dangerous—"out of the mainstream." Dukakis listened impassively; he made no comments.

An advertising unit called the Future Group was set up, with Kiley as its manager and Scott Miller as its creative director. Miller had been the former creative director of McCann-Erickson, who had designed the commercials for Coca Cola ("Coke is it!") and had gone into political media work. He promptly recruited Michael Kaye for his team. Kaye had made promotional films and ads for Disney and produced spots for Jerry Brown and Senator Bill Bradley.

About two weeks after the convention, Miller and Kaye flew to Boston, where they met with the staff's high command. Kaye entered the campaign without having had any previous contact with Dukakis. His optimism was unalloyed. But he had a few concerns—the furlough issue, for example. Kaye was told not to worry, that it would be dealt with. He also observed that the positive feeling from the convention about Dukakis was evaporating. An ad, he suggested, could sustain it. So he was given the assignment.

That evening, Miller and Kaye and about six others met with Dukakis. Kaye explained that he would be making a spot about the convention. Dukakis nodded. Then Miller said, "We should put some comparative material in the can." "Hold it a second," said Dukakis. "I don't know about that. I don't want to get negative. I'm real nervous about getting negative." "I don't understand," Kaye interrupted. "What do you mean by negative? We have to say to the American people that there are differences. They don't pay attention. We have to do it. You say you don't want to go negative. You've already gone negative." Just a few days before, on July 30, in a self-righteous reflex, without forewarning anyone in his campaign, Dukakis had criticized President Reagan on the ethics of his administration by saying, "A fish rots from the head first."

"What should I say then?" Dukakis replied to Kaye. Miller told Dukakis that if he didn't define himself, Roger Ailes would. Miller suggested a media plan that would run through September. "Yes," said Dukakis. Two days later, a disappointed Estrich called Miller and said: "He's decided not to go on the air until Labor Day. He said the Republicans are going to dominate the news during their convention. There's no use even trying to get into it."

After the meeting with Dukakis, Miller begged Kaye to produce his spot instantly. The Republicans were filling the lull between the conventions with negative attacks on Dukakis. No positive message was being communicated. Over the weekend, Kaye worked feverishly, making five commercials featuring pictures of Dukakis with "America the Beautiful" played on the harmonica in the background. Miller was ecstatic. The spots were as polished as any he had ever seen, and they bathed the candidate in warm feelings. In one of them, pictures of Roosevelt, Truman and Kennedy faded into a picture of Dukakis, making him the natural successor to the Democratic tradition. The ads were quickly shipped to Dukakis for his approval. Soon, Kaye was informed that the music had to go—bigger music, please; Dukakis's voice didn't sound deep enough—put an echo on it; the pictures of Dukakis weren't positive enough—more smiles; Dukakis's accomplishments weren't listed—mention balanced budgets; the cheering crowd wasn't shown—adoring faces, please.

"Listen," Kaye told Miller, "nobody is going to have credibility with this guy. He's not going to trust anyone. He doesn't know you or me. Nobody has his trust." In spite of Miller's imploring, Kaye quit. Miller finally revised the spot to Dukakis's specifications, making it into a clichéd snippet of candidate adoration. By the time it aired, Dukakis's lead had begun to vanish.

Dukakis believed that the feeling he had aroused for a brief moment at the convention could be prolonged by mechanical means. He ascribed the success of his acceptance speech partly to his use of the teleprompter. Afterwards, he became addicted to it. Almost everywhere he went, he demanded the device. His performances became more wooden than ever. And he began to regard the events of the campaign as rude intrusions.

A week after the Democratic convention, Kirk O'Donnell had received a telephone call from a contact, informing him that the Republicans were going to try to make an issue of Dukakis's mental health. O'Donnell believed his source and prepared himself for the moment when the innuendo started circulating. He knew how bogus issues, if not dealt with, could damage politicians. At the first sign of trouble, O'Donnell went directly to Dukakis and told him he could stop it cold by releasing his medical records. Dukakis, however, didn't believe that anything so obviously base could hurt him. He told O'Donnell he didn't trust his judgment. By the time Dukakis released his records to the press, putting an end to the speculation a week later, his lead had been halved to 7 points. O'Donnell's advice would have forced the candidate to descend from his pedestal into the arena to play politics in a way he disdained. But O'Donnell did not have Dukakis's implicit trust and, therefore, could not play the Sasso role.

Then, unexpectedly, the Dukakis campaign was delivered a gift: Dan Quayle. Bush's running mate was a heaven-sent reason for Dukakis to avoid defining the issues. Quayle was Bush cubed, his faults raised to the nth degree, especially reflected in his fractured speech, which signified an immense, immeasurable intellectual vacuum. The Dukakis camp believed that whatever boost Bush had gotten from his acceptance speech would be undone by Quayle. The beauty of it was that the press, in a "feeding flurry," according to a horrified Bush, was doing all the dirty work. But immediately after the convention, Roger Ailes choreographed a confrontation between the press and Quayle in his hometown of Huntington, Indiana, where the reporters appeared like a lynch mob and Quayle a victim. The townsfolk, playing the chorus, were naturally aroused to denounce the press and defend the native son. On television, the tableau looked like *The Ox-Bow Incident,* with Quayle in the role of the innocent.

Dukakis did not realize that he had to provide his own interpretation of the events in order to turn them in the political direction he wanted. The reporters, following their empirical method, had uncovered Quayle's hypocrisy by exposing the facts of how he entered the National Guard. But the facts do not always speak for themselves. The underlying issue here was privilege, but raising it into the spotlight was the task of the politician. But Dukakis had never liked the theme of privilege anyway. He never grasped, according to his aides, that the attacks on Bush as a figure of privilege made by speakers at the Democratic convention were part of his campaign. He had rejected anything that smacked of economic populism since the beginning of his campaign, even the potentialities that had been on vivid display ("Bush was born on third base and thinks he hits a triple," etc.) at the Democratic convention.

With Quayle's emergence, Dukakis's strategists saw a chance to portray the Republicans as out of the mainstream. Attack lines were scripted for Bentsen and Dukakis to be delivered the day after the GOP convention. "A mardi gras for the Moral Majority," said Bentsen. "They've gone so far right, they're wrong," Dukakis was supposed to have said. But he balked at the last minute, with his speech in hand and the crowd before him, undermining the tactic and losing the initiative. The "tone," he complained, bothered him.

Dukakis had come to believe that his staff was forcing a negative campaign on him. Within a campaign devoted to "consensus-building," there was no consensus. The internal conflict grew greater as Dukakis became more paralyzed. He had the idea that the public wanted a positive effort and that his staff was getting between him and the people. He envisioned the voters flocking to him because of his evident virtues. He could not imagine that anyone would fail to see his honesty and competence. To do so would be irrational.

Bush was now following every command of his consultants to the letter, as though he had been coded by software programmers. The decision to go negative had become a double imperative; his campaign was seized with panic by Quayle's presence on the ticket. Thus, as soon as the GOP convention ended, Bush, Quayle and a host of surrogates were launched on a ferocious blitz—the last political offensive of Cold War conservatism. The fact that the Cold War had been declared "another time" by no less than Reagan himself was beside the point. This campaign wasn't about reality; it was about ideology.

On August 22, Bush defended Quayle before a Veterans of Foreign Wars convention. "He damn sure didn't burn the flag," he said, implying that there were those in the opponent's camp who had.

On August 23, Bush accused Dukakis of favoring a "weak defense," which was obvious from his position on the Pledge of Allegiance. "Teachers should open the day with the Pledge of Allegiance."

On August 24, Quayle said: "Dukakis' defense and foreign policy positions amount to a litany of retreat . . . a replay of the McGovern, Carter, Mondale dogma that has shoved the modern Democratic Party over to the far left."

That day, Senator Steve Symms revealed: "I heard that there are pictures around that will surface before the elections are over of Mrs. Dukakis burning the American flag while she was an antiwar demonstrator during the 60s." But there were no such pictures because there was no such incident. Nevertheless, Symms's claim was widely reported.

"What is it about the Pledge of Allegiance that upsets him so much?" demanded Bush.

On August 25, Bush conflated all his themes in one speech: "I can't help feel but his fervent opposition to the Pledge is symbolic of an entire attitude best summed up in four little letters: ACLU. I think it's time [Dukakis] let the Pledge of Allegiance out on furlough. . . . It's one thing to give peace a chance. But we cannot afford a president who would take a chance with peace. I don't understand why my opponent seems to oppose the development of every new weapons system since the slingshot."

On August 28, Bush claimed: "He fought tooth and nail to keep that outrageous furlough program that lets murderers, rapists and drug dealers out of jail."

On August 29, Bush justified his attacks: "It isn't negative campaigning to try to help the American people understand the differences." The next day, Senator Orrin Hatch called the Democratic

Party "the party of homosexuals," a charge broadcast on the network news programs.

By now, Bush had gained a lead over Dukakis that he would never relinquish. The negative campaign had succeeded in knocking down Dukakis, leaving him lying face-flat in the mud. During the whirlwind week in which Bush was mercilessly pummeling a straw man he called "the liberal governor," Dukakis spent most of his time wandering around western Massachusetts, inspecting state facilities and programs. At the moment when the electorate wanted the campaign to expand to a national and even a global scale, he was contracting it to the size of his home state. He had achieved presidential stature for an instant with his acceptance speech, but now he was shrinking himself. He had virtually barricaded himself in a far corner of New England, remote not only from the voters but from his own helpers. The springs of his character were tightening. He hardly ever deigned to speak with Susan Estrich, who usually wound up hectoring him when he did. But the more he withdrew into himself, the more he was besieged by bewildered and stricken Democrats, who inundated him with advice for action. Senator Paul Simon, among many others, urged him to leave Massachusetts, go anyplace else, even across the border into Vermont. But Dukakis stubbornly kept to his own schedule, as if he were frozen in time and space.

The press, which his advisers had hoped would swallow Quayle, instead began to devour Dukakis. At every stop, they took another bite out of him: Governor, how do you respond to George Bush's latest charge? The press instinctively believed that its on-the-one-hand-he-said, on-the-other-hand-you-said approach was the platonic form of balance and fairness. But those members of the press who adhered to the conventions of "objectivity" became the Bush campaign's best surrogates by broadcasting its distortions unfiltered. In an election notable for its manipulativeness, the reporters who believed their "straight" craft insulated them were the most manipulated figures in political society. Thus the press, too, played its role in the Cold War drama of 1988. Its performance was disturbingly similar to the press performance in the early Cold War, when an "objective" press was essential to the rise of Senator Joseph McCarthy. Historian Robert Griffith, in *The Politics of Fear*, writes of McCarthy:

> He turned to his own advantage the structure and functioning of the press itself. The "straight" news story, for example, played directly into his hands, for while it might not be a fact that Philip Jessup had "an

unusual affinity for Communist causes," it *was* a fact that McCarthy had said so, and thus the story would be printed. . . .

If the functioning of the press created publicity for McCarthy, so did the nature of his charges. Once leveled, an accusation did not wither and die, but tended to bounce back in the form of denials, qualifications, and countercharges, thus generating a chain reaction of publicity. This in turn would allow McCarthy opportunity for further comment, for a repetition of the charges, a well-chosen epithet, or some other new twist. If carefully managed, even the most unfounded charge could produce almost a week of notices.

Dukakis's first formative political experience was his viewing of the fall of McCarthy in the televised Army–McCarthy hearings. It had made Dukakis an unshakeable civil libertarian. It was precisely on these grounds—for being a "card-carrying member of the ACLU," for example—that he was being slurred. Dukakis believed that McCarthyism was something in the past. He could not conceive of its irrational methods being revived in a modern, enlightened world that had already rejected them. He told his advisers that the lies and distortions about him would fall harmlessly to the ground; they were so patently preposterous that no one would really give them credence. But his refusal to dignify the calumnies by defending himself allowed them to hang in the air. His aloofness appeared as passivity. He played the victim hauled before the House Un-American Activities Committee, blinking into the flashing cameras, as the relentless interrogator demanded: Are you now or have you ever been . . . a liberal? Dukakis kept taking the Fifth Amendment. By acting out the role of the accused, he was Bush's chief co-conspirator in perpetrating the Cold War drama.

Dukakis was isolated and dejected. His campaign had been devoted to separating himself from Democrats of the past. This disconnection was one of its fundamental premises: Who he wasn't was who he was. But his beleaguerment was reminiscent of Jimmy Carter's. His western Massachusetts tour recalled nothing so much as Carter's Camp David retreat. Carter had withdrawn to the mountaintop to discover a new inspiration, to be born again—again. When he came down, what he delivered was not engraved tablets but the famous "malaise" speech. Dukakis seemed even more lost than Carter. His campaign was sunk deep in a malaise. And he had no big message in reserve; rather, he believed that his problem could be cured by a double dose of managerialism. If only the campaign could be made orderly, it would be restored.

On September 2, John Sasso returned. One of Dukakis's greatest appeals to Democrats in the primaries had been that he had learned from defeat, that it had made him a complete person and politician. Now all the vulnerabilities that he had supposedly dealt with in his first defeat were exposed again. As in a recurring nightmare, he summoned Sasso to perform the phoenixlike miracle of raising him. The secret of his decline after the convention was not that the candidate who had won the primaries had changed but that he had not really changed at all. Sasso was back because Dukakis was dead again.

The first thing that Sasso discovered was that there was no strategy—not even a strategy memo—that Dukakis had agreed on. Virtually overnight, Sasso singlehandedly imposed economics on the campaign as the main theme. Its motifs were the "middle class squeeze" and "making America number one again." The former was supposed to appeal to women, playing to their desire for security, and the latter to men, playing to their notions of strength.

On Labor Day, September 5, the formal opening day of the fall campaign, Dukakis's first rally in Philadelphia was disrupted by antiabortion militants. He flew next to the traditional site where Democratic presidential campaigns are kicked off, Cadillac Square in Detroit. His new theme was supposed to be unveiled here. The best speechwriter in the Democratic Party, Robert Shrum, had been recruited to write this all-important speech. Shrum was that rare bird, an intellectual politico, who had been a senior aide to Senator Edward Kennedy, gone into the consulting business and been a mastermind behind the rise of Dick Gephardt's presidential candidacy. He composed a stirring speech, almost all of which wound up on the cutting-room floor. Dukakis delivered only a few of the lines written for him. "Bring the prosperity home," he said. But even these lines irritated him. As he walked off the stage, he turned to an aide and scowled. "I don't want to see this anymore," he said. "This is divisive."

The Bush campaign, in the meantime, continued to paint Dukakis satanic black. It was never to let up. Every day, until election day, there was a new charge, a new smear. On September 4, for example, Secretary of Education William Bennett, donning the robes of the Grand Inquisitor, his favorite costume, declared that the "Brookline–Cambridge world . . . have disdain for the simple and basic patriotism of most Americans. . . . the crowd with which Mike Dukakis runs. . . . They don't like what most Americans think and believe."

That month alone, an independent expenditure committee, Americans for Bush, spent $540,000 on television ads about Willie Horton. In Texas, the Republican Party mailed hundreds of thousands of brochures reading: "Here are the words Dukakis doesn't want your child to have to say." The words were the Pledge of Allegiance. Another flier distributed by the GOP warned that Dukakis "doesn't want your children to say the words of the Pledge of Allegiance, and wants special privileges for gays and lesbians under the civil rights laws." Radio ads paid for by the Bush campaign were broadcast in areas with large defense plants, warning that hundreds of thousands of workers would lose their jobs because of Dukakis's weakness on national security. Twelve separate ads in this series were made for Texas alone: "He's not just talking about America losing ground. He's talking about Texans losing jobs." The Illinois Republican State Central Committee issued a pamphlet saying, "All the murders and rapists and drug pushers and child molesters in Massachusetts vote for Michael Dukakis." The Republican National Committee published a pamphlet, "The Hazards of Duke," portraying him as a "coddler of criminals" who "grants free passes to murderers." Another section was headlined: "Dukakis Grants Sasso Political Furlough." In Maryland, the state GOP distributed a flier featuring the pictures of Michael Dukakis and Willie Horton: "Is This Your Pro-Family Team for 1988?" In California, at the state Republican convention, Representative Newt Gingrich, a leader of the House GOP, said, "It's not that Dukakis is not a patriot; it's that Dukakis is nuts." He received a standing ovation. And Roger Ailes called Dukakis the "dirtiest campaigner in America."

As it happened, Michael Dukakis was not the only one who had supported prison furlough programs. On September 8, the *Houston Chronicle* reported that George Bush "provided key help in the founding of a Houston halfway house, New Directions, to which hundreds of felons are admitted each year after receiving parole or early release from the Texas Department of Corrections. . . . One of its residents raped and murdered the wife of a Pasadena minister the year before." Scott Miller believed that this was the break the campaign needed. That very day he made an ad throwing the furlough issue back in Bush's face. He sent it into the black hole of campaign headquarters, and it never emerged.

Earlier, angered by the Bush campaign's use of the Pledge of Allegiance to smear Dukakis's patriotism, Miller had proposed to make a spot in which Senator John Glenn would label the Bush charges "lies." Miller had been the media adviser to Glenn during his 1984 presidential campaign, and Glenn agreed to make the commercial. But the idea was killed.

A week before the *Houston Chronicle* story, on September 1, Bush had sailed around Boston Harbor in a boat, decrying Dukakis's responsibility for its pollution, thereby besmirching his reputation as an environmentalist. As Bush was on the water, his campaign aired a new ad, featuring pictures of polluted waters shot elsewhere: "And Michael Dukakis promises to do for America what he has done for Massachusetts." Miller was outraged. He knew that Bush's record as an environmentalist was soiled. And he knew that the lack of federal funding had been a factor in the slowness in cleaning up the harbor. Miller worked all through the night making a response ad, detailing Bush's negative record. The spot was almost instantly unreeled before a focus group that Miller's consulting group was conducting on Long Island. All those who saw it turned against Bush and toward Dukakis. So Miller sent it into the campaign, and it disappeared. He heard back later that Dukakis thought it was too negative.

Bush now claimed that Dukakis's goal was to strengthen Russia and weaken America. "Remember the [nuclear] freeze movement?" he said. "My opponent supported it. . . . He wanted to restrain us, not the Soviet Union." The freeze proposal, of course, called for a mutual, verifiable freeze. Dukakis's advisers desperately wanted him to defend himself. Kirk O'Donnell urged Dukakis to call Bush's statements "lies." By labeling them "lies," he argued, the press would be forced to do more than report what Dukakis had said. It would be obligated to investigate whether Bush was actually lying. The stories would fill the media for days. If that happened, the mud would begin to be wiped off Dukakis. On September 11, Dukakis compared Bush's tactics to "McCarthyism." But when he came to the word "lies" in his speech, he refused to say it; instead, he said "garbage." He had made the story one the press could not recycle.

That day, the House Republicans attempted and failed to force a vote on a bill that would have required the Congress daily to recite the Pledge of Allegiance.

The following day, Zbigniew Brzezinski endorsed George Bush. "Dukakis' views are a lot closer to Jesse Jackson and Jane Fonda," he said. Dukakis had spent his entire campaign trying to avoid guilt by association with the last Democratic president. Conversely, Bush had devoted considerable efforts to making Dukakis appear as Carter redux. Right after the Democratic convention, a television ad produced by the Republican National Committee had featured Carter and scenes of gas lines and Arab sheiks as the soundtrack played: "I remember you— you're the one who made me feel so blue." Now, Bush was running against Dukakis as the embodiment of the Carter foreign policy with

Carter's national security adviser acting as his surrogate.

Brzezinski flew his mission against Dukakis accompanied by Brent Scowcroft, Henry Kissinger's business partner and Bush's future national security adviser. On Louis Rukeyser's television show, Scowcroft explained what "I believe has motivated . . . Dr. Brzezinski to the move that he took today." It was, Scowcroft said, his "concerns" about Dukakis's "fundamental instincts, and those instincts seem clearly to be outside the mainstream of American policy, as practiced by both Republican and Democratic presidents."

Dukakis seemed paralyzed by Bush's Cold War barrages, though he had plenty of forewarning. In fact, the attacks had been precisely predicted by John Marttila, the central figure in the most important political consulting firm in Massachusetts. (Tom Kiley was his partner and Dan Payne a former partner and friend.) Marttila had managed Morris Udall's 1972 presidential campaign, been a senior strategist in Gary Hart's 1984 bid and was the chairman of Joe Biden's ill-fated effort. After Biden's withdrawal, Marttila raised funds for a project he called Americans Talk Security (ATS), which became the most thorough inventory of public opinion on national security in the country. Marttila's partner in this venture happened to be the firm operated by Robert Teeter, George Bush's pollster. The same information was therefore available to both sides.

In late 1987, Martilla wrote a memo to Dukakis urging him to develop a clear position on U.S.–Soviet relations. But Dukakis rebuffed him. In March, Marttila delivered a paper at O'Donnell's think tank. In it, he noted Gorbachev's approval rating of 71 percent. But he cautioned that 68 percent still wanted American leaders to "go slow." A Democratic presidential candidate, Marttila said, could take advantage of the changing attitudes so long as he did not "allow the Republicans to position him as soft on the Kremlin."

Immediately after the Republican convention, Marttila submitted a lengthy memo to the Dukakis campaign, entitled "Evaluating the Political Potential of George Bush's Anti-Soviet Strategy." "With each passing week," he wrote, "the broad outlines of the Bush campaign's political strategy are becoming increasingly clear. . . . What is surprising to many analysts, especially in the light of the Reagan–Gorbachev negotiations, is the extent to which George Bush is emphasizing a hard line approach toward the Soviets." But Marttila pointed out the political uses of the issue. "Throughout most of this year, the American people have believed Mike Dukakis would be a stronger president than George Bush, but the Bush campaign knows they cannot win unless they permanently turn this perception around—and they will do every-thing in their power to achieve this vitally important objective. In this context, Bush's anti-Soviet campaign should be seen in a broader strate-gic perspective; he is clearly using the issue as an opportunity to portray himself as the stronger candidate. . . ."

Marttila listed the ways in which Bush's strategy would work: First, he would depict Dukakis as "naïve" in order to draw out distrust of the Soviets, "the Gorbachev reforms notwithstanding." Second, Dukakis's hold over "key Democratic audiences" would be loosened. Marttila pointed to ATS data showing that "lower income, lower education" voters, who comprised the Democratic base, remained the most skepti-cal of the Soviets. Surprisingly, the most suspicious group in the popula-tion was "non-college women," who were the most economically vul-nerable. "I believe," Marttila wrote, "the Bush campaign sees the anti-Soviet views of non-college women as a strategic opportunity to help close the gender gap!" Third, the tough stance would help Bush deal with the "wimp" image. Fourth, it would polarize the electorate ideologically at a time when the liberal designation was a stigma. Fifth, Bush's "anti-Soviet strategy helps him deal with the 'vision-thing' be-cause it allows him to present a coherent, if slightly old-fashioned, vision of the world which resonates with forty years of American experi-ence." Sixth, it helped him justify the military buildup, when Ameri-cans "want to spend less on defense today." Seventh, it helped him defend Star Wars, which ATS surveys showed had declining support. Eighth, it enabled Bush to characterize all foreign policy by reference to U.S.–Soviet relations.

Bush's strategy would work, Marttila warned, in the "absence of a countervailing vision." Dukakis's imperative was to demonstrate strong leadership by his actions in the campaign itself. "This goal cannot be realized through advertising slogans or one-liners in the press. Rather, it must be revealed gradually, as the campaign and its dominant issues unfold, as the Dukakis priorities emerge, and as MSD responds to events around him." Neither criticism of the Reagan administration nor of Bush's negative campaign would "convey strong leadership qualities." If that were all Dukakis did, then Marttila suggested that "the public will conclude *both* campaigns are too negative. Therefore, as truly regrettable as the tone of the Bush campaign is, I believe it is more important for Mike Dukakis to be seen fighting for his political beliefs than fighting the negative tactics of the Republicans."

Dukakis's strategy of evading the national security issue, as Marttila suggested, had not removed him from Bush's line of fire. So Sasso decided that Dukakis had to make an assault on this redoubt. Graham Allison, who had hired Dukakis for the Kennedy School faculty after his first political demise, was put in charge of coordinating a big, new Dukakis speech on U.S.–Soviet relations. Allison had helped Secretary of Defense Weinberger devise a policy dubbed "competitive strategies"—a justification of the high-tech aspect of the arms race. Bush hailed it as "visionary" and claimed it as his own. Thus Allison was brought in to help Dukakis after indirectly helping Bush—"competitive strategies" indeed.

At the same time, Sasso convened a group of campaign strategists to map out what was called "national security week." Their plan was to link the campaign's scheduling, themes and media opportunities in a way that had not yet been done. It was decided that Dukakis should project the image of the commander-in-chief. (Larry Smith, who had been Gary Hart's assistant, taught at Harvard and became director of Business Executives for National Security, had proposed in detail in the early spring how Dukakis could make his program and his image coherent if he presented himself as a military reformer, but that idea was dismissed.) At the instigation of his Kennedy School advisers, Dukakis had already advocated beefing up conventional forces. "A tank!" someone said. It was an epiphany. Yes, everyone agreed, Dukakis needed a photo opportunity with a tank. Then the candidate would be poised to repel the Soviets and the Republicans; he would be as tough as armor; he would be invulnerable to attack; he would be the commander-in-chief.

Drafts of his new speech on U.S.–Soviet relations were sent around. Marttila received a copy. "No, no, no," he told the campaign advisers. The speech had conflated Gorbachev with Soviet leaders of the past. Gorbachev, he explained, was different. It was an elementary point, but it was one that Dukakis was not making.

On September 13, the two tracks of "national security week"—the style and the substance—converged. In the morning, Dukakis unveiled his new policy. The man who had assiduously avoided new thinking during his campaign set himself up as the judge of Gorbachev's. Dukakis said he was ready for "testing the limits of what is called 'new thinking' in the Soviet Union." It was time for "a strategy of our own to protect American interests and translate Soviet economic weakness into improved Soviet behavior in world affairs." Bush, he continued, wanted to "pretend that Soviet leadership today is as tired and as paralyzed and as heavy-handed" as before. Dukakis then cited an authority to support his position. "President Reagan understands the danger of that course and so do I." Point by point, Dukakis enumerated a program that did not go beyond anything already elaborated by the Reagan administration. In the end, his "new thinking" turned out to be Reagan's.

"Junk," said Robert Legvold, the director of the Harriman Institute for Advanced Russian Studies at Columbia, who had been sent an early draft. "No vision or framework. No underlying theme. This certainly wasn't a leader saying we're approaching a historical turning point. The campaign was more concerned with how it could get hurt by pushing too much on the Soviet issue than with the historic opportunity."

That afternoon, Dukakis flew to a General Dynamics tank factory in Michigan. He put on a flak suit and a helmet with his name written across it and climbed into a camouflage-painted M1 tank. As he held on to a 30-mm machine gun, the driver wheeled the tank around the field. At last, Dukakis was riding out to do battle with the Red Storm Rising. He was training a tank cannon on the image of himself as a Cold War wimp. He was ready to blast to smithereens the curse of the L-word. "So what did you think? Did I look like I belonged up there?" he shouted to the reporters, as the theme from the movie *Patton* blared over the loudspeakers.

That day, in another place, Dan Quayle was entertaining a Republican audience: "Want to hear a sad story about the Dukakis campaign, another sad story? The governor of Massachusetts, he lost his top naval adviser last week. The rubber duck drowned in his bathtub."

Dukakis's tank ploy was defeated by the network cameras. He was a man of the utmost seriousness who now appeared ridiculous. The army uniform he wore was like a clown suit. He had become a figment of George Bush's imagination. "The tank kept veering to the left," jeered Bush. On September 20, Bush literally wrapped himself in the flag at a New Jersey flag factory known as Flag City. "My friends," he said, "American flag sales are doing well, and America is doing well." Bush's flag and Dukakis's tank had become the chief symbols of a campaign that gave the public no choice but to vote on the emotional subtexts of these iconographic displays, referring backwards in time, not to the new realities.

By now, the candidates had cloistered themselves to prepare for the first debate. Two new valuable players were brought into the Dukakis campaign to help. The first was Robert Squire, a media consultant involved in Democratic presidential campaigns since 1968, exceedingly clever and canny—and a literary man. His films about Faulkner and Melville had been aired on public television; his aestheticism was often disguised by his side-of-the-mouth political shoptalk, but even the negative commercials he produced betrayed an artfulness. He also had a will to power that was sometimes lacking in his clients.

Squire traveled to Dukakis's house in Brookline "to get him fired up," he said. "I engaged him in political small talk to get him going. What smaller talk can there be than to ask a candidate how he came to this. It's often helpful. The campaign wears them down. They lose their way. If you ask, they can get back to the original idea. Dukakis' recollection of it was more mechanical than inspirational. He said that Sasso believed that the time was right, that it was doable; the more Sasso explored it, the more he explained it, the more committed Dukakis said he became to the race. If Sasso was able to go out in the country and find this presidency, he was willing to accept it. John was sitting there. He had a smile on his face—guilty as charged."

The second new figure admitted into the campaign was Tom Donilon, a young Washington lawyer who had been a political aide to Jimmy Carter and who was put in charge of Dukakis's debate training. Donilon's soft-spoken manner and choirboy appearance belied his partisan ferocity. He wanted to fight the Republicans on land, sea and in the air, using knives when the bullets ran out. To him, a presidential debate was the Thunderdome: two men went into the metal cage, only one emerged. Donilon had been through the ordeal before, as a coach for Carter and Mondale. For Dukakis, he developed a precise plan. Each statement Dukakis made should contain an affirmative theme, which should be repeated about ten times during the course of the debate. It should be coupled with negative thrusts at Bush, repeated early and often. If Dukakis did not wither, Donilon told him, he would cross an "invisible threshold" in the public's perception; he would begin to be seen as a president.

After conferring with Sasso, Donilon presented three themes to Dukakis and asked him to choose one: economic populism, or standing up for the interests of working families; making America number one in the global economy; or, simply, change. Perhaps, his handlers felt, the gladiatorial contest would force him to pick a thematic weapon. Dukakis rejected the first one, as he had all along. It was "divisive," he said. Then he rejected the second one. It sounded to him like protectionism, which he associated with Gephardt. Finally, he rejected the third one. "I don't know what this means," he said. " 'Change'—that doesn't mean anything. I want to know the words. What do I say?" But Sasso pressed him, and Dukakis reluctantly agreed to take up the theme of change.

At last, the candidates were locked in the arena. Bush was overprogrammed and diffuse, spewing out almost at random the one-liners that had been stuffed into him. For example: "We're going to have to, the MX, MX, we're going to have to do that. It's Christmas. It's Christmas. Wouldn't it be nice to be perfect, wouldn't it be nice to be the ice man so you never make a mistake?" The first sentence was a reference to the MX missile, which Dukakis opposed as redundant and wasteful. Bush was trying to make the case that Dukakis was weak on defense. Bush's non sequitur about "Christmas" harkened back to a statement he had made on September 7, declaring it the anniversary of the Japanese attack on Pearl Harbor, which, of course, was December 7. He had been told by Ailes before the debate that if he felt he was tripping over his tongue, he should make a self-deprecating joke, referring to his Pearl Harbor Day mistake by announcing that it was now Christmas. This, he had been advised, would show him to be warmer than Dukakis. This allusion, inaccessible to the audience, prompted Bush's next cryptic line about the "ice man," which was an oblique reference to Dukakis, whom he was trying to depict as unfeeling.

Dukakis was crisp and tart. He showed an aggressiveness that had been lacking before, especially on the issue of his patriotism. In one long exhalation, Bush attacked him for being a "card-carrying member" of the ACLU, a "liberal," out of the "mainstream of America," and opposed to the Pledge of Allegiance. Then, Bush slyly concluded, "I'm not questioning his patriotism."

"Of course, the vice president's questioning my patriotism," Dukakis shot back. "I don't think there's any question about that. And I resent it."

Almost all observers agreed afterwards that Dukakis had won the debate. But his own advisers knew what he had failed to do. He had not communicated any theme. Dukakis was buoyant again, but he had not used the debate to resolve his central problem. Nobody listening to him could say in twenty-five words or less what his campaign was about.

John Sasso expected that that would finally be answered by advertising. He had spent his exile handling public affairs at Hill Holiday, one of the biggest ad agencies in Boston. He immediately installed the ad executive of its chief client as the head of advertising. David D'Alessandro was a young man with vast self-confidence but without any political experience. At the John Hancock insurance company he had been responsible for managing the ad campaign, produced by Hill Holiday, whose slogan was "real life, real answers." It was shot in black-and-white, had an unsteady camera to convey the threat of instability, and featured vignettes in which actors played "real people" agonizing over their finances. The Hill Holiday doctrine was the theme of anxiety communicated in the cinema verité style. After the Hancock success, this "reality-based" approach was applied in other clients' ads, each time a success. In the small pond of Boston advertising, those associated with these ads were acclaimed as geniuses. Sasso's brief sojourn in this world was now to provide the intellectual capital of the Dukakis campaign.

D'Alessandro offered more than the John Hancock approach; he offered order. He presented to Dukakis a complete campaign, with charts, colored paper, transparent strips, and arrows. Dukakis liked the approach, as Sasso knew he would; he felt comfortable with its neatness and thoroughness.

A few days before the debate, D'Alessandro summoned the campaign's various media consultants to a room in the Lafayette Hotel for a similar presentation. "This is not going to be your typical aldermanic political media," he informed them. After he finished, Robert Squire was still perplexed. He noticed storyboards of future ads displayed across the room, with pictures of Dukakis and writing below his face. *This* must be the theme, Squire thought; the talking head spots will spell out the theme. He walked over to the storyboards to discover what he had not learned from the presentation. In small letters, the message read: "Blah, blah, blah, blah, blah."

On September 30, the new wave of Dukakis advertising began rolling out. The screen turned black—and white words appeared: "The Packaging of George Bush." Five middle-aged men sat around a table. They were talking about George Bush and his campaign tactics. What should he do next? "He'll do anything," said one of the men. "Wrap himself up in the American flag," said another. "That again?" "They'd like to sell you a package," said the voiceover. "Wouldn't you rather choose a president?"

Nearly twenty years earlier, Michael Dukakis had read Joe McGinness's book on the Nixon campaign, *The Selling of the President 1968* (starring Roger Ailes). "He was appalled," said Frank Sieverts, one of Dukakis's oldest friends, his roommate at Swarthmore and now the public relations director of the Senate Foreign Relations Committee. McGinness's tale of manipulation offended "his brand of good government," according to Sieverts. "He considered it to be a cautionary tale."

Dukakis's "packaging" ad was a sixty-second video version of *The Selling of the President*, produced in the "real people, real answers" mode. The format of the spot was intended to be the backbone of the Dukakis campaign until its end. Every week, the actors, who had been hired to play the Bush handlers through election day, were to be given a new script that would comment on Bush's latest transgression. Dukakis was not really going negative; he was showing how Bush was going negative. But it was an attempt to attack artifice with artifice. It was a campaign ad about campaign ads, a glimpse of advertising executives at work made by advertising executives. It tried to deflect Bush's smears without answering them. In docudrama style, it purported to show Bush's aides having conversations that had never actually taken place.

Thus the ad was itself a fabrication on the subject of fabrication. More importantly, the voters neither knew nor cared much about the Bush consultants. What they had been made anxious about was Dukakis. But his ad, following the Hill Holiday doctrine, conveyed anxiety. His true message was that politics was corrupt. More than anything else, the spot reflected Dukakis's antipolitics: it identified the enemy— the politicos. The total message was that campaigns were not to be trusted. If they were exposed, virtue could triumph. The ad, however, primed the public's mood of general disgust by providing an object for it. Dukakis had made the campaign's repellence an issue without transcending it. He may have heightened voters' distrust of campaigns, but he was not the beneficiary.

The commercial about the "packaging" of a presidential candidate was also a clear sign that the campaign was not about "The Making of the President" as the readers of Theodore H. White had come to expect—a romantic quest by a hero of the American Century who seeks power and discovers a deeper understanding of himself and the world. It was instead a campaign that had turned inward, whose subject was itself. This solipsism was a symptom of the candidates' failure to face the radical transformations of global politics.

The week the new Dukakis ads started running, Victor Navasky, the editor of *The Nation*, the liberal weekly magazine, sent Dukakis an article he had just published. It was written by Stephen Cohen, the Princeton Sovietologist who had been Gary Hart's chief adviser on Russia. The point of the article was that the campaign was ignoring the paramount issue of the next four years:

> The next American president will have both a historic opportunity and an obligation to end the decades-long cold war between the United

States and the Soviet Union. The opportunity already awaits him in Moscow—in the anti-cold war thinking and foreign policy reforms adopted by Mikhail Gorbachev since he was chosen Soviet leader in 1985. If the president lacks the vision and courage to seize the opportunity, he will be neglecting the best interests of the United States.

Navasky was an old friend of Dukakis, a classmate at Swarthmore. He had even written a warm recollection of Dukakis's Swarthmore years in *Esquire*. Navasky believed, he said, that Dukakis was being "campaign cautious." He wanted to get his friend to think about something besides campaign tactics. So he sent Cohen's article to Dukakis at his home and to his issues director, Christopher Edley (Swarthmore '71). He received a nice note back from Edley but nothing from Dukakis. Asking him to address the issue was a quixotic gesture, like trying to get a grounded airplane to fly by shoving it.

In spite of trailing Bush, the Dukakis campaign still maintained optimism. Its hope rested in great part on the vice presidential debate. Here the campaign believed that it had two assets: Dan Quayle and Lloyd Bentsen. Quayle's performance was turning into a dunciad. He had asked the press for "a little respect and dignity for the things I did not do." During the first two weeks of September, the Bush campaign did not allow him to give a single press conference. Finally, risking spontaneity, Quayle was permitted to speak. He compared his flaws to Roosevelt's, Kennedy's and Churchill's. "Winston Churchill was not a great student," he said. Then, he talked about the Holocaust, which he called "an obscene period in our nation's history." The reporters politely told him that it was the Nazis who had committed the Holocaust. "I didn't live in this century," he explained.

Lloyd Bentsen, by contrast, was the biggest surprise of the campaign. He was the most assured and capable politician of the four men running in the general election. He was also the least passive. His image as a dull, courtly reactionary was dispelled by his appearance as a sharp campaigner. He knew how to appeal to different crowds in direct and forceful language. He communicated his pleasure in campaigning, which contrasted with Dukakis's air of sufferance. When Dukakis was smeared, he immediately urged him to address the point and counterattack—advice that was ignored, as was all such advice.

In the debate, Quayle had a glassy-eyed look of fear. He sought shelter by trying to wrap the image of Kennedy around himself. "Senator," said Bentsen, with that one word alone putting Quayle in his place by invoking the institutional status system in which he was the Finance

Committee chairman and Quayle a junior, marginal member. "I served with Jack Kennedy. Jack Kennedy was a friend of mine. Senator, you're no Jack Kennedy." Quayle gulped and turned a shade of red, and his body stiffened. The duel was over.

It was the second false dawn provided to the Dukakis campaign by Dan Quayle. The election, however, was not close enough for the vice presidential factor to be decisive. More, Quayle was not the only one claiming to be the reincarnated Kennedy. Dukakis, too, kept identifying himself with the late president from Massachusetts. But no one in the race resembled Jack Kennedy in his charm, physical presence, will to power, and ability to identify and grasp the historical moment.

After Bush's and Quayle's weak debate performances, the Bush campaign made a massive media buy. Willie Horton was back. The most potent ad of the entire campaign was staged in four scenes, in ominous black-and-white, opening with the words "The Dukakis Furlough Program," as if that were a movie title. Scene one: As dark, portentous music sounded, a faceless prison guard raced up a watchtower, grasping a rifle. Scene two: A faceless prison guard, holding a rifle and packing a pistol on his hip, slowly walked along the perimeter of a prison wall. Scene three: Prisoners, mostly black and Hispanic, walked in single file through a revolving door. "268 Escaped" flashed on the screen. Scene four: A watchtower was silhouetted against the twilight. On top of the nearby prison wall stood a faceless guard, his rifle at the ready. "Michael Dukakis wants to do for America what he's done for Massachusetts," said the voiceover. "America can't afford that risk."

In 1984, Ronald Reagan's advertising depicted America as a mythical small town where no one was unfriendly or had a reason for discontent: "It's morning again in America." In Bush's ad, if it was morning, it was a cold, grim dawn. The threat in his ad was not just the escaping criminals; it was the concrete walls, the tall towers, the guards, the guns. This is where the voters would be sentenced to live if Dukakis were elected. It was a vision of America as a prison.

Nothing could have been more ironic and perhaps more traumatic than the appearance of this issue for Dukakis's campaign manager, Susan Estrich. The issue was not simply a matter of politics or images to her; she had been raped by a black man. In 1987, before she joined the campaign, her book *Real Rape* was published. It began with a description of her own rape: " . . . a man held an ice pick to my throat. . . ." Six months after the election, she wrote: "A lot of women who are raped have trouble dealing with men afterward. They're afraid of men. Not me. Not all men, at least. Just black men." She emphasized that she had "managed to conquer my fear," but that because of the experience "I never underestimated the power of the Willie Horton story." And yet she dismissed the warnings.

Before the Democratic convention, Ken Swope, a Boston media consultant with experience in several presidential campaigns who had made ads for Dukakis during the primaries, burst into Estrich's office holding up a picture of Willie Horton published that day in the *Boston Herald*, the tabloid used by Bush's staff to carry the campaign against Dukakis into his home territory. "There can't be a more insidious subliminal attack than this," Swope said. He also raised the Pledge of Allegiance issue. "That's what the campaign is going to be about, patriotism and racism. It's not going to be about competence." Estrich, however, assumed the lofty, distanced role of Professor Estrich of the Harvard Law School, where she indeed taught rape law. The Horton case, she insisted, could be argued on its legal merits and, in effect, ruled out of order. Her approach perfectly dovetailed with that of the lawyerly Dukakis, who had never made a summation to a jury. "If they think they're going to get anywhere with the Pledge issue they're wrong," she said. "We've got the Supreme Court answer." Swope left Estrich's office thinking the campaign was in deep trouble.

He felt sure that Estrich's confidence was misplaced. His mind kept echoing with what she had said in a recent meeting: *"We're* going to be president." His constant carping that the campaign was going to suffer for not dealing with Bush's charges turned him into an irritant to the campaign leaders. Like his friend Dan Payne, the other Jeremiah, Swope was shunted to the side.

On the eve of the second debate almost everyone in the campaign agreed that the crime issue finally had to be confronted. Tom Donilon ran the candidate through a drill almost a dozen times. Dukakis was to give the reply that he had given in his 1982 race for governor, a reply that had transformed perceptions of him. He was to talk about how he knew about crime firsthand, that his father and brother had been crime victims, that anyone who said he was soft on crime didn't know who he was.

The first question in the debate was directed to Dukakis. "Governor, if Kitty Dukakis were raped and murdered, would you favor an irrevocable death penalty for the killer?" Willie Horton was now stalking Dukakis on the stage. And Horton was not only terrorizing him; he had "raped and murdered" his wife. The fact that the question was posed by a black man, Bernard Shaw, the CNN anchor, subliminally heightened the effect. Dukakis did not give the answer he had been prepared to give. Rather, he delivered a generic, digressive answer in an impersonal monotone: "No, I don't, Bernard. And I think you know I've opposed the death penalty during all my life. I don't see any evidence that it's a deterrent, and I think there are better and more effective ways to deal with violent crime. We've done so in my own state. And that's one of the reasons why we have had the biggest drop in crime of any industrial state in America. . . ." In an instant, Michael Dukakis inhabited the weak, unfeeling image of Michael Dukakis projected by the Bush campaign.

After the debate, nearly every commentator faulted Dukakis for his failure to show emotion when his wife was being hypothetically violated and hacked to death before his eyes. But this was not necessarily a consequence of excess cerebration. Dukakis's intellectual failure had laid the groundwork for the issue of his emotional deficit. Nowhere was that more apparent than in this debate. In the previous debate he had lashed out at Bush for assailing his patriotism. Now he faced his tormentor directly and flattered him: "I didn't hear the word 'liberal' or 'left' one time. I thank you for that." Thus Dukakis offered a new positive message against himself—an appreciation of Bush for not slandering him with the awful L-word.

Bush was free now to say or do whatever he wanted. There was almost nothing standing between him and the presidency. Once again, he tackled the "vision thing." On October 18, he traveled to Westminster College in Fulton, Missouri, where Winston Churchill in 1946 had delivered his famous "Iron Curtain" speech, the greatest peroration of the early Cold War. Bush did not come to Fulton to revise Churchill, but to proclaim his eternal verities—"the truth," he called it. He quoted extensively from Churchill's address, point by point. " 'From what I have seen of our Russian friends and allies during the war,' " Bush read aloud, " 'I am convinced that there is nothing they admire so much as strength, and there is nothing for which they have less respect than for weakness, especially military weakness.' " Bush commented: "And, I might add, so it continues to be." What was true then was true now. "My generation has lived in the shadows of war—world war and Cold War. We have lived our lives partly in the sunlight but always in the shadow of struggle, of rivalry with the Soviet Union. That struggle, that rivalry, is not yet over." He acknowledged that the Iron Curtain was "rusting," that the new leadership in Moscow offered "promise," but this evidence simply confirmed for him his prior beliefs. He argued that to "abandon" the policy of forty years "is to invite trouble." The mental universe of the World War II generation, as interpreted by the Republican, had been completely unchallenged in the campaign and thus was politically preserved. Bush's campaign could continue as an act of taxidermy.

The next day a new Bush ad was broadcast, illustrating in thirty seconds a motif of his latest "vision" speech. It consisted entirely of film footage of Dukakis riding in the tank. "Michael Dukakis has opposed virtually every defense system we developed." As a helmeted Dukakis pointed a gun at the camera, aiming at the viewer, the voice-over concluded: "America can't afford that risk."

A week later, Dukakis's campaign reached rock bottom. "Let me ask you for a definition," said Ted Koppel, interviewing the candidate on "Nightline" on October 25. "And—and you'll know where I'm coming from as soon as you hear the word. How do you define the word liberal? What is a liberal in 1988?"

"That's maybe a question we ought to ask George Bush—if he had been here." That very day, Bush had accused Dukakis of advocating "socialism"—graduating from the L-word to the S-word.

"No, no, I'd like to hear your definition," said Koppel.

"Well, I think all of us have combinations of liberal and conservative about us, Ted. I'm not a liberal."

"I'd like to hear you define—what is a liberal?"

"Well, if one is a liberal in the tradition of Franklin Roosevelt and Harry Truman and John Kennedy . . ."

"1988, Governor."

"One is somebody who cares deeply about people, sees concerns, sees opportunities to make a real difference in the lives of real people, and works hard in public service to help make that difference in a way that will improve the quality of life of all our people, but like most people, I have certain conservative instincts as well. I've balanced ten budgets in a row. In many ways I'm a lot more conservative than George Bush."

Michael Dukakis had now come to the end of this evasive line. Instead of restating his party's tradition, he had abandoned it.[1]

1. During the fall campaign of 1960, John F. Kennedy, speaking to the New York State Liberal Party, made an open defense of liberalism. "What do our opponents mean when they apply to us the label 'liberal'?" he asked. "If by 'liberal' they mean, as they want people to believe, someone who is soft in his policies abroad, who is against local government, and who is unconcerned with the taxpayer's dollar, then the record of this party and its members demonstrate that we are not that kind of 'liberal.' " He continued: "But if by a liberal they mean someone who looks ahead and not behind,

Robert Reich was a professor of government at the Kennedy School who strove to bridge the gap between policy and politics. He had been influential with Gary Hart, and he had sent Dukakis memo after memo throughout the campaign. In early August, he gave Dukakis one that explained: "For the past eight years the United States has been governed as much by a public philosophy as by a particular president or party." Reich proposed "reestablishing the connection between prosperity and social justice." In another memo, given Dukakis in late August, he continued stressing this theme: "America's greatness has been based on equal opportunity and equal contribution. In the last eight years we've strayed from these core principles. It's time to reassert them."

"Why don't you try 'heightist' humor?" asked Reich, as he rode in a car with Dukakis to a speech. "What's 'heightist' humor?" asked Dukakis. Reich, who is four feet eleven inches tall, told him that short people can generate sympathy and affection by using self-deprecating humor. "Why not say that this campaign is about who represents the little man in America? And then steal a line from Bush and say, 'I am that man.' " Dukakis did not laugh or even smile. About a week later, on October 20, at the annual Al Smith Dinner in New York, Dukakis shared the stage with Bush. "Mr. Vice President," he said, "You said many times that you want to give America back to the little guy. . . . Mr. Vice President, I am that man." He received a roar of laughter.

"That was the most influence I had on this campaign," said Reich.

Lloyd Bentsen, in the meantime, without prior approval from the Boston headquarters, had taken it upon himself to say that Bush's campaign had "elements of racism." "A campaign tactic!" charged Bush. On the stump, Bentsen began speaking lucidly about the loss of American economic independence, the maldistribution of wealth and industrial decline. These speeches were his own; they were not prompted by Boston or any pollster. Bentsen shook his head as he

---

someone who welcomes new ideas without rigid reactions, someone who cares about the welfare of the people—their health, their housing, their schools, their jobs, their civil rights, and their civil liberties—someone who believes that we can break through the stalemate and suspicions that grip us in our policies abroad, if that is what they mean by a 'liberal,' then I'm proud to say that I'm a liberal."

Dukakis, in fact, was invited to address the Liberal Party dinner, just as Kennedy was, but declined because of fear of the label. Mario Cuomo spoke in his place, delivering a ringing defense of liberalism in the spirit of Kennedy's speech. "Liberalism properly understood is not just consistent with the American idea," he said. "Liberalism properly understood *is* the American idea."

received canned speech after speech from Dukakis central. "That's not what the audience is interested in," he said to an aide. "I want to be out talking about the issues people are thinking about."

Dukakis had run the campaign on his own terms, but now this was no longer possible. In the effort to maintain consistency and his own sense of integrity, he had steeled himself against his own experience. He had rejected the idea that the campaign could in any way transform him and that he could learn from it. If he were allowed to continue, however, the Democrats might lose every state; if he did not start sounding like a Democrat, he risked losing even his Democratic base. His own campaign staff was in rebellion. The state organizations were refusing to run the national ads. The surrogate speakers were rejecting the speeches sent them from the headquarters. The activists in the field were swamping Boston with complaints about the campaign's vacuousness. His advisers knew that he was not communicating any message, that all was bleakness.

Before the second debate, Sasso had sent Paul Bograd, a seasoned operative who had managed Dukakis's primary effort in New York, on a mission to Ohio. He was commissioned to play with themes and messages there and to come up with a way to "change the equation." Bograd developed a shadow presidential contest between two candidates he made up. Candidate A wanted to continue the strong growth of the economy, supported a strong military, was tough on crime and for traditional values. In short, this was George Bush as he wished to be seen. Candidate B promised to be on the side of working families and stand up to foreign competition and favored guaranteed health care for all. In short, this was a Democratic candidate as his campaign wished he were seen in the industrial heartland. The race between Candidate A and Candidate B was held every day in the tracking poll of Senator Howard Metzenbaum of Ohio, who was running for reelection. Candidate B trounced Candidate A, winning more than 60 percent of the votes. What was more, Candidate B won by about the same margin every day. (He even won on election day.) Bograd called him "Working Class Hero."

Out in California, Tony Podesta, the state Dukakis campaign director, who had battled the right wing throughout the 1980s as the president of People for the American Way, was conducting a similar hypothetical campaign. Candidate A was again an idealized description of George Bush. Candidate B was a governor of a large state, an innovator, someone who wanted to get America ready for the twenty-first century, in favor of exporting our products, not our jobs. Candidate

B soundly beat Candidate A. "Usually," said Podesta, "the 'what ifs' start after the campaign. This time it started even before the second debate."

Dukakis's campaign was descending into fantasy as a response to his failure to be real. In the beginning, Sasso thought that Dukakis was the next best thing to a blank slate. He could be all things to all people, missing only the liabilities of Democrats who had lost elections. But Dukakis had the defects of his rigidity, and he fought off anyone who tried to correct them. "I am who I am," he said repeatedly. His campaign now tried to reinvent him by spawning android candidates. This exercise proved that a Democrat could be elected in the abstract, just not a Democrat as abstract as Michael Dukakis.

John Sasso, once again playing the ghost of politics future, took Dukakis by the hand. This time he did not show him the road to glory. Instead, he pulled back a curtain to reveal the scene of a political graveyard, with the miserable tombstone that awaited Dukakis if he did not mend his ways. He gazed into the abyss and his legs buckled. All eyes were on the ticking clock. It was two weeks to election day. Dukakis's campaign of competence was finally overthrown by the activists of the Democratic Party who had helped nominate him, led by the man who had made him run for president.

"George Bush is on their side, I'm on your side!" shouted a new Dukakis. Every refrain of his rewritten stump speech pounded on the theme of us versus them: "Easy Street" versus "Main Street," "family fortune" versus "family budget," "have it made" versus "chance to make it." He experienced something he had not seen since the convention—large, enthusiastic crowds. He seemed to draw energy from them. He no longer seemed gloomy. At last, he appeared to be a happy warrior. And he started gaining in the polls.

When Walter Mondale became a full-throated populist in the last two weeks of his campaign, he was returning to his roots, to the language of the Democratic Farmer-Labor Party that had cradled him from his political birth—and his political father, Hubert Humphrey, and his actual father, the Reverend Theodore Mondale, who had been a crusader for the Social Gospel. When Dukakis echoed the same words, he was saying things he had never uttered before. He always regarded the populist appeal as an expression of unreason and therefore false. He associated the rhetoric of class antagonism with the chicanery and demagogy of local Massachusetts politicians; it was stale and besotted, reeking of cigars, liquor and late-night sessions of the state legislature. His whole career had been intended to cleanse the process of such contamination. Since the campaign's inception he had rejected the theme of economic populism every time it had been presented to him. Now he was forced to take it up. Dukakis had found a voice; it was not his own, but it was a voice.

David Kusnet was a principal author of the "On Your Side" speech. A former Mondale speechwriter, he had been a consultant to public interest groups and unions. For more than a year, since he had begun working for Dukakis, Kusnet tried to slip bread-and-butter Democratic messages into Dukakis's speeches. Without exception, Dukakis crossed them out. One phrase Kusnet kept inserting was "country club," as in "country club Republicans." At the preparation session for the first debate, Dukakis was told that Kusnet was responsible for this tic that kept reappearing in his speech drafts. During a break, the candidate sought out the speechwriter. "You shouldn't put in that stuff about country clubs," he said. "A lot more people belong to country clubs than used to be the case. You can't attack country clubs anymore." But a month later Dukakis was now the "divisive" candidate he had abhorred.

The first advertising to use the "On Your Side" slogan was broadcast on October 26. It was made by Dukakis's state organization in California without his permission. Tony Podesta was the producer. He got the speechwriters to put a line into a Dukakis speech: "I want an America that's in charge of its own destiny—not an America that's selling off its land and assets to foreign interests." Then he got Tony Bill, the actor and director, to shoot the speech. And then he arranged for a group of campaign workers to crowd around Dukakis afterwards, cheering and hugging him. Everything went according to plan. After the spot was produced, Podesta pleaded with the Boston headquarters not to show it to Dukakis, who had overseen every single ad in the campaign and mangled most of them. Podesta argued that by speaking the line in his speech the candidate had in effect already approved it. Everyone was so frustrated with Dukakis and had so little faith in his political instincts that the ad went on television without him ever knowing about its existence. Within days, Dukakis was campaigning in California. He asked Podesta what he should be saying there. "You should reinforce the paid media with your speeches. You know, putting America in charge of its economic future. Don't sell off our assets." "I'm not comfortable with bashing the Japanese," replied Dukakis. It was clear that he was unaware of the new advertising, that he was so numbed by campaigning that he didn't recall a line he had read off a teleprompter. "I said to myself that I shouldn't have said anything about the paid media," recalled Podesta. "So I said, 'This campaign is basically about economics.' "

Meanwhile, Dukakis was still being hounded by the L-word. Every day, Bush hastened to pin it on him. "The L-crowd doesn't like it," Bush taunted. Dukakis, he charged once again, was weak on defense, unlike Democrats of the past, such as Truman and Kennedy, who "never believed in this nuclear freeze." JFK, of course, had been assassinated two decades before the freeze was proposed. "I'm on your side!" Bush shouted to crowds, blatantly lifting Dukakis's new slogan in order to create confusion about a message that was having an effect. A new television ad charged Dukakis with lying about Bush's record. Huge letters appeared on the screen: "Dukakis is *Un*believable." Over and over again, on Bush's campaign plane, a tape played "Don't Worry, Be Happy."

On October 30, Dukakis stood on the rear platform of a train carrying him near Bakersfield, California, one of the most conservative sections of the state, and declared, "Yes, I'm a liberal." Back in Boston, before his blurted confession, his campaign staff had decided that he should deal with the L-word problem by defining himself as a Democrat in the tradition of Roosevelt, Truman and Kennedy. When he named his forebears he was to enumerate their accomplishments and associate himself with them. The L-word itself was not to be used; "Democrat" was the preferred designation. This gambit, which the staff dubbed "Dead Democrats," was communicated to the candidate on the road. The arrival of the "Dead Democrats" memo prompted him to announce that, after all, he was a liberal. "Miracle of miracles!" exclaimed Bush. "Headlines! Read all about it! He's using the liberal label again!"

But all the candidates were running in the reflected light of the "Dead Democrats." Quayle had presented himself as a young Kennedy. And Bentsen punctured the image by saying "Jack Kennedy was a friend of mine." Bush talked about Truman and Kennedy, evoking them as cold warriors, as much as he talked about Reagan. (He never, ever talked about Nixon.) And Dukakis frequently pointed out that he and Kennedy had the same state of residence. Only Dukakis belatedly defined himself as the "Dead Democrats" had defined themselves: liberal. But Dukakis did not even begin to define liberalism in the contemporary context.

The day after he called himself a liberal, Dukakis's polling operation conducted a focus group of voters in New Jersey. About 40 percent said that prison furlough was the number one issue. Clean government, or competence, made little impression. For the majority, Bush represented the rich, Dukakis the poor and neither stood for middle-class concerns. The campaign was something happening far away from them that existed only as a few minutes of distraction every night on television.

On November 3, a ten-year-old boy in a Philadelphia suburb where Dukakis was campaigning told him that he was playing the role of "Dukakis" in a school debate and asked what he should do. "Respond to the attacks immediately," Dukakis answered without hesitation. "Don't let them get away with a thing." He was now running a posthumous campaign, having defeated much of the political talent within the Democratic Party before he himself was defeated, giving advice to children that he had not followed.

As Bush and Dukakis exchanged mutual recriminations, the president began to ruminate, almost absentmindedly, that the Cold War was probably ending. "Right now we have hopes—and for the moment we must remember that they are only hopes—that our children might see 1988 as the turning point in the great twilight struggle known as the Cold War," said Reagan on October 28. These hopes rested on Mikhail Gorbachev. "I think it would be a great setback if anything happens to prevent him from continuing the program that he has set out. I hope that he can continue and will continue on this path." Reagan had been a man of myths, fantasies and illusions. Now he was saying something that neither of his would-be successors was willing to hazard; he was speaking the unspeakable. His engagement with reality seemed out of character. But, in a sense, Reagan was casting himself back in the role in which he had been comfortable before his political career. "Jimmy Stewart for governor, Ronald Reagan for best friend," quipped Jack Warner upon hearing that Reagan was running for office. Reagan was now Gorbachev's best friend. Let Reagan be Reagan.

In spite of all his negative campaigning and his overall lead, Bush was ahead in California only by 1 point. So, on the last weekend before election day, Reagan was dispatched to his home state. It was his last campaign tour. He left Washington in sunshine and arrived in a mist at Long Beach. When he left there it was sunny, but he arrived in San Diego in rain. Several local officials apologized to him about the weather; the president was entitled to blue skies. But Reagan, ever cheerful, told them it was a good omen. He had learned at the Washington summit of a Russian saying that sunshine at the beginning of a journey and rain at the end means success. He had arrived in the presidency determined to act on the dogmas of Cold War conservatism and was departing it repeating folk sayings he had learned from the Russians.

In front of the White House, George Bush was shaking hands with Gorbachev. Reagan stood to the side. It was a photograph in one of the final Bush spots. The camera closed in on Bush and Gorbachev. Reagan had disappeared. "Somebody is going to find out if he is real," said the voiceover. "This is no time for uncertainty." Bush walked past a line of Special Forces soldiers in red berets, standing at attention with rifles on their shoulders. "This is the time for strength."

The culminating Bush commercial was a collage of scenes of idealized rural and small-town life, George Bush hugging his grandchild and George Bush with his large family. Highlighting the cavalcade of emotions was country singer Lee Greenwood, reprising "I'm Proud to Be an American," which was the 1984 Reagan campaign anthem. As he sang the lyric, "The flag still stands for freedom, they can't take that away," Gorbachev's face loomed on the screen. It was rapidly followed by acts of patriotic piety: a flag-raising ceremony and children reciting the Pledge of Allegiance. But did Gorbachev really want to lower the American flag and take away our freedom? If he didn't, would we still need the endless lines of soldiers? Such questions were out of order. They created uncertainty, and the true enemy, according to Bush's ad, was "uncertainty." Bush capped his campaign with a flash of Cold War dread, offering himself as the agent of reassurance.

At the campaign's end, an official at the Soviet embassy in Washington reflected: "We are only just coming to democracy, just discovering its virtues. But, in some ways, Russia might be more liberal, in terms of discussing alternatives." The L-word had been a bad word in the Soviet Union since its founding. For a Soviet official to use the L-word as a grace-note was a break with the totalitarian language of Marxism-Leninism. It was paradoxical that at the moment that liberalism had become the principle of hope in Russia and Central Europe, it had become a malediction in America. "There's a degradation of political debate here," the Soviet said, "that parallels the starting of the political debate there."

The world beyond the Cold War was already forming when the campaign began; it was a process that accelerated when the campaign concluded. The Cold War's end was not a photo opportunity, a sound bite, a media-generated controversy, a revelation of "character," a political consultant's tactic, or even a theme. It was a global sea change as profound as the Cold War's beginning. But the candidates did not wish to understand that a new world was dawning, so they struggled amid the shadows and phantoms of the old.

On election day, November 8, George Bush won the presidency, 54 to 46 percent, with 426 votes in the Electoral College to 112. The degradation of political debate produced the lowest voter turnout since 1924.

Dukakis's advisers believed that his campaign had been whiplashed by history. It was not apparent in 1988, they argued, that events would play themselves out as they did. Even if Dukakis had been prescient, the public was unprepared. Their justification had a tone of fatalism. In the words of Joseph Nye: "The end of the Cold War? It came up. There was still some uncertainty of whether the Soviets were going to follow up good rhetoric with good proposals. To declare the Cold War over when there were no changes in Soviet force structure was a little bit early. Were people a little bit cautious? Yes. It was unclear. We struck a cautionary note. We were not there yet. It was almost conventional wisdom that a Democrat on defense issues had to be cautious and careful in order not to be painted into a position that George Bush eventually painted Dukakis." But in spite of the caution, he was reminded, Bush succeeded. "That's the irony."

The day after the election, Michael Dukakis took the Green Line to Park Street, from where he walked to his corner office in the State House overlooking the Boston Common. He was back where he wanted to be all along, where he felt he belonged. Two years earlier, when he had first contemplated running, he allowed himself to be convinced that he would be risking nothing. He could always return to Massachusetts. It was what he wanted to hear, so it was what he heard. He seemed to believe that even after running for president he could go back to the beginning and everything would be as it was.

Dukakis's politics had always been based on the divorce between emotion and action. His premise was that his competence would compensate for the absence of feeling. But the entire state had felt itself part of his campaign. With his defeat, a pall descended. His obvious relief at being home only deepened the depression. Before he could settle in, the glitter fell off the "Miracle of Massachusetts," partly for reasons beyond Dukakis's control. The state's debt ballooned, expenses could not be met without new taxes, the legislature balked and Dukakis promised a display of competence that would resolve the crisis. As a token of his good faith, he announced that he would not run again for governor, that he would not be guided by any political considerations, that his only goal was good government. But there was no solution and the problems worsened. The public disappointment that had been rife after the election curdled into a seemingly bottomless anger. Dukakis was wildly unpopular, his name a curse. Then his wife, who had been treated for alcoholism, was rushed to the hospital after drinking rubbing alcohol. It seemed to some observers who knew them both that she was acting out the despair he could not, or would not, express.

If Dukakis attempted to divide emotion from action, Bush tried to split politics from policy. Politics had to be conducted in the arena, where the candidate was at the mercy of a public drama. It was ruled by the law of the jungle, the survival of the fittest. Policy, however, was guided by "the best people," as he once called them. It was crafted within the bureaucracies of Washington in which Bush had risen over the decades. Precisely because Bush was so obviously one of "the best people," he had had to prove himself by claw and fang. The Darwinian struggle was the price he paid for the opportunity to be himself.

"The American people are wonderful when it comes to understanding when a campaign ends and the work of business begins," said President-elect Bush in his first postelection news conference. The week of his inauguration, Bush was interviewed on ABC "News" by Barbara Walters, who asked him about the campaign by which he had won the White House. "That's history," he said. "That doesn't mean anything anymore." The campaign had been an unpleasant necessity, but was otherwise of no consequence. It had illumined no truths about the country or the candidates that had meaning beyond election day. "That's history" was among Bush's favorite phrases. He used it whenever he did not want to be held accountable for what he had done before, even if it had happened yesterday. The past is weightless; history is bunk.

George Bush had won the presidency by arousing fear about the future. He defined his opponent as "risk," the most common word in his commercials. He had campaigned for a mandate to preserve the status quo, a world bequeathed him like a patrimony. But his presidential campaign had not laid the groundwork for presidential policies. During the campaign, Bush had refused to account for the upheaval in the world order that was already in progress and instead flourished the symbols of the Cold War that was passing. As president, however, he would face not Michael Dukakis but Mikhail Gorbachev. "Somebody," claimed his advertising, "is going to find out if he is real." What the ad did not say was what it would mean if he were. Thus the new president unthinkingly entered one of the most revolutionary years of the twentieth century.

14

Absent at the Creation

Democracy isn't our creation. It is our inheritance.
—GEORGE BUSH

One month after the election, George Bush had lunch with Ronald Reagan and Mikhail Gorbachev. The Soviet leader had come to New York to address the United Nations. His meeting with Reagan was his last with the president. For all their differences, Gorbachev and Reagan shared a common sense of themselves as makers of history. Reagan had come into office determined to roll back the "evil empire," an enterprise that landed him in the swamps of the Iran-contra scandal. A year after it was exposed, he found himself sitting side by side with Gorbachev at a long table signing a treaty. Reagan saw himself doing more than making a deal. He believed he was ending an era and ending a drama, leaving the Cold War on the cutting room floor. He had a set of convictions that carried him in spite of his ignorance and a sense of role that carried him in spite of his convictions. Thus Reagan's presidency was salvaged.

Gorbachev stood against the drift of Russian history in which every effort at reform from the time of Peter the Great had met defeat. He was also presiding over a system that had been presumed to be the penultimate stage in human development, the way station to utopia, but in a place where soap was scarce. Gorbachev was possessed with the idea that if he could not reverse the country's course, it would lapse into the long dark night of Oriental despotism. "The tradition of all the dead generations weighs like a nightmare on the brain of the living," wrote Marx. Gorbachev was ending the Cold War in order to wage war against Russian history. It was the reason he had come to speak to the United Nations.

"The world in which we live today is radically different from what it was at the beginning or even in the middle of this century," he said. "Life is forcing us to abandon established stereotypes and outdated views. It is forcing us to discard illusions." Totalitarianism, he said, could not be maintained. "Today, the preservation of any kind of 'closed' society is hardly possible." It was outmoded as a system of values and impossible in any case because of modern communications and economics. "The world economy is becoming a single organization, and no state, whatever its social system or economic status, can develop normally outside it." This notion of the "normal" was completely heretical, running against the grain of communist schematics in which history has an apocalyptic resolution. In this new world, national security must be rethought. "One-sided reliance on military power ultimately weakens other components of national security," he said. With that, he announced a unilateral cut of a half-million Soviet soldiers and 10,000 tanks. He was reversing the rules of the game, gaining prestige and influence by forfeiting military counters. Some critics, he suggested, might regard his post–Cold War vision as "a little too romantic." He granted that "the legacy and inertia of the past continues to be felt," but added: "I am convinced that we are not floating above reality."

Gorbachev's speech was an effort to define the next era in the most sweeping terms. But even he did not grasp how sweeping those terms would be and how immediately they would be applied. He had delivered an invocation to the revolutions of 1989. His speech also had the effect of making clear that the presidential campaign that had just concluded was a dramatic irrelevance. George Bush did not see that even though his campaign had succeeded in electing him it was a larger failure. Against Dukakis, he managed to sustain Cold War atmospherics until election day. But he had neglected to grasp the new reality, which could not be held off indefinitely. He could put his campaign to no real use in governing. Bush had run a campaign that defined him at the beginning of the era of his presidency as absent at the creation.

For the first time in his career, Bush was not in the shadow of a father figure. However, Reagan had prepared the scene to alter U.S.–Soviet relations, a transformation that undergirded Bush's election. President-elect Bush could claim a major political achievement within a matter of months by making a strategic arms reduction treaty. This aspect of Reagan's legacy was instantly available to him. At lunch precisely to claim his inheritance, Gorbachev's handshake, Bush suffered a moment of confusion. He didn't know how he should address the Soviet leader. Should he call him General Secretary Gorbachev? President Gorbachev? Mr. President? Or Mr. Gorbachev? "Anything you like," Gorbachev told him. What to call Gorbachev was a problem that continued to plague Bush throughout his first year in office.

The three leaders posing on Governor's Island in New York harbor appeared to form a picture of smooth transition, a tableau vivant reproducing Bush's concluding campaign spot. The president-elect did not see himself as Reagan's stand-in. He had identified himself with Reagan to win the job, but he did not want to be Reagan. He wished to escape from the force field of Reagan and Gorbachev that encircled him. Bush rejected Reagan's instinctive approach to the presidency and resisted the view of Gorbachev as a driven world-historical figure.

"Euphoria" was the watchword of members of the Bush team—a word put into play in 1987 by Kissinger to deride the atmosphere surrounding the Washington summit. "Euphoria" described Reagan's attitude toward Gorbachev. It was what must be guarded against. Bush believed that he had a superior sense of realism that demanded a deliberate pause. He wanted the world to slow down to the speed of his caution.

A private battle for Bush's allegiance was waged before his inauguration. During the transition, a bipartisan organization of policy professionals based in Washington, calling themselves the Annapolis Group, presented him with a memo. Their recommendations were based upon more than 125 extensive interviews with the key players on national security policy: 20 senators, 13 congressmen, former high officials, generals and experts. These interviews revealed a consensus view that Bush had an extraordinary opportunity that was politically safe and rewarding: "You possess a unique inheritance from Ronald Reagan: a strategic arms reduction negotiation which is very far advanced. If you accept and embrace this inheritance, you may enhance American security and your own political fortunes at the same time," said the memo. "Reagan's gift" was how it was described in an article in *The Atlantic* by Jack Beatty, one of the magazine's editors and a member of the Annapolis Group. "For George Bush, time is not a free good," said Alton Frye, the Washington director of the Council on Foreign Relations and another member of the group.

The memo was presented to Brent Scowcroft, newly appointed national security adviser, and John Sununu, the new White House chief of staff. The presenter was carefully chosen, someone whom they would trust: Jeff Bergner, staff director of the Senate Foreign Relations Committee when the Republicans were in the majority. He made the case, then was politely but firmly shown the door. The new administration had something else in mind besides "Reagan's gift."

"The Cold War is over," said Reagan, flying away from Washington on *Air Force One* on Inauguration Day. For eight years, he had dominated American politics, but overnight he had vanished. Within the Bush White House, the former president became a figure of fun. Presidential assistants openly joked to journalists about how he had been a dunce, out of touch, lazy, manipulated. One reporter, Owen Ullman of Knight-Ridder, wrote that Bush's aides, "hoping to make their man look good at Reagan's expense . . . point out how hard Bush works, how knowledgeable he is on the issues and how much he hates being managed by the staff." Ullman's article was published on March 24 in the New Jersey *Bergen Record,* where it was read by an interested subscriber living in Saddle River: Richard Nixon. Immediately, he scribbled a note to Sununu instructing him to squelch the belittling of Reagan. On hearing of it, Bush telephoned Reagan to apologize.

Reagan had departed, and Nixon returned. His presidency (before Watergate)—not Reagan's—was Bush's true model. Bush saw himself in the line not of the Reagan succession but of the Nixon succession. So, too, did Nixon, the seminal Republican figure in Cold War politics. "The claim that Bush has no mandate is a myth," wrote Nixon a week after Bush's election. "He has a mandate for a strong national defense and a strong, pragmatic foreign policy."

Nixon wasted no time in filling in the details of Bush's mandate. In an article magisterially entitled "The Bush Agenda," Nixon wrote that "those who parrot a fashionable slogan—'the cold war is over'—trivialize the problems of Western security." Published in *Foreign Affairs,* it appeared as Bush was assuming the presidency. In the tone of a game plan, Nixon's piece argued that Gorbachev was unlike Soviet leaders of the past; he had "star quality" and was "in a class of his own." But Gorbachev's motives were not different from his predecessors. "He is a different but, from the West's point of view, not necessarily a better type of leader." A new *Realpolitik* was required, a new balance of power diplomacy, a new strategy of "linkage"—the heart of the old Nixon policy. "Gorbachev's public relations experts have made many Western policymakers forget that a more benign Soviet image does not mean a more benign Soviet foreign policy." The Reagan version of a strategic arms agreement, according to Nixon, must be junked. Its terms had to be completely recast. "President Bush should continue to reject the advice of those who urge that he schedule a quick summit with Gorbachev in order to have a foreign policy 'victory' early in his term." Progress can be made toward the goal of stability, but, Nixon warned, "our two nations cannot be friends. . . ." The tensions might be reduced; but the tensions will "still endure." Thus the circular Nixon policy, the policy of waging the Cold War in order to draw down the Cold War so that it could be better waged.

George Bush began his administration by ordering a complete "strategic review" of U.S.–Soviet relations. He had won the presidency by promising continuity with Reagan. Now he announced that all policy decisions would be postponed for months, including a new arms agreement, until he had rethought how to deal with Gorbachev. "The thinking thing," cracked a Soviet diplomat.

In asking for a "strategic review," Bush was in effect demanding that the national security bureaucracy produce a rationale for him not to govern like Reagan. Bush was not going to be a romantic utopian, veering from visions of astrodomes in space to visions of a world without nuclear weapons. Reagan had stood for innocence to Bush and his circle. He was willing to brandish the symbols of this innocence, including the image of Reagan himself, yet he saw himself in many ways as Reagan's antithesis—not as an outsider, but as a Washington player who was finally on top of his town. To him, the language of American exceptionalism was no more than an occasionally useful political tactic.

Reagan had occupied the extremes. Bush thought he was going to occupy the middle. His foreign policy was calibrated partly according to his fears about domestic politics. Like Nixon, he wished to use foreign policy to achieve a favorable balance of power at home, too: neutralizing the Democrats by combining belligerence with promising steps toward détente, all done on a calculating basis that would forestall any attack from the right. Bush's fears were deeply impressed upon him and his entourage after Nixon's fall, during the interregnum of the Ford administration, when they were whipsawed by the right-wing assault on détente and the Democrats' post–Watergate ascendancy. Bush did not want to repeat the Ford experience. But in his revival of the Nixonian and Kissingerian mindset, which he would never publicly acknowledge because of the taint of scandal still attached to the former president, Bush seemed unaware (or did not acknowledge) that Reagan's rise had been made possible by Nixon's failure.

Under Nixon, the *Realpolitik* system of a balance of powers had replaced the American Century system in which the U.S. enjoyed unchallenged dominance. Nixon fought the Cold War as he fought a hot one in Vietnam. His *Realpolitik* had a backdrop of daily body counts. Waging the Cold War was presented as ending the Vietnam War. He was able to justify action on one front by reference to another, whether it was the opening to China, détente with the Soviets or the Christmas bombing of Hanoi. Nixon's triangular diplomacy, however, came unstuck after Watergate. Kissinger attempted to maintain the system, but it was turning chaotic even before Ford was defeated.

Jimmy Carter paid the full political price for the collapse of Nixon's and Kissinger's system—from Iran to Afghanistan. Carter the engineer, Cyrus Vance the case lawyer, Harold Brown the lab technician—all tried to make détente and the arms control process rational, offering an early take on Dukakis's theme of competence. Unfortunately, they did not fully appreciate the degree to which they were operating within the framework of those they had supplanted. In the meantime, Zbigniew Brzezinski, the Kissinger manqué, played the compulsive maneuverer, the agent of incoherence. When the system did not hold, Carter was left standing in the center. Reagan's blunt attacks on Carter were unintentionally ironic judgments on the consequences of Nixon and Kissinger.

Bush, who had been their underling, sought to revive their approach in another time and another setting. Like them, he adopted the methods of secrecy and indirection, which he had honed at the CIA. His realism would replace Reagan's vision, masked before the masses by intermittent flourishes of Reaganesque rhetoric. But the differences between Nixon's world and Bush's world were fundamental. Unlike the Nixon era, when Vietnam bloodied his plans, Bush was operating with a sterile slate. Nixon had grasped as early as 1971 that the American Century had passed, that it had been superseded by a world of "five powers," in his words, requiring an adroit balance of power policy. Even so, Nixon made claims of U.S. omnipotence, while raising fears of America as a "pitiful, helpless giant." He overextended the system of alliances, ultimately rationalizing every ad hoc move by an all-encompassing anti-communism. Bush was more constrained by his budget than Nixon was, but he, too, had pledged that the American Century was endless. Though Bush was Nixon's hidden legatee, he had not thought out global strategy as deliberately as Nixon had two decades earlier; nor, apparently, had he considered the fate of Nixon's policy.

Détente had helped bring about the ultimate Kissingerian goal of stability. Now the greatest movement of destabilization since the close of World War II was loose in Europe. "The Cold War is over" was more than a "fashionable slogan," as Nixon would have it. The Cold War's end would bring about a more peaceful and yet a more tumultuous world. In the face of the unimaginable, Bush imagined that a balance could be struck by a hesitant man moving one degree or another—not that the world was turned upside-down. His *Realpolitik* was not a hard-edged empiricism, in which the glistening, cold facts slice through the generalities, but a form of wishful thinking, an effort to make the outside world seem subject to the mastery of his uncertain mind. "I'm not going to hypothecate that it may—anything goes too fast," he said incoherently on the day the Berlin Wall fell. "The emotional part is hard for me to describe because I'm not an articulate emotionalist," he said at the Malta summit. "Uncertainty" was how he described the biggest problem in the world, at a press conference at the end of his first year in office. Bush had run a campaign in 1988 against uncertainty—or "risk"; now it dogged him.

Bush projected himself as a commanding realist, but from the beginning his approach was improvisational. During the campaign he had broken from his unbending loyalty to Reagan only to adopt the Kissinger line on arms control—making Reagan's START agreement contingent on a conventional arms agreement, which might take years to negotiate—a classic example of "linkage." Even before Bush assumed office, though, his position had been overtaken by events. At the U.N., Gorbachev had startled him by unilaterally reducing his conventional forces in Europe. These reductions were not symbolic, not for the benefit of the world press, but deep, significant cuts, undermining the case for linkage. Gorbachev was not waiting for Bush. He had little time to waste, particularly in anticipating a president who had already sent a signal that he wanted to slow down. Gorbachev's speech was an indication that he was going to accelerate history on his own. The old, elaborate rules of the game, which had been developed under Nixon and Kissinger into an endless management of the arms race, were suddenly obsolescent. After forty years of stalemate on the Western front, Gorbachev was starting to throw his weapons away. What was even more disorienting was that he would not stop. Larger and larger piles of tanks, planes and missiles accumulated on the junk heap. Without negotiating, Gorbachev was disarming. At the negotiating table, he was instantly accepting one-sided U.S. proposals calling for massive reductions in the Soviet army, which further disoriented the new administration.

President Bush had surrounded himself with the Kissingerians, appointing two senior partners in Kissinger Associates to high positions: Brent Scowcroft to head the NSC and Lawrence Eagleburger as deputy secretary of state. Other Kissingerians honeycombed the national security bureaucracy. "The Cold War is not over," said Scowcroft two days after Bush's inauguration, on ABC's "This Week with David Brinkley." Gorbachev, he claimed, was "interested in making trouble within the Western Alliance," and his diabolical method was a "peace offensive." There might be, Scowcroft said, "light at the end of the tunnel," but he wondered "whether the light is the sun or an incoming locomotive."

A week later, Bush was asked at a press conference about Scowcroft's remark. "So I—but if the—in the—I want to try to avoid words like Cold War . . . ," explained the president. "But if he—if it's used in the context of—Do we still have problems? Are there still uncertainties? Are we still unsure of—in our predictions on—on Soviet intentions? I'd have to say, yes, we should be cautious."

"I think," said Dan Quayle, "the root of the matter all comes back to a hatred of God." The Soviet Union, according to the new vice president, was irredeemably "evil."

The new secretary of state, James Baker, the man closest to the president, who had managed his campaign to victory, was unfamiliar with his job. He was a pragmatist who came to it without any fixed ideas and spent much of his time studying briefing books and assembling his team. In the meantime, the bureaucracy, set in motion by Bush, was running ahead of him while proceeding at a glacial pace in its work on the "strategic review." Gorbachev kept making proposals for faster and greater disarmament, which only served to agitate Bush. "We'll be ready to react when we feel like reacting," he said on April 7, with obvious irritation.

Within the administration, there was much discussion about whether or not the U.S. should "help" Gorbachev. The ideological

Cold War conservatives argued that little should be done to "help" him because he was an aberration who would prove to be short-lived. The Kissingerians argued that Gorbachev had to be engaged in a step-by-step balance of power game. They stressed that he had to be handled carefully, so that he did not win political battles in his effort to divide the Western Alliance. Both of these tendencies were susceptible to the argument being circulated by certain right-wing think tanks that Gorbachev was the Great Pretender, that his reforms were merely a way to obtain *peredyshka*—breathing space—after which he would embark on aggressive ventures against the West.[1]

In early May, the deliberations on the inside burst upon the public. "I would guess that he would ultimately fail," said Secretary of Defense Richard Cheney about Gorbachev. "And that when that happens, he's likely to be replaced by somebody who will be far more hostile." Bush weakly countered this position: "I made clear to Mr. Gorbachev . . . that we wanted to see perestroika succeed."

The conservatives' logic had at least as much to do with their own situation as Gorbachev's. Their belief in his fall was wish-fulfillment that what had already happened would not really happen. That it had indeed happened was implicit in their corollary argument that the military buildup of the 1980s had been the cause of Gorbachev's reforms. Totalitarianism, they had long insisted, could not change, which was why we had needed to spend hundreds of billions more on armaments. Yet the conservatives were now justifying the buildup by the Soviet transformation they had previously said was impossible. What was at stake was not moral credit for conservative arguments of the past, but the future of the military-industrial complex, the organization of the economy and the dynamic of American politics.

All those involved in the internal debate over "helping" Gorbachev

1. A new neoconservative think tank, the Center for Security Studies, was the chief proponent of the *peredyshka* line. In a paper circulated around Washington the week of Bush's inauguration, entitled "The New Soviet Challenge," the Center argued that "Gorbachev's use of perestroika and glasnost to advance Soviet foreign policy constitutes a sophisticated form of Lenin's classic adversarial strategy of 'peaceful coexistence' to woo the democracies while rebuilding strength." And: "Gorbachev is using perestroika and glasnost as tactical devices in domestic politics." Finally: "Western policy should not be based on the notion that 'helping' Gorbachev shape a strengthened Soviet system will necessarily create a safer world for the Western democracies."

The Center for Security Studies was directed by Frank Gaffney, former deputy assistant secretary of defense, who had been the chief aide to Richard Perle, the most tenacious opponent of arms control within the Reagan administration. After Perle left the administration for the private sector in 1987 and the INF Treaty went forward, Gaffney attempted to mount an internal opposition but was ousted.

were brought together by the latest Cold War crisis. Germany, always the focal point of Cold War tension in Europe, would be the main battleground if World War III ever broke out. In the early 1980s, during the controversy over installing Pershing missiles there, the German opposition had raised the cloud of "Euroshima." Now, Gorbachev's disarmament proposals electrified German public opinion. The Bush administration picked this moment, in the spring of 1989, to make an issue of placing new short-range Lance missiles in Germany, inflaming the country. Helmut Kohl, the conservative chancellor, fearful that endorsing the missiles would doom his party in the 1990 elections, resisted U.S. pressure. Bush responded by doubling it, posing the question as a test of political will. If the Germans were allowed to reject the missile, Gorbachev would achieve his objectives of undermining resolve, damaging credibility and splitting the Alliance. The entire issue was viewed through the Cold War lens as a classic case of East–West competition, not as evidence that the old model was breaking down. Bush, for his part, did not want to blink.

In his office in a glass tower overlooking Beverly Hills, Ronald Reagan was not happy. He did not believe that his vice president was truly acting as his successor. Reagan disapproved of Bush's hesitancy in approaching Gorbachev, his slowness in making an arms agreement, his "strategic review," his roiling of the Germans over missiles. "Reagan's friends say that one of his frequently repeated 1988 campaign statements about Bush—'he's been part of everything we've done for the past eight years'—now has an ironic aftertaste for the former president," reported Lou Cannon on May 6 in *The Washington Post.* Cannon was the most knowledgeable journalist in the country on the subject of Reagan, having covered his entire political career. On leave from the newspaper, Cannon had moved to California to write his account of the Reagan presidency. The "Reagan view," according to Cannon, was that Bush was "behaving the way new presidents do when replacing someone from the opposing party with different views." He concluded: "Both in Bonn and in Beverly Hills, they are wondering if Bush's only strategy is to react to events as they unfold."

On May 12, after five months in the White House, George Bush unveiled his long-awaited "strategic review." He began his speech at Texas A & M University by paying homage to the architects of the Cold War. "Wise men—Truman and Eisenhower, Vandenberg and Rayburn, Marshall, Acheson, and Kennan—crafted the strategy of containment," he said. Bush wished to be seen as their heir. In the light of their success, he suggested, it was now possible to move "beyond containment." Still, he echoed the skeptical tone of those who argued that the Cold War was not over but had just entered a new phase: "The Soviet Union has promised a more cooperative relationship before, only to reverse course and return to militarism. Soviet foreign policy has been almost seasonal: warmth before cold, thaw before freeze. . . . Many dangers and uncertainties are ahead."

Bush's idea of bringing the Soviet Union into the "community of nations" was twofold. First, he advanced a maximalist position that the nations of Central Europe be granted self-determination and that the Iron Curtain be torn down. This was not really a policy, but an assertion of preconditions to a policy. Bush was testing Gorbachev with the stock rhetoric that had been in the arsenal of every president. (Bush took no notice in his speech that on May 2 the Hungarians had dismantled barbed-wire sections of the Iron Curtain.) Second, the president proposed that the U.S. and the Soviets agree to surveillance flights over each other's territory. The so-called Open Skies proposal, in fact, had been proposed thirty-four years before by President Eisenhower. It had since been rendered a technological anachronism because the U.S. and the Soviets were already surveying every inch of ground with spy satellites. The only new element in Bush's new grand strategy, therefore, was a symbolic gesture.

Before Bush's speech, a senior member of the National Security Council who had been a principal author of the "strategic review" held a special background briefing for foreign policy analysts in Washington so that they could gain insight into its profundity. After lavishly praising the president's "long-term vision," the aide summarized it in a phrase that tellingly captured its spirit: "status quo plus." As the historians of science have pointed out, an intellectual system in crisis, which has lost the ability to make sense of an increasing number of anomalies, often provokes its adherents to qualify the old paradigm in order to make it less recognizable as the old paradigm. "Status quo" was the Ptolemaic view of the Cold War; "plus" was the epicycles. "Status quo plus" was an oxymoronic admission of change and denial of change.

Bush's slogan—"beyond containment"—was another way of saying "status quo plus." The world, he explained, was changing because of what had happened in the past. He lauded the fathers of the American Century for the recent shifts in global politics. "Containment worked," Bush said. But he could not describe what lay "beyond" it. His image of America was of a static power; his language reiterated the language of the ancestors. He was standing on the edge of the flat earth, peering into the unknown. "To put it mildly," read an editorial in *Pravda*, "we are bewildered at the attempts of the president to pose conditions under which the U.S. will work to include the USSR in the world community." Bush's speech, it concluded, displayed a "poverty of ideas."

The day after the May 12 speech, James Baker arrived in Moscow. In his long private discussions with Soviet Foreign Minister Eduard Shevardnadze, he was astonished by his counterpart's candor. Shevardnadze told him of the wretched state of the Soviet economy, of how criminal the past Soviet leadership had been, that Gorbachev understood that only a radical transformation could deal with the problems, and that this massive upheaval was not only unavoidable but necessary. As Baker attempted to assimilate this information, Gorbachev himself turned up at his press conference. Gorbachev then startled him by suddenly accepting Baker's proposals for Soviet force cuts and announcing the withdrawal of five hundred nuclear weapons from Central Europe. Baker's instinct was a political instinct, and he accused Gorbachev of "politics," as though politics were something Bush's master politician found distasteful.

The Bush administration believed it was in a public relations war with Gorbachev, who had succeeded in inducing "euphoria" in Reagan and was trying to outflank Bush with his "peace offensive," which was inducing "euphoria" in Europe. Cold War conservative Dick Cheney dismissed Gorbachev's latest move as meaningless. "He has got so many ratholes over there in Eastern Europe that five hundred is a pittance," said the defense secretary. (On the eve of his talks with Baker, Shevardnadze, in an interview with *Time* magazine, had called Cheney's comments about Gorbachev's prospects "incompetent and not serious.")

Gorbachev then upped the ante again by offering to cease sending arms shipments to the Sandinistas. The White House was in a fury. "Public relations gambits," fumed Marlin Fitzwater, the president's spokesman, as though "public relations gambits" were completely alien. He said the administration was "very leery" of Soviet intentions. And he called Gorbachev a fraud—a "drugstore cowboy." Paul Wolfowitz, the Pentagon's new policy director, a neoconservative and contributor to the "strategic review," chimed in, saying that the Soviet Union "continues to challenge U.S. interests around the world" and that it remained "a powerful threat to the West."

Gorbachev, in the meantime, landed in Beijing, where Tiananmen Square was filled with one million people demanding democracy and chanting his name: "Gorbachev! Gorbachev! Gorbachev!" He had come to end the Sino–Soviet conflict, but his presence further aroused the gigantic crowds protesting the old-style Communist regime, which was clinging to Stalinism just as desperately as Gorbachev was trying to escape it.

From Washington, the insults increased. Dan Quayle accused Gorbachev of "phoniness." Quayle was "troubled," he said, seeing "the general secretary in China talking about liberty, freedom, democracy." To the vice president, the sight of a Soviet leader helping to instigate a revolt against communism on behalf of "liberty, freedom, democracy" was an occasion not for pinching oneself but for protest. Gorbachev had "stolen our issues," Quayle complained.

Bush was like an ambassador who makes fine speeches and awaits instructions. But everyone had turned to him looking for direction. His response was to cast blame on the man of action. Bush acted as if he were in a campaign against Gorbachev for the allegiance of the world. His positive themes—"status quo plus," "beyond containment"—had not worked. So he reverted to the negative techniques from the 1988 campaign. Having his surrogates call Gorbachev a "drugstore cowboy," however, did not have the same effect as calling Dukakis a "liberal."

The Germans were unimpressed, and so was elite opinion in America. Bush was extremely sensitive to the criticism. When the "strategic review" was charged with emptiness, he altered its nuances. In a speech at Boston University on May 21, he delivered another version. Now he declared himself "optimistic" about the "extraordinary changes" taking place in the Soviet Union. But, he warned, we should let not let down our guard: "While an ideological earthquake is shaking asunder the very communist foundation, the West is being tested by complacency. We must never forget that twice in this century, American blood has been shed over conflicts that began in Europe." What he recommended, above all, was "prudence."

Bush's speech, however, was a smokescreen for what was occurring offstage. During the two days before his Boston University address, the president had met with his advisers at his Kennebunkport home. Almost exactly a year earlier, Bush and his handlers had met there to plot the turnabout in his campaign; it was then that he had decided to go negative. Now the president was distressed that his extravagantly advertised grand strategy was receiving such bad reviews. James Baker, who had followed the initial lead of the Kissingerians and had even tried to make the Lance missile issue his own, strongly urged a change of course. He had been deeply affected by his talks with Shevardnadze; he did not want this presidency to appear irrelevant; he could envision dire political consequences. Bush agreed that he had to act quickly. The NATO summit, less than a week away, was bringing everything to a head.

But Bush had already scheduled yet another speech on the "strategic review." He went through the motions, even though his approach had shifted. His address at the Coast Guard Academy on May 24 was an anthology of his previous rhetoric, devoid of proposals; it seemed an anticlimax. When he reached his conclusion, however, he made what were among the most revealing and important remarks of his career. "I began today by speaking about the triumph of a particular, peculiar, very special American ideal: freedom," he said. "And I know there are those who may think there is something presumptuous about that claim, those who will think it's boastful." From his childhood, George Bush had been admonished by his mother to avoid boastfulness. In his talk about "freedom," he explained that he was not being boastful— "for one simple reason." Here he came to the crux of the matter. "Democracy," he said, "isn't our creation. It's our inheritance." Bush had inherited much, including the succession to the presidency. The ancestors had been present at the creation, not us. Democracy was not something we made, but something we received. "We can't take credit for democracy," Bush said, "but we can take that precious gift of freedom, preserve it and pass it on as my generation does to you and you too will do one day." Bush was the inheritor, the conservator. Change was not for people like us, but for those who wished to be like us. Democracy in America was not about change; the point was preservation—the "status quo plus," as it were. And Bush projected that role for America.[2]

He came to the NATO summit to announce that he had accepted the notion that the Cold War was ending. He had mounted a mock Cold War crisis that he would now resolve. It was not urgent, after all, to place new missiles in Germany. That decision, he said, was postponed. In order to prevent a major failure at his debut on the world

2. Bush's homage to the Founding Fathers, however, did not reflect their own sentiments about the obligations of the present to the past or about the character of democracy. Jefferson, for example, fervently argued that every generation had a duty to remake the world. "The earth belongs to the living," he was fond of saying. In his old age, Jefferson remarked: "Some men . . . ascribe to the preceding age a wisdom more than human, and suppose what they did to be beyond amendment. . . . We might as well require a man to wear still the coat which fitted him when a boy, as civilized society to remain ever under the regime of their barbarous ancestors." Shortly before his death, he wrote: "Nothing then is unchangeable but the inherent and unalienable rights of man."

stage, Bush deferred the issue he had raised. He also proposed symbolic cuts in U.S. troops and aircraft in Europe and significant Soviet cuts. "The world has waited for the Cold War to end," he said. "The world has waited long enough. The time is right. Let Europe be whole and free."

But Bush's retreat from the "strategic review" was not a retreat from a certain balance of power diplomacy. His rhetoric was implicitly counterposed to Gorbachev's vision of a "common European house," which the Kissingerians feared might be a ploy to split the Western Alliance. "There cannot be a common European home until all within are free to move from room to room," said Bush. He called for the razing of the Berlin Wall: once again, the maximalist demand. As he delivered his speech in Germany, the first tumultuous session of the Congress of People's Deputies was convening in Moscow. Bush's triumph at the NATO summit was less over Gorbachev than over his past position.

Every time Bush appeared to command the tides, they crashed in. His performance in Germany was almost immediately overtaken by a far more momentous event in China. The Stalinist leadership there decided that it would tolerate the clamor for democracy no more. On June 4, in the darkness of the early morning, columns of tanks rolled into Tiananmen Square and ground the protestors under their treads. "I think this perhaps is a time for caution," said Bush.

The U.S. and China, in his view, had a special relationship. Nixon's balance of power diplomacy had begun with his playing of the China card. Under Ford, Bush turned down ambassadorships to Britain and France, asking instead to be appointed the U.S. plenipotentiary to China, where he would be on the pivot of the balance of power. His self-image as a China hand was also a self-image as an aspiring Kissingerian. Now the Beijing massacre threatened to upset the centerpiece of the Nixon–Kissinger strategy.

Bush consulted both Nixon and Kissinger. It was Kissinger who, in *The Washington Post,* openly made the case for *Realpolitik.* "No government in the world would have tolerated having the main square of its capital occupied for eight weeks by tens of thousands of demonstrators who blocked the authorities from approaching the area in front of the main government building," he wrote. " . . . China remains too important for America's national security to risk the relationship on the emotions of the moment. The United States needs China as a possible counterweight to Soviet aspirations in Asia, and needs China also to remain relevant in Japanese eyes as a key shaper of Asian events."

The Cold War might be ending, but the Nixonian balance of power still had to be preserved. At the NATO meeting, Bush had recognized that the old order was passing. Yet he played the China card to balance the Soviet Union as if the past were still intact: the Nixonian game without the Nixonian context. In a parody of the opening of China, Bush sent Brent Scowcroft, Kissinger's former partner, twice on secret trips to Beijing. The first was on July Fourth. "President Bush still regards you as his friend," said Scowcroft, toasting Deng Xiaoping, who had given the orders to crush the movement for democracy. *"A friend forever."*

In the weeks following the Tiananmen Square massacre, the dynamic in Central Europe rapidly accelerated. Virtually the whole population of Budapest turned out to give a hero's reburial to Imre Nagy, who had been executed for leading the 1956 revolt. In Poland, Solidarity candidates defeated the Communists in the country's first postwar free election. Clearly, these amazing events were made possible by the tacit permission of the Soviets.

American politics registered none of it. In late June and early July, the main political controversy, overwhelming all other discussion, involved respect for the flag. A year had passed since Bush had introduced the Pledge of Allegiance issue. Now the Supreme Court ruled that flag-burning was protected as a form of free speech. Standing before the Iwo Jima Marine Memorial, the president unfurled a constitutional amendment to make flag-burning a crime. As the enemy outside was receding, he attempted to mobilize the country against an invisible enemy within. Bush's amendment expressed the political need for an overbearing threat. But when no such threat materialized, the issue simply drifted away after some months. The symbol of nationality had been reduced to sheer symbolism. Once again, the vacuum in American politics was laid bare.

On July 10, Bush addressed the newly elected Polish parliament. "Being there is an enormous signal," he said before he left. "It's what Woody Allen said—ninety percent of life is just showing up." Bush's trip was partly intended to offset Gorbachev's reception in Germany by huge, excited crowds. But the turnout in Warsaw's streets for Bush was sparse. He was not seen as a heroic figure. "Today," said Bush, "the scope of political and economic change is indeed Copernican—a fundamental change in perspective, that places the people at the center." The collapse of communism, according to the president, had brought about a revolution in worldview. But he suggested that the transformation applied only east of the Oder River. Bush took the overturning of communism to be proof of his principles. The Copernican revolution at the end of the Cold War was happening in a world elsewhere.

On the night before Bush flew to Poland, members of the National Security Council hurriedly scraped together $100 million to offer as a loan. It was a paltry sum, eventually tripled by the Congress, but still two-thirds less than the amount offered by the Japanese. The Polish loan exposed a secret premise of the Bush presidency: America's radically diminished place in the world. Bush's inertia reflected not only his temperament but the economic circumstances he had inherited.

Throughout the 1980s, Reagan's control of political debate rested in great part on his paralyzing hold on the budget. His military buildup and regressive tax cuts had fostered an unprecedented deficit. So long as the military buildup continued, the Republicans were the arbiters of what constituted strength and weakness within the four corners of the Cold War. And so long as taxes were cut, new projects for social reform were out of the question. The Democrats were cast as weak and spendthrift but blocked at every turn; they began to appear as ineffective as the stereotype.

The Reagan legacy that Bush chose to continue was the crisis of American solvency. In 1988, Bush had defined the Republican future: "Read my lips, no new taxes." Unlike Reagan, he admitted to the existence of widespread social ills. His adoption of the theme of a "kinder, gentler nation" was his effort to separate himself from Reagan's blind indifference. But Bush's natural interest was in maintaining the Republicans' control over political society. "We have more will than wallet," he said, in the most memorable phrase of his inaugural address. The budget deadlock frustrated the Democrats from enacting new programs and gaining the initiative, and the crisis of solvency sharply curtailed American influence in the world. Bush's foreign policy was in deficit partly because of a defense budget calculated to deal with an enemy from the past; and it was especially hostage to his domestic politics, which were calculated to contain the enemy at the other end of Pennsylvania Avenue. Even if he wished to act like the Wise Men he had cited as his forebears, he had made it impossible for himself to do so. His commitment to the policies of insolvency, in the interest of partisan advantage, drastically limited his means. His conundrum was a reversal of the situation that faced the makers of the American Century. "There is no Marshall," remarked Sergey Plekhanov, the deputy director of the Institute of the U.S.A. and Canada Studies. "And there is no plan."

The summer of 1989 was a curious interlude. While an explosive pressure gathered beneath the crust of Central Europe, it seemed in

Washington as though time were standing still. George Bush was at his estate on the Maine coast. Daily coverage of the presidency consisted mostly of fishing reports. And political society spent July and August arguing whether history had come to an end. The discussion was precipitated by an abstruse article in a small neoconservative journal, *The National Interest,* by Francis Fukuyama, deputy director of the State Department's policy planning staff. Entitled "The End of History?," it read: "What we may be witnessing is not just the end of the Cold War, or the passing of a particular period of postwar history, but the end of history as such: that is, the end point of mankind's ideological evolution and the universalization of Western liberal democracy as the final form of human government."

Fukuyama appealed to authority in the form of Hegel, whom he observed had first seen the victory of "universalization" in Napoleon's defeat of the Prussians. (Napoleon himself took a less abstract view. "What have we to do with destiny now?" he remarked to Goethe. "Politics are destiny.")

Fukuyama's tone was not jubilant but mournful. "The end of history will be a very sad time," he wrote. The great struggle in which there was "the willingness to risk one's life for a purely abstract goal" will be replaced by "the endless solving of technical problems." The State Department policy planner did not call for new policies but cast himself and his colleagues as bystanders. "I can feel in myself, and see in others around me, a powerful nostalgia for the time when history existed."

At the end of the American Century one discovers the beginning of the American Century. History doesn't repeat itself, the first time as tragedy, the second as farce; it just repeats itself. The near-universal triumph of America and the end of ideology—these were the themes of the late 1940s and 1950s. (It was a man of the 1950s generation, Michael Dukakis, of course, who had staked his presidential campaign on the theme of "the endless solving of technical problems.") Forty years earlier, the postwar world was approached with immense self-confidence and optimism by its makers. Henry Luce's labeling of it as the American Century captured the intoxication of supreme power. Fukuyama was Luce with footnotes and self-pity. At end of history, he suggested, there was nothing really useful or interesting to do. In particular, there was nothing to do in America that would call forth "daring, courage, imagination, and idealism"—the romance of anti-communism. Ahead lay only "centuries of boredom." The end of history was a victory that heralded the wasteland.

The currency that Fukuyama's piece gained was itself a telling his-

torical incident. Was the Cold War the beginning of history so that
he should talk about history's being at an end when it was concluded?
If the god that failed had truly failed, what became of all those—East
and West—who had organized their lives around it? Those who had
defined themselves exclusively as Cold War combatants were losing
their roles. For them, it may have seemed that history was winding
down because it couldn't be explained in the old way. They were
without an intellectual template, a root metaphor. But this was more
than an intellectual dilemma. The crisis was not just of their explana-
tory systems but of their nervous systems. Their fierce passions had lost
their object; their polemics now aroused little response. They were like
Civil War veterans who endlessly recounted battle stories and waved
the bloody shirt. In extreme cases, they sounded like political pentacos-
talists. The devil was out there, they insisted, but only they could see
him. They were talking in tongues indecipherable to others.

"In the post-historical period," wrote Fukuyama, striking an existen-
tial pose, "there will be neither art nor philosophy, just the perpetual
caretaking of the museum of human history." Coincidentally, the
White House was occupied by a president who saw himself as a curator,
his mission being the preservation of "our inheritance."

When Washington reconvened, having put aside its summer reading, the debate within the administration about Gorbachev was still
unsettled. The first important event of the fall season was a speech by
one of the leading Kissingerians, Deputy Secretary of State Eagleburger, at Georgetown University on September 14. It was a wistful
look backward at the Cold War, which he claimed had been "characterized by a remarkably stable and predictable set of relations among
the great powers." (He did not mention the Korean or Vietnam wars,
or any other unpredictable episodes.) The static and reassuring past was
unlike the present confusion, "in which power and influence is diffused
among a multiplicity of states and where the dangers [exist] that change
in the East will prove too destabilizing to be sustained." Eagleburger
seemed to prefer the past to the present because it better reflected the
great Kissingerian ideal of stability. Gorbachev, who had shaken the
Cold War structure, might be shaken from power. He personified
instability. In any case, Gorbachev was following in the footsteps of
Lenin and Stalin. "This is not the first time," Eagleburger warned,
"that the Kremlin has engineered an ideological retreat in order to
stimulate national recovery." This interpretation of Gorbachev was the
peredyshka line being propagated by various right wingers around
Washington. "Already," continued Eagleburger, "we are hearing it

said that we need to take measures to ensure the success of Gorbachev's reforms. This, however, is not the task of American foreign policy, nor should it be that of our Western partners." In the realist's view, there was no linkage between the American interest and Gorbachev's survival.

Eagleburger's speech crystallized the suspicion that Bush was more comfortable with continuing the Cold War than with ending it. The administration seemed "almost nostalgic about the Cold War," said Senate Majority Leader George Mitchell, who criticized Bush for "timidity" in his responses to the changes in the Soviet Union. "Let me address [it] this way," replied James Baker. "When the president of the United States is rocking along with a seventy-percent approval rating on his handling of foreign policy, and [if] I were the leader of the opposition party, I might have something similar to say." Baker acted as though criticism of policy could be dismissed by flourishing opinion polls. But he himself had not approved Eagleburger's speech beforehand, and he did not approve of the Kissingerian approach.

Just as criticism before the NATO summit had forced Bush to shift his position, renewed criticism inspired another movement. The turn began on September 22, at Jackson Hole, Wyoming, where Baker and Shevardnadze staged an artful *pas de deux*. The Soviet foreign minister stepped back on a minor point and the secretary of state leaped to declare victory, thereby clearing the way for negotiating a strategic arms agreement. At the same time, they also planned a summit between Bush and Gorbachev. With the success of this meeting, Baker had gained the upper hand within the administration over Soviet policy. "Let me sum it all up," he said in a speech three weeks later. "We want perestroika to succeed at home and abroad. . . ." Baker's speech was an open refutation of the arguments of the internal opposition within the administration. Perestroika was not, as they had suggested, *peredyshka*. "Perestroika is different than earlier, failed attempts at reforming the state Lenin founded and Stalin built." Gorbachev's actions were, in fact, in our interest. "Thus," said Baker, "our mission must be to press the search for mutual advantage."

Baker prevailed within the inner councils, but he had not convinced the Kissingerians. When he sent a draft of his speech to Scowcroft for his comments, the national security adviser returned it with a notation at the top: "It is euphoric in tone." There was no more damning word in the Kissingerian lexicon than "euphoric"; it was the antonym of "realistic." All the same, Baker's dominance was demonstrated a week later when he succeeded in suppressing a speech by Scowcroft's deputy,

Robert Gray, who had prepared a pessimistic reading on Gorbachev and his prospects.

The crossed ambitions, the speculative theories, the Washington jockeying—all this was now drowned out. World politics was being played in thundering chords. Gorbachev had visited East Germany on October 7 as its regime celebrated its fortieth anniversary. As the crowds paraded by the reviewing stand, they chanted, as the Chinese had a few months earlier: "Gorbachev! Gorbachev!" Soon thousands, then tens of thousands, then millions of East Germans were on the march, day and night, in every city. Eleven days after Gorbachev's visit, the Stalinist dictator Erich Honecker was toppled.

"The fundamental Germany cannot revolutionize without revolutionizing from the foundation." What the exiled Karl Marx hoped his whole life to see had now materialized: the German revolution. " . . . the day of German resurrection will be proclaimed by the crowing of the Gallic cock," he wrote in 1844. But the crowds of Berlin had been anticipated by the crowds of Beijing.

The Tiananmen Square massacre was the hinge of 1989. What followed turned on it. The movement in China, after all, had not been contained. One nation's upheaval led to another's—and another's and another's. The revolution was televised, and it became global. The Chinese students had not stopped the People's Liberation Army, but their martyrdom helped keep the Red Army in its barracks half a world away. "The political and moral choice that we faced was formulated after Tiananmen Square," Andrei Grachev, one of Gorbachev's senior aides, told Michael Dobbs of *The Washington Post*.

In China, Gorbachev had vividly seen that repression would lead to a nightmarish end to reform. The Chinese students had received enormously favorable coverage on Soviet television and in the Soviet press. When the blood began to run, a shudder ran through Soviet society. The Tiananmen experience was heavily underlined by the deadly suppression of Georgian nationalists on April 7, which Gorbachev had reacted to by removing the local Communist bosses who had given the orders. After Tiananmen Square, the course of repression, if it were ever a real option for Gorbachev, was decisively ruled out. He was determined to avoid the tool of force, willing to let the old politically bankrupt regimes of Central Europe face their people alone and inevitably fall.

The week after Tiananmen Square, the Kremlin spokesman, Gennadi Gerasimov, held a luncheon in Bonn for former Moscow correspondents at which he casually announced a momentous shift in policy.

The Brezhnev Doctrine, which had asserted implacable Soviet control over its satellites, was henceforth null and void. With all seriousness, Gerasimov disclosed the new policy as "the Frank Sinatra Doctrine." It had been inspired, he said, by Sinatra's signature song "My Way." Now the countries of Central Europe were free to do it their way.

Within the White House, as the old regimes began to break, the mood was muffled to the point of silence. It was a deliberate policy. Bush had decided that not being boastful would be his signal contribution. When asked in mid-October about the changes in Central Europe, he replied that he was not going to be "stampeded into overreacting." In private, his advisers prided themselves on how low-key they were. On Halloween, Bush announced that he would hold a "nonsummit" summit with Gorbachev. "I just didn't want to, in this time of dynamic change, miss something," he said.

On November 9, the Berlin Wall came down. One minute it divided Europe, the next it was a million souvenirs. The cracking of the chisels was more than the sound of an era being dismantled. In the shadow of the Brandenburg Gate, the twentieth century—the century of total war—was coming to a close.

Reporters admitted into the Oval Office that afternoon found the president sitting at his desk, distractedly playing with a pen. Twice, in major addresses that year, he had called for the wall to be removed. "Well," he said, "I wouldn't want to say this kind of development makes things move—be moving—too quickly at all—the kind of development that we would—we have long encouraged. . . ." In short, he said: "We are not trying to give anybody a hard time." "You don't seem elated," observed a reporter. "I'm elated," said Bush. "I'm just not an emotional kind of guy." "Well, how elated are you?" "Oh, I'm very pleased, and I've been very pleased with a lot of other developments."

That night, on NBC "Nightly News," which had broken the story of the fall of the wall, the broadcast ended with a long segment showing President Kennedy delivering his famous speech in Berlin—"Ich bin ein Berliner"—an image of American leadership at the height of the Cold War that was missing at its end. On Soviet television that same night, the evening news program opened with Kennedy in Berlin. The torch was being passed to a new generation of Europeans.

"Mind-boggling," said Bush the day after. "We must not be euphoric," cautioned Secretary of Defense Cheney.

The possibility that the Berlin Wall might be opened had not occurred to the administration. It did not have a best-case scenario, only worst-case scenarios. For years, sections of the Pentagon, the State Department and the National Security Council had been devoted to devising such plans. When the turmoil started in East Germany, various red-alert scenarios were instantly cranked out. What was not imagined was what happened. Almost overnight, the Warsaw Pact became a phantom; NATO had lost its overriding purpose. The prospect of a reunified Germany and its immense economic power immediately supplanted the military power of a crumbling Soviet empire as the chief issue in European politics. The question at the beginning of the century was restated at its end: the German Question.

Eight days after Germans danced atop the wall, riot police broke up a demonstration of Czech students singing "We Shall Overcome" in Wenceslas Square. A week later, the government fell. A month after that, Vaclav Havel, the dissident playwright, released from prison in May, became president.

The revolutions of 1989 were a successful 1848, a successful 1968. They were the ultimate commentary on the bicentennial of the French Revolution. "Revolutions are the festivals of the oppressed and the exploited. At no other time are the masses of the people in a position to come forward so actively as creators of a new social order as at a time of revolution. At such times the people are capable of performing miracles. . . ." So wrote Lenin.

Bush had begun his presidency by gingerly treating developments in the East bloc as the second phase of détente—the Ford years in a new key. They represented instead a revolutionary upheaval in the world system. Bush's ultimate goal, both at home and abroad, was to project stability. Any major disturbance might trigger a reordering of the federal budget and, therefore, domestic politics. Assuming the stance of the spectator who sits on his hands was at the same time Bush's foreign and domestic position. His aides argued that by not gloating, the administration contributed to change in the East. By acting unruffled, as if everything were under control, Bush also attempted to minimize change in American politics. Thus he defined passivity as action.

The situation was pregnant with the greatest expectations—the German chancellor had just called for reunification, the Czech Communists had ceded power, the Soviet leader was about to meet with the Pope. Within a week, the president would have his summit with Gorbachev. But Bush called a press conference on November 29 to warn against "euphoric expectations." His aides scurried to give background briefings to reporters, emphasizing that the summit would not resemble Reykjavik. Bush himself explained that the "surprise" would be "no surprise." Part of his hidden agenda at the summit was to dispel the lingering image of Reagan, the naïve romantic carried away by "euphoria." In Rome, that same day, Gorbachev raised the question of the "end of history" and suggested an alternative. "The Cold War has ended, or is ending, not because there are victors and vanquished but because there is neither one nor the other," he said. "Therefore it is perfectly possible to avoid a period of 'cold peace' and to proceed with greater courage toward a period of peace for human history."

The summit took place on Malta, an island renowned for its anachronisms. The legendary Maltese falcon was deadly but extinct. The Knights of Malta, the oldest military order in the world, founded in 1113, was a remnant of the first Crusade. On December 4, Bush and Gorbachev held a joint news conference at which it seemed that the Cold War was a relic from a bygone age. "We stand at the threshold of a brand new era of U.S.–Soviet relations," said Bush. "The world leaves one epoch of Cold War, and enters another epoch," said Gorbachev. The strategic arms agreement, stalled by the abortive "strategic review," was back on track. A year before, at lunch on Governor's Island, Reagan had assured Gorbachev that his successor would continue his work, especially on arms control. It had taken Bush most of 1989 to escape from Reagan's shadow and yet to return to Reagan's position.

In Brussels, on his journey home, when asked if he believed the Cold War was finally over, Bush replied: "Let me tell you something. We're fooling around with semantics here. I don't want to give you a headline. I've told you areas where I think we have progress. Why do we resort to these code words that send different signals to different people? I'm not going to answer. I can— . . . But in terms of if you want me to define it—is the Cold War the same?—I mean, is it raging like it was before in the times of the Berlin blockade?—absolutely not. Things have moved dramatically. But if I signal to you there's no Cold War, then you'll say—well, what are you doing with troops in Europe? I mean, come on."

Luck followed Bush from the summit in the form of trouble. In his inaugural address, he had called for a total war on drugs; it was the moral equivalent of the Cold War. Quickly, however, the war turned into a quagmire. The enemy, the ideology and the solution were all murky. But an evil foreign villain loomed in the personage of Manuel Noriega, the Panamanian dictator, who had been on a CIA contract when Bush had been the agency director and had since turned free agent, cutting deals with the Medellín cartel and Cuba. Inside the

Reagan administration, Bush opposed a plan in which Noriega would have left Panama in exchange for the U.S. dropping all prosecution against him. Bush feared that this deal might somehow be leaked to the public, like the Iran-contra scandal, and haunt his effort to become president. Noriega's prominence in the American imagination was mostly a byproduct of the artificiality of the campaign. He was a symbol, like the flag, the tank, the revolving door: the weak spot in Bush's image as a macho, law-and-order man. Dukakis had raised the issue only sporadically. Now Bush's war on drugs sustained Noriega's symbolic importance. He had become Bush's personal demon. In September, a coup against Noriega failed, in great part because of the Bush administration's hesitance at the crucial moment. Again, Bush was excoriated as a wimp. Senator Lloyd Bentsen, the erstwhile vice presidential candidate, told a roaring crowd of Democrats that Bush had let Noriega out "on furlough."

The triumphant dictator soon overreached, waving a machete before a gathering of his confederates, declaring that a "state of war" existed with the U.S. Then, one of his thugs killed an American soldier. On December 20, the U.S. invaded Panama. To the extent that the invasion expunged the vestiges of Yankee imperialism—namely Noriega and the Panamanian Defense Force—it succeeded. To the extent that it gave ideological ammunition to the Soviet conservatives trying to block Gorbachev, the effect of Bush's "prudence" was canceled. (Predictably, U.S.–Latin relations were drastically set back.) The historic significance of Operation Just Cause lay beyond Panama. It was the first U.S. intervention in more than forty years that had not been justified by reference to the Cold War.

While Noriega was holed up in the Vatican embassy, bombarded with eardrum-shattering rock music to make him surrender, another dictator was falling. Nicolae Ceauşescu, the self-designated Genius of the Carpathians who had bulldozed much of Bucharest for the massively bleak Avenue of Socialist Victory, and his queen, Elena, whose many posts included the presidency of the Romanian Academy of Sciences, were executed by a firing squad for which there was a surfeit of volunteers.

In those countries where the Soviets exercised influence, the overthrow of Stalinism had been almost bloodless. But in Romania the blood literally flowed in the streets. Following a policy of *Realpolitik*, the U.S. since the Nixon administration had courted Ceauşescu because of his independence from Moscow. That independence, in the end, made his regime the most difficult to uproot. The Romanian revolution had been secretly encouraged by the Kremlin, but it burst upon Washington as a surprise.

While the battle for Romania was still in the balance, Secretary of State Baker issued a call for Soviet intervention. This complete reversal of Cold War policy was far "beyond containment." The Soviets, adhering to the Sinatra Doctrine, declined the invitation. With that gesture, the curtain fell on 1989. But the revolutionary drama had more acts still to unfold.

The new decade opened with President Bush establishing his character as a *Realpolitik*er. He played the China card, vetoing a bill that would have ensured that no Chinese students in America would ever be sent home against their will. "And I point back to the original relationship with China, and I don't believe you'd ever had it if there hadn't been some secret diplomacy," he said, irrelevantly justifying his own China policy. His rationale revealed how wedded he was to a strategy and self-image rooted in the Nixon years. His determination to protect the Chinese rulers from losing face implied his belief in the whole balance of power game that had been superseded by the end of the Cold War. Bush felt so strongly that he enlisted Nixon himself to join in lobbying the Senate to sustain the veto. It was the first public issue the former president had been openly and directly involved in since he resigned his office.

With Bush's blessing, Nixon spent October 28 to November 2 in China, conferring at length with Deng Xiaoping and other top Chinese leaders. Upon his return, he briefed the president over dinner in the White House. Immediately afterward, Nixon circulated a memo to congressional leaders, labeled "Personal & Confidential," in which he pointed out that "every Chinese leader I met rejects" the idea that "the cold war is over. . . ." Gorbachev, to be sure, was a "new kind of leader," he wrote, repeating the formula from his *Foreign Affairs* piece at the beginning of the year. But "in not implementing the Brezhnev Doctrine in Hungary, Poland, and East Germany . . . Gorbachev is simply making a virtue out of necessity. He is using his head. At a time when he is using his head, we should not lose ours." Nixon noted that the Malta summit was approaching. "His handshake will be warm, but based on his past record we can assume he will have a card or two up his sleeve." One of the cards he might play was the China card. "But it would not serve our interests if Gorbachev was able to do so. . . . Now we must once again adopt a policy toward China that serves our geopolitical interests, and such a policy will require high-level contacts." The great anti-Communist, seeking to preserve his place in history, had come to the aid of the last Stalinist great power.

Thirty-seven loyal Republicans stood by the president in his battle of the veto, and he gained his victory. "Let me share with you what President Nixon has shared with me," Senator Alan Simpson, the Republican whip, said afterwards. "Our foreign policy," he quoted Nixon as telling him, "should not be a salve for our own offended sensibilities—a mechanism for making us feel noble and true. Our foreign policy should be a tool for protecting our interests. . . ." As always, Nixon argued for *Realpolitik*. His rationale for American foreign policy was clearer and more straightforward than any yet offered by President Bush.

Nixon's emergence was a mark of the strategic vacuum within the Bush administration, a vacuum that was widening as the post–Cold War world came into broader view. The president's agenda was recast every day without any overarching design in mind. Every week seemed like a non sequitur; every month saw a new crusade, sometimes a crusade that had receded a few months earlier. The war on drugs, for example, made irregular reappearances.

The running battle between the Kissingerians and Baker within the bureaucracy was a subdued but continuing struggle. In January, Kissinger was so upset by it that he openly challenged Baker's competence on the "American Interests" television show, claiming that he was "influenced by judgments of domestic politics of being on the side of peace and good relations with the Soviet Union"—that is, Baker's position was invalid, not based on the merits of the issues. The secretary of state, the president's closest adviser, chose not to answer the charge of his distinguished predecessor, one of the president's icons. So long as the battle was not waged in public and the president did not have to take sides, Baker was able to scuttle ahead. He moved quicker than the Kissingerians, but he was still trailing the slipstream of events. The conflict between the present and former secretary of state was hardly trivial, not solely a matter of personalities; at stake was Bush's concept of strategy.

George Bush piloted the ship of state like his fast-moving cigarette boat, energetically but without direction. He sped here and there and nowhere in particular. He was popular without really engaging anybody in what he was doing. Indeed, his extraordinary popularity, among the highest levels ever recorded, was largely due to events in which he had played a little role. At the beginning of 1990, less than a majority approved his handling of the economy, in spite of continuing prosperity. It was for his mastery of foreign policy that he was acclaimed. Even before Operation Just Cause ("a political jackpot," in the words of Lee Atwater), Bush's approval rating was nearly 80 percent. He was the accidental beneficiary of the changes Gorbachev had unleashed. As a candidate, Bush had been subordinate to Reagan's popularity, which was restored by his relationship with Gorbachev. In a yearlong pivot, the new president slowly faced the main action, all the while declaiming that the Cold War was not over. But communism, in dreamlike sequences, was collapsing on his watch. Bush had inherited the credit for forty years of American policy. His popularity appeared to have been achieved effortlessly because, for the most part, it was.

"There are singular moments in history: dates that divide all that goes before from all that comes after," said the president, in his first State of the Union address. "And many of us in this chamber have lived much of our lives in a world whose fundamental features were defined in 1945. . . . 1945 provided the common frame of reference—the compass points of the post-war era we've relied upon to understand ourselves. And that was our world. Until now."

With a dramatic flourish, he unveiled a new arms control proposal that would cut U.S. and Soviet troops to 195,000 each in Europe. When he demanded that the Soviets accept 30,000 more U.S. soldiers—the sort of asymmetrical proposal that in the past had ground arms talks to a halt—the Soviets almost instantly agreed. Hailed as a breakthrough, it was hardly the endgame. The military alliances of East and West, premised on the division of the Center, were losing their hold as the Germans hurtled over the rubble of the wall toward reunification. The same day the troop levels were agreed upon, the U.S. and the USSR also agreed on a framework to negotiate German reunification. Bush had offered numbers as if they were principles. But the numbers lacked magical properties; they were tossed by the tides.

"The events of the year just ended—the revolution of '89—have been a chain reaction, changes so striking that it marks the beginning of a new era in the world's affairs," said Bush. But he did not say specifically what in the "common frame of reference" of 1945 was now obsolete; nor did he outline the shape of things to come. His rhetoric was detached from his budget, which was based on the presumption of a timeless Cold War. Though he had proposed that spending on education be cut, military spending was to increase by $5 billion: more for Star Wars to stop a Soviet first strike, or unnamed terrorists who happened to possess an ICBM; more for the MX missile, the Midgetman missile, the Lance missile for placement in West Germany to launch against East Germany; more for the B-2 Stealth bomber to deliver a second strike, the ultimate weapon for the postnuclear holocaust. To fracture Clausewitz, the end of the Cold War was the Cold War pursued by the same means.[3]

The week after the State of the Union, Bush played the role of spectator at the beginning of World War III. He donned an army camouflage uniform to watch a mock tank battle staged in the Mojave Desert between the "Warsaw Pact" and "NATO." In these maneuvers, the "Warsaw Pact" broke through the "Fulda Gap" in "Germany" and plunged westward, in the direction of Anaheim. "Now, back to war," Bush ordered the soldiers. War games were the health of the state. At that very moment, Gorbachev was arguing at a heated Central Committee plenum for the Communist Party to give up its constitutional monopoly of power.

"The world is moving too fast," Bush complained the next day, in a speech in San Francisco. He admitted he could not follow the story line, because he could not "forecast with absolute certainty what will happen next." Once again, he warned against "euphoria" and pleaded to be "called cautious," not "reckless." He also summarized his policies in a phrase: "I think we can avoid doing dumb things." He then traveled to the Strategic Air Command, the nerve center where orders would be given to launch missiles in the event of nuclear war. Again, he cautioned against "uncertainty." "And for you missile crews," he said, "the pointy end is up."

Bush operated within a closed universe that was running down. Circumstances no longer fit the story he wanted to tell. More than anything else, he conveyed a wish not to be overwhelmed by chaos. At least once a week, he described the main problem in the world as "uncertainty." The Soviet enemy was now replaced. "The enemy is unpredictability," said Bush on February 25, 1990.

The Cold War had been an easy story line to follow. It was the main narrative since George Bush had left the navy as a young man. With its ending, the world no longer made much sense to him; its randomness, its disorder seemed only to be increasing. But his bafflement was

3. "Uncertainty," according to Cheney, was the justification for such spending. He also called the "peace dividend" a "myth." There could be no cuts, he said, until a START agreement was signed, progress on which the administration had delayed for a year. "We see little change in Soviet strategic modernization," said Bush.

In May 1989, the Pentagon had presented a classified study to the president laying out the "broad agreement within the U.S. intelligence community" that Gorbachev "has decided to reverse a 20 year pattern of growth in Soviet military spending and force structure. . . ." The Soviets, moreover, were already tailoring their forces to the strictures they anticipated in a START treaty.

not unique. When the future fell on American politics, everyone was free from the past and everyone froze. The Cold War had polarized the elements of politics for so long that there was no idiom with which to speak about the new conditions. Concepts of weakness and strength, good and evil, optimism and pessimism—all had been politically defined within the old common frame of reference. Both Cold War liberalism and Cold War conservatism were now at an end, but no one of political consequence stepped forward to suggest what was next. There was a vast silence. Political society as a whole was stricken with aphasia. The end of the Cold War was like a stroke.

In the golden age of Democratic power, liberalism and the Cold War had fused. The long twilight struggle was used to argue for domestic reforms, and liberalism cast the Cold War as a progressive crusade. "We discuss tonight domestic issues," said John F. Kennedy in his first debate with Richard Nixon, "but I would not want . . . any implication to be given that this does not involve directly our struggle with Mr. Khrushchev for survival." The Democratic candidates for president in 1988 (and Bush and Quayle, too) had attempted to wrap themselves in Kennedy's aura. Their failure to evoke his persona was more than just personal; they were, in a larger sense, out of sync with history.

Cold War liberalism, after all, could not be reconstructed. It had unraveled forever in the Vietnam War, which split the Democrats, lost them the presidency and ushered in a long conservative era. But, with the end of the Cold War, the issue that tore apart the Democratic Party for more than a generation was removed. The problem facing the Democrats was not the restoration of an earlier age but the invention of a political language and program for a new one.

By the time of Bush's first State of the Union, not a single prominent Democrat had ventured a speech on the possibilities of the post–Cold War world. Since 1946, the election in which Richard Nixon was first elected by Red-baiting his opponent, a defensive instinct on the Cold War had become deeply ingrained in their politics. From Harry Truman onward, the effort to escape the accusation of favoring "appeasement of communism at home and abroad," as the 1952 GOP platform put it, was a Democratic tradition. More than forty years of smears about their patriotism reached a crescendo in 1988. In the aftermath of Dukakis's defeat, the party elites in Washington looked back in sorrow, determined not to repeat his error of being depicted as weak on national security. The tradition of fear and self-loathing, however, could no longer be acted upon, except in a vacuum; the party could not remake its Cold War image because there was no more Cold War.

Already, the discourse of the 1980s had become a faint echo, growing fainter by the day. Early in 1990, Cold War conservatism made its last doctrinal stand. "Now, in the nick of time, comes substantial intellectual underpinning for the don't-save-Communism gang," wrote *New York Times* columnist and former Nixon speechwriter William Safire. He was touting an article in *Daedalus*, entitled "To the Stalin Mausoleum," by an anonymous author who called himself "Z." A version of the piece filled most of the *Times'* op-ed page, alongside Safire's encomium. The pseudonym "Z" seemed deliberately calculated to evoke Cold War history; in *Foreign Affairs*, under the name "Mr. X," George Kennan, then the State Department's policy planner, had introduced the idea of containment. Perhaps "Z" was cloaking his identity because he was as important as "X"—a "Mr. X for Our Time," wrote Safire.

"Z" 's task was the defense of the "totalitarian interpretation." His mastery of Soviet history was apparent on every page, but his argument drew its power from its determinism. "Z" 's tone was that of a brilliant Bolshevik. The "Party-state," he wrote, was the "institutional essence of totalitarianism." This "unitary and increasingly petrified" system was entering its "terminal crisis" under Gorbachev. His "aim" was to "salvage what can be saved of the existing system." The U.S. should stand aside as the Soviet Union was inevitably reduced to "economic and social rubble. . . . any aid the West might render to the Soviet state to save or improve the existing system would be futile: on this score, Gorbachev is beyond our help." The Soviet leader, "Z" contended, was fundamentally hostile to "effecting a transition from a Party-state and a command economy to democracy and the market. . . . such a transition would bring the end of the cardinal leading role [of the party] and hence would amount to the self-liquidation of communism, something Gorbachev clearly does not intend to do."

What "Z" claimed the dictate of history had made impossible was precisely what happened less than a month after the publication of his article.[4] "Z," as it happened, was not a high U.S. government official or even tangentially connected to influential political circles. He was unmasked by the *New Republic* as a respected but relatively obscure historian at the University of California at Berkeley named Martin Malia. Malia denied that he was "Z," but the evidence seemed incon-

4. Perhaps "Z" 's article was undercut most ironically when it was republished by the *Moscow News*, the liberal weekly, in the form in which it had appeared in the *New York Times*, along with commentaries considering "Z" 's argument about implacable totalitarianism in the Soviet Union.

trovertible. He had briefly gained renown for hiding his identity, and with this seriocomic episode, Cold War conservatism as an ideological movement fizzled out. There were no more intellectual arguments left to make.

Almost all the talk at the end of the Cold War was of the Soviet future, the German Question, the New Europe, the awakening of Central Europe. The ancient questions that had been closed for decades were now reopened. But one question strangely went unasked: the American Question. While the Old World was transforming itself, the American political scene was a study in torpor. Change had always been the essential American property. But Bush reversed this tradition; for him, America must be unchanged. He was on guard against "uncertainty," "unpredictability" and "euphoria." America was an estate he had inherited, and he wanted to leave it as he had received it, with some new tree-plantings.

Just as the Cold War's beginning had radically transformed American politics, so would its ending. If the rest of the world was changed, America would change, too. To believe otherwise was to embrace a new, futile brand of isolationism. Indeed, the changes in the world had already moved American politics. Gorbachev had helped save the Reagan presidency, thereby indirectly fostering the environment for Bush's election; Gorbachev's decision to abet the overthrow of the Stalinist regimes of Central Europe then helped raise Bush to the heights of popularity. Now Gorbachev's actions were impacting again: The unintended agent of change in American politics was creating the preconditions for the revival of liberalism.

The aphasia of American political life was connected to the frustration of reform, enforced by an insolvency built up over the 1980s. Bush's military budget, in the absence of the Communist threat, had become an instrument to keep pressure on the domestic budget. He played war games to try to prevent the political game from slipping out of his control. The crisis of solvency kept the Republican Party liquid. *Cui bono?*

With the introduction of Bush's budget, the reaction of the congressional Democratic Party, reluctant to play the role of the opposition for so long, was at first predictably muddled. As natural incumbents, with a 97 percent rate of reelection, they wanted to act "responsibly" and to strive for "bipartisan accord." The advance word on the budget, leaked by the administration to a compliant press, was that the military would be cut and social programs increased. But when the full budget was released, cutting many social programs and increasing the military, the Democrats in the House began to rage that the "kinder, gentler nation" was a Potemkin Village. The military cuts, such as they were, included twenty-one base closings, nineteen of which were in districts represented by Democrats. Once again, the Democrats were to be politically victimized by the Republican budget. In this atmosphere of anger and frustration, a new, awkwardly formulated issue—the "peace dividend"—was galvanized. It first surfaced, in the House, between the fall of the Berlin Wall and the State of the Union. No one in particular was responsible for naming it. The term could be traced to the short-lived expectations of a one-time windfall after the Vietnam War. The battle over the "peace dividend" marked the beginning of a protracted battle over spending and priorities, the beginning of post–Cold War legislative politics.

As Bush understood it, the issue was still the proper care and handling of the inheritance. He vehemently denied that there would ever be a "peace dividend." "That's like the next of kin who spent the inheritance before the will is read," Bush told a business group in Cincinnati on January 12. "And, unfortunately, what is being packaged as a 'dividend' is not money in the bank. It is more like a possible future inheritance." The Cold War had not died yet, but the Democrats were already behaving as wastrels. "Whenever a potential inheritance looms there are those eager to rush out and squander it." He would prevent the inheritance from falling into their hands. "That's not going to happen," he said.

Bush saw himself as worthy of serving as the executor of this estate. He had earned the position by his years of deference as the good political son. He had inherited the Reagan legacy: the automatic transference of popularity in 1988, enabling him to assume Reagan's place in the Oval Office; the solvency crisis that boxed in the Democrats. Bush had also inherited the Nixon legacy: the constant tending of his career; the higher education in party politics; the received doctrine of *Realpolitik*. He had even inherited the Ford legacy: the collapse of détente; the attacks from left and right; the anxiety of being caught in a room whose walls were closing in. All of these legacies were variously marshaled by Bush on behalf of his presidency.

One could even imagine him running for reelection in 1992 as Richard Nixon had run in 1972, directed by many of the same handlers. The candidate campaigned as having brought peace with Russia but was still wary and tough. Nixon's advertisements showed him with the Soviet leader, signing an arms treaty and placing a wreath at the cemetery in Leningrad. The danger, represented by his opponent, was uncertainty and risk. The slogans: "Change without Chaos" and "You Need Nixon." In early 1990, Lee Atwater, who had given a speech in praise of Nixon at the groundbreaking of the Nixon Library and had spent weeks immersed in the second volume of Stephen Ambrose's biography of Nixon, which ended with the triumphant 1972 campaign, was already talking about how Bush could present himself as the victor of the Cold War. The political future would be an unbroken line with the past. This would be possible because of yet another legacy available to Bush: the Republican permanent campaign team, that group of media specialists, pollsters and strategists who had guided Republican presidential campaigns since Nixon won the White House.

Bush's presidency, however, would not ultimately be judged by his stewardship of these legacies. Bush was the heir to another legacy, far more relevant and pressing. It was an inheritance he had not expected.

When President Roosevelt returned from the Yalta Conference, he believed that he had laid the foundation for the postwar order. A month before his death, he spoke to the Congress of "the end of the system of unilateral action, the exclusive alliances, the spheres of influence, the balances of power. . . ." Roosevelt had been the assistant secretary of the navy under Woodrow Wilson, and he had witnessed Wilson's failure in making the peace after World War I. Roosevelt sought to vindicate the legacy by not repeating the mistakes. His rhetoric was Wilsonian, but he was among the subtlest practitioners of power. He sought a peace that was at the same time idealistic and realistic. FDR had no illusions whatsoever about democracy in the Soviet Union. Still, he believed that the Grand Alliance of the war could be transformed into the Four Policemen—the U.S., Britain, the USSR and China, the guardians of international peace, the keepers of the balance, later to be incarnated as the permanent members of the United Nations Security Council.

Crucial elements of Roosevelt's Grand Design of liberal internationalism were realized by the Wise Men extolled by Bush; other elements were postponed, seemingly forever, by the onset of the Cold War. Yalta itself was turned into a powerful myth in American politics by the right wing. Without a factual basis, "Yalta" became a byword for Roosevelt's treachery in handing over Central Europe to Stalin. It was the first issue of Cold War conservatism, and it helped make the national reputation of Richard Nixon, for Alger Hiss had been a member of the U.S. delegation at Yalta.

Astonishingly enough, what came into view at the end of the Cold War was the view at the beginning. After an enormous hiatus, the central issues of 1945 returned: the settlement of Europe and the triumph of democracy. Roosevelt's task was now Bush's task. The job of transcending the "exclusive alliances" and the "spheres of influences" had fallen to him. History had handed him a greater assignment than any president had been given since the end of World War II.

Gorbachev's conception of the "common European home" was the Soviet response to Roosevelt's vision, delayed by forty years. It was no longer unimaginable to visualize a Great Power consortium, a new Concert of Europe, including the U.S. and the USSR—the Cold War rivals even as members of the same security order. But the fulfillment of Roosevelt's Grand Design rests in great part on Bush's statecraft in creating a new internationalism. In the final analysis, the president will be judged on his ability to deal with the consequences of the peace, a world he never anticipated.

Since he first began campaigning for president, Bush had been searching for "the vision thing." For years, it eluded him. After he took up residence in the White House, he invited the historian David Donald to lecture a select audience there on the sixteenth president. Bush was seeking a vision of himself in the light of Lincoln.

On the eve of the summit, on December 1, 1989, as he arrived on Malta, Bush praised Gorbachev for being "a dynamic new Soviet leader, willing, as Lincoln said to 'think anew.' " The president's coupling of a Soviet leader with the greatest redemptive figure in American history was only the latest of unthinkable events that had come to pass. Unfortunately, Bush did not give the full quotation. Lincoln's words had been delivered exactly one hundred twenty-seven years earlier to the day. On December 1, 1862, in his Second Annual Message to Congress, Lincoln said: "The dogmas of the quiet past are inadequate to the stormy present. . . . As our case is new, so we must think anew, and act anew. We must disenthrall ourselves, and then we shall save our country."

We now take leave of George Bush and how he came to be and act as president, at the conclusion of the summit and the beginning of a new era, nearing the peak of his popularity, as he stepped off a small craft that carried him between the Soviet and American ships in dangerously high sea waters. A reporter asked if he were "hotdogging" and taking a risk by braving the waves. "You know these charismatic, macho, visionary guys," the president said. "They'll do anything."

Notes

CHAPTER 1 *A Long Twilight Struggle*

On "imperial overstretch," see Paul Kennedy, *The Rise and Fall of the Great Powers* (Random House, 1988), p. 514. For Acheson's thinking, see Dean Acheson, *Present at the Creation* (Signet, 1970), p. 922. For Lippmann's analysis, see Walter Lippmann, *The Cold War: A Study in U.S. Foreign Policy* (Harper Torchbooks, 1972), pp. 14–16, 50. On Cold War liberalism, see Arthur M. Schlesinger, Jr., *The Vital Center* (Houghton Mifflin, 1949), p. 250. For Robert Taft's position, see William L. O'Neill, *American High: The Years of Confidence, 1945–1960* (Free Press, 1986), p. 99. On the early formulation of Cold War conservatism, see James Burnham, *Containment or Liberation?* (John Day, 1953), p. 41. For Acheson's response to the right-wing attack, see Acheson, op. cit., pp. 462–483. For Dilling's attacks on Franklin Roosevelt, see Elizabeth Dilling, *The Roosevelt Red Record and Its Background* (published by the author, 1936). On Truman's Cold War politics, see Richard M. Freeland, *The Truman Doctrine and the Origins of McCarthyism:*

Foreign Policy, Domestic Politics, and Internal Security, 1946–1948 (Knopf, 1972), pp. 85, 236–238. On Eisenhower's role in Roosevelt's and Truman's foreign policy, see Stephen Ambrose, *Eisenhower: Soldier, General of the Army, President-Elect, 1890–1952* (Simon and Schuster, 1983), p. 530. For the 1952 Republican Party convention platform, see ibid, p. 543. On Nixon's smears, see Fawn Brodie, *Richard Nixon* (Norton, 1981), p. 310, and Robert Griffith, *The Politics of Fear: Joseph R. McCarthy and the Senate* (Hayden, 1970), p. 199. On the Gaither Commission and Lovett's response, see John Newhouse, *War and Peace in the Nuclear Age* (Knopf, 1989), p. 119. On Carter's reaction to the Soviet invasion of Afghanistan, see ibid, p. 331. For Revel's neoconservative formulation on the Soviet Union, see Jean-François Revel, *The Totalitarian Temptation* (Doubleday, 1977), p. 26. For Kirkpatrick's version of the theory of totalitarianism, see Jeane Kirkpatrick, "Dictatorships and Double Standards," in *Keeping the Tablets: Modern Conservative Thought*, edited by William F. Buckley, Jr. and Charles R. Kesler (Harper & Row, 1988), pp. 392, 410, 413. For Podhoretz's neoconservative polemics, see Norman Podhoretz, *The Present Danger: "Do We Have the Will to Reverse the Decline of American Power?"* (Simon and Schuster, 1980), p. 12. For Will's dismissal of Gorbachev, see George Will, *The Morning After: American Successes and Excesses 1981–1986* (Free Press, 1986), p. 339; for his statement on Brezhnev, see p. 333. For Marx's vision of the revolutionary crisis, see Karl Marx, *Capital* (International Publishers, 1967), p. 762. For Gorbachev's view of the Soviet position, see Seweryn Bialer and Michael Mandelbaum, editors, *Gorbachev's Russia and American Foreign Policy* (Westview Press, 1988), p. 297.

CHAPTER 2   *Waiting for Gorbachev*

For Casey's view of the Cold War, see Jane Mayer and Doyle McManus, *Landslide: The Unmaking of the President 1984–1988* (Houghton Mifflin, 1988), p. 77. For Phillips's view of Reagan and the Iran-contra affair, see *Howard Phillips' Washington Report*, "Coup D'Etat!," Vol. 3, No. 1 (January 1987). On conservatives in the federal bureaucracy under Reagan, see Terrel Bell, *The Thirteenth Man: A Reagan Cabinet Memoir* (Free Press, 1988), p. 53. On the Moonie influence, see Andrew Ferguson, "Can Buy Me Love: The Mooning of Conservative Washington," *The American Spectator* (September 1987). For Buchanan's view of the Iran-contra affair, see Patrick Buchanan, "No One Gave the Order to Abandon Reagan's Ship," *The Washington Post*, December 8, 1986. For his view on contra aid, see Patrick Buchanan, "The Contras Need Our Help," *The Washington Post*, March 5, 1986. On Oliver North's mental instability, see Ben Bradlee, Jr., *Guts and Glory: The Rise and Fall of Oliver North* (Donald I. Fine, 1988), pp. 107–110. On North's belief in his divine inspiration, see ibid, p. 422. For the conservative equation of Democrats and Soviets, see J. Michael Waller and Joseph Sobran, "Congress's Red Army," *National Review* (July 31, 1987). On the failure of the Movement

State, see Irving Kristol, "Why Did Reagan Do It?," *The Wall Street Journal,* December 17, 1986. On Reagan's acceptance of the Arias peace plan on Nicaragua, see "Reagan's Bay of Pigs," *The Wall Street Journal,* August 11, 1987. On the shortcomings of the conservative movement, see R. Emmett Tyrrel, "The Coming Conservative Crack-Up," *The American Spectator* (September 1987). On the failure of the Reagan Revolution, see Joseph Sobran, "The Old Right's Lament," *The Washington Times,* October 27, 1987. On Reagan's request for plans on nuclear disarmament, see Newhouse, *op. cit.,* p. 339. On Star Wars and Reagan's movies, see Garry Wills, *Reagan's America: Innocents at Home* (Doubleday, 1987), p. 361. On Reagan at Reykjavik, see Newhouse, *op. cit.,* p. 392. On Bush and Gorbachev, see *Time* Magazine, *Mikhail S. Gorbachev: An Intimate Biography* (Signet, 1988), pp. 232–233.

CHAPTER 3.   *The Vision Thing, or Whatever*

On the Wise Men of the eastern establishment, see Walter Isaacson and Evan Thomas, *The Wise Men: Six Friends and the World They Made* (Simon and Schuster, 1986). The six friends were Robert Lovett, John McCloy, Averell Harriman, Charles Bohlen, George Kennan, and Dean Acheson. The term "the wise men" appears in Dean Acheson's memoir, *Present at the Creation (op. cit.).* For the definition of internationalism, see Thomas L. Hughes, "The Twilight of Internationalism," *Foreign Policy,* No. 61 (Winter 1985–1986). For George Bush on Prescott Bush, see Garry Wills, "The Ultimate Loyalist," *Time* (August 22, 1988). For George Bush's account of his father's political defeat, see George Bush, "Foreword," in Phyllis Tilson Piotrow, *World Population Crisis: The United States Response* (Praeger, 1973), p. vii. For Reagan's response to Bush's background, see *Time, The Winning of the White House* (Signet, 1988), p. 83. On Bush's desire for independence from his father, see Margaret Garrard Warner, "Bush Battles the 'Wimp Factor,'" *Newsweek* (October 19, 1987). For Bush's view of Texas, see *Time* (December 3, 1979). On Bush as Harris County Republican Party chairman, see *Time, The Winning of the White House,* p. 92, and Barry Bearak, "Team Player Bush: A Yearning to Serve," *Los Angeles Times,* November 22, 1987. For Bush's opposition to the Civil Rights Act of 1964, see *The Boston Globe,* June 12, 1988. For Colson's memo on negative campaigning, see Bruce Oudes, editor, *From: The President: Richard Nixon's Secret Files* (Harper & Row, 1989), p. 167. For Bush on running for the Senate, see Warner, *op. cit.* For Bush on positioning against Bentsen, see Bearak, *op. cit.* For Colson on Bush, see Oudes, *op. cit.,* p. 169. For Ehrlichman's account of Nixon on Bush, see Walter Pincus and Bob Woodward, "George Bush: Man and Politician; A Public Life Courting the More Powerful," *The Washington Post,* August 8, 1988. For Colson on Bush following the Nixon line, see Oudes, *op. cit.,* p. 302. For the U.N. appointment, see Walter Pincus and Bob Woodward, "George Bush: Man and Politician; Presidential Posts and Dashed Hopes," *The Washington Post,* August 9, 1988. For Nixon on Bush as a loyalist and the RNC appointment, see Nicholas Lemann, "Bush and Dole: The Roots of a Feud," *The Washington Post,* February 2, 1988. For Bush's denial of knowledge of the meaning of the word "patrician," see *Time* (December 3, 1979). For Bartley's advocacy of Bush, see Robert L. Bartley, "Bush Is Hounded for Reaffirming Ties with Right," *The Wall Street Journal,* January 16, 1986. On Bush's ties to Jim Bakker, see William Scott Malone, "Bush and the Bakker Connection," *The Washington Post,* December 18, 1988. For the Atwater memo, see *Time, Winning, op. cit.,* p. 60. For Bush's "wimp factor" and his motives, see Warner, *op. cit.*

CHAPTER 4: *The Nixon Succession*

On the cycle theory, see Arthur M. Schlesinger, Jr., *The Cycles of American History* (Houghton Mifflin, 1986). On Nixon's Red-baiting of Voorhis, see Roger Morris, *Richard Milhous Nixon* (Henry Holt, 1990), p. 326. For Chotiner's statements, see Garry Wills, *Nixon Agonistes* (Signet, 1971), p. 82 and Gore Vidal, *An Evening with Richard Nixon* (Random House, 1972), p. 21. For Nixon on Dole, see Lemann, *op. cit.*

CHAPTER 5: *The Pretenders*

For Kristol's promotion of Kemp, see Irving Kristol, *Confessions of a Neoconservative* (Basic Books, 1983), pp. 109–113. On the rise of the religious right see Sidney Blumenthal, *Our Long National Daydream* (Harper & Row, 1988), pp. 149–161, and A. James Reichley, "The Evangelical and Fundamentalist Revolt," in *Piety and Politics,* edited by Richard John Neuhaus and Michael Cromartie (Ethics and Public Policy Center, 1987). On the political shift of Southern Baptist ministers, see James L. Guth, "The Christian Right Revisited: Partisan Realignment Among Southern Baptist Ministers," paper delivered at the 1985 meeting of the Midwest Political Science Association, Chicago, Illinois. For the portrait of Senator Robertson, see Harry McPherson, *A Political Education: A Washington Memoir* (Houghton Mifflin, 1988), p. 53. On Robertson's view of his relationships with his father and Jesus Christ, and Robertson's wife's view of his mental state, see Hendrik Hertzberg, "Robertson's Oedipus Complex," *The New Republic* (March 28, 1988). On Robertson's refusal to help his father in his Senate campaign, Robertson's vision of Armageddon and his view of Reagan's election, see Jim Castelli, "Pat Robertson: Extremist," paper published by People for the American Way, 1987. For Falwell on nuclear war, see Reichley, *op. cit.,* p. 87.

CHAPTER 6: *The Strategies of Zeus*

On the neoconservatives, see Sidney Blumenthal, *The Rise of the Counter-Establishment* (Times Books, 1986). On the 1972 Republican Party convention and platform, see Jonathan Schell, *The Time of Illusion* (Knopf, 1976),

p. 278. On Nixon's advertising, see Edwin Diamond and Stephen Bates, *The Spot: The Rise of Political Advertising on Television* (MIT Press, 1984), pp. 185–220. On the reputations of McGovern and Nixon, see Jonathan Schell, *Observing the Nixon Years* (Pantheon, 1989), p. 268. For Hart on Tolstoy, see Gary Hart, *Right from the Start: A Chronicle of the McGovern Campaign* (Quadrangle, 1973), pp. 103, 238. For Hart's theory of power, see ibid, p. 323. On his view of the bankruptcy of liberalism and generational succession, see ibid, pp. 328, 330. For Hart on military reform, see Gary Hart, *A New Democracy* (Quill, 1983), p. 125. For Hart on postindustrialism, see ibid, p. 80. For Bell's definition of postindustrialism, see Daniel Bell, *The Coming of Post-Industrial Society* (Basic Books, 1973), p. 112. For Reich on the postindustrial transition, see Robert B. Reich, *The Next American Frontier* (Times Books, 1983), p. 254. For Hart's citation of Buchan, see Hart, *A New Democracy*, p. 8. For Bell on "intellectual technology," see Bell, *op. cit.*, p. 27. For Bell on the class structure of postindustrial society, see ibid, pp. 374–375. For Hart in Colorado, see David Maraniss, "The Evolution of Gary Hart," *The Washington Post*, April 15, 1984. For Cohen on the American debate on U.S.–Soviet policy, see Stephen F. Cohen, *Sovieticus: American Perceptions and Soviet Realities* (Norton, 1986), pp. 166–167. For Cohen's early assessment of Gorbachev, see ibid, p. 155. For Machiavelli on the fox and the lion, see Niccoló Machiavelli, *The Prince* (Modern Library, 1950), p. 64. On Hart's cryptic self-depiction, see Sally Quinn, "Gary Hart: It's Better Not to Lose," *The Washington Post*, August 7, 1972. On the myth of the hero in American politics, see Sarah Russell Hankins, "Archetypal Alloy: Reagan's Rhetorical Image," *Central States Speech Journal* (Spring 1983). For Tolstoy on power, see Leo Tolstoy, *War and Peace* (Signet, 1968), p. 1421. For Hart's description of his fictional hero, see Gary Hart, *The Strategies of Zeus* (Worldwide, 1988), p. 30. For Hart's depiction of "Father Tolstoi," see ibid, p. 422. On William Broadhurst, see Liz Galtney, "The Real Monkey Business," *The Washington Monthly* (February 1988).

CHAPTER 7:   *The Vacuum*

For political fixer Masiello on Dukakis, see Richard Gaines and Michael Segall, *Dukakis and the Reform Impulse* (Quinlan Press, 1987), p. 173. For Dukakis's view of the "Massachusetts Miracle," see Michael S. Dukakis and Rosabeth Moss Kanter, *Creating the Future: The Massachusetts Comeback and Its Promise for America* (Summit Books, 1988), p. 178. For *The Nation*'s poll, see Victor Navasky, "The Hart Poll," *The Nation* (August 15, 1987). For Biden on Caddell, see Paul Taylor, "Scolding on the Stump," *The Washington Post*, March 3, 1986. For Biden's appeal to history for his lack of program, see Ron Brownstein, "The Politics of Passion," *National Journal* (February 22, 1986). For the only report on Babbitt's view of the end of the Cold War, see "Democratic Contender Says Cold War Could Be Ended," Associated Press, September 29, 1987. For poll numbers showing the lack of support for Democratic primary candidates, see Mark J. Penn and Douglas E. Schoen, "Hart's Return: A Benefit for Democrats," *The New York Times*, December 17, 1987.

CHAPTER 8: *Born in the U.S.A.*

For Gephardt's early conservatism on social issues, see Bill Lambrecht, "Focus on Gephardt: Candidate Takes Center Stage After Just 10 Years in Congress," *St. Louis Post-Dispatch*, June 8, 1987. For Dukakis's sense of his contest with Gephardt, see David Nyhan, *The Duke* (Warner Books, 1988), p. 115.

CHAPTER 9: *The Cat in the Hat*

For Jackson's view of campaigns as drama, see Elizabeth O. Colton, *The Jackson Phenomenon* (Doubleday, 1989), p. 1. For Jackson's view of himself as representing all blacks, see Adolph L. Reed, Jr., *The Jackson Phenomenon* (Yale University Press, 1986), p. 36. On Jackson's mistreatment of his aides, see Colton, ibid, and Mary Summers, "The Front-Runner," *The Nation* (November 28, 1987). Colton served as a press secretary, Summers as speechwriter. On Jackson as the Cat in the Hat, see Gerald Early, *Tuxedo Junction* (Ecco Press, 1990), pp. 13–14. For Jackson's stepfather's view of Jackson's secure economic upbringing, see Barbara Reynolds, *Jesse Jackson: America's David* (JFA Associates, 1985), pp. 30–31. On Jackson at the Chicago Theological Seminary, see David Maraniss, "Jackson Playing to the Camera," *The Washington Post*, December 27, 1987. For Abernathy's account of hiring Jackson for the SCLC, see Thomas Landess and Richard Quinn, *Jesse Jackson and the Politics of Race* (Jameson Books, 1985), p. 18. For Jackson on the Cicero march, see ibid, p. 30. For King's view of Jackson, see Priscilla Painton, "Jackson's Charisma, Principles Winning Converts, but Contradictions Linger," *The Atlanta Constitution*, October 19, 1987. On King's conflict with Jackson, see David Maraniss, "Jackson and King: A Troubled Legacy," *The Washington Post National Weekly Edition*, April 11, 1988; also see David J. Garrow, *Bearing the Cross* (Morrow, 1986), p. 616. On Jackson's publicity strategy immediately after King's death, see Reynolds, *op. cit.*, p. 97. On Jackson's messianic self-image, see ibid, pp. 103, 411, and Painton, *op. cit.* For DuBois' view of the black dilemma, see W.E.B. DuBois, *Dusk of Dawn* (Harcourt, Brace, 1940), p. 199. For Malcolm X on violence, see *The Autobiography of Malcolm X*, with the assistance of Alex Haley (Grove Press, 1965), p. 367. For Malcolm X on world revolution, see *Malcolm X Speaks*, edited by George Breitman (Grove Press, 1965), p. 217. For Fanon on decolonialization, see Frantz Fanon, *The Wretched of the Earth* (Grove Press, 1963), p. 30. On Malcolm X's political strategy, see Paulette Pierce, "The Roots of the Rainbow Coalition," *Black Scholar* (March/April 1988). For King on Vietnam, see Martin Luther King, Jr., "Beyond Vietnam," in *Vietnam and Black*

America, edited by Clyde Taylor (Anchor, 1973), pp. 79–98. For Jackson on King and Malcolm, see Pierce, *op. cit.* For examples of LeRoi Jones's anti-Semitism, see Werner Sollops, *Amiri Baraka/LeRoi Jones: The Quest for a "Populist Modernism,"* (Columbia University Press, 1978), p. 198. For Jackson on a black "third force," see Pierce, *op. cit.* On Singer and Jackson, see Lally Weymouth, "Running with Jesse," *New York* (March 4, 1984). On Jackson's attack on McGovern, see Reynolds, *op. cit.,* p. 263. For Jackson's doubts about integration, see ibid, pp. 372–373. On Linowitz and Jackson, see Bob Faw and Nancy Skelton, *Thunder in America: The Improbable Presidential Campaign of Jesse Jackson* (Texas Monthly Press, 1986), p. 63. On Jackson's appeal for Arab money, see Rick Atkinson, "Peace with American Jews Eludes Jackson," *The Washington Post,* February 13, 1984. On Reagan and Jackson, see Reynolds, *op. cit.,* p. 410. On Goodman and Jackson, see Landess and Quinn, *op. cit.,* p. 205. On Jackson's self-image as a Third World person, see Atkinson, *op. cit.* For Jackson on his alliance with Farrakhan, see Faw and Skelton, *op. cit.,* p. 113, and Lerone Bennett, interview with Jesse Jackson, "I Could Have Won," *Ebony* (August 1984). On Hagen and Jackson, see Faw and Skelton, *op. cit.,* pp. 79–80. On Jackson in Chicago after Harold Washington's death, see David K. Fremon, *Chicago Politics Ward by Ward* (Indiana University Press, 1988), pp. 343–358. For Jackson about drugs, see Jesse Jackson, "Drug Use Is a Sin," *New Perspectives Quarterly* (Summer 1989). On underclass pathologies, see William Julius Wilson, "The Black Underclass," *The Wilson Quarterly* (Spring 1984). On the limits reached by the civil rights movement, see William Julius Wilson, *The Declining Significance of Race* (University of Chicago Press, 1977). On the economic situation of the underclass, see Wilson, *The Black Underclass.* On blacks since the Kerner Report, see William Julius Wilson, Robert Aponte, Joleen Kirschenman, and Loic J.D. Wacquant, "The Ghetto Underclass and the Changing Structure of Urban Poverty," in *Quiet Riots: Race and Poverty in the United States,* edited by Fred R. Harris and Roger W. Wilkins (Pantheon, 1988), pp. 139–140. On the difficulties for the black working class, see ibid, p. 98. On the limits of black politics, see Wilson, "Ghetto Underclass," *op. cit.,* p. 143.

CHAPTER 10:   *Gotham*

For the Pittsburgh Pirates' scouting report on Cuomo, see Robert S. McElvaine, *Mario Cuomo* (Scribner's, 1988), p. 108. For Mead on the Democratic Party, see Walter Russell Mead, *Mortal Splendor: The American Empire in Transition* (Houghton Mifflin, 1987), p. 321. On the Cuomo Commission and Cuomo's view, see The Cuomo Commission on Trade and Competitiveness, *The Cuomo Commission Report* (Touchstone, 1988), pp. xxvi–xxvii. For Cuomo's view of Koch, see *The Diaries of Mario M. Cuomo* (Random House, 1984), p. 179. On ethnic and racial models of politics, see Nathan Glazer and Daniel Patrick Moynihan, *Beyond the Melting Pot* (MIT Press, 1970), p. xxiv.

On corruption in New York City during Koch's administration, see Jack Newfield and Wayne Barrett, *City for Sale: Ed Koch and the Betrayal of New York* (Harper & Row, 1988). For Koch's contempt for non–New Yorkers, see McElvaine, *op. cit.,* p. 289. For Will on Gore, see George Will, "Albert Gore, Raging Moderate," *The Washington Post,* April 16, 1987. For Muravchik on Gore, see Joshua Muravchik, "Albert Gore, A Dove in Hawk's Feathers," *The Wall Street Journal,* January 12, 1988. On the origins of the Willie Horton furlough issue, see Sidney Blumenthal, "Willie Horton and the Making of an Election Issue; How the Furlough Factor Became a Strategem of the Bush Forces," *The Washington Post,* October 28, 1988. On Dukakis's wonderment at winning the primaries, see Patricia O'Brien, "Representing the Candidate," *Gannett Center Journal* (Fall 1988).

CHAPTER 11: *The End of Ideology*

On the bromides of public management, see Harrison Rainie, "The Making of Mike Dukakis," *US News and World Report* (March 21, 1988). On the need for historical consciousness, see Richard E. Neustadt and Ernest R. May, *Thinking in Time: The Uses of History for Decision Makers* (Free Press, 1986). For Nye on deterrence, see Joseph S. Nye, Jr., *Nuclear Ethics* (Free Press, 1986), pp. 128–129. On national balance, see Kennedy, *op. cit.,* p. 546. For Kennedy on the imbalances upsetting the U.S. position in the world, see Kennedy, *op. cit.,* p. 515. For Nye on the U.S. position, see Joseph S. Nye, Jr., "Understating U.S. Strength," *Foreign Policy,* Number 72 (Fall 1988). For Nye's optimistic assessment, see ibid. For Dukakis on the end of the Cold War, see Robert Scheer, "Dukakis Not Ruling Out First Use," *Los Angeles Times,* May 26, 1988. For Dukakis aides' view of him as different from McGovern, see Don Oberdorfer, "Dukakis Adopts Centrist Stance," *The Washington Post,* June 16, 1988. For Nye on Dukakis's position, see Joe Fitchett, "Dukakis Aide Assures Europe on Arms," *International Herald Tribune,* June 20, 1988. On the absence of American leadership, see Robert Legvold, "The Revolution in Soviet Foreign Policy," *Foreign Affairs* (Spring 1989). For Jackson's supporters on Ferraro, see Peter Goldman, Tony Fuller, et al., *The Quest for the Presidency 1984* (Bantam, 1985), p. 223. On the political possibilities of the nonvoters, see Francis Fox Piven and Richard A. Cloward, *Why Americans Don't Vote* (Pantheon, 1988). On voter turnout in the 1988 election, see Ruy A. Teixeira, "Registration and Turnout," *Public Opinion* (January/February 1989).

CHAPTER 12: *The Birth of a Kinder, Gentler Nation*

For Will's criticism of Reagan's foreign policy, see George F. Will, "The President's Foreign Policy: Incoherence and Incompetence," *Manchester Guardian,* June 12, 1988, p. 19. For Kissinger on Bush, see Henry Kissinger,

White House Years, Volume Two (Little, Brown, 1979), p. 902. On Kissinger's views, see James Chace, "Bismarck & Kissinger," *Encounter* (June 1974), and Ronald Steel, "All About Henry," *The New York Review of Books* (September 19, 1974). For Kissinger's skepticism of Gorbachev, see Henry Kissinger, "The Dangers Ahead," *Newsweek* (December 21, 1987). For Bush on the Cold War, see John Mashek, "Bush Comfortable If Election Becomes Referendum on Reagan Administration," *The Atlanta Constitution*, July 20, 1988. For Bush's poem about Walker's Point, see Bearak, *op. cit.* On the permanent campaign, see Sidney Blumenthal, *The Permanent Campaign* (Beacon Press, 1980); for additional material see the revised edition (Touchstone, 1982). On the "interregnum state," see Walter Dean Burnham, "The Reagan Heritage," in *The Election of 1988*, edited by Gerald M. Pomper (Chatham House, 1989), p. 21. For Ailes in the 1968 Nixon campaign, see Joe McGinniss, *The Selling of the President 1968* (Trident, 1969), p. 103. On Ailes, see Lloyd Grove, "The Image Shaker; Roger Ailes, the Bush Team's Wily Media Man," *The Washington Post*, June 20, 1988. For Ailes on the use of racism, see McGinniss, *op. cit.*, p. 101. On Bush and Ailes, see Grove, *op. cit.* For Atwater on the permanent campaign, see Lee Atwater, *The White House Office of Political Affairs: Its Origins, Growth and Role in the Campaign to Re-Elect the President 1981–84*, unpublished paper. On Atwater, see Thomas B. Edsall, "New GOP Chief Renowned for Dividing Foes; Atwater Relishes Hardball Reputation," *The Washington Post*, January 20, 1989. For Bush on policy and politics, see Peter Goldman, Tom Mathews and the Newsweek Special Election Team, *The Quest for the Presidency: The 1988 Campaign* (Touchstone, 1989), p. 185. On the "paranoid style" of the "pseudo-conservative revolt," see Richard Hofstadter, *The Paranoid Style in American Politics* (Vintage, 1967). On technique as the source of negative campaigning, see Goldman et al., *The Quest for the Presidency: The 1988 Campaign*, p. 418. On the history of the Pledge of Allegiance, see David Whitman, "Behind the Pledge Flap," *The Washington Post*, September 18, 1988. On nativism and loyalty, see John Higham, *Strangers in the Land: Patterns of American Nativism 1860–1925* (Atheneum, 1969), p. 330. On rape and race, see W.J. Cash, *The Mind of the South* (Doubleday Anchor, 1954), p. 125. On charges of Dukakis's apostasy, see Rowland Evans and Robert Novak, "A Question of Orthodoxy," *The Washington Post*, May 18, 1988. On Quayle, see George Lardner, Jr. and Dan Morgan, "Quayle Drew on Energy, Affability in Political Rise," *The Washington Post*, October 2, 1988. On Marilyn Quayle and Colonel Thieme, see Garry Wills, "The Private Ministry of Colonel Thieme," *Wigwag* (October 1989); also Elinor J. Brecher and Robert T. Garrett, "Marilyn's Thieme," *The New Republic* (November 14, 1988). On Marilyn Quayle in her husband's first campaign, see Lardner and Morgan, *op. cit.*, and Wills, *op. cit.* For Quayle on Gorbachev, see David Broder, "Thoughts from Quayle on the Campaign Trail," *The Washington Post*, September 6, 1988. For Quayle on his own mind, see the *Louisville*

Courier-Journal, August 29, 1988. For Quayle's mother on her son, see John Seabrook, "Why Dan Quayle's Life Is Like His Golf Game," *Manhattan, Inc.* (November 1988). On the origins of "a thousand points of light," see Peggy Noonan, *What I Saw at the Revolution* (Random House, 1990), p. 312.

CHAPTER 13:   *The Dead Democrats*

On the post–Watergate Democrats, see William Schneider, "JFK's Children: The Class of '74," *The Atlantic* (March 1989). On McCarthy's manipulation of the press, see Robert Griffith, *op. cit.,* p. 140; see also Edwin R. Bayley, *Joe McCarthy and the Press* (Pantheon, 1981). On Bush's involvement with an early release and parole program for prisoners, see *Houston Chronicle,* September 8, 1988. For Marttila's analysis of Dukakis's prospects in the light of U.S.–Soviet relations, see John Marttila, "Democrats, U.S.–Soviet Relations and National Security: New Opportunities for the Democratic Party as Americans Cope with our Changing Role in the World," Center for National Policy (March 30, 1988). For Cohen on the end of the Cold War, see Stephen F. Cohen, "The Next President's Historic Opportunity," *The Nation* (October 10, 1988). For Navasky's account of Dukakis's college days, see Victor Navasky, "Big Mike on Campus," *Esquire* (September 1988). For Estrich's account of her rape, see Susan Estrich, *Real Rape* (Harvard University Press, 1987), p. 1. For Estrich on Willie Horton, see Susan Estrich, "Willie Horton and Me," *The Washington Post Magazine* (April 23, 1989). For John F. Kennedy's remarks on liberalism, see E.J. Dionne, "Describing Liberalism," *The New York Times,* November 1, 1988.

CHAPTER 14:   *Absent at the Creation*

For Marx on the weight of the past, see Karl Marx, "The Eighteenth Brumaire of Louis Bonaparte," in Karl Marx and Friedrich Engels, *Basic Writings on Politics & Philosophy,* edited by Lewis S. Feuer (Anchor, 1959), p. 320. On the Annapolis Group, see Jack Beatty, "Reagan's Gift," *The Atlantic* (February 1989). On Nixon's response to Bush aides' criticism of Reagan, see Rowland Evans and Robert Novak, "A Note from Saddle River," *The Washington Post,* April 10, 1989. For Nixon on Bush's mandate, see Richard Nixon, "Bush: The Battle to Come!," *The Sunday Times* (London), November 13, 1988. For Nixon on Bush's agenda, see Richard Nixon, "American Foreign Policy: The Bush Agenda," *Foreign Affairs,* Vol. 68, No. 1. On Nixon's foreign policy, see James Chace, *A World Elsewhere* (Scribner's, 1973), and Earl C. Ravenal, "Large-Scale Foreign Policy Change: The Nixon Doctrine as History and Portent," Institute of International Studies, University of California, Berkeley, 1989. For Reagan's criticism of Bush, see Lou Cannon, "Reagan Is Concerned About Bush's Indecision," *The Washington Post,* May 6, 1989. On revolutions and paradigms, see Thomas S. Kuhn, *The*

Structure of Scientific Revolutions (University of Chicago Press, 1970). For Pravda on Bush's strategic review, see Don Oberdorfer, "Bush Finds Theme of Foreign Policy: 'Beyond Containment,' " *The Washington Post,* May 28, 1989. For Shevardnadze on Cheney, see John Kohan and Ann Blackman, "Shevardnadze: 'Allow Me to Disagree,' " *Time* (May 15, 1989). For Jefferson on democracy, see Richard Hofstadter, *The American Political Tradition* (Knopf, 1948), p. 44. For intelligence reports on the Soviet build-down, see Patrick E. Tyler and R. Jeffrey Smith, "Bush Alerted in May to Soviet Military Cuts," *The Washington Post,* December 11, 1989.

Bibliography

These citations are not intended to encompass all the literature that I consulted during the writing of this book, but, with few exceptions, those sources that are direct references.

Books

Acheson, Dean. *Present at the Creation.* Signet, 1970.

Ambrose, Stephen. *Eisenhower: Soldier, General of the Army, President-Elect, 1890–1952.* Simon and Schuster, 1983.

Bayley, Edwin R. *Joe McCarthy and the Press.* Pantheon, 1981.

Bell, Daniel. *The Coming of Post-Industrial Society.* Basic Books, 1973.

Bell, Terrel. *The Thirteenth Man: A Reagan Cabinet Memoir.* Free Press, 1988.

Bialer, Seweryn, and Michael Mandelbaum, eds. *Gorbachev's Russia and American Foreign Policy.* Westview Press, 1988.

Blumenthal, Sidney. *Our Long National Daydream.* Harper & Row, 1988.

——. *The Permanent Campaign.* Beacon Press, 1980; revised edition, Touchstone, 1982.

——. *The Rise of the Counter-Establishment.* Times Books, 1986.

Bradlee, Ben, Jr. *Guts and Glory: The Rise and Fall of Oliver North,* Donald I. Fine, 1988.

Breitman, George, ed. *Malcolm X Speaks.* Grove Press, 1965.

Brodie, Fawn. *Richard Nixon.* Norton, 1981.

Burnham, James. *Containment or Liberation?* John Day, 1953.

Cash, W. J. *The Mind of the South.* Doubleday Anchor, 1954.

Chace, James. *A World Elsewhere.* Scribner's, 1973.

Cohen, Stephen F. *Sovieticus: American Perceptions and Soviet Realities.* Norton, 1986.

Colton, Elizabeth O. *The Jackson Phenomenon.* Doubleday, 1989.

The Cuomo Commission on Trade and Competitiveness. *The Cuomo Commission Report.* Touchstone, 1988.

Cuomo, Mario. *The Diaries of Mario M. Cuomo.* Random House, 1984.

Diamond, Edwin, and Stephen Bates. *The Spot: The Rise of Political Advertising on Television.* MIT Press, 1984.

Dilling, Elizabeth. *The Roosevelt Red Record and Its Background.* Published by the author, 1936.

DuBois, W.E.B. *Dusk of Dawn.* Harcourt, Brace, 1940.

Dukakis, Michael S., and Rosabeth Moss Kanter. *Creating the Future: The Massachusetts Comeback and Its Promise for America.* Summit Books, 1988.

Early, Gerald. *Tuxedo Junction.* Ecco Press, 1990.

Estrich, Susan. *Real Rape.* Harvard University Press, 1987.

Fanon, Frantz. *The Wretched of the Earth.* Grove Press, 1963.

Faw, Bob, and Nancy Skelton. *Thunder in America: The Improbable Presidential Campaign of Jesse Jackson.* Texas Monthly Press, 1986.

Freeland, Richard M. *The Truman Doctrine and the Origins of McCarthyism: Foreign Policy, Domestic Politics, and Internal Security, 1946–1948.* Knopf, 1972.

Fremon, David K. *Chicago Politics Ward by Ward.* Indiana University Press, 1988.

Gaines, Richard, and Michael Segall. *Dukakis and the Reform Impulse.* Quinlan Press, 1987.

Garrow, David J. *Bearing the Cross.* Morrow, 1986.

Germond, Jack W., and Jules Witcover. *Whose Broad Stripes and Bright Stars?* Warner, 1989.

Glazer, Nathan, and Daniel Patrick Moynihan. *Beyond the Melting Pot.* MIT Press, 1970.

Goldman, Peter, Tony Fuller, et al. *The Quest for the Presidency 1984.* Bantam, 1985.

——, Tom Mathews, and the Newsweek Special Election Team. *The Quest for the Presidency: The 1988 Campaign*. Touchstone, 1989.

Griffith, Robert. *The Politics of Fear: Joseph R. McCarthy and the Senate*. Hayden, 1970.

Hart, Gary. *A New Democracy*. Quill, 1983.

———. *Right from the Start: A Chronicle of the McGovern Campaign*. Quadrangle, 1973.

———. *The Strategies of Zeus*. Worldwide, 1988.

Higham, John. *Strangers in the Land: Patterns of American Nativism 1860–1925*. Atheneum, 1969.

Hofstadter, Richard. *The American Political Tradition*. Knopf, 1948.

———. *The Paranoid Style in American Politics*. Vintage, 1967.

Isaacson, Walter, and Evan Thomas. *The Wise Men: Six Friends and the World They Made*. Simon and Schuster, 1986.

Kennedy, Paul. *The Rise and Fall of the Great Powers*. Random House, 1988.

Kissinger, Henry. *White House Years, Volume Two*. Little, Brown, 1979.

Kristol, Irving. *Confessions of a Neoconservative*. Basic Books, 1983.

Kuhn, Thomas S. *The Structure of Scientific Revolutions*. University of Chicago Press, 1970.

Landess, Thomas, and Richard Quinn. *Jesse Jackson and the Politics of Race*. Jameson Books, 1985.

Lippmann, Walter. *The Cold War: A Study in U.S. Foreign Policy*. Harper Torchbooks, 1972.

Machiavelli, Niccoló. *The Prince*. Modern Library, 1950.

Malcolm X, with the assistance of Alex Haley. *The Autobiography of Malcolm X*. Grove Press, 1965.

Maloney, Gary, ed. *The Almanac of 1988 Presidential Politics*. The American Political Network, 1989.

Marx, Karl. *Capital*. International Publishers, 1967.

Mayer, Jane, and Doyle McManus. *Landslide: The Unmaking of the President 1984–1988*. Houghton Mifflin, 1988.

McElvaine, Robert S. *Mario Cuomo*. Scribner's, 1988.

McGinniss, Joe. *The Selling of the President 1968*. Trident, 1969.

McPherson, Harry. *A Political Education: A Washington Memoir*. Houghton Mifflin, 1988.

Mead, Walter Russell. *Mortal Splendor: The American Empire in Transition*. Houghton Mifflin, 1987.

Morris, Roger. *Richard Milhous Nixon*. Henry Holt, 1990.

Neustadt, Richard E., and Ernest R. May. *Thinking in Time: The Uses of History for Decision Makers*. Free Press, 1986.

Newfield, Jack, and Wayne Barrett. *City for Sale: Ed Koch and the Betrayal of New York*. Harper & Row, 1988.

Newhouse, John. *War and Peace in the Nuclear Age*. Knopf, 1989.

Noonan, Peggy. *What I Saw at the Revolution*. Random House, 1990.

Nye, Joseph S., Jr. *Nuclear Ethics*. Free Press, 1986.

Nyhan, David. *The Duke.* Warner Books, 1988.

O'Neill, William L. *American High: The Years of Confidence, 1945–1960.* Free Press, 1986.

Oudes, Bruce, ed. *From: The President: Richard Nixon's Secret Files.* Harper & Row, 1989.

Piven, Francis Fox, and Richard A. Cloward. *Why Americans Don't Vote.* Pantheon, 1988.

Podhoretz, Norman. *The Present Danger: "Do We Have the Will to Reverse the Decline of American Power?"* Simon and Schuster, 1980.

Reed, Adolph L., Jr. *The Jackson Phenomenon.* Yale University Press, 1986.

Reich, Robert B. *The Next American Frontier.* Times Books, 1983.

Revel, Jean-François. *The Totalitarian Temptation.* Doubleday, 1977.

Reynolds, Barbara. *Jesse Jackson: America's David.* JFA Associates, 1985.

Schell, Jonathan. *Observing the Nixon Years.* Pantheon, 1989.

———. *The Time of Illusion.* Knopf, 1976.

Schlesinger, Arthur M., Jr. *The Cycles of American History.* Houghton Mifflin, 1986.

———. *The Vital Center.* Houghton Mifflin, 1949.

Sollops, Werner. *Amiri Baraka/LeRoi Jones: The Quest for a "Populist Modernism."* Columbia University Press, 1978.

Time Magazine. *Mikhail S. Gorbachev: An Intimate Biography.* Signet, 1988.

———. *The Winning of the White House.* Signet, 1988.

Tolstoy, Leo. *War and Peace.* Signet, 1968.

Vidal, Gore. *An Evening with Richard Nixon.* Random House, 1972.

Will, George. *The Morning After: American Successes and Excesses 1981–1986.* Free Press, 1986.

Wills, Garry. *Nixon Agonistes.* Signet, 1971.

———. *Reagan's America: Innocents at Home.* Doubleday, 1987.

Wilson, William Julius. *The Declining Significance of Race.* University of Chicago Press, 1977.

Articles and Papers

Associated Press. "Democratic Contender Says Cold War Could Be Ended." September 29, 1987.

Atkinson, Rick. "Peace with American Jews Eludes Jackson." *The Washington Post,* February 13, 1984.

Atwater, Lee. The White House Office of Political Affairs: Its Origins, Growth and Role in the Campaign to Re-Elect the President 1981–84. Unpublished paper.

Bartley, Robert L. "Bush Is Hounded for Reaffirming Ties with Right." *The Wall Street Journal,* January 16, 1986.

Bearak, Barry. "Team Player Bush: A Yearning to Serve." *Los Angeles Times,* November 22, 1987.

Beatty, Jack. "Reagan's Gift." *The Atlantic*, February 1989.

Bennett, Lerone. Interview with Jesse Jackson, "I Could Have Won." *Ebony*, August 1984.

Blumenthal, Sidney. "Willie Horton and the Making of an Election Issue; How the Furlough Factor Became a Strategem of the Bush Forces." *The Washington Post*, October 28, 1988.

Brecher, Elinor J., and Robert T. Garrett. "Marilyn's Thieme." *The New Republic*, November 14, 1988.

Broder, David. "Thoughts from Quayle on the Campaign Trail." *The Washington Post*, September 6, 1988.

Brownstein, Ron. "The Politics of Passion." *National Journal*, February 22, 1986.

Buchanan, Patrick. "The Contras Need Our Help." *The Washington Post*, March 5, 1986.

————. "No One Gave the Order to Abandon Reagan's Ship." *The Washington Post*, December 8, 1986.

Burnham, Walter Dean. "The Reagan Heritage." In *The Election of 1988*, edited by Gerald M. Pomper. Chatham House, 1989.

Bush, George. "Foreword." In *World Population Crisis: The United States Response*, by Piotrow, Phyllis Tilson. Praeger, 1973.

Cannon, Lou. "Reagan Is Concerned About Bush's Indecision." *The Washington Post*, May 6, 1989.

Castelli, Jim. Pat Robertson: Extremist. People for the American Way, 1987.

Chace, James. "Bismarck & Kissinger." *Encounter*, June 1974.

Cohen, Stephen F. "The Next President's Historic Opportunity." *The Nation*, October 10, 1988.

Dionne, E.J. "Describing Liberalism." *The New York Times*, November 1, 1988.

Edsall, Thomas B. "New GOP Chief Renowned for Dividing Foes; Atwater Relishes Hardball Reputation." *The Washington Post*, January 20, 1989.

Estrich, Susan. "Willie Horton and Me." *The Washington Post Magazine*, April 23, 1989.

Evans, Rowland, and Robert Novak. "A Note from Saddle River." *The Washington Post*, April 10, 1989.

————. "A Question of Orthodoxy." *The Washington Post*, May 18, 1988.

Ferguson, Andrew. "Can Buy Me Love: The Mooning of Conservative Washington." *The American Spectator*, September 1987.

Fitchett, Joe. "Dukakis Aide Assures Europe on Arms." *International Herald Tribune*, June 20, 1988.

Galtney, Liz. "The Real Monkey Business." *The Washington Monthly*, February 1988.

Grove, Lloyd. "The Image Shaker; Roger Ailes, the Bush Team's Wily Media Man." *The Washington Post*, June 20, 1988.

Guth, James L. "The Christian Right Revisited: Partisan Realignment

Among Southern Baptist Ministers." Paper delivered at the 1985 meeting of the Midwest Political Science Association, Chicago, Illinois.

Hankins, Sarah Russell. "Archetypal Alloy: Reagan's Rhetorical Image." *Central States Speech Journal,* Spring 1983.

Hertzberg, Hendrik. "Robertson's Oedipus Complex." *The New Republic,* March 28, 1988.

Hughes, Thomas L. "The Twilight of Internationalism." *Foreign Policy* 61 (Winter 1985–86).

Jackson, Jesse. "Drug Use Is a Sin." *New Perspectives Quarterly,* Summer 1989.

King, Martin Luther, Jr. "Beyond Vietnam." In *Vietnam and Black America,* edited by Clyde Taylor. Anchor, 1973.

Kirkpatrick, Jeane. "Dictatorships and Double Standards." In *Keeping the Tablets: Modern Conservative Thought,* edited by William F. Buckley, Jr. and Charles R. Kesler. Harper & Row, 1988.

Kissinger, Henry. "The Dangers Ahead." *Newsweek,* December 21, 1987.

Kohan, John, and Ann Blackman. "Shevardnadze: 'Allow Me to Disagree.'" *Time,* May 15, 1989.

Kristol, Irving. "Why Did Reagan Do It?" *The Wall Street Journal,* December 17, 1986.

Lambrecht, Bill. "Focus on Gephardt: Candidate Takes Center Stage After Just 10 Years in Congress." *St. Louis Post-Dispatch,* June 8, 1987.

Lardner, George, Jr., and Dan Morgan. "Quayle Drew on Energy, Affability in Political Rise." *The Washington Post,* October 2, 1988.

Legvold, Robert. "The Revolution in Soviet Foreign Policy." *Foreign Affairs,* Spring 1989.

Lemann, Nicholas. "Bush and Dole: The Roots of a Feud." *The Washington Post,* February 2, 1988.

Malone, William Scott. "Bush and the Bakker Connection." *The Washington Post,* December 18, 1988.

Maraniss, David. "The Evolution of Gary Hart." *The Washington Post,* April 15, 1984.

———. "Jackson Playing to the Camera." *The Washington Post,* December 27, 1987.

Marttila, John. "Democrats, U.S.–Soviet Relations and National Security: New Opportunities for the Democratic Party as Americans Cope with our Changing Role in the World." Center for National Policy, March 30, 1988.

Marx, Karl. "The Eighteenth Brumaire of Louis Bonaparte." In Karl Marx and Friedrich Engels, *Basic Writings on Politics & Philosophy,* edited by Lewis S. Feuer. Anchor, 1959.

Mashek, John. "Bush Comfortable If Election Becomes Referendum on Reagan Administration." *The Atlanta Constitution,* July 20, 1988.

Muravchik, Joshua. "Albert Gore, A Dove in Hawk's Feathers." *The Wall Street Journal,* January 12, 1988.

Navasky, Victor. "Big Mike on Campus." *Esquire,* September 1988.

———. "The Hart Poll." *The Nation,* August 15, 1987.

Nixon, Richard. "American Foreign Policy: The Bush Agenda." *Foreign Affairs* 68 (1).

———. "Bush: The Battle to Come!," *The Sunday Times* (London), November 13, 1988.

Nye, Joseph S., Jr. "Understating U.S. Strength." *Foreign Policy* 72 (Fall 1988).

Oberdorfer, Don. "Bush Finds Theme of Foreign Policy: 'Beyond Containment.'" *The Washington Post,* May 28, 1989.

———. "Dukakis Adopts Centrist Stance." *The Washington Post,* June 16, 1988.

O'Brien, Patricia. "Representing the Candidate." *Gannett Center Journal,* Fall 1988.

Painton, Priscilla. "Jackson's Charisma, Principles Winning Converts, But Contradictions Linger." *The Atlanta Constitution,* October 19, 1987.

Penn, Mark J., and Douglas E. Schoen. "Hart's Return: A Benefit for Democrats." *The New York Times,* December 17, 1987.

Phillips, Howard. "Coup D'Etat!." *Howard Phillips' Washington Report* 3 (1) (January 1987).

Pierce, Paulette. "The Roots of the Rainbow Coalition." *Black Scholar,* March/April 1988.

Pincus, Walter, and Bob Woodward. "George Bush: Man and Politician; A Public Life Courting the More Powerful." *The Washington Post,* August 8, 1988.

———. "George Bush: Man and Politician; Presidential Posts and Dashed Hopes." *The Washington Post,* August 9, 1988.

Quinn, Sally. "Gary Hart: It's Better Not to Lose." *The Washington Post,* August 7, 1972.

Rainie, Harrison. "The Making of Mike Dukakis." *US News and World Report,* March 21, 1988.

Ravenal, Earl C. "Large-Scale Foreign Policy Change: The Nixon Doctrine as History and Portent." Institute of International Studies, University of California, Berkeley, 1989.

Reichley, A. James. "The Evangelical and Fundamentalist Revolt." In *Piety and Politics,* edited by Richard John Neuhaus and Michael Cromartie. Ethics and Public Policy Center, 1987.

Scheer, Robert. "Dukakis Not Ruling Out First Use." *The Los Angeles Times,* May 26, 1988.

Schneider, William. "JFK's Children: The Class of '74." *The Atlantic,* March 1989.

Seabrook, John. "Why Dan Quayle's Life Is Like His Golf Game." *Manhattan, Inc.,* November 1988.

Sobran, Joseph. "The Old Right's Lament." *The Washington Times,* October 27, 1987.

Steel, Ronald. "All About Henry." *The New York Review of Books,* September 19, 1974.

Summers, Mary. "The Front-Runner." *The Nation,* November 28, 1987.

Taylor, Paul. "Scolding on the Stump." *The Washington Post,* March 3, 1986.

Teixeira, Ruy A. "Registration and Turnout." *Public Opinion,* January/February 1989.

Tyler, Patrick E., and R. Jeffrey Smith. "Bush Alerted in May to Soviet Military Cuts." *The Washington Post,* December 11, 1989.

Tyrrel, R. Emmett. "The Coming Conservative Crack-Up." *The American Spectator,* September 1987.

The Wall Street Journal. "Reagan's Bay of Pigs." August 11, 1987.

Waller, J. Michael, and Joseph Sobran. "Congress's Red Army." *National Review,* July 31, 1987.

Warner, Margaret Garrard. "Bush Battles the 'Wimp Factor.'" *Newsweek,* October 19, 1987.

Weymouth, Lally. "Running with Jesse." *New York,* March 4, 1984.

Whitman, David. "Behind the Pledge Flap." *The Washington Post,* September 18, 1988.

Will, George. "Albert Gore, Raging Moderate." *The Washington Post,* April 16, 1987.

———. "The President's Foreign Policy: Incoherence and Incompetence." *Manchester Guardian,* June 12, 1988.

Wills, Garry. "The Private Ministry of Colonel Thieme." *Wigwag,* October 1989.

———. "The Ultimate Loyalist." *Time,* August 22, 1988.

Wilson, William Julius. "The Black Underclass." *The Wilson Quarterly,* Spring 1984.

———, Robert Aponte, Joleen Kirschenman, and Loic J.D. Wacquant. "The Ghetto Underclass and the Changing Structure of Urban Poverty." In *Quiet Riots: Race and Poverty in the United States,* edited by Fred R. Harris and Roger W. Wilkins. Pantheon, 1988.

Index

Abernathy, Ralph, 181, 183
Abortion, religious right and, 100
Abrams, Elliott, 21, 212
Acceptance speeches: Bush, 280–83; Dukakis, 227–28, 242–47
Acheson, Dean, 6
Ackerman, Barbara, 138
ACLU. *See* American Civil Liberties Union
Adelman, Kenneth, 277
Agnew, Spiro, 79, 114; and Gore, Sr., 216
Ailes, Roger, 75, 89, 256–57, 259, 280, 291, 296
Albright, Madeleine, 232, 235–36
Allen, Woody, 335
Allison, Graham, 231–32, 300
Ambrose, Stephen, 10, 353
America, King's views, 186–87
American Century, 6, 11, 13, 211–12, 337; Bush and, 281–82; Nixon and, 325

American Civil Liberties Union (ACLU), 9, 264; Dukakis and, 294
American Enterprise Institute (AEI), 28
American history, cycles of, 77
American politics: change in, 351; Cold War and, 6; Soviet views, 2–3
An American Renaissance, Kemp, 94
Americans for Democratic Action, 59–60
Americans Talk Security (ATS), 298–99
Anderson, John, 192
Annapolis Group, 322–23
Anti-Semitism of Jackson, 190–91, 194, 196, 197, 202
Arafat, Yasir, 191
Arbatov, Georgi, 4–5, 47
Arias, Oscar, 38
Armed Services Committee, Hart and, 116–17
Arms control: Biden and, 152; Bush and, 73–74, 252–55, 322, 326–27, 333–34,

Arms control *(cont.)*
     343, 347; Gephardt and, 171; Kissinger
     and, 251; Quayle and, 277; Reagan
     and, 40–46
Arms reduction, Bush administration, 323
Assad, Hafez al-, 191, 192–93
Atlanta Journal and Constitution, 103
Atlantic Council, Dukakis speech, 234–35
Atwater, Lee, 65, 67, 71, 87, 257–59,
     264, 347, 353
Austin, Gerald, 199

Babbitt, Bruce, 156–57
Babbitt, Hattie, 157
Baker, Howard, 30, 38, 39, 47, 51
Baker, James, 39, 259, 272, 327, 331,
     332–33, 339–40, 345, 346
Bakker, Jim, 69, 102, 103
Bakker, Tammy Faye, 69
Balance of power, 250, 325, 334–35
Baldwin, James, 185
Baraka, Amiri. *See* Jones, LeRoi
Bartley, Robert, 68
Bayh, Birch, 275
Beatty, Jack, 323
Beatty, Warren, 127, 158
Beckel, Bob, 197
Beers, Orvas E., 274
Beijing massacre, 334, 340
Bell, Daniel, *The Coming of
     Post-Industrial Society,* 118, 120
Bell, Terrell, 27
Bellamy, Francis, 263
Bennett, William, 28, 268, 295
Bentsen, Lloyd, 238–39, 291, 311–12,
     315, 344; debate, 306–7; Senate
     election, 60
Bergen Record, 323
Bergner, Jeff, 323
Berlin Wall, fall of, 341–42
Beyond the Melting Pot, Glazer and
     Moynihan, 214
Biden, Joseph, 149–54, 242, 298
Bill, Tony, 314
Birth control, Bush and, 57n1
The Birth of a Nation (movie), 265
Bitter Fruit, Schlesinger and Kinzer, 145
Black America, Jackson and, 179
Black Muslims, 195; Jackson and, 185
Black Power, Jackson and, 183–84
Blacks, 200–201; and Jackson, 194; in
     Massachusetts, 202–3; voters, 241
Blackwell, Morton, 100
Bograd, Paul, 312
Boland Amendment, Casey and, 21
Bolling, Richard, 166

Bork, Robert, 38–39, 249, 268–69
Borosage, Robert, 199
Boston Globe, 268
Boston Herald, 267
Bradlee, Ben, Jr., 35
Bread 'n' Butter Party, 188
Brezhnev, Leonid, 15, 86; Hart and, 109
Brezhnev Doctrine, 341
Broadhurst, William, 131–32
Brokaw, Tom, 90
Brooke, Edward, 203
Brookline, Massachusetts, 135–36, 137
Brountas, Paul, 162, 238, 239
Brown, Harold, 325
Brzezinski, Zbigniew, 297–98, 325
Buchan, John, 119
Buchanan, Mary Estill, 117
Buchanan, Patrick J., 30–33
Budget deficit, 336, 351–52; Dole and,
     85, 88
Bukharin, Nikolai, Cohen's biography,
     124
Bundy, McGeorge, 54
Bundy, William, 54–55
Burnham, James, 8n1; *Suicide of the
     West,* 32; *The Struggle for the World,*
     8
Burnham, Walter Dean, 261n2
Burns, Helen, 180
Bush, Barbara, 58, 69
Bush, George, 19, 46, 51–54, 56–67, 239,
     249–50; acceptance speech, 280–83;
     and birth control, 57n1; and black
     vote, 241; and Cold War, 252–55,
     309–10; Democrats and, 298–99; Dole
     and, 80, 81, 87–91; Dukakis and,
     242–43, 286; election of, 318; and
     Gorbachev, 47–48, 317; Kissinger and,
     251–52; Nixon and, 85; nomination
     campaign, 65–76, 107; as president,
     319–20, 322–54; presidential campaign,
     255–72, 292–93, 303, 315; prison
     furlough issue, 296; and Quayle, 278;
     Reagan and, 49–51, 66; Robertson and,
     106
Bush, George, Jr., 53
Bush, Prescott, 56–57, 59, 63, 85, 264

Caddell, Patrick, 138, 150–54
Calero, Adolfo, 98
California, 1988 campaign, 316–17
Campbell, Joseph, *The Hero with a
     Thousand Faces,* 128
Cannon, Lou, 329
Capital, Marx, 15–16
Carlucci, Frank, 30

Carmichael, Stokely, 186
Carter, Jimmy, 3, 12–13, 32, 99, 118, 138, 190, 234, 253, 325; Bush and, 64; Caddell and, 150–51; Dukakis and, 294, 297–98; Gephardt and, 167; Jackson and, 189, 240; and Kennedy School, 231; Kirkpatrick's view, 14; presidential campaign, 23; SALT II Treaty, 86
Casey, William, 14, 19–22, 33, 131
Cash, W. J., *The Mind of the South*, 265
Castellanos, Alex, 82
Castro, Fidel, Jackson and, 196
Catholicism of Cuomo, 208
Ceausescu, Nicolae, 344
Center for Security Studies, 328n1
Central Europe, 335, 340–41, 342
Central Intelligence Agency (CIA), 63–64
Centrism: of Gephardt, 167–68; of Gore, Jr., 218, 219, 225
Change: Bush and, 351; as debate theme, 302; Republicans and, 271
Channell, Carl "Spitz," 29
Cheney, Richard, 30, 328, 331, 341, 348n3
Chernenko, Konstantin, 19, 109
Chicago: Democratic politics, 192; Jackson in, 183, 188–89, 198–99; King in, 181–82
China, 340; Bush as ambassador, 63; Bush policies, 334–35, 345; Gorbachev in, 331–32; Nixon and, 61, 345
Chisholm, Shirley, 188
Chotiner, Murray, 78–79
Christian Broadcasting Network, 102
Churchill, Winston, 309
CIA (Central Intelligence Agency), 63–64
Civil rights: Bentsen and, 239; Bush and, 59; Dole and, 84; Dukakis and, 264, 294; Gore, Sr., and, 216; Reagan and, 192; Republican Party and, 98–99
Civil rights movement, 180–83, 186
The Clansman, Dixon, 265
Class issues: Dukakis and, 313–14; Republican, 80. *See also* Social class
Cleaver, Eldridge, 186
Clifford, Clark, 175–76, 178
Coelho, Tony, 169, 171
Cohen, Stephen, 124–26, 305–6
Colby, William, 64
Cold War, 6–13, 154, 281–82; Babbitt and, 156–57; Bush and, 74–75, 107, 252–55, 309–10, 317, 327–54; CIA and, 63–64; Cuomo and, 212; Democratic platform, 237; Dole and, 87; Dukakis and, 146–47, 234–35, 239,

305–6; ending of, 3–5, 107–8, 317–18; Gephardt and, 164–66, 170–71; Gorbachev and, 343; Gore, Jr., and, 219–20; Hart and, 108, 123–25, 158–59; Jackson and, 179, 205; Kennedy, John F., and, 245n2; Kennedy, Paul, and, 233–34; Kennedy School and, 229; Kissinger and, 250–51; McGovern and, 112–13; Nixon and, 79, 113, 324–26; and political campaigns, 5–6, 261–62, 292, 297–301, 317–18; Reagan and, 248–49, 316, 323; religious right and, 104–5; Republican Party and, 81; Robertson and, 105; Third World and, 185–86
Colson, Charles, 60, 61, 113n2
Colton, Elizabeth O., 177
Columnists, conservative, 32
The Coming of Post-Industrial Society, Bell, 118
Commentary, 28; Kirkpatrick article, 14
Commission on National Goals, 11
Committee on the Present Danger, 14–15
Communists, former, Cold War politics, 8
Competence: as campaign theme, 24, 137; Dukakis and, 146, 228–29, 244–46, 318
Congress, Bush's record, 59–60
Congress of African People, 187
Connally, John, 79, 239
The Conscience of the Majority, Goldwater, 26
Conservative Caucus, 45
Conservative movement, 25–30, 92–93, 99; Bush and, 67–68, 260–61; and Iran-contra affair, 70–71; Kemp and, 95
Conservative politics, 26–27, 30–37; and arms control, 41, 45, 249; Cold War and, 7–9, 350–51; and Gorbachev, 328; and Iran-contra affair, 25; Reagan and, 37–39; Roosevelt and, 353
Containment or Liberation?, Burnham, 8
Containment policy, 6–8; Hart and, 123–24; Republicans and, 11
Continuity, as Bush theme, 280
Controversy, Dukakis and, 285
Council on Foreign Relations, 54–55, 64; Cuomo and, 212–13; Robertson and, 105
Courter, James, 33
Cox, Archibald, 62, 135
Creating the Future: The Massachusetts Comeback and Its Promise for America, Dukakis, 144

Crime issue, 1988 campaign, 139, 224, 227–28, 264, 265, 296, 307–9
Criswell, W. A., 100
Cuomo, Mario, 141, 142, 208–14; and Biden, 152; Dukakis and, 221–23; Koch and, 214, 215–16; liberalism of, 311n
Czechoslovakia, 342

D'Alessandro, David, 303–4
Daley, Richard J., 176, 181, 187–88
D'Amato, Alfonse, 215
The Day the Earth Stood Still (movie), 42
Deaver, Michael, 40
Debates: Bush-Dukakis, 301–4, 308–9; Kennedy-Nixon, 349; Reagan-Mondale, 257; Republican candidates, 1987, 72–73; vice presidential, 306
The Declining Significance of Race, Wilson, 200–201
Defense, Hart and, 116–17. See also Arms control; Cold War
Democracy, Russian views, 3
Democratic Leadership Council, 167
Democratic nomination, 1984, 121–22; Jackson and, 196–97
Democratic nomination, 1988, 158; Babbitt, 156–57; Biden, 149–54; Dukakis, 141–49, 235–47; Gephardt, 163–71; Gore, 217–21; Hart, 122–32, 155–56, 158; Jackson, 199–206; Simon, 169–70, 172–74
Democratic Party, 12, 99, 151–54, 167–68; and budget deficit, 351–52; candidates, 147–48; Chicago, 192; and Cold War, 9–10, 171, 349; Cuomo and, 210; Gore, Jr., and, 219; Illinois, 173–74; and Iran-contra affair, 24; Jackson and, 177–79, 193, 199, 202, 240–41; Kennedy School and, 231; New York, 207–26; 1972 campaign, 111–15; 1984 convention, 196–97; 1988 campaign, 284–319; 1988 convention, 240–47; 1988 platform, 237; and Reagan, 19; Soviets and, 110–11
Deng Xiaoping, 335
Department of Education, 27
Des Moines debates, Hart and, 158
Des Moines Register, 105
Détente, 326
Detroit News, 267
Dewey, Thomas, 80, 81
Diamond, Neil, "Coming to America," 243

Dilling, Elizabeth, The Roosevelt Red Record and Its Background, 8–9
Dinkins, David, 225
Direct mail fund-raising, 99
Dixiecrat Party, 98
Dixon, Thomas, The Clansman, 265
Dobbs, Michael, 340
Dolan, Terry, 28, 29
Dole, Doran, 82–83
Dole, Elizabeth Hanford, 87
Dole, Kenny, 83
Dole, Robert, 70, 73, 75, 80; Kirkpatrick and, 95; 1988 primary campaign, 81–91
Donald, David, 354
Donilon, Tom, 302, 308
"Doonesbury," Trudeau, 53–54
Dreyer, David, 148
Drug issues, 343–44; Jackson and, 200
Du Bois, W. E. B., 184
Dukakis, Euterpe, 135
Dukakis, Kitty, 142, 148, 319
Dukakis, Michael, 133–49, 226, 262, 264, 337; acceptance speech, 242–47; after defeat, 318–19; and Biden, 154–55; and black vote, 241; Cuomo and, 221–23; foreign policy, 232–37; and Gephardt, 170; Gore, Jr., and, 224; Illinois campaign, 173–74; Jackson and, 204–6, 240–42; and Kennedy, 239; and Kennedy School, 230–31; Koch and, 223; Michigan caucus, 203–4; New Hampshire primary, 168, 170; New York primary, 225–26; nomination campaign, 159–62, 171–72; presidential campaign, 284–319; and racial issues, 202–3; Republican campaign strategies, 259–72; vice presidential choice, 238–39
Dukakis, Olympia, 243
Dukakis, Panos, 134–35
Dukakis, Stelian, 155
Du Pont, Pierre S., IV, 72, 95–96
Dusenberry, Phil, 96

Eagle Forum, 268
Eagleburger, Lawrence, 252, 327, 338–39
Eagleton, Thomas, 112, 188
Early, Gerald, 177–78
East Germany, 340
Economic issues, 170–71; Cuomo and, 211–12; Dukakis and, 143–44, 160–61, 222, 295, 302; Gephardt and, 163–66, 168; Jackson and, 200, 201, 205; Simon and, 173
Economic theories: Hart, 118–19; Kemp, 94–95

Economy, American, 336, 351–52
Edley, Christopher, 235–36, 306
Edwards, Edwin, 131
Efficiency, Democrats and, 285
Ehrlichman, John, 60, 62
Eisenhower, Dwight, 10, 81, 330
Elections, U.S., Soviet views, 1–4
Eliot, T. S., 280
Ellison, Ralph, 176
Ellsberg, Daniel, 12
The Emerging Republican Majority,
    Phillips, 26
Emerson, John, 131
ENA (École Nationale d'Administration),
    229
"The Enterprise," 21–22, 29–30
Environmental issues, 1988 campaign,
    297
Establishment, 230; Bush and, 54–55, 64,
    66, 67–68; CIA and, 63; Democratic,
    and Jackson, 178; Nixon and, 60–62,
    81
Estrich, Susan, 159–61, 287, 293; and
    Horton, 307–8
Evangelicals, 99; and Robertson, 106
Evans, M. Stanton, 274
Evans, Rowland, 267

Fallows, James, *National Defense*, 117
Falwell, Jerry, 69, 99, 103, 104, 269
Fanon, Frantz, 186
Farrakhan, Louis, 194–95
Ferguson, Andrew, 29
Ferraro, Geraldine, 238; Dukakis and,
    141
Feulner, Edwin, 29–30
Finances of Jackson, 184–85, 191
Fitzwater, Marlin, 331
Flag-burning, issues of, 335
Flournoy, Houston, 51
Ford, Gerald, 3, 50–51, 63, 259
Foreign affairs: Biden and, 152; Bush and,
    66, 252–55; campaign issues, 292,
    297–301; Cuomo and, 212; Dole and,
    86–87; Dukakis and, 144–46, 232–37;
    Gephardt and, 171; Hart and, 158–59;
    Jackson and, 179, 185–86, 192–93,
    198, 205–6. *See also* Iran-contra affair
Foreign Affairs magazine, 6, 78, 323–24;
    containment policy, 350
Foreign policy, 6–8, 81; Bush
    administration, 324–27, 329–54; Hart
    and, 123; Reagan administration, 34
Foreign Policy magazine, Nye article,
    233–34
Former communists, Cold War politics, 8

Fortune magazine, 19
Founding Fathers, 333n2
Franken, Al, 170
Frost, David, 56
Frye, Alton, 323
Fukuyama, Francis, 337–38
Fullbright, J. William, 216
Fuller, Craig, 70
Future as campaign theme: Dole, 82, 88;
    Dukakis, 140–41, 142; Gore, Jr.,
    218–19
Future Group, 288–89

Gaffney, Frank, 328n1
Gaither Report, 11
Gans, Curtis, 241
Garth, David, 223–24
Gary, Indiana, black convention, 187
Generational politics, 120–21, 147,
    149–54, 258
Geneva, Reagan-Gorbachev meeting, 42
Gephardt, Richard, 160, 163–72, 174, 221
Gephardt Amendment, 168, 171
Gerasimov, Gennadi, 340–41
Germany, 340, 342, 347; Bush policies,
    332–34; Cold War and, 329
Gibson, Kenneth, 187
Gingrich, Newt, 37, 296
Glazer, Nathan, *Beyond the Melting Pot*,
    214
Glenn, John, 296
Global economy, 118, 211–12
Goldman, Peter, 261n1
Goldwater, Barry, 26, 59, 89, 99, 273;
    The Conscience of the Majority, 26
Goodman, Robert, 64, 192–93
Gorbachev, Mikhail, 15, 16, 86, 108–11,
    125, 321–22, 328–54; arms reductions,
    326–27, 329, 331; Bush and, 73–74,
    317, 319; Cuomo and, 212; Democratic
    platform and, 237; Dukakis and, 146,
    227–28, 236, 300; and generational
    politics, 154; Gore, Jr., and, 219, 220;
    Hart and, 125–26, 156; Jackson and,
    197; Kissinger's views, 250–51; Nixon's
    views, 324, 345; Quayle's view, 277;
    Reagan and, 19, 42–47, 248–49, 316;
    United Nations visit, 320–22
Gore, Albert, Jr., 217–21, 223–25
Gore, Albert, Sr., 170, 216–17
Gore, Tipper, 218
Government, Dukakis' view, 140
Grachev, Andrei, 340
Graham, Philip, 239
Gramm, Phil, 268
Gramsci, Antonio, 261

Gray, Robert, 340
Great Society, Nixon and, 79
Greenwood, Lee, 317
Gregg, Donald, 70
Griffith, D. W., *The Birth of a Nation*, 265
Griffith, Robert, *The Politics of Fear*, 293–94
Gromyko, Andrei, Hart and, 109
Grunwald, Mandy, 160
Guevara, Ché, 186

Hagen, Tim, 196
Hahn, Jessica, 69
Haig, Alexander, 32, 73, 270
Haldeman, H. R., 61
Hamilton, Lee, 36
Hankins, Sarah Russell, 128–29
Harriman, Roland, 56
Harriman, W. Averell, 56
Hart, Gary, 111, 115–23, 126–32, 141, 148, 154, 158, 298; Biden and, 150; Caddell and, 151; and Cold War, 108; Dukakis and, 140, 147; Gorbachev and, 109–11, 155–56; and McGovern, 114–15
Hart, Lee, 111
Hatch, Orrin, 292–93
Hawks, Doves, and Owls, Nye and Allison, eds., 232
Helms, Jesse, 32
Heritage Foundation, 28, 29–30, 251
Herman, Tom, 244
The Hero with a Thousand Faces, Campbell, 128
Heroic models, 128–29
Hertzberg, Hendrik, 101
Higham, John, 263
Hill Holiday advertising agency, 303–4
Hiss, Alger, 10, 12, 353
History: cycles of, 77; Dukakis's view, 145; end of, 337–38
Hofstadter, Richard, 260
Hollywood, politics of, 127
Holmes, Oliver Wendell, Jr., 210
Holocaust, Jackson and, 191
Honecker, Erich, 340
Horton, Willie, 224, 227–28, 264–65, 295–96, 307–9
House Democratic Caucus, 168
Houston Chronicle, 296
Hughes, Thomas L., 55
Human Events (publication), 267
Humphrey, Hubert, 112–13, 172–73
Hyland, William, 85, 252
Hypothetical campaigns, 312–13

Ideology, 27, 260–61, 269; Dukakis and, 146, 228–30, 244–46, 285–86; Kissinger and, 251
Illinois, Democratic Party, 173–74
Industrial policy, 118, 140, 167
INF (Intermediate Nuclear Force) treaty, 44–46, 73; Dole and, 86–87; Kemp and, 97; Kissinger and, 250, 251; Quayle and, 277; religious right and, 104–5; Robertson and, 105
Inouye, Daniel, 36
Insight magazine, 29
Institute of the U.S.A. and Canada Studies, 2–4, 134; Hart at, 109
Intellectuals, Russian, 3
International affairs. *See* Foreign affairs
Internationalism, 353–54; Bush and, 55
Interregnum state, 261–62n2
Iowa caucus: 1980, 64; 1988, 88, 97, 105, 158, 168, 169, 220
Iran-contra affair, 19–24, 32, 36–37, 70–71; Bush and, 75; Dole and, 85–86; Dukakis and, 142; Kemp and, 96–97
Iran hostage crisis, 13
Isolationism, 7–8, 81; Hart and, 123

Jackson, Angela, 32
Jackson, Charles Henry, 180
Jackson, Henry, 113
Jackson, Jesse, 158, 172, 176–206, 237–38; Dukakis and, 240–42; Koch and, 223, 225; and New York primary, 226
Japan, Gephardt's views, 165–66
Jatras, James, 267
Jefferson, Thomas, 333n2
Jehovah's Witnesses, 263
Jews: Gore and, 223–24; Jackson and, 190, 195, 197, 202, 223
John Birch Society, 273; Bush and, 58
Johnson, Lyndon, 11–12, 173, 239, 273
Jones, LeRoi, 186, 187

Kahane, Meier, 195
Kanter, Rosabeth Moss, *Creating the Future: The Massachusetts Comeback and Its Promise for America*, 144
Kaplan, Martin, 160–61
Kaye, Michael, 289–90
Kean, Tom, 269–70
Kemp, Jack, 50, 73, 92–98, 268
Kennan, George, 6, 350
Kennebunk, Maine, 263
Kennedy, Edward, 12–13, 120
Kennedy, Jacqueline, 208
Kennedy, John F., 11, 71, 129, 135, 171,

208, 237, 310–11n1; acceptance
speech, 245n2; in Berlin, 341; Hart
and, 121, 128; identification with, 239,
243–45, 307, 315, 349; Nixon debate,
349
Kennedy, Paul, *The Rise and Fall of the
Great Powers*, 4, 232–34, 285
Kennedy School of Government, 228–32,
246
Khrushchev, Nikita, 20
Kiley, Tom, 287–89, 298
King, Coretta Scott, 196
King, Edward, 134, 138–39
King, Martin Luther, Jr., 186–87; Jackson
and, 176, 181–83
King, Mel, 203
Kinnock, Neil, 153
Kinzer, Stephen, *Bitter Fruit*, 145
Kirkpatrick, Jeane, 14, 95, 269
Kissinger, Henry, 50–51, 110, 230,
250–54, 322, 325; and Baker, 346;
Bush and, 61–62; and China, 334
Klein, Herbert, 94
Koch, Edward I., 213–16, 223–25
Kohl, Helmut, 329
Koppel, Ted, 255, 310
Korean War, 10
Kristol, Irving, 37, 94
Ku Klux Klan, 263
Kundera, Milan, 16
Kusnet, David, 314

Lacy, William, 82
Lamm, Richard, 121
Lance, Bert, 199
Lance missiles, 329, 333–34
LaRouche, Lyndon, 267
Laxalt, Paul, 49, 50, 51
Leadership, Dukakis's views, 228
Lee, Bernard, 182
Left wing politics, 113
Legvold, Robert, 235–36, 301
Lehrman, Lewis, 209
Leland, Mickey, 194
Lewis, Ann, 199
Liberal Party, Dukakis and, 311n
Liberalism, 266, 351; Cold War and, 7,
9–10, 349; Democratic Party and, 167;
Dukakis and, 284–87, 310, 315; Hart
and, 116; Kennedy and, 310–11n1;
religious right and, 99–100; Russians
and, 317
Liberty Federation, 69
Lincoln, Abraham, 354
Lincoln's Preparation for Greatness,
Simon, 172

Lin Piao, 186
Linowitz, Sol, 190
Lippmann, Walter, 6–7, 233
Loeb, William, 68
Lofton, John, 33
Lovett, Robert, 11
Luce, Clare Booth, 56, 63
Luce, Henry, 282, 337

McCain, John, 270
McCarthy, Joseph, 57, 293–94
McCarthyism, Dukakis and, 145
McFarland, Robert, 22, 29
McGinniss, Joe, *The Selling of the
President 1968*, 257, 304
McGovern, George, 84, 111–16, 188–89,
286
McLaughlin, John, 32
"McLaughlin Group," 32
McPherson, Harry, 101, 112
*Magical Mike: The Real Story of Michael
Dukakis*, 269
Malcolm X, 185–87; and Farrakhan, 195
Malia, Martin, 350–51
Malta summit, 343, 354
Management, Kennedy School and, 229
Manchester *Union Leader*, 32
Marshall, George C., Taft's view, 7
Marttila, John, 298–99, 300
Marx, Karl, 321, 340; *Capital*, 15–16
Marxist views of American politics, 2–3
Masiello, William, 139
Massachusetts: blacks in, 202–3; politics
in, 136–41, 318–19
Mathews, Tom, 261n1
May, Ernest, *Thinking in Time: The Uses
of History for Decision Makers*, 230
Maynes, Charles William, 212–13
Mayoralty: Chicago, 192, 198–99; New
York City, 215
Mead, Walter Russell, 211–12; *Mortal
Splendor: The American Empire in
Transition*, 211
Meany, Francis, 138
Media, 261; Bush and, 75; in Republican
campaigns, 256–57. *See also* Press
Meese, Edwin, 23, 27, 232
Mental breakdown of North, 35
Mental health issues, 267–68, 290
Metzenbaum, Howard, 312
Meyer, Eugene, 58
Michigan caucus, 174, 175, 203–4
Military budget: buildup, 15; Bush and,
347–48; cuts, 352; Hart and, 116–17
Military issues, Dukakis and, 300
Military obligations, and status, 4–5

Miller, Richard, 29
Miller, Scott, 289–90, 296–97
The Mind of the South, Cash, 265
Mitchell, George, 37, 339
Mitropoulis, Nick, 222
Mitterand, François, 123
Mondale, Theodore, 313
Mondale, Walter, 85, 119–20, 172, 194, 313; Caddell and, 151; Cuomo and, 209; Dukakis and, 140–41; and Hart, 121–22; Jackson and, 196–97, 238
Moon, Sun Myung, 29
Moonstruck (movie), 243
Moral Majority, 69, 99
Mortal Splendor: The American Empire in Transition, Mead, 211
Movement State, 27–28, 30
Moynihan, Daniel Patrick, 79; *Beyond the Melting Pot*, 214
Muravchik, Joshua, 219
Murder in the Air (movie), 42n2
Murphy, Daniel, 64
Murphy, Michael, 82, 90
Muskie, Edmund, 23, 111, 112, 140, 236

Nagy, Imre, 335
Napoleon Bonaparte, 337
National Black Political Convention, 187, 195
National debt. *See* Budget deficit
National Defense, Fallows, 117
The National Interest, Fukuyama, 337–38
National Press Club, Bush speech, 74
National Review, 21, 28, 32, 37, 269
National security: Bush administration, 322–23, 324; Cold War and, 6
"National security week," 300–301
Nationalism: black, 184; economic, 166, 170
NATO, 333–34, 342
Navasky, Victor, 305–6
NCPAC (National Conservative Political Action Committee), 28
Negative campaigns, 9, 31, 258; Bush-Dole, 89–90; Dukakis and, 155, 170, 289, 291; Gephardt, 170; Mondale, 122–23; Nixon, 60, 78–79; Republican, 1988, 259–72, 287, 292–93, 295–97, 307
Neoconservatives, 13–15, 28, 113; Gore, Jr., and, 219; Kemp and, 94–95; Quayle and, 277; and Reagan, 37
Neustadt, Richard, *Thinking in Time: The Uses of History for Decision Makers*, 229–30
New class politics, 120–21, 140

New Deal: Hart and, 116; Taft's view, 7
A New Democracy, Hart, 109, 119
New Hampshire primary, 88, 90, 97–98; Gephardt and, 168, 169–70; Hart and, 121; Robertson and, 105
New right, 99
New York City politics, 207–26
New York primary, Jackson and, 195–96
New York Times Magazine, 119
Newsweek, 71, 261n1
Newton, Huey P., 186
The Next American Frontier, Reich, 119
Nicaragua, 196; North's views, 34–35
"Nightline," 255, 310
1999: Victory without War, Nixon, 78
Nir, Amiram, 70
Nitze, Paul, 14–15, 40–41
Nixon, Richard, 3, 11, 12, 20, 77–80, 81, 114, 216, 253, 353; black vote, 98; Bush and, 60–62, 67, 107, 323–26; campaign strategies, 256–57; and China, 345; and Cold War, 10–11; conservatives and, 26–27; foreign policy, 334, 346; and Kemp, 94; Kissinger and, 251; 1968 campaign, 23, 99; 1972 campaign, 113–14; and 1988 campaign, 85; Republican Party and, 270–71
Nonalignment, political strategy, 185
Nonvoters, 241n1
Noonan, Peggy, 90, 279–80, 283n3
Noriega, Manuel, 205–6, 343–44
North, Oliver, 21, 22, 29, 33–38, 39
Northern states, civil rights, 181–82
Novak, Robert, 267
Nuclear Ethics, Nye, 232
Nuclear Weapons and Foreign Policy, Kissinger, 230
Nunn, Sam, 37
Nye, Joseph S., Jr., 232–34, 235, 318
Nyhan, David, 170

Oberdorfer, Don, 234
O'Brien, Patricia, 226
O'Donnell, Kirk, 288, 290, 297
Ogilvie, Richard, 189
Oil industry, conservatives and, 28
O'Neill, Tip, 202; and Dukakis, 137
"On Your Side" speech, Dukakis, 313–14
Open Skies proposal, 330
Operation Breadbasket, 184
Operation Just Cause, 344
Organization of Afro-American Unity, 186
Organized labor, McGovern and, 112–13

Panama, 343–44; Jackson and, 205–6
Payne, Dan, 161–62, 170, 286, 287, 298
Peace dividend, 352
Pearson, Drew, 57
Perle, Richard, 41, 43, 212, 277, 328n1
Permanent campaign system, 256–62
PFIAB (President's Foreign Intelligence
    Advisory Board), 63–64
Phillips, Howard, 25, 30, 32, 45, 95, 99
Phillips, Kevin, *The Emerging Republican
    Majority*, 26
Pinkerton, James, 224, 259
Pipes, Richard, 64
Plagiarism, Biden and, 153
Planned Parenthood, 57
Platforms: Democratic, 237; Republican,
    10–11, 113, 269
Pledge of Allegiance, as campaign issue,
    262–64, 292, 296, 308
Plekhanov, Sergey, 336
Podesta, Tony, 312–15
Podhoretz, Norman, 249, 251; *The
    Present Danger*, 14
Poland, 335–36
Policy, Bush and, 319
Politics: Bush and, 260, 319; Dukakis
    and, 137, 285–87, 291, 318; Kennedy
    School view, 229
The Politics of Fear, Griffith, 293–94
Populism: Dukakis and, 159–60, 205, 291,
    302, 313–14; Gephardt and, 170; Gore
    and, 221
Portrait of a President (Nixon film), 113
Post-industrial society, 118
Power, views of, 23–24, 115, 218
Pravda, on Bush policies, 330–31
Present at the Creation, Acheson, 6
The Present Danger, Podhoretz, 14
Presidential election, 1972, 111–15
Presidential election, 1988, 1–6, 19, 23,
    37, 107, 318; Cold War and, 10–13;
    Jackson and, 199–206; Nixon and, 77;
    Democratic campaign, 284–319;
    Republican campaign, 255–72. *See also*
    Primary elections
Presidential nomination, 1984, Jackson
    and, 196–97. *See also* Primary elections
Press: Bush and, 71, 75; Cuomo and, 209;
    and Dukakis, 293
Primary elections, 1980, 49–52, 64–65
Primary elections, 1984, 121
Primary elections, 1988: Biden, 149–54;
    Bush, 67–76; Dole, 81–91; Dukakis,
    141–49, 235–47; Gephardt, 163–71;
    Gore, 217–21; Hart, 122–32; Jackson,

199–206; Kemp, 92–93; Robertson,
    103–6; Simon, 169–70, 172–74
Public opinion polls, 103, 271, 346–47;
    Bush-Dole contest, 89; Democratic,
    287, 315–16; Republican, 259, 266
Public safety issues, 265
Public service, views of, 230
Pulliam, Eugene, 272–73
PUSH (People United to Save
    Humanity), 184, 199

Quayle, Dan, 264, 272–79, 290–92, 301,
    306–7, 315, 327, 332
Quayle, James, 273
Quayle, Marilyn Tucker, 274–75
Quinn, Robert, 137
Quinn, Sally, Hart interview, 126–27

Racial issues, 200–203, 214–15, 223,
    257–58, 264–65
Rainbow Coalition, 193
Rather, Dan, 75, 204
Reagan, Nancy, 39, 40
Reagan, Ronald, 8n1, 19–20, 33, 46–47,
    51, 57, 96, 253–54, 320–21, 336;
    acceptance speech, 122; and arms
    control, 40–46; Bush and, 66, 322–24;
    and Bush administration, 329; and
    Cold War, 14, 248–49, 316, 323;
    conservatives and, 27–28, 32, 37–39,
    92–93; Dole and, 84–85; Dukakis and,
    245–46, 300–301; Gephardt and, 167;
    and Gorbachev, 42–47, 109; Hart and,
    117–18; and Iran-contra affair, 23–24,
    70–71; Jackson and, 191–93; Koch and,
    215; and 1988 campaign, 271–72,
    316–17; Noonan and, 279; and North,
    35; presidential campaign, 13, 49–51,
    257; Quayle and, 278; and religious
    right, 100–101; Republicans and,
    22–23; Robertson and, 104–5; Soviets
    and, 3; Watergate and, 79
Real Rape, Estrich, 307–8
Regan, Donald, 39, 44
Reich, Robert, 140, 311; *The Next
    American Frontier*, 119
Reilly, Ed, 170
Religion: of Dukakis, 267; of North, 35
Religious right, 28, 29, 98–100, 106; Bush
    and, 68–69
Religious Roundtable, 100
Republican National Committee, 62, 80
Republican Party, 2–3, 58, 59, 68, 80–81,
    85–91, 107, 110; and Bush nomination,
    65–66; and Cold War, 7, 10–11;
    conservatives and, 26–27; Jackson and,

Republican Party (cont.)
189–90; Massachusetts, 141;
conventions, 113, 268–72; platforms,
10–11, 113, 269; Nixon and, 77–78;
presidential campaign, 255–72, 292–96,
298–99; Reagan and, 22–23; in South,
98–99
Resentment, politics of, 26, 78, 257–59
Resurrection City, 183
Revel, Jean-François, The Totalitarian
Temptation, 14
Revolutions, 1989, 342
Reykjavik summit, 43–44, 109–10
Reynolds, Barbara, 183
Richardson, Elliot, 62, 135
Right wing, 8–9; Bush and, 58–68, 249;
and Gorbachev, 328, 338–39; Kissinger
and, 250; and neoconservatives, 28, 95;
Nixon and, 81
Riley, Pat, 256
Ringe, Don, 275–77
Ripon Society, 60
The Rise and Fall of the Great Powers,
Kennedy, 4, 232–34, 285
Roberts, Oral, 69
Robertson, Marion "Pat," 28, 69, 88, 92,
97, 98, 101–6
Robertson, Willis, 101
Robinson, Noah, 180
Rockefeller, David, 230
Rockefeller, Nelson, 59, 63, 230
Rodriguez, Felix, 70
Romania, revolution in, 344–45
Roosevelt, Franklin D., 6, 8–9, 353–54;
Cuomo and, 209–10; Reagan and, 51
The Roosevelt Red Record and Its
Background, Dilling, 8–9
Roosevelt, Theodore, 71
Rose, Don, 182
Rukeyser, Louis, 298
Rusk, Dean, 236
Rutherford, William, 182

Safire, William, 350
Sakharov, Andrei, 44, 212
SALT II Treaty, 13, 86; Quayle and, 277
Sargent, Frank, 137
Sasso, John, 134, 138–44, 146, 159, 168,
242, 287, 294–95, 299–300, 302, 303,
313; and Biden, 154–55
Sawyer, David, 160
Scheer, Robert, 234
Schell, Jonathan, 114
Schlafly, Phyllis, 268
Schlesinger, Arthur M., Jr., 77, 120; The
Vital Center, 7

Schlesinger, Stephen, 211; Bitter Fruit,
145
Schroeder, Patricia, 121
SCLC. See Southern Christian
Leadership Conference
Scowcroft, Brent, 23, 85, 252, 298, 323,
327, 339; China trips, 335
The Secret Kingdom, Robertson, 102–3
The Selling of the President 1968,
McGinniss, 257, 304
Senate: Bush campaign, 60; Gorbachev
and, 86; Hart campaign, 115–16;
Quayle in, 277
Sexual life of Hart, 127
Shamir, Yitzhak, 223–24
Shaw, Bernard, 308–9
Shevardnadze, Eduard, 110, 331, 332, 339
Shrum, Robert, 295
Sidd, Allan, 136, 138
Sieverts, Frank, 304
Simon, Paul, 169–70, 172–74, 293
Simpson, Alan, 346
Sinatra Doctrine, 341, 345
Singer, William, 188
Sledge, Percy, 258
Smith, Bailey, 100
Smith, Larry, 116, 300
Snapp, Constance, 104
Sobran, Joseph, 38
Social class: Biden and, 150; Bush and,
53–55, 57, 59, 61, 64–66, 68, 71–72;
Democrats and, 221–22; Dukakis and,
135–36, 313–14; Republicans and, 80;
Robertson and, 101–2
Social contract, Cuomo and, 211–12
Social issues, 114, 200–201
Sorensen, Theodore, 237
South Carolina primary, 106
South Dakota primary, Gephardt and,
170
Southern Baptist Convention, 100
Southern Christian Leadership
Conference (SCLC), 186; Jackson and,
182, 184, 191
Southern states, 98–99; Bush and, 69–70;
Dukakis and, 288; Gore and 220
Soviet Union, 1–4, 13–17, 43, 110–11,
340, 348n3; Bush and, 282, 309; Dole's
view, 86; Gorbachev and, 321; Hart's
view, 123; Jackson's view, 198
Squire, Robert, 117, 301–2, 304
Stability, Kissinger's idea, 250
Stalin, Joseph, 6
Star Wars, 41–43
START Treaty, 251; Bush and, 254, 326
State Department, conservative views, 8

Will, George, 15, 32, 124, 218, 249, 284
Wills, Garry, 42n2, 56, 274
Wilson, William Julius, *The Declining
    Significance of Race,* 200–201
Window of vulnerability, 15, 40–41
Wirth, Tim, 121
Wirthlin, Richard, 51
Wisconsin primary, 205–6
Wittgraf, George, 87
Wolfowitz, Paul, 331
The World and I (magazine), 29

World War II, 57–58, 83
Writhlin, Richard, 89

"X," *Foreign Affairs* article, 6, 350

Yalta Conference, 8, 353
Yarborough, Ralph, 59, 60
Young, Andrew, 190–91, 194, 196

"Z," article on Soviet Union, 350
Zeibert, Duke, 48

State of the Union address, Bush, 347
States Rights Party, 98
Status, politics of, 68
Stevenson, Adlai, 11; Dukakis and, 144–45
Stockman, David, 167
Stone, I. F., 145
Strategic arms agreement, 343. *See also* START Treaty
Strategic Defense Initiative, 41–43
The Strategies of Zeus, Hart, 129–30
Strauss, Robert, 40
The Struggle for the World, Burnham, 8
Suicide of the West, Burnham, 32
Sullivan, Brendan, 36
Summit meetings: Bush-Gorbachev, 339, 342–43, 354; Reagan-Gorbachev, 42–48
Sununu, John, 323
Super Tuesday, 68–69, 170, 171–72, 221
Supply-side economics, 94–95
Swaggart, Jimmy, 69, 103, 106
Swope, Ken, 308
Symms, Steve, 292

Taft, Robert, 7–8, 10, 81
Taft, William Howard, 81
Tanks, Dukakis and, 117, 300–301
Taxes, Bush and, 336
Technocrats, 230–31
Teeter, Robert, 66, 71, 89–90, 259, 262, 265, 266, 271, 298
Teleprompter, Dukakis and, 290
Teller, Edward, 41
Thieme, Robert, 274
Thinking in Time: The Uses of History for Decision Makers, Neustadt and May, 230
Third World, 185–86; Gorbachev and, 198; Jackson and, 179, 190–96, 205
Thornburgh, Richard, 30
Thurmond, Strom, 98, 99
Tiananmen Square massacre, 334, 340
Tolstoy, Leo, 129
The Totalitarian Temptation, Revel, 14
Tower, John, 23
Tower Commission report, 23–24, 146
Trade issues, 165–66, 168, 170–71
Trbovich, Marco, 159–60
Trilateral Commission, 55, 64, 105
Trudeau, Garry, "Doonesbury," 53–54
Truman, Harry, 7, 9–10, 98; Bush and, 315
Truman Doctrine, 10
Tucker, Marilyn (Quayle), 274
Tyrrell, R. Emmett, Jr., 38

Udall, Morris, 298
Ullman, Owen, 323
Unification Church, 29
United Nations, 61; Gorbachev and, 320–21
United States, nuclear power, 40–41
United States Senate: Gorbachev and, 86
Upper-class political figures, 71–72
USA Institute. *See* Institute of the U.S.A. and Canada Studies

Vance, Cyrus, 190, 236, 325
Vanderbreggen, Cornelius, 101
Vice presidency, 51; Bush and, 50–54, 65–67; Jackson and, 202, 237–38
Vice presidential debate, 306
Vietnam War, 11–12, 349; Dukakis and, 145; Gore, Jr., and, 217; Gore, Sr., and, 216; King and, 186; McGovern and, 112; North's views, 34; Quayle and, 274
Viguerie, Richard, 28, 29, 45
The Vital Center, Schlesinger, 7
Voorhis, Jerry, 78
Voter turnout, 200–201, 241, 241n1, 318

Walcott, Louis. *See* Farrakhan, Louis
Walker, G. Herbert, Jr., 58
Wall Street Journal, 38, 94, 153
Wallace, George, 99, 256
Wallace, Henry, 10; McGovern and, 112
Walters, Barbara, 319
Wanniski, Jude, 94, 96
Warner, Jack, 316
Warner, Margaret Garrard, 71
Warsaw Pact, 342
Washington, Booker T., 185, 201
Washington, Harold, 192, 198–99
Washington, D.C., 127, 183; Bush and, 66–67; Reagan-Gorbachev meeting, 45, 47–48, 73–74
The Washington Post, 31, 334
Washington Times, 29, 38, 45, 267–68
Watergate scandal, 12, 20, 26, 31, 79; Bush and, 62–63
Watt, James, 27
Weinberger, Caspar, 232
Welch, Joseph, 145
Welch, Robert, 273
Weyrich, Paul, 99
White, John, 175
White, Theodore H., 252
Whitehead, Ralph, 142
Wilkins, Roger, 199